MONONGAHELA NATIONAL FOREST HIKING GUIDE

Seventh Edition

Allen de Hart and Bruce Sundquist

with the cooperation of the
Monongahela National Forest Staff
and Volunteer Hikers

Published by:

West Virginia Highlands Conservancy
P. O. Box 306
Charleston, West Virginia 25321

MONONGAHELA

NATIONAL FOREST

HIKING GUIDE

Seventh Edition

Printed in the United States of America

Copyright © 1999, 2001, 2004 by

West Virginia Highlands Conservancy

Allen de Hart- author
Bruce Sundquist- editor

Front Cover:

Hikers Helen Payne and Catherine Hatchett at Dolly Sods

Clothing furnished by Pathfinder Outdoor Store, Morgantown, WV

Photograph by Roger Spencer, Middlebourne, WV

FOREWORD

The purpose of this guide is to help you have an enjoyable outing in the Monongahela National Forest. The MNF is a very special area. As you become acquainted with its natural beauty, wildlife habitat, and recreational opportunities, I hope you will join our efforts to protect it. The predecessors of this guide were a collection of Wilderness proposal/trail guides for Cranberry Backcountry, Otter Creek and Dolly Sods published by WVHC between the late 1960s and early 1980s.

This seventh edition is the product of countless hours of volunteer effort, but the real stalwarts are our editors. Allen de Hart is a writer and veteran hiker. Allen's first-hand knowledge of West Virginia's trails is without equal. Over the past few years he has hiked every trail on the Monongahela National Forest. Besides co-authoring the fifth, sixth and seventh Editions of this guide, he is also the author of *Hiking The Mountain State: the Trails of West Virginia* (Appalachian Mt. Club, 1997), *North Carolina Hiking Trails, South Carolina Hiking Trails, Hiking the Old Dominion: The Trails of Virginia, Hiking and Backpacking Basics, Adventuring in Florida, Trails of the Triangle and Trails of the Triad* (both in North Carolina). He has hiked over 1855 miles of West Virginia trails and over 32,000 miles in 48 states and 18 foreign countries.

Since September of 1972, Bruce Sundquist has selflessly and tirelessly edited the successive editions. These guides have introduced the MNF to thousands of hikers, and many of the conservation projects undertaken by the West Virginia Highlands Conservancy would not have been successful without the financial support derived from the guide sales. Bruce has also authored or co-authored *Hiking Guide to Laurel Highlands Trail, Hiking Guide to Western Pennsylvania, Canoeing Guide to Western Pennsylvania, Hiking Guide to Allegheny National Forest and Ski-Touring Guide To Southwestern Pennsylvania.*

Working together, Allen and Bruce have produced a significantly improved edition: updated trail descriptions and distances; made trail descriptions more consistent; divided the trails into segments to make the description easier to use, and provided more information about wildlife and fauna likely to be seen along the trails. Recognizing the growing interest in cross-country skiing on the MNF, they have added information on ski trails and ski-touring opportunities. We are indeed fortunate to have the talents of Allen and Bruce.

Your help in sending the editors descriptions of the trails you have hiked or skied will continue to be as important as it has been in the past.

Hugh Rogers, President
West Virginia Highlands Conservancy

ACKNOWLEDGEMENTS

This guide was originally researched and put together by a committee of about 20 people who recognized the Monongahela National Forest as a "Special Place"; as an outstanding source of dispersed recreation opportunities in the heart of the densely populated northeastern United States.

We will always be grateful to the original committee that established and laid the foundation for the first few editions: Craig and Pricilla Moore, Jane Showacre, Redding Crafts, John Sutton, Bernie Johnson, Ned S. Vanderven, Frank and Judy O'Hara, John Walker, Ray Cole, the West Va. University Outing Club, Ron Hardway, Bill Riley, Helen McGinnis, Bob Burrell, Vince Berinati and Bob, David, Ann and Jean Woods.

We are all grateful for the cooperation of many members of the U.S. Forest Service staff in the Elkins Office and in the six District Ranger offices. It was the untold thousands of hours of hard work and thoughtful planning of USFS personnel that made the trails of the Monongahela National Forest what they are today. Without them the guide would not be possible. For this seventh edition we wish to give particular thanks the following members of the Monongahela National Forest staff: Joe Robles (forest recreation specialist), Linda White (forester/Wilderness Manager), Steve Chandler (land-use planning specialist), and William Kerr (landscape architect).

This edition, as previous editions, is a product of the hiking community--hikers willing to share the benefits of their experiences. Major contributors to this edition include: Chris Addison, Dale Bowman, Jeff Brewer, Keith Brooks, Cliff Brummitt, Richard Byrd, Ray Carpenter, Travis Combest, Frank Duke Jr., Alvin Edwards, David Fisher, Wayne Gibbs, Ellen Haney, Greg Hippert, Kelly Horton, David Hutson, Charles Isley, Lisa Kiley, Sheri Lanier, Sharon Leonard, Ed Liberatore, Greg Murphy, Dennis Parrish, David Porter, Wade Potter, George Rosier, David Salling, Wendie Schaller, Todd Shearon, Joe Smith, Clint Snow, Gary Stainback, Scott Stalls, Chip Suttles, Jeanne and Steve Swingenstein, Carol Anne Thompson, Ryan Watts, Travis Winn and Doug Wood.

We are also grateful to organizations such as the West Virginia Chapter of the Sierra Club, Highlands Nature Conservancy, Boy Scouts, Girl Scouts, West Virginia Scenic Trails Association, and college- and university organizations.

We hope that the efforts of these people and many others have produced a guide of sufficient merit to attract many further contributions for the next edition.

Allen de Hart
Bruce Sundquist
May, 1999

Previous Editions:

First-Sept.1972 (1500 copies):	Second-Jan.1974 (1500 copies)
Third-July,1977 (5097 copies):	Fourth-Aug.1982 (5119 copies)
Fifth- Feb.1988 (7393 copies):	Sixth- May,1993 (12631 copies)

TABLE OF CONTENTS

INTRODUCTION TO MONONGAHELA NATIONAL FOREST

"It became clear in the public comments on the Draft Plan that
West Virginians consider the Monongahela National Forest a special, even unique, place where the public can take part in dispersed recreation activities available nowhere else in the State."

Monongahela National Forest Summary,
Land and Resource Management Plan, 1986

(A) PURPOSE

As with other forms of dispersed, primitive recreation, the simple pleasures and rewards of hiking, backpacking and ski-touring are hard to describe
to the uninitiated. Yet such activities have a clearly significant effect on the
attitudes and outlook-on-life of those who partake. This effect seems particularly relevant to the searchings of present-day society. In the densely populated northeastern U.S. the Monongahela National Forest (MNF) provides an
exceptional environment for such recreation. It also provides outstanding
scenery, wildlife habitat and watershed protection, often in large blocks where
natural values, rather than urban values predominate. This greatly enhances
the diversity of habitats for plants and animals, and the diversity of scenery
for people to visit and enjoy.

It is little wonder then that thousands of citizens provided input to the
last (1986) MNF Land Management Plan. They urged the U.S. Forest Service
(USFS) to give greater recognition to the MNF as a "Special Place". This
Guide was born over a decade earlier, but out of the same concerns and
desires. The public clearly senses that management practices on the MNF
need continued public input to maintain a proper balance among short-term
commodity values, long-term economic values, natural values and aesthetic
values.

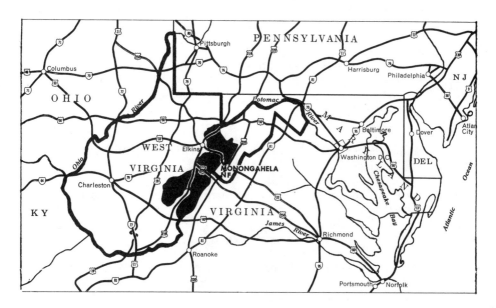

1

Millions of us have come to know and cherish the MNF. There are few better ways to come to know the forest than to walk its trails. This book is devoted to helping you plan and carry out your foot travel on the MNF. Hopefully you, too, will soon come to think of it as a "special place".

(B) GENERAL DESCRIPTION OF THE AREA

The MNF is basically an eastern hardwoods forest with some notable areas of red spruce at high-elevations. As a result of its geographic location and topography it contains a great diversity of species of trees. Some highland areas suggest the forests of eastern Canada while, elsewhere, trees more common to southern states are found. Fall colors are particularly attractive in the hardwood forests of West Virginia's Highlands.

Most of the MNF was cut in the late 1800s and early 1900s. As a result, a large fraction of the tree population is 70-90 years old. The USFS intends to eventually achieve a condition whereby roughly the same timber acreage is devoted to each tree age class from zero to about 100 years. Currently you see more middle-aged trees and fewer "mature" and young trees than you will in years to come.

For hikers and backpackers, the MNF offers much. It occupies some of the highest elevations in West Virginia; the headwaters of five major river systems (Monongahela, Potomac, Greenbrier, Elk, Gauley) lie within the Forest boundaries. Many trails travel along clear mountain streams. The rugged terrain also offers spectacular views of forested valleys and peaceful countryside. Highland bogs and open areas are also found, where the climate is so harsh, and the soil so thin and poorly drained, that little except mosses, ferns and small shrubs survive. A large variety of wildlife can also be seen, including black bear and wild turkey. The forest floor is usually beautiful and fascinating. Mosses and ferns in great variety are everywhere. Rhododendrons and laurel add waxy green beauty to the forest scene. Although the stumps from the logging days of old have largely vanished, one can still find remains of old logging camps, such as horseshoes, logging tools, stove parts, barrel hoops, and bottles. In some areas the crowns of the trees are far overhead and nearly continuous, creating a "cathedral-like" atmosphere that adds to hiking pleasures.

The Monongahela National Forest is a land of variety--rich in plant and animal life, outstanding in scenic values, and diverse in recreation opportunities. Its 1420 square miles (909,000 acres) of public land contain:
19 Developed campgrounds
16 Picnic sites
 4 swimming sites
 5 Impoundments (fishing and boating)
825 Miles of hiking trails
    (165 in Wilderness; 660 are all-purpose, non-motorized)
570 Miles of roads offering outstanding scenery
700 Miles of fishing streams (Trout and Bass)
 5 Wilderness Areas totaling 122 sq. miles
 3 Designated Scenic Areas totaling 4.4 sq. miles
  Spruce Knob--Highest Point in West Va.--4,862 ft.
  Seneca Rocks--a 900-ft.-high vertical rock formation
  Spruce Knob--Seneca Rocks National Recreation Area--156 sq. miles
  Several National Natural Landmarks

The Forest is mountainous; elevations range from 900 ft. at Petersburg to over 4800 ft. along Spruce Mountain in Pendleton County. A "rain shadow" effect drops about 60 inches of precipitation on the west side and half that on the east. The Forest is underlain by sedimentary rocks that result in beautiful scenery, valuable minerals, excellent timber, grazing opportunities, and generally good water quality.

Minerals include commercial quantities of coal, natural gas, limestone and limited amounts of iron, silica, and gravel.

Grazing for sheep and cattle occurs on 11 sq. miles of land, primarily on limestone and limy shale soils.

Northern hardwoods merge on the Monongahela with oak-hickory forests typical of the Ohio Valley and trees from the south to form complex and diverse ecosystems. Ample rainfall and good soils contribute to excellent tree growth. Much is lost in generalizations like this however. Black locusts and sycamores have much different minimum requirements for rainfall (soil moisture). Black cherry and red spruce require much different definitions of "good" soils.

The scenic and recreational attributes of the Forest support over a million visitor-days of recreation use each year. Recreation activities on the Forest include:

Berry picking	Spelunking	Hunting	Cross-country skiing
Nature study	Swimming	Fishing	Whitewater boating
Picnicking	Backpacking	Trapping	Driving for pleasure
Rock climbing	Camping	Hiking	Mountain biking

Water quality is generally good. The Monongahela is astride the Eastern Continental Divide and is drained by the Potomac and Ohio River Systems.

Populations of deer, bear, wild turkey and squirrel are found, as well as a large variety of upland game, fur bearers, and non-game species. Both warm-water and cold-water fishing is available. Two species of endangered bats and one species of endangered flying squirrel are found on the Forest.

The 1997 Annual Report of the 1420-square-mile MNF contains some information of interest to Forest visitors:

Recreational Use:	1,100,000 Visitor-Days	
Timber Volume Sold:	13 million board-feet	
Timber Volume harvested:	25 million board-feet	
Land Acquired:	52 acres	(0.1 sq. miles)
Natural Regeneration:	983 acres	(1.5 sq. miles)
Even-aged regeneration:	691 acres	(1.1 sq. miles)
Oil and Gas Leased: (1994)	200,000 acres	(312 sq. miles)
Trail Maintenance:	100.miles	
Road Construction:	2.5 miles	
Road Reconstruction:	5.4 miles	
Roads Abandoned:	6.0 miles	
Returns to U.S. Treasury:	$7,200,000 *	
Returns to W. Va. Counties:	$1,800,000 **	

* $6.6 million from timber, $400,000+ from oil/gas royalties, $150,000
        from recreation (not including savings from concession campgrounds)
**   does not include payments in lieu of taxes.

Seneca Rocks Hiking Trail (TR563). Photo by Allen de Hart

(C) WEST VIRGINIA'S HIGHEST MOUNTAINS

In and near the MNF, particularly along the Allegheny Front, are the highest knobs and ridges in West Virginia. In some states it is a popular sport to visit each mountaintop on a list of the state's highest peaks. For those interested in pursuing this sport in West Virginia, see the table below.

West Virginia's Ten Highest Peaks

No.	Mountain	Elev.	Topo Map	Ownership
1	Spruce Knob	4863	Spruce Knob NE	MNF
2	Bald Knob	4842	Cass	St.Park
3	Thorny Flat	4839	Cass	Private
4	Unnamed knob on Back Allegheny Mountain	4810	Cass	Private
5	Unnamed knob on Cheat Mtn. North of Snowshoe	4772	Cass	Private
6	Mt. Porte Crayon	4770	Laneville	MNF
7	Unnamed knob on Cheat Mtn. (N of RR)	4760+	Cass	Private
8	Hosterman Knob	4757	Cass	Private
9	Red Spruce Knob	4703	Woodrow	MNF
10	Snyder Knob	4700	Snyder Knob	Private

(D) TREES ON THE MONONGAHELA NATIONAL FOREST

About 75 different tree species are found on the MNF. The more common species are listed below, along with a summary of major attributes of each species.

Eastern Hophornbean		Serviceberry	(W,R)
American Beech	(W,S)	Sourwood	(R)
Sugar Maple	(T,S)	Scarlet Oak	(W,T)
Flowering Dogwood	(W,R)	Butternut	(now rare)
Red Maple	(T)	Yellow Poplar	(T)
Basswood	(T,S)	Sassafras	(R)
Black Gum	(W)	Black Cherry	(W,T)
Sweet Birch		Aspen	(W)
Fraser Magnolia	(W)	Black Locust	(S,T)
Cucumber Tree	(T,W)	Pin Cherry	(W)
White Ash	(T,W)	Red Spruce	(W,T,F,S,R)
Yellow Birch	(T)	Eastern Hemlock	(W,R,T)
White Oak	(W,T)	Eastern White Pine	(T,W,R,F)
Northern Red Oak	(W,T)	Pitch Pine	(W,R,T)
Black Oak	(W,T)	Virginia Pine	(R,T)
Chestnut Oak	(W,T)	Red Pine	(F,R,T)
Slippery Elm	(T)	Norway Spruce	(T,R)
Hickories	(W,T)	Black Walnut	(W,T)

W = Wildlife   F = Fire Control   S = Soils   T = Timber   *R = Recreation
*Species choices for aesthetics are a variety rather than a monoculture or a given preferred tree species.

Tree identification can make your hike more interesting and educational. Most book stores have several good field guides to trees and shrubs.

The 75 tree species on the MNF can be grouped into eight types. The relative abundance of these types is charted below.

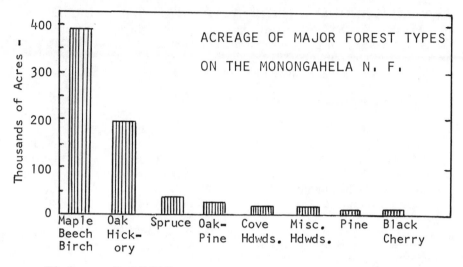

ACREAGE OF MAJOR FOREST TYPES ON THE MONONGAHELA N. F.

Timber on the MNF is generally middle-aged. As a result of extensive timber harvest between 1890 and 1930, 67% of the area classed as productive forest land supports timber stands 60-89 years old. About half are 70-89 years old. (see table below) The USFS hopes to develop a more balanced age class distribution as a means of improving wildlife habitat, timber management and visual appeal in those portions of the Forest in which vegetation management through timber harvest is permitted. However, the MNF Land and Resource Management Plan of 1986 does not permit timber harvests on about 25% of the Forest, provides for development and management of uneven-aged stands on some areas, and has scheduled harvests to regenerate young stands on less than 0.25% of the forest annually during the planning period. The following table gives the February, 1988 and January, 1995 distributions of timber age classes on productive forest land on the MNF in square miles and percent of total.

Age Class	(1988)	(%)	(1995)	(%)
0-19 years	36	(3)	34.1	(2.5)
20-39	29	(3)	52.7	(3.9)
40-49	28	(3)	18.7	(1.4)
50-59	133	(13)	63.3	(4.7)
60-69	278	(27)	226.3	(16.8)
70-79	245	(24)	395.2	(29.4)
80-89	109	(11)	276.0	(20.5)
90-99	45	(4)	98.6	(7.3)
100+	65	(6)	#108.3	(8.0)
Uneven-aged	23	(2)	-	(-)
Two-aged	41	(4)	-	(-)
No Age	-	(-)	71.7	(5.3)
Total Area	**1032	(100%)	1344.9	(99.8)
Total MNF Area*	1381	(1987)	1420.0	(1997)

* Includes water, unproductive land, Wilderness, scenic areas etc.
** Excludes water, unproductive land, Wilderness, scenic areas, etc.
#   42.9 (100-109)   27.4 (110-119)   14.9 (120-129)
     9.2 (130-139)   6.4 (140-149)   7.4 (150+)

(E) THE MONONGAHELA NATIONAL FOREST LAND MANAGEMENT PLAN

The current MNF Management plan and Environmental Impact Statement was published in July of 1986. All 156 national forests are required to prepare land management plans every 10-15 years, and the MNF expects to begin planning in 2001, though Congress may change this. Some of the issues present during the 1986 planning process are no longer issues. New ideas and concerns have been raised. MNF management and planning are constantly adjusting.

The 3,600 public responses to the 1986 draft plan contained about 35,000 comments and suggestions regarding the Forest Plan. Many comments referred to it as a "special place". There can be no doubt that the MNF is near and dear to the hearts of many people.

The main items of concern to the public were the following projections of the Draft Plan:

- decreases in remote wildlife habitat;
- huge increase in road construction;
- large amounts of leasing of public land for coal-related developments,
- conversion of excessive areas from hardwood forest to conifer (softwood) forest.

There was also much public interest in land acquisition and recreation management practices.

The final Land Management Plan appeared to make a sincere attempt to address these concerns. Planned road construction dropped significantly. The final Plan calls for 372 miles of road construction in 10 years and 1799 miles in 50 years. The Plan projected 10 miles of trail construction annually through 1990 and 43.2 more miles of trails between 1990 and 2000. The area with restricted motor vehicle use should increase. Area under conifer management should be less than projected in the draft. Area with extended-rotation timber management should increase. All these changes should enhance the quality of the hiking experience on the MNF in coming decades. Increasing the rotation age at which timber is harvested should increase the sawtimber-value productivity of the forest. At the same time, it will increase the amount of wildlife habitat, scenic values and natural values that result from big trees--and reduce that which comes from little trees. Timber outputs will shift toward the higher-quality end of the spectrum and therefore probably compete less with the timber outputs of private- and industrial forests. Future hiker may experience more "cathedral" areas (a leafy canopy far overhead, with relatively little understory).

A number of major land acquisitions have occurred in Greenbrier Ranger District. So that area should see significantly expanded recreation use in years to come. (The public seems to most enjoy the parts of the Forest with large contiguous blocks of public land.)

About 195 sq. miles will be managed for semi-primitive, non-motorized recreation. Hiking trail development will focus on these areas. These areas are in addition to the 122 sq. miles of Wilderness on the MNF. The table below lists the areas to managed for semi-primitive, non-motorized recreation.

North Fork Mtn. (left), Germany Valley (center left), Fore Knobs (cntr. right),

Area	Sq. Miles	Area	Sq. Miles
North Fork/Hopeville	7.2	Little Mountain	16.3
Flat Rock/Roaring Plains	12.1	Peters Mountain	3.7
Cheat Mountain	11.8	Tea Creek/Turkey Mtns.	16.2
Seneca/Gandy Creeks	30.7	Cranberry Back Country	12.3
East Fork of Greenbrier	11.9	Spice Run	12.0
Laurel Fork	4.9	Big Draft	12.5
Canaan Mountain	21.1	Upper Middle Mountain	12.8
Smokehole	4.2	Laurel Run	4.7
		Total	194.4

Natural succession will be the primary vegetative objective in these areas, with vegetation management used only to protect the resource or complement recreational values. A variety of dispersed recreation activities may take place. Recreation management may include limited, rustic facilities such as Adirondack shelters and primitive sanitary disposal, as well as publicity, to maximize the semi-primitive recreation potential of the area. The transportation system will be closed to public motorized use; no additional system roads will be built. Wildlife management compatible with the recreation objective will occur, and wildlife species that prefer a low level of disturbance will be favored.

Of particular interest to hikers and other Forest visitors is the many new Special Areas called for in the Plan. These areas are listed below.

<u>Allegheny Front (right), and Seneca Rocks (lower right).</u> Photo by Carl Belli

Special Areas For The Monongahela National Forest
(Some are still pending NEPA analysis.)

NAME	DIST.	ACRES	CLASS*	PRESCRIPT.**	FEATURE
Bear Rocks Bog	Potomac	10	RN	B,RNA	
Bickle Slope	Cheat	10	RN	B	
Big Draft	Wh.Sul.	71	RN	B	Trillium
Big Run Bog	Cheat	660	SPM	NNL,B,RNA	Boreal bog
Black Cherry	Green.	120	RN	RNA	Typical type
Black Mtn.	Marlin.	10	RN	B	Rhododendron
Blister Rn.Swamp	Green.	260	RN	NNL,B	Balsam fir
Blue Rock	Potomac	264	RN	Geol.	Limestone
Cran. Glades	Gauley	750	RN	NNL,B,RNA	Boardwalk
Dolly Sods	Potomac	2470	SPM	SA	Boreal Plants
Fls of Hills Cr.	Gauley	114	RN/SPN	SA	Waterfall
Fanny Bennett Hemlock Grove	Potomac	70	RN	B	Virgin Hemlock
Fernow Expt. For.	Cheat	5556	RN		
Fisher Spr. Run Bog	Potomac	410	SPN	NNL,B,RNA	Boreal bog
Gaudineer	Green.	140	SPN	NNL,SA	Virgin Spruce
Glade Run Swmp.	Green.	60	RN	B	
Hawthorne RNA	Green.	8	RN	RNA	Typical type

Max Rothkugel Plantation	Green.	150	RN	B		Norway Spruce
Meadow Creek	Wh.Sul.	17	RN	B,RNA		Shale Barron
Mt.Porte Cray.	Potomac	392	SPN	B,RNA		
N.Fork Mtn. Red Pine	Potomac	10	RN	B		Red pine
Red Spruce RNA	Greenb.	60	RN	RNA		Acid rain res.
Rohrbaugh Pl.	Potomac	136	SPN	B,RNA		Northern forest
Shavers Mtn. Spruce-Hemlock	Cheat	68	SPN	NNL,B		Virgin Spruce & Hemlock
Stuart Knob	Cheat	350	RN	B,RNA		Red Spruce
Virgin White Pine	Wh.Sul.	13	RN	B		Large trees
White's Draft	Wh.Sul.	67	RN	B,RNA		Shale Barron
Yellow Poplar	Gauley	112	RN	RNA		Typical type
Flying Squirr.	Gauley	586	-	Zool.		Threatened spec
TOTAL ACRES		12366				

*Classes: RN= Roaded Natural;   SPM= Semi-primitive, Motorized
        SPN = Semi-primitive, Non-motorized
**Prescriptions: NNL= National Natural Landmark; SA= Scenic Area;
        B= Botanical; RNA= Research Natural Area; Geol.= Geologic,
        Zool.= Zoological

The entire Plan weighs 15 lbs. However a 40-page Summary is available for review in any of the six ranger stations or at the MNF headquarters in Elkins. These locations are normally closed on weekends, but the Summary is available by mail from the Elkins office. Many libraries in West Va. carry the complete plan. Addresses and telephone numbers of MNF headquarters and district ranger offices are given below.
  Supervisor's Office, 200 Sycamore St., Elkins 26241 (304-636-1800)
  Cheat Ranger Dist., P.O. Box 368,   Parsons 26287 (304-478-3251)
  Potomac Ranger Dist., HC 59, Box 240, Petersburg 26847 (304-257-4488)
  Greenbrier Ranger Dist., P.O. Box 67, Bartow   24920 (304-456-3335)
  Marlinton Ranger Dist., P.O. Box 210, Marlinton 24954 (304-799-4334)
  Gauley Ranger Dist., P.O. Box 110, Richwood   26261 (304-846-2695)
  White Sulphur R.D., 410 E.Main St, W. Sulphur Spr. 24986 (304-536-2144)

(F) THE MONONGAHELA NATIONAL FOREST NEEDS YOU!

In 1972, Congress passed special legislation to enable interested citizens to assist in the important conservation work of the Forest Service. If you like people and are concerned about natural resources, the Monongahela National Forest needs your skills and talents in its volunteer program.

Anyone who wants to become involved may apply. The volunteer program has something for about everyone: retirees, professionals, housewives, students, teenagers, and youngsters. Volunteers under 18 years of age must have written consent from a parent or guardian. Students may volunteer for work to earn college credits, based on agreements between their colleges and the Monongahela. Retired professionals have a wealth of knowledge they may wish to share.

Some opportunities for volunteers may include working at Seneca Rocks Discovery or Cranberry Mountain Nature Centers assisting the director in putting on tours, conducting environmental studies, or doing routine maintenance. You may know a lot about a subject which you could tell to Forest visitors.

You can choose to be involved in outdoor work with other volunteers working in crews to build and maintain trails, rehabilitate campgrounds, improve wildlife habitat, assist in fire prevention activities, and perform other useful and important conservation services. Also, you may have a special interest, such as archaeology or geology, where your skills can be utilized and your knowledge enhanced by working with professionals on the staff.

Much satisfaction can be gained from helping others to understand our American heritage and resources. If you are interested, contact the Forest Supervisor's Office, or the District Ranger's office in the area where you wish to serve, and ask for an application. All addresses are given above. Indicate on the application any special interest area in which you wish to be involved or special skills you wish to use.

Your hiking group may also be interested in the Forest Service's "Adopt-A-Trail" program in which a responsible group volunteers to maintain one or more of the trails on the MNF according to a set of guidelines provided by the USFS. For more information, contact the Forest Supervisor's office or any District Ranger offices (See page 10). If you would like to join a group involved in trail maintenance on the MNF, consider the WV Rails-Trails Council, Highlands Trail Foundation, WV Mountain Bike Association, WV Chapter of the Sierra Club, WV Scenic Trails Association, or the WV Trails Coalition. Non-Wilderness trails need the most help.

A large fraction of the annual maintenance required by a trail can be done most efficiently by hikers themselves as they walk the trail. Carrying a long-handled pruner or use bow saws weighing only a few pounds and cutting branches, saplings and fallen logs is something almost any hiker can do easily, and without detracting noticeably from the fun of hiking. It is also easy to carry a plastic garbage bag for packing out rubbish from remote camping areas, trailhead parking areas and trails. Below are a few hints for maintaining trails.

(1)   Do not do any blazing. The USFS prefers to do this using its own procedures, and they do not blaze in Wilderness areas. Also, do not pound blaze-holding aluminum nails all the way in. Nail heads are left sticking out about 3/4 inch to give the tree room to grow.

(2)   Do not remove logs that are laying flat on the ground and positioned so as to serve as "water bars". (These reduce trail erosion.)

(3)   It may be faster and easier to carry or pull an entire fallen log off a trail than to saw it up first.

(4)   Inexpensive cotton gloves are handy for trail maintenance.

(5)   Hatchets and axes are too heavy and dangerous for trail maintenance. An exception is the Swedish bush axe which is under two pounds and is recommended by professional trail maintenance people. Obtain these axes from forestry supply houses since they are rarely carried by hardware stores or gardening shops.

(6)   Report major trail problems (large blow-downs, serious erosion problems, trail-sign damage) to the district ranger's office. In that way their limited resources can be spent on fixing trail problems instead of finding them.

HIKING AND BACKPACKING IN MONONGAHELA
NATIONAL FOREST

(A) WHEN AND HOW TO ENJOY HIKING

Personal preference has a lot to do with hiking habits, so little can be said here that is not disputable. May and October are the most popular times to hike in the MNF. At higher elevations spring comes a few weeks later, and fall a few weeks earlier. The least desirable periods are when the leaves are off the trees and no snow covers the ground, i.e. November, early December, late March and early April. Wildflowers can make late April and early May pleasant. Although problems with icy roads are encountered, winter offers more by way of broad views and beautiful snowy landscapes. The USFS does not plow snow on any of its roads. Only state roads and back roads used as school bus routes are plowed.

Winter travel off regularly maintained highways should not be taken lightly, even if only a short day hike is planned. From early November to mid-April have snow tires, several blankets or sleeping bags, a shovel, tire chains, extra food and matches in your car. If the weather begins to turn bad while on the trail, and you are uncertain of your ability to continue on foot or to drive back to a highway, get out quickly. Don't delay and get trapped. Dolly Sods and Spruce Knob are particularly treacherous in this regard.

Enjoying hiking and backpacking frequently involves correcting misconceptions and revising priorities. Among the more common misconceptions are:

(1)   that hikes involves some sort of struggle between people and nature, and people must be prepared to beat nature into submission to enjoy hiking:
(2)   that a major purpose of hiking is to cover as many miles as possible, and
(3)   the more people in the group the merrier.

Rethinking priorities often produces suggestions like the following:

(1)   Do not carry axes or hatchets (dangerous, heavy, unneeded).
(2)   Carry a minimum of gear and simple, readily prepared foods. But be prepared for accidents and bad weather.
(3)   Go to bed early and get up shortly after sunrise. You will hear and see more wildlife; a lower sun often creates better conditions for photographs, and in summer you walk farther before it gets hot.
(4)   Take more breaks. Wade in a mountain stream. Explore interesting rock formations. Try to get artistic photographs. Listen to the wildlife and the wind. Take leisurely lunch breaks. Linger longer at that overlook. Try to identify plants, trees, birds, footprints. Eight miles per day for a hike and six for a backpack trip are reasonable. There is so much else to see and do than just covering miles.
(5)   Keep your group size down to 10 or less. The maximum allowed group size in MNF Wilderness Areas is 10 people. Car shuttles and economics of travel to and from the area recommend two carloads of people. (one carload if no shuttle is needed). Hiking alone can be risky.

The MNF is within a day's drive of a third of the population of the U.S. and its popularity keeps growing. Your enjoyment of the MNF is made possible by the care that visitors before you exercised, and by the dedication of

Spruce Knob Lake Trail (No #). Photo by Allen de Hart

USFS personnel. Ethically then, you have the same obligation to the visitors who follow you as those before felt toward your visit. In case you are wondering how to exercise your social conscience, below are a few suggestions.

(1) Solitude is fragile. Bring no radios (except perhaps a weather radio) and minimize the area you disturbe by keeping shouting to a minimum.

(2) Leave gates as you found them; stay away from farm animals; do not damage fences or walls, even by climbing on them.

(3) Do not contribute to erosion by cutting across switchbacks or by using boots with excessively deep lugs on the soles.

(4) Camp at least 150 ft. off the trail and out of sight of the trail. Avoid camping on especially scenic areas. Leave your campsite looking more natural than when you arrived. If an established campsite already exists, usually obvious because of a fire ring and sparse vegetation, use the established site. Avoid sites where vegetation is still present but disturbed (flattened, scuffed) because environmental damage accelerates in areas of bare soil.

(5) Enjoy flowers, plants, animals and minerals in their natural setting, not by taking them home with you.

(6) Never cut boughs for a bed, dig hip-holes for sleeping, or dig trenches around your tent.

(7) Clear some fallen limbs from the trail (leaving those that are laying flat on the ground).

(8) If you packed it in, pack it out. And, for good measure, pack out some litter that was not yours. Aluminum cans and pull-tabs can last 80-100 years along a trail; plastic film 20-30 years; plastic baggies 10-20 years; paper containers 5-10 years, and orange peals can last up to 5 months. Standard practice is to to pack all unburnable rubbish out in plastic garbage bags. Aluminum foil DOES NOT BURN! "Pack it out" is a rule stressed in all national parks, national forests, wildlife refuges and BLM lands. The importance of this has increased greatly in recent years due to the popularity of backpacking and because of the decrease in the number of areas suitable for backpacking. "Leave nothing but footprints; take nothing but pictures, kill nothing but time" is the first rule of backpacking.

(9) Never put soap, food particles, or body wastes in or near water bodies. Two drops of liquid soap for the main meal of the day is all a backpacker needs to avoid GI problems from grease residues in the eastern US. Dump soapy water under bushes well away from streams and from where people walk. When packing before your trip, plan serving sizes so as to eliminate excessive amounts of cooked, but uneaten, food. You reduce pack weight and volume, make cleanup easier, and keep wild animals from developing bad eating habits.

(10) Cook with backpacker stoves. Substitute warm clothes and small campfires for ordinary clothes and large campfires. Use established fire sites.

(11) Dig a "cathole" for feces and toilet paper about 6 inches deep, away from water and trails. Mix feces with soil to aid break-down, then cover with the remaining soil to provide sanitation. Urine, which is sterile, does not need a hole, but do not do it near trails and water. Some people pack used toilet paper out in a zip-lock-type plastic bag.

(12) Report trail conditions to the district ranger in writing. Report the nature and location of major problems in detail.

(13) For more information on low impact hiking and camping techniques, call Leave No Trace, a non-profit organization, at 1-800-332-4100, or see their web site at http://www.nols.edu/LNT/LNTHome .

(B) GEAR AND FOOD FOR HIKING AND BACKPACKING

Numerous books have been written on equipment for hiking and backpacking. Many books have also been written on food and cooking under hiking- and backpacking conditions. It is not clear that presenting a brief summary of these books here would do more good than harm. If you are an experienced hiker thinking about getting into backpacking, by all means choose a few books and read them carefully. There is much to learn, and no matter how much you read, your first few backpacking experiences are going to be real learning experiences. People who have backpacked for 20 years say they learn something new on every trip they take. Many excellent books deal with equipment for hiking and backpacking. Among them:

Backpacking: One Step at a Time (1986) by Harvey Manning;

The National Outdoor Leadership School's Wilderness Guide (1983), by Peter Simer and John Sullivan,

Minimum Impact Camping (1994) by Curt Schatz and Dan Seemon.

If you want something more condensed and less expensive, try the Sierra Club's "Basic Backpacking Course Lecture Notes". It covers topics like: buying backpacking gear and supplies, equipment checklist, food-related checklist, first-aid checklist, the packing part of backpacking, using map and compass, cooking stoves, choosing campsites, setting up camp, breaking camp, disaster avoidance, equipment maintenance, wilderness ethics, and inclement-weather backpacking. The 120-page packet is available from Allegheny Group, Sierra Club, P.O. Box 8241, Pittsburgh, PA 15217 for $6.00 + $1.24 book-rate postage. The document is also available on floppy disk as word-processing files for groups running their own backpacking courses.

(C) MAPS

Topographic maps (1"= 2000 ft.) can be obtained from the U.S. Geological Survey, Printing and Distribution Center, Denver Federal Center, Box 25286, Denver, CO 80225 (Tel. 303-236-7477). The cost is $4.00/map plus $3.50/order (1998). Discounts are available for large orders. First order a free index to topographic maps of West Va. and the Survey's leaflet's "Topographic Maps". Topographic maps are indispensable on any hike. Even if one knows the trail well, topo maps can suggest interesting side trips and alternative routes. The Trail Notes in this Guide are written under the assumption that the appropriate topo map(s) is visible to the reader.

The full usefulness of this Guide is realized only after the reader has obtained one or more of the following maps from the USFS (200 Sycamore St., Elkins, WV 26241) (Checks must be made out to USDA Forest Service.):

(1) Forest Visitor Map (1994)

One half of the Forest is shown on one side and the other half on the reverse side. These maps include streams, roads, county lines, communities, trails and recreation sites but do not have contour lines. These maps are suit able for auto-touring, locating sites, and general use, but are not detailed enough for cross-country travel. Available folded only. Scale: 0.5 inch = one mile. $4.00 each.

(2) Secondary Base Series Maps

Basic map details (roads, trails, county lines, etc.) are printed in black; water features are in blue; urban areas are in red. A green overprint shows National Forest Lands. No contour lines. Scale: 1/2" = 1 mile.
(A) Northern half of the Forest, 33"x46", 1983, $4.00 each.
(B) Southern half of the Forest, 33"x46", 1983, $4.00 each.
NOTE: These maps were apparently discontinued in early 1999.

(3) Topographic Maps

Topographic maps similar to those available from the USGS (See above.) are also available from the U.S. Forest Service for $4.00 each, plus a $3.50 handling fee per order. These topo maps (1"=2000 ft.) have been specially updated for the USFS and hence are more useful that the corresponding maps obtained from the USGS. An index to the 81 topo maps covering the MNF is available free.

(D) WATER

Trail Notes later in this Guide comment on water available for drinking. These comments are based only on surmises made by trail scouts, based only on their impressions of what lies upstream--not on any sort of chemical analysis or bacteria count. MNF managers recommend treating all water from springs, streams and lakes on the MNF. Water at offices and campgrounds is tested for bacteria and need not be treated. You should know that serious diseases can be carried in unpurified streams and springs, so act accordingly. No guarantees of any kind are implied in this Guide. Using one's own judgment is risky at best, so always carry a canteen. Human enteric diseases have been acquired in remote wild areas from water contaminated by wildlife. You won't necessarily get hepatitis, but you could get a 24-hour vomiting-diarrhea syndrome that could leave you dangerously dehydrated and too weak to carry a backpack.

Below are three ways of treating water for drinking. Methods (1) and (2) produce a certain amount of "off-taste".
(1)   (safest) Boil for one minute. To restore taste, pour rapidly back & forth between two containers to re-aerate.
(2)   Water purification tablets (may not inactivate viruses capable of causing enteric disease, particularly hepatitis, giardiasis, and polio).
(3)   Water purification pump. Many are now on the market, priced from $35 to $300, which weigh one pound or less.

(E) TRESPASSING

A few trails described in this guide cross private property. Nothing in this Guide should be construed to mean that permission has been obtained for hikers to use the trails described. Whenever "No Trespassing" signs are seen, ask the land owner for permission to cross the land. Inform the editors of any problem. (See page 35.)

View from north end of North Fork Mountain Trail (TR501).
Photo by Steve Swingenstein and Bill Battenfelder

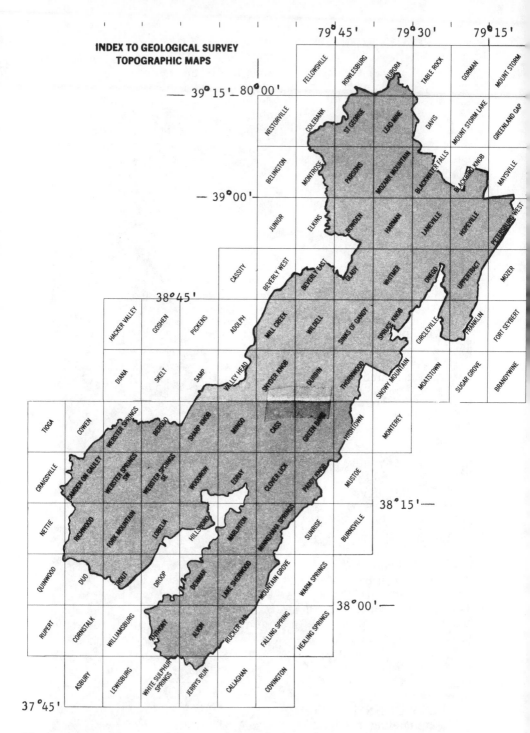

INDEX TO GEOLOGICAL SURVEY
TOPOGRAPHIC MAPS

Obtain topographic maps from U.S. Geological Survey, Printing and Distribution Center, Denver Federal Center, Box 25286, Denver, CO 80225 (Tel. 303-236-7477) or from Monongahela National Forest, 200 Sycamore St., Elkins, WV 26241

(F) OFF-ROAD VEHICLES

Certainly some of the most agonizing problems facing public land managers, law enforcement agencies, property owners, and those seeking to enjoy the peace and serenity of the forests and countrysides have arisen with the increased use of trail bikes, snowmobiles, and ATVs in recent years. "No Trespassing" signs are going up; sections of major hiking trails that cross private land are being closed down by irate landowners, and ever-tighter restrictions are being placed on the use of such vehicles. By now there are few who have not heard the protests and arguments concerning the damage these vehicles do to plant and animal life, the erosion of trails and hill sides, the vandalism at remote structures and fences, the disturbances to the tranquility of rural and wooded areas, and any number of others.

Those considering purchasing an ORV should consider the following:

(1)   A noise level of 80 decibels is sufficient to cause (eventually) permanent damage to the human ear.
(2)   Telephone guy wires are almost capable of decapitating people traveling at snowmobile speeds. Barbedwire fences, deep ruts, and other obstructions can inflict serious injuries.
(3)   Cars, trucks, buses, and locomotives have run-down ORV users unable to hear their approach.
(4)   Mechanical breakdowns in remote areas can cause serious problems.
(5)   At least one Michigan doctor, with considerable experience in the problem, claims that all snowmobile users have hairline cracks in their backbones after three or fewer seasons.
(6)   The trailer and other accessories, repairs, maintenance, and storage make ORVs much more costly than one often anticipates.
(7)   Much of the appeal of most remote areas arises from the peace and tranquility found in these areas.
(8)   If ORVs are used extensively by hunters to gain access to remote areas this will most probably reduce the size of the herd to the point that the average annual kill, averaged over the years, is reduced for everyone.
(9)   The use of ORVs over fallen logs, across deep ravines, and on steep slopes often causes serious erosion problems.
(10) A 1990 survey by the Michigan Association of Conservation Districts estimated that the cost of restoring Michigan land damaged by off-road vehicles would be $1.2 billion.

The USFS annually reviews its "Road and Trail Management Program" which governs the use of all types of motorized use on Monongahela National Forest roads and trails. Information on the current policy is available from the Forest Supervisor (200 Sycamore St., Elkins, WV 26241). The public is invited to participate in the review and revision of this program. Currently the standard on the MNF is no ORVs, and open Forest Roads are only open to state-licensed vehicles. This means no ATVs and snowmobiles since WV does not license them.

(G) SAFETY CONSIDERATIONS

During hunting season, especially, wear bright-colored outer garments: reds, oranges, and yellows (for safety). The most dangerous time is deer (gun) season which begins in late November and runs through most of December. Archery season and small game season is not as dangerous

19

View looking east from Allegheny Front, looking across the Fore Knobs, North Fork Mountain (N end of TR501) and four ridges beyond. Photo by Steve Swingenstein

because hunters get closer to their prey, and the projectile is not as powerful.

Lyme disease, a bacterial infection spread by certain ticks (about the size of a poppy seed), is also becoming a threat to be reckoned with. If left untreated, the disease causes joint pain, impairment of nerves, lungs, and heart, blindness, severe eye- and speech problems, and, in rare cases, death. The disease can be detected fairly accurately with a blood test (after 4-6 weeks), and can be cured, even in its advanced stages, with antibiotics (though oral antibiotic taken early can save intravenous antibiotic therapy later on). It is often mistaken for arthritis, multiple sclerosis and other neurological disorders. Nationally, 5000 cases were reported in 1988, and the number has doubtlessly gotten much larger since then. The disease is spreading across Pennsylvania, so presumable it will become more common over the years in the MNF as well. Be sure to check your skin for ticks after returning from the woods. Remove them carefully with tweezers. Symptoms of Lyme disease include a rash or a ring-shaped red spot like a bull's eye that grows larger every day, plus flu-like symptoms (fever, chills and headache), a stiff neck and difficulty concentrating. Two or three weeks later there will be pain and swelling of the joints.

Crossing streams during periods of high water can be dangerous or cause death. Forest soils have tremendous capacity for absorbing rain water, but once that capacity is exceeded, rain water runs rapidly down steep hillsides and converts babbling brooks into raging torrents. Thin soils (e.g. Dolly Sods) can result in extreme stream-crossing dangers after only 2-3 days of rain. It's a good idea to check with the district ranger's office just before you leave for a trip to the MNF. If they report rain for the past few days, you should probably postpone your trip even though the forecast for the days of your trip sounds good. Dolly Sods Wilderness and Otter Creek Wilderness are places where troubles with stream crossing are most often reported.

If you are backpacking and need to cross a stream with a significant flow rate, unbuckle your backpack belt buckle so you can exit your pack quickly in case of emergency. Use a walking stick for balance, but otherwise keep both hands free to balance yourself and grab onto rocks. Some people carry 3/8" rope for use in crossing sizeable streams. If you do that, make sure you are experienced in using the rope by practicing without a pack on a non-ferocious stream. The stretch of nylon rope can make the procedure very tricky. Cold weather greatly compounds the dangers involved in crossing streams. Crossing streams barefoot can also increase the difficulty, especially for people who aren't used to walking barefoot. Many people now carry "water shoes" on hikes and backpack trips because they are light, cheap, and greatly increase foot comfort when crossing streams. Tie your hiking boots to the outside of your pack, don't carry them in your hands.

(H) WILDERNESS TRAILS

Five Wilderness areas (78,131 acres) are found in the MNF: Cranberry Wilderness (35,864 acres) in the Gauley Ranger District; Dolly Sods Wilderness (10,215 acres) in the Potomac Ranger District; Laurel Fork Wilderness (North) (6,055 acres) and Laurel Fork Wilderness (South) (5,997 acres) in the Greenbrier Ranger District, and Otter Creek Wilderness (20,000 acres) in the Cheat Ranger District. All are forested, with extensive trail networks, and a major stream either flowing through, or near, the Wilderness boundaries.

Otter Creek and Dolly Sods were designated as Wilderness under the Eastern Wilderness Act of 1975. Cranberry Wilderness and Laurel Forks Wilderness were designated as such under the West Virginia Wilderness Act of 1983.

Wilderness management takes its guidelines from the Wilderness Act of 1964, whose purpose it to preserve and protect natural ecosystems and values, and to provide opportunities for solitude or a primitive- or unconfined type of recreation. Therefore, a Wilderness area is considerably different from other forest lands, and visitors need to be aware of the contrasts.

Wilderness is not just a place for recreation; it is not a "park" within a national Forest, and it is not a nice place to take the kiddies for a safe walk. It is special. It is designated by Congress because it has unique opportunities for education, scientific study, preservation of our heritage, and scenic wonder. It has the appearance of being influenced primarily by the forces of nature. It carries with it the implication that those who would go there for any single or combination of the above opportunities have a responsibility to:
- be prepared for whatever situations they may encounter,
- insure that their actions do not impair the opportunities for future generations.

Wilderness is both non-motorized (no ORVs, no chainsaws) AND non-mechanical (no bikes, carts, or wagons).

Heavy maintenance on MNF Wilderness areas stopped around 1993. Light maintenance is expected to decrease in coming years. This is an attempt to make these eastern Wildernesses even more wild. Around 1993, wide trail-clearing limits and the replacement of damaged signs and blazes stopped. Since then the MNF limited maintenance to clearing trails just wide enough for a person with a pack, and clearing anything that couldn't be ducked under or stepped over. In the future the MNF is only going to clear wide enough for a person with a pack and clear anything that may cause unacceptable environmental damage by people going around it. Trails scoured by flooding will not have the tread reestablished. Visitors will be encouraged to spread out to lessen impact where a treadway can't be distinguished, or to find safe detours around deadfalls on trails. This will enhance the naturalness of the areas and increase the challenge of hiking the wilderness. Signs explaining this policy will be placed at trailheads.

Timber harvests, construction of reservoirs, power projects, transmission lines and roads are all prohibited in Wilderness. Recreational usage is not promoted. Trail shelters are being phased out. Bridges and blazes are non-existent. Wilderness usage is by non-motorized, non-mechanical means. Exceptions are allowed for the USFS to deal with health- and safety issues, fire suppression, and insect- or disease control. The maximum group size in MNF Wilderness areas is 10. Camp stoves are strongly encouraged, and campfires must be from only dead and down wood. Camping is not permitted near trailheads or trail intersections to assist in a feeling of solitude. In Dolly Sods, camping is not permitted within 100 yards of FR19 and FR75. Use of horses is discouraged because of the resultant excessive degradation of trails and limited trail maintenance. Hunting, fishing, and trapping may occur, subject to appropriate state and federal laws. To monitor user treatment of Wilderness areas, law enforcement is utilized for litter, vehicle, and fire rule violations. Read the brochure "Leave No Trace Land Ethics" offered free by the US Forest Service, National Park Service, and the Bureau of Land Management.

A frosty Bald Knob on Cabin Mtn. near Dolly Sods Wilderness. Photo by Nick Broskovich

MONONGAHELA NATIONAL FOREST WINTERS

(A) WINTER BACKPACKING
(Contributed by Helen McGinnis and Craig Moore, past WVHC members who have had much experience backpacking on the MNF in winter.)

Few people take advantage of opportunities to visit their favorite backpacking areas in the winter. With the leaves off the trees, vistas open up. Frozen waterfalls of icicles appear. Deep snow creates scenes of incredible beauty and the satisfying crunch of undisturbed snow under snowshoes or skis. There is more solitude, and more tracks of forest dwellers. Some people fear they will spend part of the trip being cold, wet, and miserable, but if they are properly equipped, they almost certainly will be more comfortable than they would be walking city streets.

Snow camping is advanced backpacking, and isn't for beginners. Packs are heavier because of the extra gear and clothing. Snow makes the going more strenuous. Days are short, leaving less time to reach your goal. And problems arising from getting lost, injured, or falling into an icy stream are more serious than at other times of the year.

If you're not a moderately skilled skier you are better off on snowshoes. Look for an intermediate-sized shoe with upturned toes.

The most dangerous part of a winter backpack trip is the drive there. USFS gravel roads are not plowed; some are even gated in winter. Check with the district ranger's office to make sure you can get to the trailhead. County and local roads may not be plowed until well after a storm. You could be snowed-in for a while. Carry a snow shovel to dig out of drifts. Tire chains are excellent for winter travel on icy or unplowed roads.

Local law enforcers and USFS personnel become concerned if they find a car seemingly abandoned in a remote area in the dead of winter. Avoid becoming the object of a search party by leaving a note in your car--visible from the outside--explaining what you're doing and when you'll be back.

On the MNF, temperatures below zero and balmy weather can occur on the same weekend. Snow usually doesn't accumulate too deep, melting away between storms. During unseasonably warm weather, streams can turn into icy torrents.

Snow creates problems in route finding by obscuring the tread-way, even blazes and trail signs. In a heavy snow storm or fog, even the most familiar landscape can seem unfamiliar. A compass and maps and the ability to use them are essential. According to former Potomac District Ranger Whitney Lerer, who has rescued people in Michigan and on Dolly Sods, lost hikers frequently stay lost because they refuse to believe their compasses.

(B) SKI-TOURING
Much of the MNF is at high elevations, resulting in more snowfall, lower temperatures, and less melting between snow storms than near urban areas surrounding the MNF. For example, Pittsburgh (el.1000') averages 45" of snow yearly. Laurel Ridge (el.2700') receives around 130" of snow yearly. Canaan Valley in the MNF (el.3100') receives around 160". Showshoe (el.4800') receives 180" snow yearly.

The potential of the MNF for ski-touring is growing. Countless trails, unplowed USFS roads, logging roads, etc. offer delightful ski-touring. Unfortunately little or no information is available on most of these opportunities. So exploratory ski-touring trips to the MNF are likely to be rewarding. This edition tries to assess the potential of each hiking trail for ski-touring. Where possible, we rate each trail S1, S2, S3 and S4 (beginner, intermediate, advanced and not suitable) based on steepness, trail width, rockiness, crookedness, stream crossings, etc. The elevation range for each trail is given, permitting an approximate judgment of snow conditions.

The U.S. Forest Service has provided a list of Forest Service roads on the MNF that are unplowed and which the USFS judged to be suitable for ski-touring. Their list currently includes 200 miles of USFS roads. These roads are listed in the introduction to each ranger district.

The fact that the MNF is at high elevations also means that the terrain is rugged, so trails can be quite steep in spots. Also, stream crossings that offer the hiker only minor challenges can provide the ski-tourer with formidable challenges. In the Table of Trips, the number of stream crossings is given as an aid to planning ski-touring trips. Because of the steepness of the terrain and the frequent stream crossings, beginning skiers should stick to trails rated S1 and to USFS roads recommended in this guide for ski-touring.

The availability of snow and the charm of the MNF that is derived from its rural character create drawbacks for the ski-tourer as well as benefits. The main drawback is the driving that must be done to get to the area where you want to ski. One should be experienced as a winter driver and be prepared for emergencies both on the road and at the trailhead.

Some commercial outfitters offer ski rentals, groomed- and patrolled trails, eating facilities, guided tours, etc. In Canaan Valley one can buy a one-time lift ticket at a downhill area to get to the top of Cabin Mountain, and spend the day skiing back down to the valley floor. The area around Cranberry Backcountry is also developing facilities and accommodations for ski-touring. Maps and directories of facilities are becoming available. Below is a list of information and areas of interest to ski-tourers as known to the editors.

- Canaan Valley Resort, Davis, WV 26260 offers a map plus a description of ski-touring trails in and near the Park.
- White Grass Nordic Ski Center, Davis, WV 26260 (Tel 304-866-4114) offers trail map, groomed trails, eating facilities and ski rentals.
- Blackwater Falls State Park, Davis, WV 26260 offers a map of ski-touring trails in and near the park.
- Elk River Touring Center, Slaty Fork, WV 26291 (Tel. 304-572-3771) offers a trail map and brief guide to its system of trails.
- Snowshoe Resort, PO Box 10, Snowshoe WV 26209, 304-572-5252
- Timberline Resort, PO Box 625, Davis WV 26260, Tel. 800-766-9464.
- Richwood Chamber of Commerce, 52 Oakford Ave, Richwood WV 26261 (Tel. 304-846-6790) offers a map/brochure on 75 miles of ski-touring trails in Cranberry Backcountry and surroundings. Call for information on trail conditions. There are far more than 75 miles of trails. Many over-night accommodations are found in Richwood. Much of the Cranberry Backcountry and surroundings are at high elevations (4000+ft). This makes for good snow conditions. Numerous unplowed roads in the area also make it popular for ski-touring.

For information on other ski areas near the MNF call 1-800-CALL-WVA.

Skiing along Upper Red Creek near Blackbird Knob Trail (TR511). Photo by Mike Wardwell

STRUCTURE AND USE OF THIS GUIDE

(A) MAPS AND THE TABLE OF TRAILS

Following this introductory material is a map outlining the MNF. It shows major roads, various sub-divisions of the MNF. (See the Table of Trails and the locations of various groups of interconnected trails.) This map will find application when using the Table of Trails or the Trail Notes.

Following the map is a "Table of Trails" that summarizes the basic information on the trails described in this Guide. The idea behind this Table is that, by using it along with a USFS map, one gets an overview of the hiking opportunities and choose the trail(s) for a future hike without reading all the Trail Notes. The Table of Trails divides the area covered into sub-divisions. Usually these correspond to USFS ranger districts. Within each sub-division, trails are divided into groups. The trails of each group all inter-connect or are sufficiently close together that one could probably find abandoned logging roads and pipe lines. to make a connection.

Column 1: Number assigned to each trail for identification purposes. When the trail is a USFS trail, the three-digit number is that used by the USFS on its map and sign posts at trail junctions. The first digit of the number identifies the ranger district in which the trail is located, as can be seen from the Table.

Column 2: Name of the trail. USFS-maintained trails have the same name as that used by the USFS and seen on its sign posts. Non-USFS trails managed by State agencies have the names used by the agency.

Column 3: Starting point and finish point. These points are either junctions with roads, other trails, or obvious landmarks--all of which can be recognized on the appropriate map. The abbreviation TR means Trail. The abbreviations US, WV, CO, Rt, FS and FR refer to various kinds of roads, all easily recognized on the appropriate USFS map. (See the list of abbreviations on page 30 or 36.)

Column 4: Trail length in miles.

Column 5: A rating of each trail according to:
- character of the scenery   (1, 2, 3);
- difficulty negotiating the trail   (I, II, III);
- trail condition   (A, B, C),
- ski-touring rating   (S1, S2, S3, S4).

Ratings are defined in the Summary of Table Abbreviations which immediately precedes the Table of Trails.

Column 6: Additional comments for each trail. These are described by code letters defined in the Summary of Table Abbreviations on page 36.

Column 7: Intersecting trails and roads. Intersecting trails do not contain the standard prefix "TR", but roads have their normal prefix.

Column 8: Maximum and minimum elevations (in feet) encountered on the trail. This helps hikers and ski-tourers gauge the ruggedness of the trail and the amount of snow fall.

Column 9: Number of stream crossings encountered along the trail. Stream crossings that use bridges are not counted. This information is primarily of value to ski-tourers.

Column 10: Page number in this Guide to look to find the Trail Notes relevant to that trail, and what page to find the trail map on.

Column 11: Same as Column 1.

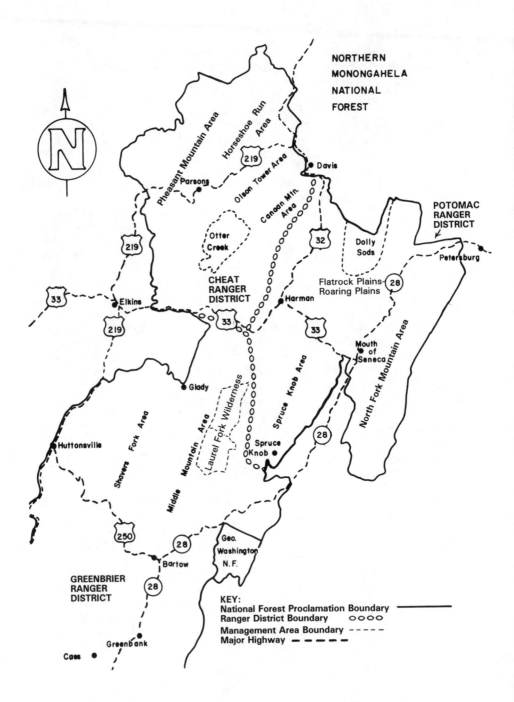

NORTHERN
MONONGAHELA
NATIONAL
FOREST

Pheasant Mountain Area

Horseshoe Run Area

219

● Davis

Olson Tower Area

● Parsons

Canaan Mtn. Area

POTOMAC
RANGER
DISTRICT

Otter
Creek

32

Dolly
Sods

● Petersburg

219

CHEAT
RANGER
DISTRICT

Flatrock Plains
Roaring Plains

28

33

● Elkins

33

● Harman

219

33

Mouth
of
Seneca ●

Spruce Knob Area

● Glady

North Fork Mountain Area

Shavers Fork Area

Middle Mountain Area

Laurel Fork Wilderness

● Huttonsville

Spruce
○ Knob ●

28

250

28

Geo.
Washington
N.F.

GREENBRIER
RANGER
DISTRICT

● Bartow

28

KEY:
National Forest Proclamation Boundary ——————
Ranger District Boundary ○○○○
Management Area Boundary - - - - -
Major Highway — — —

● Greenbank

Cass ●

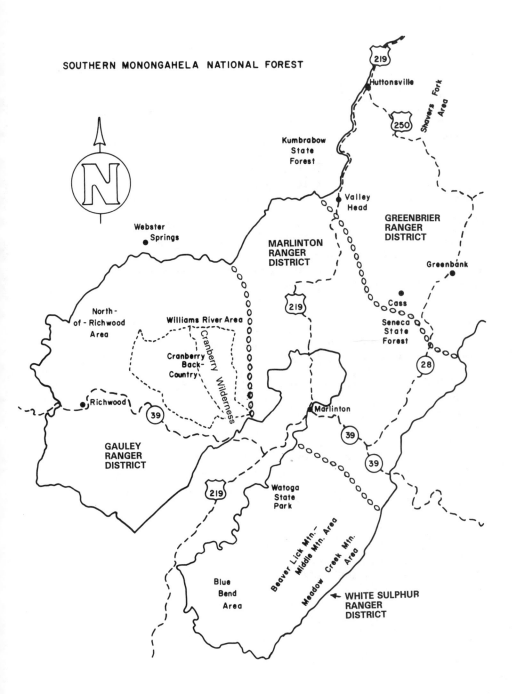

SOUTHERN MONONGAHELA NATIONAL FOREST

N

219 Huttonsville

250 Shavers Fork Area

Kumbrabow State Forest

Valley Head

GREENBRIER RANGER DISTRICT

Greenbank

MARLINTON RANGER DISTRICT

Webster Springs

219

Cass

Seneca State Forest

North-of-Richwood Area

Williams River Area

Cranberry Wilderness

Cranberry Back-Country

28

Richwood

39

Marlinton

39

39

GAULEY RANGER DISTRICT

219

Watoga State Park

Beaver Lick Mtn. Area

Middle Mtn. Area

Meadow Creek Mtn. Area

Blue Bend Area

WHITE SULPHUR RANGER DISTRICT

Following the Table of Trails is detailed information on each of the trails listed in the Table of Trails. These trail notes summarize information like: how to get to and identify access points, the location of springs, trail shelters, camp sites and points of interest, a description of the route and scenery, comments on the availability of water, necessary maps, and whatever else the trail scout thought appropriate.

(B) USING THE TRAIL DESCRIPTIONS AND MAPS

The trail descriptions following the Table of Trails comprise the bulk of this Guide. This portion of the Guide also contain topo maps of most of the trails covered by this Guide. In the interests of efficiency, a number of symbolic notations are used in these trail descriptions and Maps. You should be familiar with these to make full use of this Guide.

Trail descriptions are keyed to topo maps using notations composed of letters enclosed in squares, e.g. [D]. Such notations appear in both text and maps, so you can quickly relate a particular discussion in the description to the corresponding spot on the topo map. The topo map(s) on which a given trail appears is listed on the fifth line of each trail description.

Some trails appear on two or more topo maps. In such cases the key symbol that is mentioned first for a given map is followed by the number of the corresponding map, e.g. [K] (Map II-B-3). Subsequent map key symbols pertinent to the *same* map (Map II-B-3 in this example) are not followed by the map number.

Trail routes are shown on the topo maps in this Guide by small, closed circles, e.g. ● ● ● ● ●. Side trails (typically abandoned logging roads, abandoned USFS foot trails) noted by trail scouts (and usually mentioned in the text of the Notes) are designated by small open circles, e.g. o o o o o o. Side trails that are unexplored are shown as only a few open circles. Larger numbers of open circles indicate the approximate extent to which the side trail has been explored. These sidetrail notations are meant mainly to provide additional landmarks for hikers to identify their location along the main trail, and to help them avoid getting sidetracked. Experienced hikers who like exploratory hiking and who have the necessary maps can use these side trails as jumping-off points for their side trips (not recommended for the average hiker). Information on side trails is incomplete. Do not expect to see o o o o o on the maps for every side trail you see.

Trail descriptions contain some standard abbreviations to conserve space and reduce verbiage. The abbreviations used in this Guide are:

WV	West Virginia
MNF	Monongahela National Forest
WVHC	West Virginia Highlands Conservancy
USFS	U. S. Forest Service (U.S. Dept. of Agriculture)
DNR	West Virginia Department of Natural Resources
US19	Federal Highway Number 19 (or whatever the No.)
WV39	WV State Highway 39 (or whatever the No.)
CO48	WV Secondary (County) Highway 48 (or whatever the No.)
FR112	USFS Road No. 112 (or whatever the No.)
TR528	USFS Trail No. 528 (or whatever the 3-digit No.)
RR	Railroad
N, S, E, W	north, south, east, west

NE, SE   northeast, southeast
SW, NW   southwest, northwest
SSW, WSW south-southwest, west-southwest
NNE, ENE   north-northeast, east-northeast
3.6mi   3.6 (or whatever the No.) miles (1.0mi= 1.61km)
4.3km   4.3 (or whatever the No.) kilometers (1km=.62mi)
35ft   35 (or whatever the No.) of feet
            (used in this Guide only with reference to vertical distances)
50yd   50 (or whatever the No.) yards
2.3sq.mi   2.3 (or whatever the No.) square miles (640 acres = 1.0sq.mi)
            (Areas smaller than 64 acres (0.1sq.mi) are expressed in acres.)
topo   U.S. Geological Survey 7.5' topographic map
ORV   Off-road (motorized) vehicle
Please familiarize yourself with these abbreviations.

Trail Description Format
   Line 1: Trail name, trail number, and total length of the trail in miles and kilometers (km).
   Line 2, 3, 4: Summary of information tabulated in Columns 5, 6, 8, and 9 of the Table of Trails, i.e.:
SCENERY: Scenery rating   (from Col. 5)
DIFFICULTY: Difficulty rating (from Col. 5)
CONDITION: Trail Condition   (from Col. 5)
SKI-:   Ski-Touring Rating (from Col. 5)
NOTE: Special Notes from Col. 6 (The number in parentheses is the
               number of stream crossings from Col. 9)
ELEV: Maximum elevation/Minimum elevation encountered on the trail
               route (from Col. 8)
   Line 5: Maps useful in following the trail. The map denoted by USFS(A) is the Forest Recreation Map (1 inch = 4 miles). The map denoted by USFS(B) is the Spruce Knob-Seneca Rocks Map (1.0in= 2.0mi). The 7.5' USGS topographic map(s) (2.64in. = 1 mi) pertinent to the trail are also listed. See page 15 for more detailed information about these maps, plus information on how to obtain these maps. In most cases, relevant portions of these topo maps are reproduced in this Guide. These maps are numbered with a notation such as III-B-6. The Roman numeral indicates the ranger district. The letter indicates the region within the ranger district. See the Table of Trails to see how this numbering system works. All maps beginning with III-B are found in this Guide at the end of Section III-B (etc.) of the trail descriptions for trails located in Region III-B.
   Line 6: a table of trail segments and their lengths. Ends of segments are usually at intersecting roads and trails or other readily identifiable land-marks. The total length of all segments should equal the trail length given on Line 1.
   Subsequent Paragraphs: The first paragraph or two following the table of trail segments usually contains general information about the trail, information not specific to any particular point along the trail, or pertinent to getting to the trailheads.
   The following paragraph(s) of the trail description normally gives infor-mation on getting to the trailheads and other access points that are accessible by car, plus information about the trailhead, parking, signing, nearby camping

31

Sleeping Fawn near juncture of Allegheny Mountain Trail (TR532) and
Swallow Rock Trail (TR529). Photo by Allen de Hart

opportunities, etc. Each access point accessible by car is described in one paragraph. The first paragraph of access information is headed by the word **"Access:"**.

Subsequent paragraphs give information needed to follow the trail, plus notes on specific attractions and problems to be encountered along the trail. One paragraph is devoted to each trail segment listed in the table that started on Line 5 of the trail description. Each trail segment description is headed by **"Segment 2:"** (or whatever the segment number). This system of trail segment descriptions makes it particularly easy for you to follow routes that makes use of a number of trails.

(C) USEFUL LITERATURE

A) Dolly Sods and Otter Creek Wilderness Areas
A free pamphlet, including map, may be available on each of these two Wilderness areas from the USFS, 200 Sycamore St., Elkins, WV 26241. The USFS is (3/99) working on a web site to provide this sort of information.

B) Cranberry Back Country
A free pamphlet, including trail map, is available from the USFS (address above). Or pick one up at the Cranberry Mountain Nature Center or at the Gauley Ranger District Office on WV39 east of Richwood.

C) Wild, Wonderful West Virginia - Hotels and Motels
The West Va. Department of Commerce (Travel Division), State Capitol Complex, Charleston, WV 25305, publishes a free booklet listing all hotels and motels in West Virginia (by county). The booklet also gives the telephone number, rates, and a list of facilities available at each. Call 1-800-CALL-WVA

D) Wild, Wonderful West Virginia - Camping
The West Virginia Department of Commerce (address above) publishes a free booklet listing all the public and private camping areas in West Va. (by county). The booklet also gives the detailed location of each, the phone number, the size, the open season, and the facilities available at each area. Call 1-800-CALL-WVA.

E) West Virginia's State Parks and Forests Invite You!
This brochure lists West Virginia's state parks and forests, most of which contain hiking trails and camping facilities. Locations are shown on a map, with instructions on how to reach them. Available from Division of Parks and Recreation, Dept. of Natural Resources, Charleston, WV 25305. Tel. 304-348-6860. Free. (They also offer free brochures and trail maps on individual parks and forests if you ask about a specific area.)

F) Hiking Guide to the Allegheny Trail
The WVSTA (See page 335) offers an 108-page *Hiking Guide to Allegheny Trail* (Ed.2). The price is $8.00 postpaid (1998), with discounts available for orders of 15 or more. Orders should be sent to Vicky L. Shears, 463 Cobun Ave., Morgantown, WV 26501.

G) Forest Trees of West Virginia

This convenient pocket-sized manual describes over 100 trees seen in West Virginia's forests. Each description includes a sketch of the leaf, stem and fruit. Authored by William H. Gillespie and Earl L. Core. Available through the West Va. Division of Forestry, 1900 Kanawha Blvd. East, Charleston, WV 25305.

H) Forest Wildlife Plants of the Monongahela National Forest

This is a well written and produced field guide (5.3x8.5") by three well-known figures in West Virginia Botany, Roy B. Clarkson, W. Homer Duppstadt and Roland L. Guthrie. It is a work commissioned by the USFS to be used by the layman to identify the most common woody and herbaceous plants likely to be encountered while hiking through the MNF. It is designed for use by recreationists using the forest who are curious about flora they encounter.

The non-technical keys are written for those without the specialized vocabulary needed to use advanced guides. A feature, seldom found in manuals, is that keys and descriptions are given for plants in both summer and winter conditions.

Published by the Boxwood Press, with 285 pages. Available from the WVU Bookstore, College Avenue, Morgantown, WV 26506, or from many state park gift shops.

I) Hiking The Mountain State: The Trails of West Virginia

This recent 394-page (5x7") trail guide was written by Allen de Hart and published by the Appalachian Mountain Club Books in 1997. It covers, not only MNF trails, but also the trails on state parks, state forests and other public and private lands in West Virginia. The book is a conducted nature tour of the state's topography, flora, fauna, geology and history. Over 1700 miles of trails are covered; 38 maps with all MNF (and George Washington- and Jefferson National Forests) trails. Available at book stores and outdoor sports stores, or order from AMC, PO Box 298, Gorham NH 03581 (Tel:1-800-262-4455) or Globe Pequot Press, Inc. PO Box 833 (6 Business Park Road), Old Saybrook CT 06475 (24 hours daily) (Tel: 1-800-243-0495) ($16.95, soft-bound).

K) Miscellaneous Literature on the West Virginia Highlands

Those passing through Petersburg, W.Va. may wish to stop off at Hermitage Motor Inn (open day and night, 365 days/year). A wide selection of books, guides and other literature on West Virginia's highlands is available there. A number of other stores in the Highlands have similar selections, e.g.
- Canaan Valley State Park Gift Shop (Tel. 1-800-622-4121)
- Blackwater Falls State Park Gift Shop (Tel. 304-259-5216)
- Augusta Book Store (Elkins) (Tel. 304-636-7273)

L) Information on Nature Conservancy Reserves in West Virginia

Information on popular Nature Conservancy preserves is available from the Nature Conservancy of West Virginia free of charge. Information includes directions, special ecological features, and guidance for hikers. These areas are managed as ecological preserves, but many are quite scenic and feature trails and interpretive information. To obtain information about Nature Conservancy preserves, or about membership in The Nature Conservancy, write to TNC, P.O. Box 3754, Charleston, WV 25337 or call 304-345-4350.

(D) HELP TO IMPROVE THIS GUIDE

The trail system on the MNF is dynamic. Every year, new trails are added, while other trails are abandoned. The long-term quality of this guide depends significantly on the feedback we receive from trail users. The original edition of this guide resulted from the scouting efforts of about 20 people within the West Virginia Highlands Conservancy. Since then the scope of this guide has expanded to the point where the "committee" approach to keeping this guide up-to-date is simply not feasible, efficient or effective.

Thus an appeal is made here to all who use this guide to contribute their experiences and comments for inclusion in later editions. To encourage this, a free revised edition will be sent, as soon as it is printed, to observers who have contributed new information and corrections that are verifiable and significant for use in the new edition. Send material to: Allen de Hart, 3585 US-401 Hwy South, Louisburg, NC 27549.

Topographic maps that you send will be returned within two weeks after being received. The same holds for literature of which you wish to make the editors aware. Do not forget to include your name, address and the approximate date of the hike on which your material is based. The interests of accuracy and the editors' convenience are greatly served if you include a photocopy of whatever page(s) of this guide you think should be updated, along with the appropriate notation as to where a correction, insertion, or deletion should to be made (especially for maps). (You could also say something like "Sentence 6, paragraph 3 of page 97 is incomplete and misleading. Replace it by......").

Photographs are also needed, especially of the southern half of the MNF. Ideally they should be glossy, black-and-white, about 5x7". If you send us a print from a color negative, we will ask to borrow the negative if we decide to use the photo in the book. Unused photos will be returned. Photos used in future guides will be paid for ($10 each, plus a free copy of the new guide). Acknowledgment will be given in the caption and the photo returned, but some time after the new edition comes out. We can also use color slides but much is lost in the conversion to a black and white halftone. If your color slide is used on the front cover, you will be paid $75 for the use of your slide.

Examples of new material:

- sources of water
- possible campsites
- location of views
- interesting side trails
- exceptionally scenic spots
- location of trail signs
- describe trailhead parking
- clarify confusing text
- where trail is in poor shape
- location of gates on roads

THE TABLE OF TRAILS

SUMMARY OF TABLE-OF-TRAILS ABBREVIATIONS

(NOTE: Column numbers pertain to the Table of Trails on pages 38-47.)

Columns 1: Trail Number (normally that assigned by the USFS)
The first integer indicates which Ranger District the trail is in:
1= Cheat Ranger District   4= Marlinton Ranger District
2= Gauley Ranger District   5= Potomac Ranger District
3= Greenbrier Ranger District   6= White Sulphur R. District
7= Part of Allegheny Trail (TR701)
Column 2: Trail name assigned by the USFS unless the trail is non-USFS.
Column 3: Starting point/Finish point

US	Federal Highway
WV	State paved road
CO	County (West Va. Secondary) Road
Rt	State or County secondary road (frequently unpaved).
FR	Forest Service road
TR	Hiking trail
W.Md.RR	Western Maryland RR grade

Column 4: Distance, in miles, between the end points listed in Column 3.

Column 5: Scenery Rating:
(1)   Wild setting with exceptional scenic or natural appeal and/or points of particular interest such as scenic views, interesting geologic formations, waterfalls.
(2)   Basically wooded setting and/or little noticeable civilization, but without points of particular interest.
(3)   Mainly of a pastoral or more developed nature (scenery influenced significantly by such things as farms, unshaded logging roads, recent clearcuts, proximity to highways, strip mines, communications towers, storage tanks)
Column 5: Difficulty Rating:
(I)   Suitable for leisurely stroll. Ordinary low-heeled street shoes are adequate.
(II)   May involve moderate amounts of scrambling over rocks, and climbing steep slopes. Good walking shoes are recommended.
(III) A reasonable amount of hiking experience and good physical condition are recommended as prerequisites. Hiking boots or work boots are suggested.
Column 5: Trail Condition Rating:
(A)   Good, well blazed and maintained. No difficulty in finding trail. Few, if any, brambles, fallen logs or similar obstacles.
(B)   Average. Trail can be followed if reasonably close attention is paid to blazes, maps and treadway. Obstacles are not so bad as to obscure the trail route.
(C)   Poorly blazed and maintained; one may find difficulty in finding and staying on the trail. Hikers are likely to encounter brambles, fallen logs, washouts and similar obstacles.

Column 5: Ski-Touring Rating:
(S1) Suitable for beginner ski-tourers
(S2) Suitable for intermediate ski-tourers
(S3) Suitable for advanced ski-tourers
(S4) Not recommended as a ski-touring trail
Column 6: Additional Comments:
B	Suitable for backpacking.
H	Trail-side shelter(s) are located along the trail.
M	A topo map of this trail is included in this Guide.
S	Places to swim exist along, or near, the trail.
W	No water available. Provide your own water.

Column 7: Intersecting trails and roads. Trails are noted by the trail number only. Roads are indicated by a letter-prefix describing the type of road (as in Column 3). Numbers in parentheses denote roads and other trails that come very close to intersecting the trail. This column is useful in planning hikes involving several trails.

Column 8: The maximum and minimum elevation encountered on the trail (in feet). These numbers give hikers and ski-tourers an additional impression about the trail's difficulty and the amount of snow fall.

Column 9: The number of stream crossings that do not have bridges. Only streams involving rock-hopping or wading are counted.

Column 10: The page number, in this Guide, where the Trail Notes are found.

Column 11: The Trail Number (the same as in Column 1).

Trail NO.	**TABLE OF TRAILS** TRAIL NAME	START /FINISH		DIST. (MI.)	SCN/DIFF/ COND/SKI-
Cheat Ranger District--Canaan Mountain Area (I-A)					
101	Plantation Trail	WV32	/FR13	8.4	2/II/A/S2
102	Fire Trail No.1	WV32	/FR13	0.4	2/I/B/S4
103	Fire Trail No.2	WV32	/FR13	0.4	2/I/B/S4
104	Fire Trail No.3	TR101	/FR13	0.8	2/I/B/S1
106	Flag Run Trail	WV32	/FR13	1.0	2/I/A/S4
107	Davis Trail	FR13	/FR13	2.8	2/I/A/S2
108	Fire Trail No.6	TR101	/FR13	1.1	2/I/B/S2
109	Lindy Run Trail	FR13	/FR13	2.8	1/I/A/S2
110	Railroad Grade Trail	FR13	/FR13	3.1	1/II/A/S2
111	Firelane Split Trail	TR109	/TR107	2.0	2/II/B/S1
112	Bennett Rock Trail	TR114	/WV72	0.7	2/III/C/S4
113	Table Rock Overlook Trail	FR13	/overlook	1.1	1/I/A/S4
114	Mountainside Trail	FR13	/FR244A	4.8	1/II/B/S2
139	Pointy Knob Trail	FR13	/FR13	5.2	2/II/A/S4
Cheat Ranger District--Olson Tower-Blackwater Canyon Area (I-B)					
115	Blackwater Can. RR Gr.Tr.	WV32	/Parsons	12.2	1/II/A/S1
116	Boundary Trail	FR18	/FR18	3.5	2/II/B/S2
117	Canyon Rim Trail	FR717	/FR18	3.0	1/II/A/S2
118	Fansler Trail	FR717	/CO219	1.1	2/I/A/S2
142	Limerock Trail	CSX RR	/FR18	4.1	1/II/B/S3
Cheat Ranger District--Pheasant Mountain Area (I-C)					
120	Pheasant Mtn.Trail	TR121	/CO23	4.7	2/I/A/S2
121	Shingletree Trail (south)	US219	/TR120	3.1	2/I/B/S2
121	Shingletree Trail (north)	CO21	/TR120	1.4	2/I/B/S3
124	Clover Trail	TR120	/CO23	2.0	1/II/A/S4
126	South Haddix Trail	FR116	/SR47	10.0	2/III/B/S4
Cheat Ranger District--Horseshoe Run Area (I-D)					
153	Dorman Ridge Trail	TR155	/CO9	1.3	3/I/B/S2
154	McKinley Trail	CO7	/FR903	1.0	2/II/B/S4
155	Losh Trail	CO7	/TR153	1.8	2/III/B/S4
156	Mike's Run Trail	CO7	/TR153	4.0	2/III/C/S4
157	Maxwell Trail	CO7	/FR903	2.2	1/II/B/S4
Cheat Ranger District--Otter Creek Area (I-E)					
128	Mylius Trail	TR131	/FR162	2.4	2/II/A/S4
129	Shaver's Mountain Trail	FR91	/TR130	10.0	1/III/A/S4
130	Green Mountain Trail	TR131	/TR129	4.0	1/II/A/S3
131	Otter Creek Trail	WV72	/FR91	11.3	1/II/B/S4
132	Baker Sods Trail	TR135	/end	3.0	2/II/B/S4
135	Yellow Creek Trail	TR131	/FR324	1.3	2/I/A/S1
136	McGowan Mountain Trail	TR138	/TR135	3.5	1/II/A/S3
138	Moore Run Trail	TR131	/TR136	4.1	1/I/A/S3
140	Middle Point Trail	FR91	/TR132	1.6	2/II/B/S3
150	Turkey Run Trail	TR138	/FR701	4.0	2/I/A/S4
154	Big Springs Gap Trail	TR131	/FR701	0.9	2/I/A/S4

38

NOTES	INTERSECTIONS	Elev. Max/Min.	Stream Cr.	Page No.	Trail No.
B,H,M	104,107,108,109,110,(113)	3580/3310	8	58	101
M	(none)	3790/3560	1	61	102
M	(none)	3790/3560	0	61	103
M	101	3740/3540	1	61	104
M	(none)	3690/3210	0	61	106
B,H,M	101,111	3710/3150	1	62	107
M,W	101,111	3630/3500	0	63	108
M	101,111	3620/3100	1	63	109
B,H,M	101	3610/3210	1	65	110
M,W	107,108,109	3680/3590	0	66	111
B,M	114	2880/1830	0	66	112
M	(101)	3435/3310	0	67	113
B,M	112	3240/2440	6	67	114
B,M,H,S	(108)	4100/3240	6	68	139
B,M	142	2951/1661	0	75	115
B,M	(117)	3300/3080	1	76	116
B,M	(116)	3610/3090	1	77	117
B,M	(none)	3660/2420	0	77	118
M	(none)	3050/1800	1	78	142
B,M	121,124	2600/1850	1	82	120
B,M	120	2420/1760	0	83	(S)121
B,M	120	2450/1700	0	84	(N)121
B,M	(none)	2245/1720	3	84	124
B,M	(none)	2650/1900	2	85	126
B,H,M	155,156	2540/2400	0	88	153
B,M	(none)	2300/1720	0	88	154
B,H,M	153,156	2450/1670	2	89	155
B,H,M	153,155	2350/1620	15	89	156
B,M	(none)	2050/1680	5	90	157
B,M	129,131	3170/2320	1	97	128
B,M	128,130,165	3800/3030	0	97	129
B,M	129,131,158	3580/2200	0	98	130
B,M,S	128,130,135,138,154,158,165	3050/1780	11	99	131
B,M,S	135,140	3150/?	1	102	132
B,M	131,132,136	3150/2990	1	102	135
B,M	135,138	3900/3100	0	103	136
B,M	131,136,150	3350/2800	4	104	138
B,M	132	3850/3040	0	105	140
B,M	138,(154)	3730/2630	1	105	150
B,M	131,(150)	2450/2060	1	106	154

Trail NO.	**TABLE OF TRAILS** TRAIL NAME	START /FINISH		DIST. (MI.)	SCN/DIFF/ COND/SKI-
\multicolumn{6}{l}{Cheat Ranger District--Otter Creek Area (I-E) (Cont.)}
158	Possession Camp Trail	TR130	/TR131	3.3	1/II/A/S2
165	Hedrick Camp Trail	TR131	/TR129	1.0	2/I/A/S4

Gauley R.D.--Southern Cranberry Backcountry & Wilderness (II-A)

---	Summit Lake Trail	WV39	/WV39	1.8	1/I/A/S4
231	Fisherman Trail	FR77	/FR76	1.5	2/II/B/S4
236	Fork Mountain Trail	WV39	/TR263	21.4	1/III/B/S3
225	North Bend Trail	WV39	/TR236	2.4	1/II/A/S2
237	Big Run Trail	WV39	/TR236	1.0	2/II/B/S4
259	Eagle Camp Trail	WV39	/TR263	1.0	2/II/B/S4
263	Pocahontas Trail	FR99	/WV39	20.2	1/III/B/S3
243	South Fork Trail	TR244	/TR253	1.6	1/I/A/S3
244	Kennison Mtn. Trail	FR76	/TR263	9.7	1/II/B/S3
235	Frosty Gap Trail	TR244	/TR263	5.2	2/II/A/S1
---	Cranberry Volkswalk	CMNC	/CMNC	6.0	1/I/A/S1
253	Cow Pasture Trail	FR102	/FR102	5.5	1/II/B/S4
245	Forks of Cranberry Trail	FR102	/WV150	5.7	1/II/B/S4

Gauley R.D.--Northern Cranberry Backcountry & Wilderness (II-B)

688	North-South Trail	FR76	/TR271	15.1	2/III/B/S4
206	County Line Trail	T.F.	/FR86	9.2	2/III/B-C/S4
207	Big Beechy Trail	TR688	/TR271	5.4	2/II/B/S4
212	Lick Branch Trail	TR688	/FR76	2.1	1/II/B/S4
213	Rough Run Trail	TR688	/FR76	3.0	1/II/B/S4
214	Tumbling Rock Trail	TR688	/FR76	2.5	2/II/A/S3
242	Little Fork Trail	TR271	/TR688	3.5	1/II/A/S3
248	District Line Trail	TR207	/TR206	2.8	2/II/A/S2
250	Birch Log Trail	TR688	/FR76	3.0	2/II/A/S4
267	Laurelly Branch Trail	TR271	/TR688	3.4	2/II/C/S4
271	Middle Fork Trail	FR86	/TR688	10.0	1/II/A/S4
272	North Fork Trail	FR76	/WV150	8.9	1/II/A/S2

Gauley Ranger District--North-of-Richwood Area (II-D)

219	Hinkle Branch Trail	CO7	/Cran. R.	1.2	1/II/B/S4
223	Cranberry Ridge Trail	CO7	/FR81	5.8	2/II/B/S2
---	Bishop Knob Trail	BKC	/BKC	2.5	2/I/A/S1
228	Adkins Rockhouse Trail	FR81	/FR234	2.1	2/II/B/S2
256	Barrenshe Trail	FR76	/FR99	4.5	2/II/C/S4

Greenbrier Ranger District--Peters Mountain Area (III-A)

332	Little Mountain Trail	WV7	/TR701	2.5	2/II/B/S4
337	Hosterman Trail	CO1-24	/CO1-24	2.6	2/I/A/S2
359	Peters Mountain Trail	WV28	/WV7	5.5	1/II/B/S4
701	Allegheny Trail	CO12	/US250	21.8	1/III/A/S4

NOTES	INTERSECTIONS	Elev. Max/Min.	Stream Cr.	Page No.	Trail No.
B,M	130,131,138	3460/2780	2	107	158
B,M	129,131	3200/3000	1	107	165
M	(263)	3440/3340	2	121	---
B,H,M	272	3640/2800	1	121	231
B,M	237,263	4310/2340	4	122	236
B,M	236	3680/2780	1	123	225
B,M	236	3930/3050	1	123	237
B,M	263	3600/3310	1	123	259
B,M	231,235,236,244,(256),259	4100/3420	4	124	263
B,M	244,253	4440/3370	0	124	243
B,M	235,263,272,WV39	4440/2980	1	125	244
B,M	244,263,FR232	4400/3980	2	127	235
M	253, 263	3640/3380	3	128	---
M	(none)	3520/3350	4	129	253
B,M	(272)	4570/3160	0	129	245
B,M	267,212-4,242,250,271-2	4460/2530	0	131	688
B,M	(242),248,271	3960/2390	2	133	206
B,M	248,688,271	4440/2620	0	134	207
B,M	688	3670/2610	1	134	212
B,M	(250),688,(242)	3680/2785	6	135	213
B,M	688,(250)	3880/3080	2	135	214
B,M	(206),688,271	3650/2390	2	135	242
B,M	206,207	4420/3960	0	136	248
B,M	(213),(214),688,272	3760/3070	3	136	250
B,M	688,271	3920/2830	1	137	267
B,M,S	206,207,242,267,688	4180/2390	8	137	271
B,M,S	688,271	4470/3190	4	139	272
B	(none)	2560/2080	1	141	219
B,M,H	228	3100/2700	2	141	223
B,M	228,223	3120/3000	1	141	---
B,M	223	3060/2120	1	142	228
B,M	(263)	3780/2100	0	142	256
B	701	3200/2556	0	167	332
B	701	2960/2565	2	167	337
B	(none)	3180/2425	2	168	359
B,M,S	337,332	3478/2365	8	168	701

Trail NO.	**TABLE OF TRAILS** TRAIL NAME	START /FINISH		DIST. (MI.)	SCN/DIFF/ COND/SKI-

Greenbrier Ranger District--Middle Mountain Area (III-B)

Trail NO.	TRAIL NAME	START	/FINISH	DIST. (MI.)	SCN/DIFF/COND/SKI-
302	McCray Run Trail	FR14	/CO27	4.7	2/II/A/S2
305	Stone Camp Trail	FR14	/TR306	1.5	2/II/B/S4
306	Laurel River Trail (N)	CO40	/FR14	9.6	2/II/B/S1
306	Laurel River Trail (S)	FR97	/FR14	7.6	1/II/B/S4
307	Middle Mountain Trail	FR14	/TR306	1.2	2/II/A/S4
310	Beulah Trail (East)	TR306	/FR14	0.9	2/II/A/S4
310	Beulah Trail (West)	FR14	/FR44	3.3	2-3/II/A/S2
311	County Line Trail	FR35	/TR310	4.1	2/II/A/S2
315	Camp Five Trail	FR14	/TR306	1.6	2/II/A/S1
317	Lynn Knob Trail	FR179	/FR17	3.9	1/II/A/S3
367	Hinkle Run Trail	FR17	/FR14	3.7	2/II/A/S2
321	Span Oak Trail	FR17	/FR15	3.7	2/II/A/S3
322	Burner Mountain Trail	FR15	/FR14	3.6	2/II/B/S2
323	Forks Trail	FR183	/TR306	1.1	2/II/A-B/S4
324	Smoke Camp Trail	WV28	/FR58	1.8	1/II/A/S4
365	East Fork Trail	WV28	/FR254	8.0	1/II/A/S2-4
335	Poca Run Trail	WV28	/WV28	2.5	1/I/A/S1

Greenbrier Ranger District--Shavers Fork Area (III-C)

Trail NO.	TRAIL NAME	START	/FINISH	DIST. (MI.)	SCN/DIFF/COND/SKI-
327	Chestnut Ridge Trail	FR92	/Rt39.1	5.5	2/II/B/S4
701	Allegheny Trail	US250	/CO22	25.1	1/III/AB/S2
341	John's Camp Run Trail	TR701	/FR317	0.8	2/II/B/S2
345	High Falls Trail	FR44	/High Fls.	2.5	1/II/B/S4
350	Strip Mine Trail	SFPA	/FR227	4.0	1/II/A/S4
360	Stonecoal Trail	FR92	/FR209	4.0	2/II/C/S3
361	Whitmeadow Ridge Trail	FR92	/FR47	4.6	2/II/B/S4
362	Crouch Ridge Trail	FR92	/FR49	2.9	1/II/B/S4
372	Yokum Ridge Trail	FR92	/FR210	1.4	2/II/B/S4
312	West Fork Trail	Ch.J.	/Durbin	25.5	1/II/A/S1
701	Allegheny Trail	CO22	/US33	11.0	2/III/B/S2

Marlinton Ranger District--

Trail NO.	TRAIL NAME	START	/FINISH	DIST. (MI.)	SCN/DIFF/COND/SKI-
701	Allegheny Trail	CO23	/CO12	40.3	12/II/AB/S4

Marlinton Ranger District--Bird Run Area (IV-A)

Trail NO.	TRAIL NAME	START	/FINISH	DIST. (MI.)	SCN/DIFF/COND/SKI-
410	Flame Azalea Trail	FR441	/FR441	0.3	1/I/A/S4

Marlinton Ranger District--Laurel Creek Area (IV-B)

Trail NO.	TRAIL NAME	START	/FINISH	DIST. (MI.)	SCN/DIFF/COND/SKI-
466	Laurel Creek Trail	WV39	/WV39	8.0	2/II/A/S2
456	Two Lick Trail	WV92	/WV92	4.3	2/II/A/S4
608	Middle Mountain Trail (N)	WV39	/TR608(S)	4.6	2/II/A-B/S4

Marlinton Ranger District--Highlands Scenic Hwy, Parkway Sect (IV-C)

Trail NO.	TRAIL NAME	START	/FINISH	DIST. (MI.)	SCN/DIFF/COND/SKI-
409	High Rock Trail	WV150	/Views	1.6	1/I/A/S4
411	Cranberry Glades Overlook	WV150	/WV150	0.3	1/I/A/S4
412	Black Mtn. Trail	OVERLK	/OVERLK	4.7	1/II/A/S4
405	Red Spruce Knob Trail	WV150	/R.S.K.	1.2	1/I/A/S4

NOTES	INTERSECTIONS	Elev. Max/Min.	Stream Cr.	Page No.	Trail No.
B,M,W	306,701	3010/2780	1	174	302
B,M	306	3600/2950	3	175	305
B,M,S	302,305,307	3090/2820	9	175	(N)306
B,M,S	310,315,(317),323	3760/3100	8	178	(S)306
B,M	306	3650/3020	2	179	307
B,M	306	3610/3200	1	180	(E)310
B,M	311,FR183	3420/3000	4	180	(W)310
B,M	310	3720/3380	0	182	311
B,M	306	3620/3350	2	182	315
B,M	(306),367	3990/3150	0	183	317
B,M	317,(322)	3850/3150	5	183	367
B,M	(322)	4100/2950	0	184	321
B,M	(321),(367)	4280/3850	0	185	322
B,M	306,FR14	3420/3150	0	185	323
	(none)	4190/2900	1	185	324
B,M	FR51	3550/3000	4	186	365
B,M	(none)	4020/3281	0	188	335
M	328,331	3780/2400	2	199	327
B,H,M	302,312,341,345	4190/3940	0	200	701
B,H,M	701	3820/3640	1	202	341
B,M	701	3620/2900	2	202	345
B,M,W	(none)	4285/3940	0	203	350
B,M	(none)	4160/3650	0	204	360
B,M,S	(none)	4160/3480	0	204	361
B	(none)	4120/3560	1	206	362
B,M	(none)	3940/3360	0	206	372
B,M,S	345,701,CO22	3130/2730	0	207	312
B,M	302	3080/2640	6	208	701
B,H,M,S	CR21/4,WV39,WV28,FR1/4	3420/2220	8	221	701
	(none)	3080/3035	0	223	410
B,H,M	(none)	3000/2410	5	224	466
	(none)	3030/2490	2	224	456
B,H,W	608(S)	3220/2410	1	225	608N
B,M	(none)	4440/4350	0	229	409
M	(none)	4520/4420	0	229	411
M	(none)	4545/3880	1	229	412
M	(none)	4703/4320	0	230	405

Trail NO.	TABLE OF TRAILS TRAIL NAME	START /FINISH		DIST. (MI.)	SCN/DIFF/ COND/SKI-
Marlinton Ranger District--Tea Creek Area			(IV-D)		
446	Bannock Shoals Run Trail	TCC	/TR448	4.8	1/II/A/S1
447	Turkey Point Trail	TPCT	/TR449	1.5	1/II/A/S4
448	Saddle Loop Trail	TR447	/TR446	1.7	1/II/A/S4
449	Boundary Trail	TR448	/TR454	3.9	1/II/A/S4
454	Tea Creek Trail	FR86	/FR24	6.8	1/III/A/S4
452	Tea Creek Mountain Trail	FR86	/WV150	4.6	1/III/A/S4
450	North Face Trail	TR452	/TR454	3.1	2/III/AB/S4
453	Right Fork, Tea Creek Trail	WV150	/TR454	3.4	2/III/A/S4
439	Red Run Trail	TR453	/TR438	2.5	2/II/A/S4
440	Bear Pen Ridge Trail	TR438	/TR454	3.5	1/II/A-B/S4
438	Gauley Mountain Trail	WV150	/FR24	5.2	2/II/A-B/S1
487	Williams River Trail	FR86	/Handley	3.0	2/I/A-B/S1
Potomac Ranger District					
563	Seneca Rocks Hiking Trail	V.Ctr.	/Platform	1.3	1/II/A/S4
Potomac Ranger District--North Fork Mountain Area (V-A)					
501	North Fork Mtn. Trail	CO28.11	/US33	23.8	1/II/A/S2-4
502	Landis Trail	TR501	/CO28.11	1.4	2/II/A/S4
507	Redman Run Trail	TR501	/CO28.11	1.6	2/II/A/S4
539	South Branch Trail	Smokehole		3.5	2/II/B/S4
Potomac Ranger District--Spruce Knob Area			(V-B)		
512	Judy Springs Trail	TR515	/TR530	0.7	1/II/B/S3
515	Seneca Creek Trail	FR112	/TR530	5.0	1/I/A/S1
527	Big Run Trail	FR112	/CO29	3.1	2/II/A/S2
528	North Prong Trail	TR527	/TR532	2.8	2/II/B/S2
529	Swallow Rock Trail	CO29	/TR515	3.2	1-2/II/A/S2
530	Horton Trail	CO29	/TR515	3.5	1-2/II/B/S4
531	Bear Hunter Trail	TR515	/TR532	1.0	1-2/II/A/S4
532	Allegheny Mountain Trail	FR112	/CO7	12.4	2/III/AB/S2
533	Huckleberry Trail	FR104	/TR515	5.2	1/II/B/S4
534	Lumberjack Trail	FR112	/TR564	5.3	1-2/II/B/S2
555	Bee Trail	CO29	/TR557	1.4	1-2/II/A/S4
556	Elza Trail	CO29	/TR528	2.0	1-2/II/A/S4
557	Leading Ridge Trail	CO29	/TR532	5.1	2/II/A/S3
559	Tom Lick Run Trail	TR515	/TR532	1.1	2/II/A/S2
561	Spring Ridge Trail	CO29	/TR532	3.2	2-3/II/A/S2
562	Short Trail	FR112	/FR112	0.4	2/II/A/S4
564	High Meadows Trail	TR534	/TR533	1.9	1/II/A/S4
I-51	Gatewood Trail	FR112	/Rt10	2.4	2-3/II/A/S2
526	Back Ridge Trail	Rt10	/Rt10	5.0	2-3/II/B/S4
---	Spruce Knob Lake Trail	SKL	/SKL	1.0	1/I/A/S4
Potomac Ranger District--Roaring Plains-Flatrock Plains (V-C)					
517	South Prong Trail	FR19	/FR19	5.7	2/II/B/S4
518	Boar's Nest Trail	FR19	/FR70	2.7	1-2/II/B/S4

NOTES	INTERSECTIONS	Elev. Max/Min.	Stream Cr.	Page No.	Trail No.
B,M	(445),(209),448,449	4000/3000	1	231	446
B,M,W	448,449	4360/4200	0	231	447
B,M	447,446	4060/3920	0	232	448
B,M	448,446,447,454	4360/3840	3	232	449
B,H,M	(438),(452),453,487,449,440	4400/2980	13	234	454
B,M	(438),453,454,487,450	4535/2980	0	235	452
B,M	(none)	4000/3400	2	236	450
B,M	(438),452,454,439	4270/3550	2	236	453
B,M	453,458	4350/3820	0	237	439
B,M,H	438,454	4480/3880	0	237	440
B,M	(452),(453),(454),439,440	4440/4220	1	238	438
B,M	452,454	3160/2990	0	238	487
M	(none)	2300/1560	0	247	563
B,M,W	502,507,FR79	3795/1120	0	248	501
B,M,W	501	2800/1670	0	251	502
B,M	501	3000/2100	0	252	507
B,M	(none)	2100/1270	0	252	539
B,M,S	515,533,531,(534)	3890/3400	1	262	512
B,M,S	512,529,530-31,533,559,564	3890/2500	1	264	515
B,M	528,532	3955/3270	5	265	527
B,M	527,532,556	4120/3500	2	265	528
B,M	515,532,(557)	3974/3050	5	266	529
B,M	515,532,(533),(561),(564)	3800/2840	2	267	530
B,M	512,515,532	4020/3400	2	267	531
B,M	527,528,529-31,557,559,561	4250/2170	0	269	532
B,M	512,515,530,534,564	4840/3085	1	270	533
B,M	(512),530,533,564	4100/3950	0	271	534
B,M	556,557	4130/3100	1	272	555
B,M	528,555,557	4000/3150	2	272	556
B,M,W	532,555,556	4220/3210	1	272	557
B,M	515,532	4010/3710	1	274	559
B,M,W	(530),532	4120/2880	1	274	561
B,M,W	I-51	4000/3850	0	275	562
B,M,W	(none)	4000/3850	0	275	564
B,M	562	3980/3620	1	275	I-51
B,W	(none)	3963/2497	3	276	526
M,W	(none)	3840/3825	0	277	---
B,M	(508),(518),FR70	4130/2950	3	286	517
B,M	(517),(548)	4290/2950	2	288	518

Trail NO.	**TABLE OF TRAILS** TRAIL NAME	START /FINISH		DIST. (MI.)	SCN/DIFF/ COND/SKI-
Potomac Ranger District--Roaring Plains-Flatrock Plains (V-C) (Cont.)					
519	Flatrock Run Trail	TR548	/FR32-2	5.1	2/III/B/S4
548	Roaring Plains Trail	FR70	/TR519	3.3	1/II/B/S1
Potomac Ranger District--Dolly Sods Area (V-D)					
508	Rohrbaugh Plains Trail	FR19	/TR510	3.5	1/II/C/S2
510	Fisher Springs Run Trail	FR75	/TR514	2.3	1/II/B/S4
511	Blackbird Knob Trail	FR75	/TR514	2.2	1/II/B/S4
513	Big Stonecoal Trail	TR514	/TR553	4.4	1/III/B/S4
514	Red Creek Trail	FR19 ·	/TR511	6.1	1/III/B/S4
552	Little Stonecoal Trail	TR514	/FS Bndy.	1.8	1/II/B/S4
553	Breathed Mountain Trail	TR513	/TR514	2.5	1/III/B/S4
554	Rocky Point Trail	TR513	/TR514	1.8	1/II/A/S2
558	Dunkenbarger Trail	TR552	/TR513	1.6	1/II/B/S2
560	Wildlife Trail	FR75	/TR508	1.2	2/II/A/S2
I-52	Northland Loop Interp.Trail	FR75	/FR75	0.3	1/I/A/S4
White Sulphur R.D.--Middle Mtn. & Lake Sherwood Area (VI-A)					
608	Middle Mountain Trail (S)	TR608	/FR96	13.1	2/III/A/S3-4
610	Meadow Creek Mtn. Trail	TR701	/TR604	3.5	1/II/A/S2
601	Lake Sherwood Trail	L.Sh.	/L.Sh.	3.7	1/I/A/S4
684	Meadow Creek Trail	CO14	/TR604	2.7	2/II/A/S4
672	Upper Meadow Trail	CO14	/TR610	1.2	2/II/A/S2
685	Virginia Trail	TR601	/TR611	0.6	2/I/A/S3
611	Allegheny Mountain Trail	TR685	/TR604	3.6	1/II/A/S2
604	Connector Trail	TR610	/TR611	1.9	2/II/A/S2
668	Little Allegheny Trail	FR309	/CO14	4.2	1/II/B/S3-4
701	Allegheny Trail	CO23	/CO14	17.7	1/III/A/S4
White Sulphur Ranger District--Blue Bend Area (VI-B)					
614	Blue Bend Trail	B.B.R.	/B.B.R.	5.0	1/II/A/S4
615	South Boundary Trail	CO21	/CO36	4.8	2/II+/A/S4
618	Anthony Creek Trail	TR614	/CO21	3.8	1/II/A/S4

NOTES	INTERSECTIONS	Elev. Max/Min.	Stream Cr.	Page No.	Trail No.
B,M	(518),548	4620/2420	1	289	519
B,M	(518),519	4690/4200	0	290	548
B,M	(517),510,560	4010/3480	0	298	508
B,M	508,514	3960/3230	2	299	510
B,M	514	3970/3650	2	299	511
B,M	514,553,554,558	3930/2890	5	300	513
B,M	510,511,513,552,553,554	3930/2620	2	301	514
B,M	514,558	4000/2740	2	304	552
B,M	513,514	3950/3500	0	304	553
B,M	513,514	3580/3350	0	305	554
B,M	513,552	3670/3620	1	306	558
B,M	508	4010/3600	0	306	560
M	(none)	3870/3820	0	306	I-52
B,M,W	608(N),701	3565/2028	1	314	608
B,M	604,701,FR311	3574/3200	0	315	610
B,M,S	684,685	2720/2700	4	316	601
B,M	604	3080/2670	7	318	684
B,M	610	2970/2680	0	318	672
B,M	611,601	3050/2670	1	318	685
B,M,W	685,604	3214/3040	0	319	611
B,M	610,684,611	3480/3000	2	319	604
B,M	(none)	3341/2130	1	320	668
B,M	610,672,608	3565/2212	0	320	701
B,H,M	618	2930/1920	0	328	614
B,M,W	618	3120/1800	1	329	615
B,M,S	614,615	1920/1800	3	329	618

LONG-DISTANCE TRAILS ON

MONONGAHELA NATIONAL FOREST

ALLEGHENY TRAIL

Work on Allegheny Trail began in 1975 by members of the West Va. Scenic Trails Association (WVSTA). The trail runs from the Pennsylvania line in Preston County to the Appalachian Trail in Monroe County. All four sections are virtually complete, a total of 330 miles. The 96-mile northern section (I) is outside the boundaries of the MNF for the most part. Within the MNF, Allegheny Trail begins 26 miles north of Blackwater Falls State Park on Stemple Ridge and leaves the MNF at the W.Va.-Va. line east of Alvon in Greenbrier County. The trail has been designed and constructed, and is maintained, for human foot travel. It is not recommended for wheeled vehicles such as mountain bicycles. Neither is it suggested for horse travel. However, some parts of it are excellent for ski-touring. It is marked throughout its length with 2"x6" yellow blazes.

The northern terminus is in Preston County at the Mason/Dixon Line on the WV/Pennsylvania border. The southern terminus is on the Appalachian Trail atop Peters Mountain in Monroe County of southeastern West Virginia. It passes through four state parks, two state forests and three national forests. It skirts the Otter Creek Wilderness Area, and is only a few miles from both the Dolly Sods Wilderness and Cranberry Wilderness.

Allegheny Trail consists of a combination of previously existing and newly constructed trails and state and Forest Service roads. The location (See map on page 49.) generally leads from Blackwater Falls State Park to Canaan Valley State Park, to Glady Fork River, up Glady Fork to the town of Glady, along Shavers Mountain past Gaudineer Scenic Area, down to Durbin, across Little Mountain to Cass, through Seneca State Forest and Watoga State Park, past Lake Sherwood and south to the state line.

The Allegheny Trail is designated as TR701 where it is maintained as a foot trail on national forest land. Where it follows USFS or state roads, the road number is retained, but the trail route is marked by yellow blazes. Descriptions of sections of Allegheny Trail are found throughout this Guide. Consult the Index for page numbers.

WVSTA sells a 105-page *Hiking Guide to the Allegheny Trail* (Ed.2). To obtain a copy see page 33. For information on WVSTA see page 335.

AMERICAN DISCOVERY TRAIL

During 1990-91 an adventurous team of hikers scouted for 14 months the first coast-to-coast hiking and bicycle trail from the Pacific Ocean to the Atlantic ocean. Named the American Discovery Trail, it was a joint project by the American Hiking Society and *Backpacker* magazine. Through 12 states and more than 6,000mi it provided an alternate route in the heart of America.

The Pacific trailhead is at Limatour Beach in Point Reyes National Seashore, California. From there it crosses the Golden Gate Bridge, passes through Tahoe National Forest of California and into Virginia City in Nevada. After passing through the Dark Canyon of Utah, the trail enters Colorado to Grand Junction and follows 800mi of backcountry roads (the longest distance of any of the states through which it passes). In Denver the ADT divides for the Northern Midwest Route and the Southern Midwest Route. They recon-

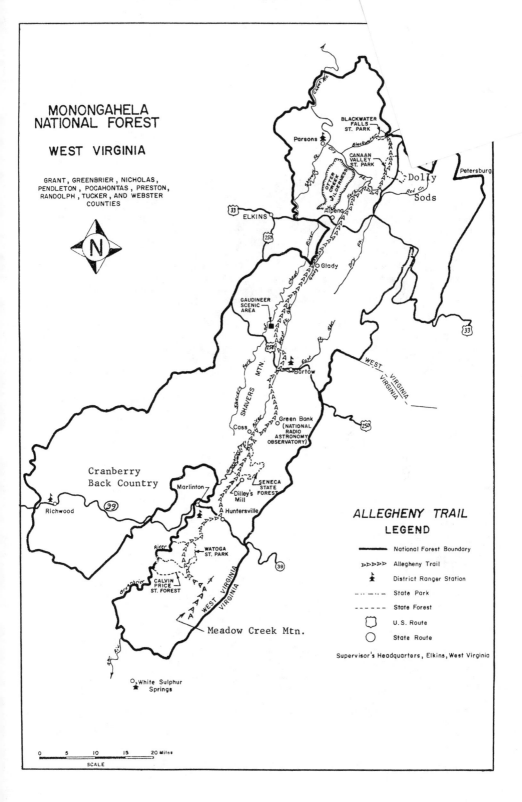

MONONGAHELA NATIONAL FOREST

WEST VIRGINIA

GRANT, GREENBRIER, NICHOLAS,
PENDLETON, POCAHONTAS, PRESTON,
RANDOLPH, TUCKER, AND WEBSTER
COUNTIES

N

BLACKWATER
FALLS
ST. PARK

Parsons

CANAAN
VALLEY
ST. PARK

OTTER CREEK W. AREA

Dolly
Sods

Petersburg

ELKINS

33

250

Alpena

Glady

GAUDINEER
SCENIC
AREA

WEST
VIRGINIA

33

250

Bartow

SHAVERS MTN.

Green Bank
(NATIONAL
RADIO
ASTRONOMY
OBSERVATORY)

Cass

Cranberry
Back Country

Marlinton

SENECA
STATE
FOREST

Dilley's
Mill

39

Richwood

Huntersville

River

WATOGA
ST. PARK

39

CALVIN
PRICE
ST. FOREST

WEST
VIRGINIA

ALLEGHENY TRAIL
LEGEND

———————	National Forest Boundary
▷▷▷▷▷	Allegheny Trail
🌲	District Ranger Station
—··—··—	State Park
— — — —	State Forest
⬡	U.S. Route
○	State Route

Meadow Creek Mtn.

Supervisor's Headquarters, Elkins, West Virginia

White Sulphur
Springs

0   5   10   15   20 Miles

SCALE

Allegheny Trail (TR701) at parking and information area on WV92.
Photo by Allen de Hart

nect at the Ohio State line. In Kansas the entry is toward Syracuse and exits at Kansas City on the Southern Midwest Route. Leaving Missouri at Alton, the ADT enters Illinois and passes through the Shawnee National Forest. Entry into Indiana is at New Haven and the exit is at Lawrenceburg. The Ohio route is through a number of state parks and parts of the Buckey Trail to cross the Ohio River to West Virginia at Parkersburg. The route through West Virginia is 275mi and passes through Wood, Ritchie, Doddridge, Harrison, Taylor, Barbour, Tucker, Grant, and Mineral counties.

From Parkersburg the ADT follows WV47 to CO-7 and then to Walker where it joins the North Bend Rail-Trail. (Plans are to use the North Bend Rail-Trail when it is extended from Parkersburg on an abandoned railroad to Walker.) The ADT follows the North Bend Rail-Trail to Wolf Summit near Clarksburg. At Clarksburg the ADT follows the Harrison County Rail-Trail along the West Fork River to Spelter where it follows back roads to Valley Falls State Park and Pleasant Creek Public Hunting and Fishing Area.

Plans call for the ADT to continue along the Tygart River from Valley Falls State Park to Grafton, past the Mothers Day Shrine, through Tygart Lake Park to Nestorville. After Netorville the ADT follows WV38 toward the MNF. From the community of Valley Furnace, the ADT goes E 1.1mi on WV38 and turns right. It then follows CO-17 (0.5mi); CO-8 (1.6mi); CO-18 (0.6mi); CO-19/4 (0.8mi); CO-21/1 (0.5mi); CO-21 (5.2mi); and CO-17 (3.0mi) to Parsons.

From Parsons it follows Brooklyn Heights Road to Hendricks (4.0mi), crosses the bridge, and turns right onto WV72 for 4.8mi. It turns left onto FR244 for an ascent to Canaan Mountain by Red Run. After 3.5mi on FR244, the trail joins FR13 and goes 1.5mi to Railroad Grade Trail (TR110) which it follows for 1.7mi. At the junction with Plantation Trail (TR101), the ADT turns right and follows Plantation Trail for 1.2mi. It then turns left onto Lindy Run Trail (TR109) and follows it for 1.5mi to FR13. It turns right and after 2.7mi meets Allegheny Trail (TR701) in Blackwater Falls State Park.

From the park stable it follows Allegheny Trail S 6.6mi to the junction with Middle Ridge Trail. After 2.3mi on Middle Ridge Trail to the park's lodge, the ADT follows 1.3mi on Deer Run Trail to the park's campground, It then goes another 0.9mi E on the park entrance road to WV32. The ADT follows WV32 for 0.8mi where it turns left (E) onto CO-45. It follows CO-45 5.9mi to Laneville where the road becomes FR19 for a climb of 3.2mi. At the ridge top the trail follows FR75. FR75 follows the Allegheny Front for 6.8mi to Bear Rocks where it descends for 4.9mi to junction with Jordan Run Road.

From here the ADT follows CO-28/17 to Maysville; CO-42/3 to Greenland Gap (a Nature Conservancy Preserve); then N/NE to Nancy Hanks Memorial; Ridgeville; Fort Ashby; Springfield Public Hunting and Fishing Area, and on to the Maryland border crossing at Green Spring. After crossing the Potomac River Bridge the ADT follows the towpath of the C & O Canal National Historic Park to Washington DC. From there it goes to Annapolis. Ahead, it crosses the Bay Bridge over Chesapeake Bay to enter Tuckahoe State Forest. In Delaware the trail follows rural roads through small towns and arrives at the Atlantic Ocean beach area in Cape Henlopen State Park.

For more information request *The American Discover Trail, Explorer's Guide* plus updates at 4838 MacCorkle Ave, SW, South Charleston, WV 25309 (Tel. 304-768-0441 or 804-340-5948 or 800-851-3442).

CHEAT RANGER DISTRICT

Cheat Ranger District is in the NW corner of the MNF. In brief, it is N of US33 between Elkins and Harman and W of WV32 between Thomas and Harman. The entire area is in the Cheat River drainage, the major streams being the Shavers Fork, Glady Fork, and the Dry Fork of the Cheat, Blackwater River, and the main Cheat itself. The district ranger's office is in Parsons (P.O. Box 368) (26287) (Tel. 304-478-3251). Five areas are of interest to hikers in this district: the Canaan Mountain area between Blackwater Falls State Park and Canaan Valley State Park, the Olson Tower area on the NW bank of Blackwater Canyon, the Pheasant Mountain area W of Parsons, the Horseshoe Run Recreation Area, and Otter Creek Wilderness S of Parsons. Most of the Otter Creek drainage was classified as a Wilderness by an act of Congress in the mid-70s. The Canaan Mountain area offers the usual beauty of the forest, plus views over Canaan Valley, the valley of the Dry Fork, and Blackwater Canyon. The Olson Tower area offers trails that go down into Blackwater Canyon. Those interested in the Canaan Mountain area may want to write to Blackwater Falls Lodge (Davis, WV 26260) for a brochure, a park map, and a simple map of the Canaan Mountain area (no substitute for a topo map).

Recreation site information is listed below. The number of campground units and user fees may change every few years. The period open for use is usually from mid-April to mid-October. Check with the district ranger office for detailed information.

- Bear Heaven Campground: picnic tables, water, toilets
- Stuart Campground: picnic tables, water, toilets, reservations available
- Horseshoe Campground: picnic tables, water, toilets, reservations available
- Stuart Picnic Shelter: reservations
- Horseshoe Group Picnic Shelter: reservations

At Horseshoe and Stuart Campgrounds, campsites can be reserved via check or credit card through MISTIX at 1-800-283-CAMP. Sites not reserved are available on a first-come-first-served basis.

Ski-Touring in Cheat Ranger District:
Canaan Mountain Area (I-A):
FR13 (Canaan Loop Road) S of Blackwater Lodge (16mi).

Davis Trail (TR107 or TR701) and Lindy Run Trail (TR109) are skiable, but are wet and rocky and require a minimum snowfall of 20" for good skiing. The area is accessible from Canaan Valley State Park and Blackwater Falls State Park, both of which offer information and rentals.

Olson Tower/Blackwater Canyon Area (I-B):
The area E of Parsons, NW and N of Blackwater Canyon includes Forest Roads FR717 and FR18 (Canyon Rim Road), Canyon Rim Trail (TR117) and Blackwater Canyon RR Grade Trail (TR115), all of which are level enough for ski-touring. The roads are not plowed.

Otter Creek Area (I-E):
FR91 (Stuart Memorial Drive) directly E of Elkins. It extends from Stuart Recreation Area to near Alpena Gap (6mi).

McGowan Mountain Road (FR324) in Fernow Experimental Forest S of Parsons is not plowed and offers good skiing.

(I-A) CANAAN MOUNTAIN AREA

This area, like the highland areas of Dolly Sods, is characterized by highland marshes covered with moss and dense vegetation. Thick hemlock- and red spruce forests, rhododendron tangles and soupy bogs block the way for off-trail hiking. Some trails themselves are often small streambeds, and some trails are rocky and root covered. Wear sturdy, waterproof hiking boots.

In compensation, the area has unique vegetation and its compact layout makes it easy to plan loop hikes. Canaan Valley Loop Road (CLR) (FR13) surrounds most of the area, providing a convenient return leg for any loop. It is scenic and provides as good a hike as can be found on a road. Plantation Trail (TR101) runs E to W across the center of the area providing a backbone to which most other trails connect from the CLR on the N or S.

For those driving WV32 S from the town of Davis the following table of distances is useful:

Center of Davis	(N of bridge over Blackwater R.)	0.0mi
Plantation Trail	(sign) (TR101)	2.2mi
Fire Trail #2	(sign) (TR103)	2.4mi
Fire Trail #1	(sign) (TR102)	2.9mi
Canaan Loop Road	(CLR) (sign) (FR13)	3.3mi
Flag Run Trail	(sign) (TR106)	5.1mi

Do not drive in from Davis on the N leg of Canaan Loop Road (FR13) because it receives only minimum maintenance between Blackwater Falls State Park and the W trailhead of Plantation Trail (TR101). It may be deeply rutted and impassable, except for four-wheel drive vehicles. The S leg of CLR (FR13) is passable by car from WV32 to the W end of Plantation Trail (TR101).

The best access to the area is the CLR from WV32 at Canaan Heights at the top of the hill. The entrance is marked with a large private sign saying, "#1 Wilderness Road" on the W side of WV32. On the E side of the intersection is a green highway department sign pointing N to Davis and S to Harman. The first 0.25mi is outside the MNF and lined with private homes. The road is well maintained for about 10mi with crushed stone. It is easily traveled in an ordinary vehicle. After the road turns N, near the W terminus of Plantation Trail (TR101), the crushed stone ends.

Along the well-maintained S leg of CLR are dozens of pull-off areas for parking and many roadside camp sites. Every trailhead has a parking area and is marked with a sign giving the trail name, the mileage to the next trail along the road and distance to the next trail intersection. All ORV access trails have been blocked by huge boulders so it is unlikely that you will see ORVs in the woods. The two main ORV trails are badly eroded and show no recent signs of use.

Used as a connecting trail, the lesser-used W end of the CLR would be a nice hike. It runs high on a steep hillside above Red Run and provides good views (in early spring before the leaves come out) of the mountains to the W as it turns N and then E back to Davis. The road offers good ski-touring.

Along the N leg of the CLR and along the Blackwater Falls State Park road on the opposite rim of Blackwater Canyon, numerous pulloffs can be found with short trails leading to great views of Blackwater Canyon. These trails are not described in this Guide, but you should have no trouble finding them.

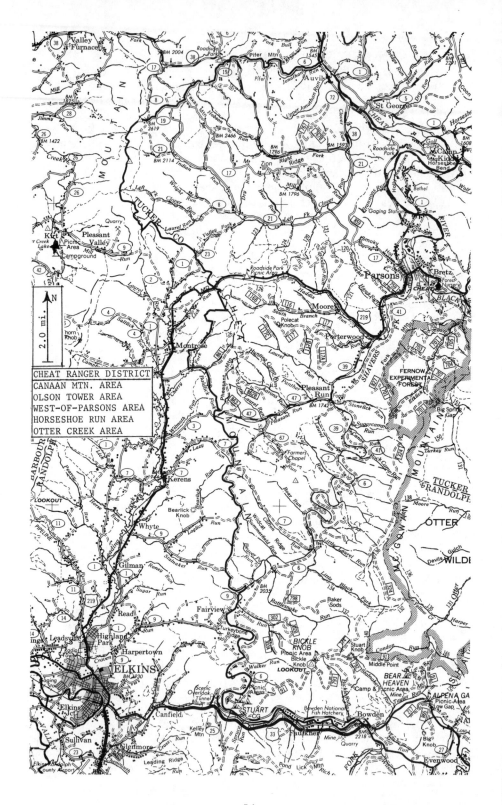

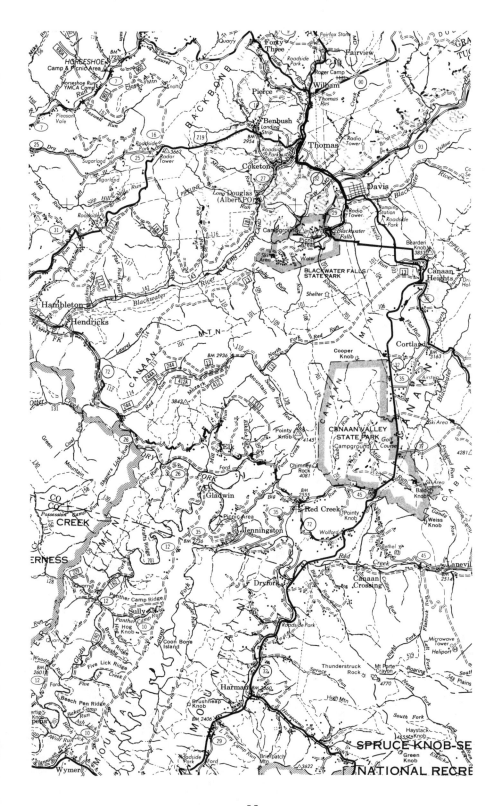

55

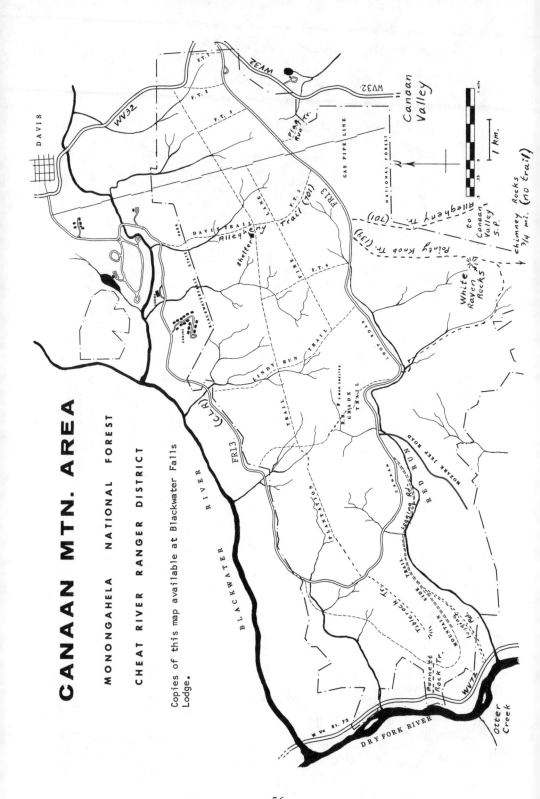

CANAAN MTN. AREA

MONONGAHELA NATIONAL FOREST

CHEAT RIVER RANGER DISTRICT

Copies of this map available at Blackwater Falls Lodge.

DAVIS

WV32

WV32

WV32

Canaan Valley

F.T. 1

F.T. 2

F.T. 3

Flag Run Tr.

GAS PIPE LINE

NATIONAL FOREST

N

1 mile

1 km.

0

DAVIS TRAIL

Allegheny Trail (701)

Allegheny Tr. (701)

shelter

Plenty Knob Tr. (139)

to Canaan Valley S.P.

chimney Rocks 3/4 mi. (no trail)

White Raven Rocks

Fire Lane

F.T. 4

STATE PARK

BLACKWATER FALLS

CABINS

LODGE

LINDY RUN TRAIL

RUN TRAIL

MAN SHELTER

R. GRADE

TRAIL

100 ROAD

FRL13

FRL13 (J.R.)

BLACKWATER RIVER

BLACKWATER

CANAAN PLANTATION

Logging Run R.R. TRAIL

RED RUN ROAD

MOZARK JEEP ROAD

MOUNTAIN SIDE TRAIL

Table Rock Tr.

Bennett Rock Tr.

W Va 72

WV72

W Va Rt. 72

DRY FORK RIVER

Otter Creek

ALLEGHENY TRAIL (TR701)　　　　　　　　47.9mi(76.6km)
SCENERY:　　1　(exceptional)　　　　　　NOTE: B,H,M,S
DIFFICULTY: I-II (easy-moderate)　　　　SKI-:　　S1-S3
CONDITION:　A　(good)　　　　　　　　ELEV: 3705/1956
MAPS: USFS(A,B), Blackwater, Bowden, Harmon, Laneville, Lead Mine,
　　　Mozark Mountain, I-A-1 and I-A-3 in this Guide
TRAIL SEGMENTS:

(1)	US33 N to FR162	8.8mi
(2)	FR162 to Jenningston Bridge (CO-35)	12.0mi
(3)	Jenningston Bridge to CO-45	3.7mi
(4)	CO45 to Canaan Valley State Park	1.5mi
(5)	Canaan Valley S.P. to FR13	4.5mi
(6)	FR13 to Blackwater Falls State Park	3.6mi
(7)	Blackwater Falls S.P. to CO-27	5.5mi
(8)	CO-27(FR18) to US219	8.3mi

Of interest to hikers is the diversity of elevation, scenery, hydrology, geology, and animal and plant species. Bear, deer, turkey, beaver, fox, skunk, owls, snakes, grouse, hawks, frogs, and box turtles are likely to be seen, or to signs of their presence. Plant life ranges from oak-hickory open forests to dense red spruce and rhododendron. Over 200 species of ferns and wildflowers have been observed in this section of trail. Trail campsites are common, and two developed campsites are on the way. Lodging and a restaurant are found near the S trailhead, in state parks, and in nearby towns such as Davis.

Access: The S trailhead is at a roadside parking space on US33, 1.3mi E of Alpena Lodge and Restaurant. Other intermediate trailheads are located: where Gladwin Road (CO12) crosses Glady Fork; at the E terminus of Mylius Trail (TR128); at the Canaan Valley State Park Restaurant and Lodge; at the two ends of Davis Trail (TR107) along FR13, and at the horse stable parking lot in Blackwater Falls State Park.

Segment 1: From the S terminus on US33, cross Flannigan Run and turn left onto an abandoned road. After a short ascent, descend to Glady Fork and follow an old RR grade off and on, and FR240 for the next 8mi. Along the way, in hardwood and rhododendron forests, are a number of good campsites near Glady Fork and its tributaries Wolf Run, Baker Camp Run, Five Lick Creek, and Brushy Creek. At 8.6mi the trail passes a USFS gate and turns left onto Gladwin Road (CO12). It then crosses Glady Fork on a bridge and, after 0.1mi, turns right onto FR162.

Segment 2: After 0.2mi on FR162 is the E terminus of Mylius Trail (TR128). For the next 8.5mi, Allegheny Trail follows an old RR grade and FR162 downstream of Glady Fork to Richford Road (CO26). Here it crosses a low-water bridge and joins a paved road in the community of Gladwin. From here the trail follows CO35/15 on the W side of Dry Fork for 3.2mi to Dry Fork Bridge in the community of Jenningston.

Segment 3: The trail continues on paved roads to CO45 where it turns right onto gravel CO45.

Segment 4: After 1.5mi on CO45, the trail turns left into Canaan Valley State Park. After 0.4mi it turns left onto Chimney Rock Trail, and soon turns right into the park's restaurant and lodge. (Another 1.0mi from the road junction is the park campground which has hot showers and hook-ups.)

Segment 5: In passing through Canaan Valley State Park, Allegheny Trail follows the 1.4mi Railroad Grade Trail and crosses Canaan Mountain

Trail and Middle Ridge Ski Trail. In a tributary cove of Blackwater River the trail ascends to reenter Cheat Ranger District. Views of Canaan Valley are outstanding. As the trail approaches the Canaan Mountain plateau, the forest becomes more dense with rhododendron and other evergreens. At 30.5mi the trail turns right onto Canaan Loop Road (FR13).

Segment 6: The trail follows FR13 for 1.2mi and turns left onto Blackwater/Canaan Cross-Country Ski Trail (Davis Trail (TR107)). At 32.9mi is a junction with Plantation Trail (TR101) where a 6-person shelter is located 70yd W. After another 1.6mi the trail reaches the horse stable parking lot in Blackwater Falls State Park. Ahead and to the left after 0.8mi is the park's lodge and restaurant. Hikers' vehicles may be left overnight at the lodge's parking area.

Segment 7: The trail turns right onto Falls View Trail and follows it 1.5mi to an exit opposite the parking area of Gentle Trail. The trail then follows paved road to the right, across Blackwater River, past a crossroads (the town of Davis is 1.3mi to the right), and past the entrance to the park's campground. The trail leaves the road near the Pendleton Lake swimming area. After 0.2mi it crosses the Pendleton Creek footbridge and enters Dobbins House Trail System. For the next 3.2mi the trail follows a scenic old RR grades and strip mine roads under tall hardwoods, hemlock and red spruce, and grassy meadows. At 41.1mi the trail turns left onto Douglas Road (CO27) and crosses the bridge over North Fork of Blackwater River. To the right 1.0mi is the town of Thomas, a source of groceries and supplies.

Note: Because of problems with private landowners, the trail from Dobbins House Trail System is now closed. So leave Blackwater Falls State Park via the entrance road, and follow WV32 to CO27 near Thomas.

Segment 8: The trail follows CO27 to the USFS boundary where CO27 becomes FR18 (Canyon Rim Road), a generally narrow, rocky, but level route. CO27 may be impassable at Tub Run in times of high water. After fording Tub Run go 0.25mi to Canyon Rim Trail. Continue on FR18 another 1.1mi to FR717. Turn right onto FR717 and follow it to US219 at 47.9mi. For information on the Cheat Ranger District portion of Allegheny Trail and the additional 82.6mi to the Pa. State Line refer to *Hiking Guide to the Allegheny Trail* published by WVSTA. (See page 33.)

PLANTATION TRAIL (TR101)   8.4mi(13.5km)

SCENERY: 2 (wooded)	NOTE: B,H,M,(8)
DIFFICULTY: II (moderate)	SKI-: S2
CONDITION: A (good)	ELEV: 3580/3310

MAPS: USFS(A,B), Mozark Mountain, Blackwater Falls, I-A-1 and
    I-A-2 in this Guide

SEGMENTS: (1) WV32 to TR104 (Fire Trail No.3)   1.0mi
            (2) TR104 to TR107 (Davis Trail)   1.7mi
            (3) TR107 to TR108 (Fire Trail No.6)   1.1mi
            (4) TR108 to TR109 (Lindy Run Trail)   1.0mi
            (5) TR109 to TR110 (Railroad Grade Trail)   1.7mi
            (6) TR110 to FR13 (Canaan Loop Road)   1.9mi

Plantation Trail is the backbone of the trail system in the Canaan Mountain Spruce Plantation. Many loop routes are possible. The trail is not shown on the topo but is shown on USFS maps. The E end of the trail is also designated for ski-touring. Ski-touring requires deep snow to cover rocks. The trail passes through rhododendron, spruce, hemlock and laurel and has few, if any, good views. It is wet and rocky in spots. Parts of the trail have been cut up badly by former ORV use. Blazing is yellow and sporadic. Segments 1 and 2 are in excellent shape.

Access: The E trailhead [A] (Map I-A-1) is on WV32, 2.1mi S of the town of Davis. Parking is available for several cars along the shoulder of the road. For backpacking trips it would probably be advisable to use one of the intersecting trails as a trailhead to secure safer parking for cars.

The W trailhead [I] (Map I-A-2) is on Canaan Loop Road (CLR) (FR13) near the westernmost point on this road. It is marked by a prominent sign. Parking is available for any number of cars along the shoulder.

Segment 1: Starting from the E trailhead [A] (Map I-A-1) descend from WV32, reaching Devil's Run at 0.5mi. Do not drink from the stream. From here ascend steadily, watching for good views to the N and W. At 1.0mi Fire Trail No.3 (TR104) [B] joins from the left. A sign marks this junction.

Segment 2: Beyond TR104, by 300yd, cross a stream with a dam and an old sign ("Pump Chance No.2"). The trail continues to ascend gradually, growing wider and crossing a pipeline [C] at 1.8mi. The trail here passes through rhododendron and spruce, passing through a rocky area at 2.3mi, where there is a view to the N. Cross a stream with a small dam at 2.5mi. Ascend briefly, to a level, open section. Descend gradually through laurel, reaching Allegheny Trail, TR701 (also known as Davis Trail, TR107) at 2.7mi. [D]. The junction is usually signed. The area around this junction is rocky, but open, with a few sites suitable for small tents. Water is found in a small stream crossing the trail 100yd W of the junction. A 6-person trail shelter is on the E side of this stream 100yd N of the trail. Just beyond the stream is an open field. The field's SW end offers dry, level tent sites.

Segment 3: Continuing on from TR701 [D], the trail is level, running just below the ridge crest through hemlock and laurel. Cross streams at 2.8 and 3.0mi. At 3.3mi reach the crest and begin a gradual descent. Cross a stream with a small dam at 3.5mi. A few sites suitable for small tents are found in this area; the ground is generally rocky. Cross Fire Trail No.6 (TR108) [E] at 3.8mi. Beware that yellow blazes turn onto Fire Trail No.6. Yellow blazes do not reappear on Plantation Trail until 0.2mi further W.

Segment 4: After leaving TR108, cross another stream with a small concrete dam at 5.0mi. The trail now becomes narrower and rocky in spots, and occasionally passes through open areas. Reach the signed junction with Lindy Run Trail (TR109) [F] (Map I-A-2) at 4.8mi. To the N, Lindy Run Trail is labeled 688 on old USFS maps.

Segment 5: Proceeding W from the junction [F] with TR109, the trail crosses Lindy Run after 100yd. The route is level and walking is easy, except at boggy sections. The junction [G] with Railroad Grade Trail (TR110) is reached at 6.5mi. This junction may be confusing because it is not at right angles.

Segment 6: Continuing W from TR110 [G], the trail is level, narrow, and passes through dense laurel. The footway is often wet. Several small streams cross the trail except during dry periods. Farther on, the trail passes through a more open section with mainly hardwoods, where it runs just below

Table Rock Overlook (TR113). Photo by Nick Broskovich

the summit, with little elevation change. At 8.0mi the trail descends into a small bog ⬚H⬚ and climbs steeply for a short distance before descending gradually to FR13 (CLR) at 8.4mi ⬚I⬚ . Sparse tent areas are found to the left, on the E side of FR13.

FIRE TRAILS NO.1 AND NO.2 (TR102, TR103)   0.8mi(1.3km)
SCENERY: 2 (wooded)   NOTE: M,(1)
DIFFICULTY: I (leisurely)   SKI-: S4
CONDITION: B (average)   ELEV: 3790/3560
MAPS: USFS (A,B), Blackwater Falls, I-A-1 in this Guide
SEGMENTS: (1) FR13(CLR) to WV32/TR103 (Fire Trail No. 2)   0.4mi
                (2) WV32 to FR13(CLR)/TR102 (Fire Trail No. 1)   0.4mi
    Fire Trails 1 and 2 run between WV32 and Canaan Loop Road (CLR) just W of the junction of these two roads. The trails are of little interest.
    Access: To access the S trailhead of TR103 (Fire Trail No.2) from the junction of FR13 (CLR) with WV32, drive W 0.7mi on CLR and park at the turnaround near the Old Canaan Tower site.
    Segment 1: From the S trailhead walk 100yd to Fire Trail No.2 (sign). The trail descends steadily through a stand of spruce. Cross Devil's Run (Do not drink the water.) and ascend briefly but steeply to WV32.
    Segment 2: The N terminus of Fire Trail #1 (TR102) is 0.3mi E of the N terminus of TR103 along WV32. The trail descends briefly, crossing Devil's Run, then ascends gradually but steadily, with private land on the left (E), back to CLR. The turnaround is 0.25mi W on CLR from the S terminus of TR102. TR102 is not on Map I-A-1.

FIRE TRAIL NO.3 (TR104)   0.8mi(0.5km)
SCENERY: 2 (wooded)   NOTE: M,(1)
DIFFICULTY: I (leisurely)   SKI-: S1
CONDITION: B (average)   ELEV: 3740/3540
MAPS: USFS(A,B), Blackwater Falls, I-A-1 in this Guide
SEGMENTS: (1) TR101 (Plantation Trail) to FR13 (CLR)   0.8mi
    Fire Trail No.3 runs N and S between Plantation Trail (TR101) and the S part of Canaan Loop Road (CLR). Virtually the entire trail is a steady, moderate descent. It is rocky, mossy, and wet in spots. A few sporadic blue blazes mark this trail. The trail is in good shape and is well-defined.
    Access: The S terminus ⬚F⬚ is on CLR near parking area #9. There is ample parking along CLR. The sign at this end says "Fire Line No. 3" and "3/4 Plantation Trail".
    Segment 1: At 0.5mi from the S terminus is a short, steep descent. The descent becomes gradual again, and Plantation Trail (TR101) is reached at 0.8mi ⬚B⬚. Water is available in a stream running alongside (and sometimes in) the trail just S of the junction with TR101.

FLAG RUN TRAIL (TR106)   1.0mi(1.6km)
SCENERY: 2 (wooded)   NOTE: M,(0)
DIFFICULTY: I (leisurely)   SKI-: S4
CONDITION: A (good)   ELEV: 3690/3210

MAPS: USFS(A,B), Blackwater Falls, I-A-1 in this Guide
SEGMENTS: (1) FR13(CLR) to WV32   1.0mi

Flag Run Trail lies outside the area bounded by CLR (FR13), and runs NW-SE between FR13 (CLR) and WV32. Recent USFS map show the trail. The trail affords a trip of moderate interest, though views are few. It also affords access from the SE to the Canaan Mountain trail system. The trail is well maintained, well defined, and has light-blue blazes.

Access: The NW end [G] is on CLR 1.9mi W of WV32 and 1.0mi W of the turnaround at the Old Canaan Tower site. There is parking for a few cars at the turnaround. This NW end of Flag Run Trail is signed.

The SE end [H] is on WV32, 5.1mi S of the main intersection in Davis (just N of the bridge over Blackwater River). It is 1.9mi S along WV32 from the junction of WV32 with FR13 (CLR). Park along the shoulder of WV32. The SE terminus is signed. The trail leads straight uphill from a point 50yd S of the crossing of Flag Run.

Segment 1: From FR13 (CLR) [G] Flag Run Trail descends S through spruce on an old wood road. At 0.25mi it crosses a clearing; just beyond is a rocky section with views of Canaan Valley to the S. At 0.5mi cross Flag Run. The descent continues through hardwoods and becomes steeper.

DAVIS TRAIL (TR107)   2.8mi(4.5km)
SCENERY: 2 (wooded)   NOTE: B,H,M,(1)
DIFFICULTY: I (leisurely)   SKI-:   S2
CONDITION: A (good)   ELEV: 3710/3150
MAPS: USFS(A,B), Blackwater Falls, I-A-1 in this Guide
SEGMENTS:
        (1) FR13 S to TR101 (Plantation Trail)   1.6mi
        (2) TR101 to TR111 (Firelane Split Trail) 0.5mi
        (3) TR111 to FR13 (CLR)   0.7mi

Davis Trail is one segment of Allegheny Trail (TR701), a long-distance trail across the MNF. It is also part of the Blackwater/Canaan Cross-Country Ski Trail. It runs N-S across the area bounded by FR13 (Canaan Loop Road). Neither water nor tent sites are found on Davis Trail between Plantation Trail (TR101) and FR13 (CLR).

Access: Its N end [I] is in Blackwater Falls (BWF) State Park, and can be reached from the town of Davis as follows:
At 0.0mi leave WV32 in Davis for BWF State Park; at 1.0mi pass a sign at the entrance to BWF State Park; at 1.3mi turn left at intersection, follow signs to BWF Lodge; at 2.2mi a sign on the left indicates beginning of the trail. Park on the right shoulder 70yd before the sign.

A prominent sign marks the S end [K], and ample parking is available along CLR.

Segment 1: From the sign at the N terminus [I], Davis Trail leads SW away from FR13. At 0.2mi pass under a power line with a stream 30yd to the right. At 0.3mi pass a sign "Entering Canaan Mtn. Spruce Plantation". A stream is to the right; cross this stream at 0.4mi. Begin a gradual ascent, following a stream on the left. The trail is pleasant here, with laurel on either side. At 0.75mi cross a small brook. The ascent becomes steeper, leading away from the stream. Near the crest, a rock formation 30yd off the trail to the right offers views of the surrounding ridges. At 1.6mi, is the junction [D] with Plantation Trail (TR101). A 6-person shelter is located 70yd W of this junction. Water can be found along Plantation Trail, 100yd W of the junction. Although the area around the junction is rocky, there are places where small tents may be pitched. Segment 1 is well-maintained and well-defined.

Segment 2: Continue S from the junction with TR101 following yellow blazes. Davis Trail ascends gradually, crossing a fire lane J (TR111) at 2.1mi. No sign marks this junction except for an arrow pointing N along Davis Trail.

Segment 3: From TR111 J the trail continues to ascend gradually to FR13 (CLR) K.

Allegheny Trail: To travel further S on Allegheny Trail (TR701), walk SW from K on CLR for 1.2mi. Allegheny Trail leaves CLR here and leads S through open woods. The first 0.1- to 0.3mi is often boggy. About 1.0mi S of CLR is a hilltop view. The junction with Canaan Mountain Trail (Map I-A-3) is obscure. Canaan Mountain Trail takes one SE to Middle Ridge Ski Trail, one of the trails in Canaan Valley State Park network. Write to the Park (Davis, WV 26260) for a free map of the trail system.

FIRE TRAIL NO.6 (TR108)

1.1mi(1.8km)

SCENERY: 2 (wooded)
DIFFICULTY: I (leisurely)
CONDITION: B (average)

NOTE: M,W,(0)
SKI-: S2
ELEV: 3630/3500

MAPS: USFS(A,B), Blackwater Falls, I-A-l in this Guide
SEGMENTS:
    (1) FR13 (CLR) to TR111 (Firelane Split Trail)   0.7mi
    (2) TR111 to TR101 (Plantation Trail)   0.4mi

Fire Trail No.6 runs N from CLR (FR13) to Plantation Trail (TR101). Nice camp sites are found in the hemlocks near the junction with the old fire lane (former TR111).

Access: Its S terminus L is along CLR, 4.2mi W of the junction of CLR and WV32. This end is signed, with a large parking area and a small camping area (with water) at the junction.

The N terminus E at TR101 may be unsigned.

Segment 1: Starting from the S terminus L, Fire Trail No.6 heads N and crosses an old fire lane (TR111) M.

Segment 2: At 0.5mi N of the fire lane the trail is a beautiful mossy path through spruce and hemlock. Plantation Trail (TR101) E is reached at 1.1mi.

LINDY RUN TRAIL (TR109)

2.8mi(4.5km)

SCENERY: 1 (exceptional)
DIFFICULTY: I (leisurely)
CONDITION: A (good)

NOTE: M,(1)
SKI-: S2
ELEV: 3620/3100

MAPS: USFS(A,B), Mozark Mountain, Blackwater Falls, I-A-1 & I-A-2 in this Guide
SEGMENTS:
    (1) FR13 to TR101 (Plantation Trail)   1.5mi
    (2) TR101 to TR111 (Firelane Split Trail)   0.9mi
    (3) TR111 to FR13 (Canaan Loop Road)   0.4mi

Railroad Grade Trail (TR110) Shelter. Photo by Allen de Hart

Lindy Run Trail follows a N-S route across the area bounded by the CLR. North of Plantation Trail (TR101), it is TR688 on old USFS maps; the S section is labeled TR109. The trail is a lovely walk through laurel and hemlocks, with Lindy Run close by for much of the first half. The trail is sporadically blazed in faded light blue. No tent sites are found along the trail. Water is available from Lindy Run along the N half. The S half has few sources of water, although the trail itself is wet.

Access: The N trailhead [A] (Map I-A-2) is along CLR, just W of where CLR crosses Lindy Run, 1.2mi W of the sled run parking area in Blackwater Falls State Park.

The S trailhead [N] (Map I-A-1) is also on CLR, 4.5mi W of WV32. This junction is signed.

Segment 1: Starting from the N, the ascent is steady but moderate. Within 0.2mi the trail skirts a large impressive rock formation. Cross Lindy Run at 0.5mi. This crossing is not difficult, even during high water. At 1.3mi the ascent becomes steeper, and Plantation Trail [F] is reached at 1.5mi. The junction is signed.

Segment 2: Continuing S from the junction with TR101, the trail ascends gradually. At 1.8mi the trail levels off as it passes over the crest. At 2.5mi a fire lane (TR111) [B], leading E is passed. A sign marks the junction, and the fire lane is easy to spot.

Segment 3: The trail ends at CLR [N] (Map I-A-1).

RAILROAD GRADE TRAIL (TR110)   3.1mi(5.0km)
SCENERY: 1 (exceptional)   NOTE: B,H,M,(1)
DIFFICULTY: II (moderate)   SKI-:   S2
CONDITION: A (good)   ELEV: 3610/3210
MAPS: USFS(A,B), Mozark Mountain, I-A-2 in this Guide
SEGMENTS: (1) FR13 S to TR101 (Plantation Trail)   1.4mi
                (2) TR101 to shelter   0.6mi
                (3) Shelter to FR13 (Canaan Loop Road)   1.1mi

Railroad Grade Trail runs N-S from the N leg of the CLR (FR13) to the S leg, parallel to, and W of, Lindy Run Trail (TR109). It follows the bed of an old logging RR. Remnants of ties can still be seen in places, although the rails have been removed.

Access: The N end [C] is 1.0mi W, along the CLR, of the N end of Lindy Run Trail (TR109), and is marked with a sign.

The S junction [E] with CLR is also signed.

Segment 1: Heading S from the N leg of CLR [C] the route is a gradual but steady ascent through the woods. At 0.75mi cross a small stream by rock hopping. Continuing the ascent, the junction [G] with Plantation Trail (TR101) (signed) is reached at 1.4mi. There are no suitable tent sites along this section of trail.

Segment 2: The trail widens S of the junction with TR101. At 1.75mi the footway improves, descending and swinging to the SE around the S side of the mountain with views of Mozark Mountain to the SW. The shelter [D] is reached at 2.0mi. It is in good condition, with a wooden table and a small outside fireplace. It sleeps six on the elevated wooden floor. Water is available from a small stream that flows in front of the shelter. A few small tents could be pitched just S or NE of the shelter, although the ground is rocky.

Segment 3: Proceeding S from the shelter, the descent continues on the old RR grade, with partially obstructed views of Mozark Mountain over the valley of Red Run. The S leg of FR13(CLR) $\boxed{E}$ is reached at 3.1mi. A short distance E along CLR are several tent sites, some of them overlooking Red Run, a convenient source of water.

FIRELANE SPLIT TRAIL (formerly TR111)   2.0mi(3.2km)

SCENERY: 2 (wooded)	NOTE: M,W,(0)
DIFFICULTY: II (moderate)	SKI-: S1
CONDITION: B (average)	ELEV: 3680/3590

MAPS: USFS(A,B), Mozark Mountain, Blackwater Falls, I-A-1 and I-A-2 in this Guide

SEGMENTS:
    (1) TR109 (Lindy Run Trail) to TR108 (Fire Trail No.6)   0.8mi
    (2) TR108 to TR107 (Davis Trail)   1.2mi

Firelane Split Trail is not officially part of the numbered trail system in the Canaan Mountain Spruce Plantation, but it is shown on the USFS map. It is marked by signs in places, and can be combined with other trails to form a variety of circuit hikes. The USFS improved this trail for fire emergency access by 4WD vehicles. There is no water.

Access: The W end $\boxed{B}$(Map I-A-2) is on Lindy Run Trail (TR109) 0.4mi N of the S end (at CLR). No sign marks either end of this trail.

The E terminus is on Davis Trail (TR107)$\boxed{J}$(Map I-A-1).

The USFS is trying to rehabilitate this old route and return it to nature. The USFS therefore asks you to stay off this trail. The number TR111 has been given to Two Camp Trail in Horseshoe Recreation Area.

BENNETT ROCK TRAIL (TR112)   0.7mi(1.1km)

SCENERY: 2 (wooded)	NOTE: B,M,(0)
DIFFICULTY: III (strenuous)	SKI-: S4
CONDITION: C (poor)	ELEV: 2880/1830

MAPS: USFS(A,B), Mozark Mountain, I-A-2 in this Guide
SEGMENTS: (1) TR114 (Mountainside Trail) W to WV72   0.7mi

Bennett Rock Trail is a short steep (1050ft. change in elevation) trail connecting Mountain Side Trail (TR114) with WV72 S of Parsons. It is not numbered on USFS maps. It provides an approach from the SW and Otter Creek Wilderness into the Canaan Mountain Trail system. It is strenuous and difficult to find.

Access: To reach the W trailhead $\boxed{K}$, follow WV72 S from Parsons through Hambleton and Hendricks. About 1.5mi beyond Hendricks is a yellow house on the right (between WV72 and the Dry Fork). About 0.3mi beyond this house is a logging road leading left up the mountain, closed off by a wire fence near the highway and by a cable 200ft. up the slope. About 50yd beyond this road is a break in the laurel where Bennett Rock Trail heads up the mountain. There is no sign, but the trail is unmistakable. If one goes beyond it, the slope is covered with boulders. Look for the trail between the logging road and the boulder-covered slope. Highway WV72 is narrow and has a narrow shoulder. Parking for a single car can be found at occasional spots on the shoulder in both directions from the trail junction, or at the USFS parking area between the road and Dry Fork River.

The E terminus [J] at Mountain Side Trail (TR114) is signed.

Segment 1: Because the trail is rarely-used, the footway is not worn. It is axe-blazed (a short slash above a longer vertical slash) but the blazes are old and often far apart. However, if the trail is lost there is no great problem, whether ascending or descending. Anyone attempting the trail should be prepared for a steep route. Bushwhacking up the mountain cannot fail to reach Mountain Side Trail (TR114); bushwhacking down will inevitably lead to WV72.

TABLE ROCK OVERLOOK TRAIL (TR113) 1.1mi(1.8km)

SCENERY: 1 (exceptional)   NOTE: M,(0)
DIFFICULTY: I (leisurely)   SKI-: S4
CONDITION: A (good)   ELEV: 3435/3310
MAPS: USFS(A,B), Mozark Mountain, I-A-2 in this Guide
SEGMENTS: (1) FR13 (Canaan Loop Road) to Overlook   1.1mi

Table Rock Overlook Trail, W of the area bounded by FR13 (CLR), leads to one of the most spectacular views in the Cheat Ranger District. The trail is blazed with blue paint (faded and sporadic). The trail is regularly used and quite evident.

Access: The NE terminus [L] is at the CLR (FR13) 65yd S of the W end of Plantation Trail (TR101). This point on the CLR is 9.8mi from WV32 and 6.6mi from Blackwater Falls State Park Lodge. The trailhead may be signed and the parking area may be boggy.

Segment 1: Starting from CLR [L], the trail climbs gradually through the woods. The footway is reasonably clear but rocky. After completing the slight incline, descend slightly to a damp area in dense rhododendron. Beyond is a large outcrop (Table Rock) [M] from which the entire Red Run Valley can be seen to the SE with Mozark Mountain near at hand. To the S, over the valley of the Dry Fork, several mountains, including Shavers Mountain, are visible in the distance. In the vicinity of the W terminus of the Trail are heavy mountain laurel thickets and one established campsite.

MOUNTAIN SIDE TRAIL (TR114) 4.8mi(7.7km)

SCENERY: 1 (exceptional)   NOTE: B,M,(6)
DIFFICULTY: II (moderate)   SKI-: S2
CONDITION: B (average)   ELEV: 3240/2440
MAPS: USFS(A,B), Mozark Mountain, I-A-2 in this Guide
SEGMENTS:
    (1) FR13(N) to TR112 (Benett Rock Trail)   3.0mi
    (2) TR112 to FR244A   1.8mi
    (3) FR244A to FR13(S)   (1.8mi)
    (Segment (3) is not part of TR114)

Mountain Side Trail is near the W edge of Canaan Mountain Spruce Plantation. Part of the trail is shown as TR688 on old USFS maps. The trail follows an old logging RR grade. Ties are still evident, but rails are gone. Changes in elevation are gradual and the route is not strenuous. Along the route there are views, first to the NW, across the valley of Blackwater River to Backbone Mountain, then to the W across the valley of Dry Fork River to McGowan Mountain, then S across the Dry Fork to Green- and Shavers Mountains, and finally across the valley of Red Run to Mozark Mountain, closer at hand.

Access: The N end [N] of the trail is at the CLR 1.0mi N of the W end [I] of Plantation Trail (TR101). This junction is signed. After looping around the SW arm of Canaan Mountain the trail becomes FR244A and FR244 which can be walked to FR13, where FR244 is gated.

Segment 1: Starting at the N end [N], Mountain Side Trail enters the woods on a dirt road. After entering USFS land, the trail passes an old hunting camp on the left. Beyond the camp the trail narrows and the old RR bed becomes evident. In the next 0.5mi the trail crosses Laurel Run five times. The area around these crossings is open, and there are several tent sites, particularly around the first two crossings. Laurel Run is a convenient source of water. The trail makes a sixth crossing, of a tributary of Laurel Run. Even in periods of high water these crossings are not difficult. The trail beyond the crossing descends gradually as Laurel Run descends steeply to the valley of the Dry Fork of the Cheat. Beware of a hairpin turnoff to the right before Bennett Rock Trail; keep going straight ahead here. Bennett Rock Trail (TR112)[J] is reached at 3.0mi.

Segment 2: The trail then swings around the SW arm of Canaan Mountain and heads E, parallel to Red Run, which is nearly 1000ft below. As one travels E, Red Run becomes increasingly audible as its elevation increases. At 4.8mi the trail reaches the signed junction [O] with Red Run Logging Road, FR244A.

Segment 3: Walk another 1.8mi on FR244A and FR244 to the NE end [P] of FR244 (gated). The NE end of FR244 is 2.0mi W of the S end of Railroad Grade Trail (TR110) [E]. About 0.5mi W of [P] is a clear view of Mozark Mountain. This is the least-obstructed view along the trail.

Circuit Hikes: Using the shelter [D] on TR110 as a base camp, the following one-day circuit hike could be made; From the shelter go N on Railroad Grade Trail to Plantation Trail (TR101) [G], then W to the CLR [I] ; N on CLR to Mountain Side Trail [N], then to FR244 which is then taken back to CLR [P]; E on the CLR to Railroad Grade Trail (TR110) [E], and return to the shelter. The total distance of 13.0mi involves less than 2.0mi on the CLR. FR244 can also be followed to WV72 and Otter Creek Wilderness, or used as part of a 5.3mi loop involving FR244A, TR114, TR112 and WV72.

POINTY KNOB TRAIL (TR139)
5.2mi(8.3km)

SCENERY: 2 (wooded)   NOTE: B,M,H,S (6)
DIFFICULTY: II (moderate)   SKI-:   S4
CONDITION: A (good)   ELEV: 4100/3240
MAPS: USFS(A,B), Blackwater Falls, Mozark Mountain, I-A-1, I-A-2 and
      I-A-3 in this Guide
SEGMENTS: (1) FR13(E) to White Raven Rocks   2.4mi
          (2) White Raven Rocks to FR13(W)   2.8mi

Pointy Knob Trail goes neither to Pointy Knob nor to Chimney Rocks. A faint side trail toward these two points of interest dead-ends at the boundary of private land. Pointy Knob Trail does however cross White Raven Rocks where there is a partial view. The trail is blue-paint blazed.

Lindy Run Trail (TR109). Photo by Allen de Hart

Access: The E trailhead [O](Map I-A-1) (el. 3630ft) is on Canaan Loop Road (CLR), 4.1mi from WV32 and 0.2mi E of TR108.

The W trailhead [Q](Map I-A-2) on CLR is signed but requires effort to locate. The sign is on the side of the stream at the parking area. One must cross the stream (North Fork of Red Run) and locate blazes to begin hiking.

Segment 1: From the E trailhead [O](Map I-A-1) on CLR look for an old forest road. Park in this area; follow the old road 0.1mi and turn left onto the trail. Follow blazes S on a slight ascent through mountain laurel, rhododendron and red spruce. Reach White Raven Rocks (el.4100ft) (Map I-A-3) at 2.4mi.

Segment 2: Turn right, W, and follow the blazes in a descent through hardwoods to cross the headwaters of South Fork of Red Run at 3.3mi. At 3.6mi is an Adirondak shelter (Map I-A-2) built by the USFS and the W. Va. National Guard in 1989. This shelter accommodates 6-8 hikers. From here the trail follows a scenic and easy treadway on an old RR grade which parallels the stream. There are a number of cascades and rock formations where mosses and ferns are prominent. At 4.8mi rock hop the stream, and three times more before turning right off the old RR grade. Descend 30yd to the confluence of South Fork and North Fork of Red Run, rock hop, and climb the stream bank to the parking area [Q] at FR13.

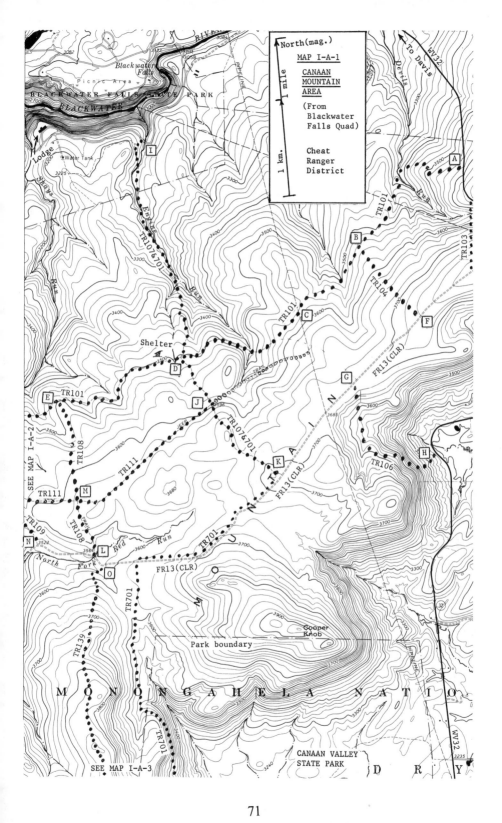

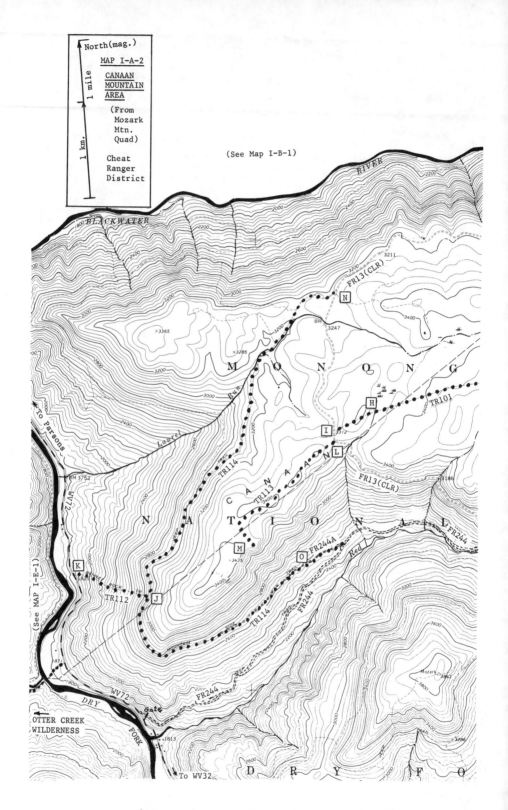

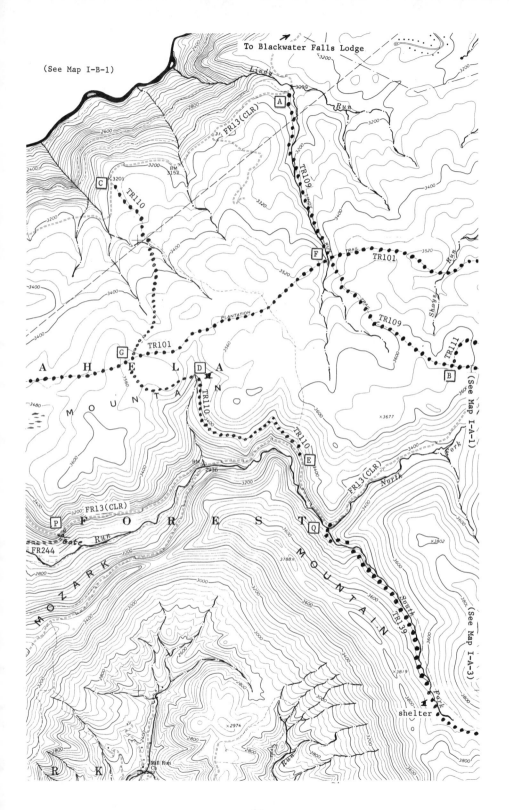

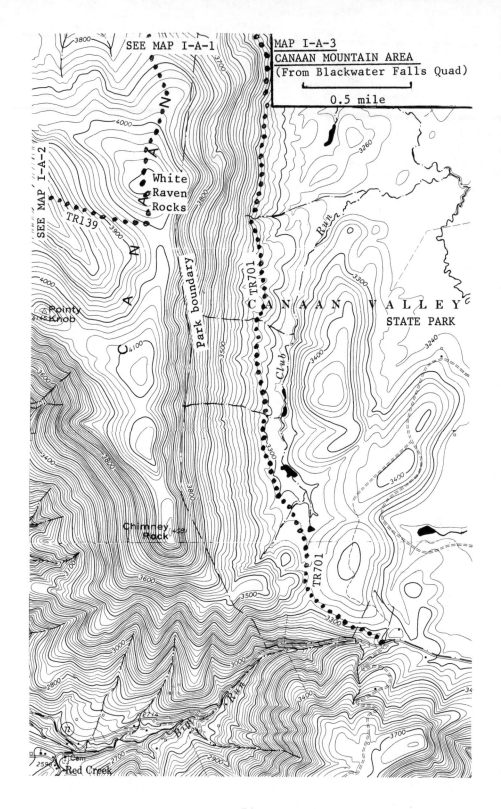

(I-B) OLSON TOWER / BLACKWATER CANYON AREA

This area is above average in beauty, isolation and diversified points of interest. The main access road, FR18, is in good condition overall, but there are rocks, ruts, and stream crossings that recommend high-clearance vehicles. To get to the E end of this road turn SW off WV32 in Thomas onto CO27 and drive through Coketon and Douglas and on to FR18 (4mi from the US219-WV32 junction in Thomas). This brings you onto the Mozark Mountain Topo map at the upper right-hand corner.

Spectacular rapids are common in Blackwater River, and canyon trails on both sides of the river lead to them. Use Maps I-A-1, I-B-1 and I-B-2 for exploring this wild canyon and for following the limited selection of USFS trails described below. The swamp shown on Map I-B-1 at the headwaters of Big Run and along FR18 shows impressive beaver activity. Please do not try to walk out on the bogs. They are fragile.

BLACKWATER CANYON R.R. GRADE TR.(TR115) 12.2mi(17.8km)

SCENERY: 1 (exceptional)   NOTE: B,M
DIFFICULTY: II (moderate)   SKI-:   S1
CONDITION: A (good)   ELEV: 2951/1661
MAPS: USFA(A), Davis, Lead Mine, Mozark Mountain, Parsons, I-B-1
       and I-B-2 in this Guide
SEGMENTS: (1) WV32 to TR142 (Limerock Trail)   7.6mi
          (2) TR142 to District Ranger Entrance   4.6mi

Blackwater Canyon Railroad Grade Trail is a section of the former Western Maryland Railroad that passes through the town of Parsons in its ascent to the town of Thomas and beyond. Its elevation change is 1290ft, and it connects with Allegheny Trail (TR701) and Limerock Trail (TR142) in the process. As of January 1999 there were no developed trailheads or even trail-head signs. The USFS hopes to someday have a trailhead parking area in the Nursery Bottom at Parson, another near the city park in Hendricks, and a third in Thomas. Land ownership issues must be resolved before this happens. A few parts of this trail border private property. Call the Ranger District office for a report of the status of clearance for through-hiking. The property line in question is between Hendricks and Spruce Lick Run. Respect any "No Tres-passing" signs. From North Fork Falls to Spruce Lick Run, the downhill half of the grade belongs to Allegheny Wood Products. Because the grade is growing in, and the treadway wiggles back and forth across the width of the grade, the USFS suggests that trail users get permission from APW to use the trail.

Access: The N trailhead is off WV32 S in the town of Thomas, about 1 block N of the Post Office. Look for a USFS gate with a brown and white sign "Foot Travel Welcome". Note: Map I-B-1 does not extend all the way to Thomas.

For the S access (Map I-B-2) choose the entrance road to the Cheat Ranger District Office in Parsons. You can park near the gate, but do not block its entrance.

Segment 1: Starting from Thomas, hike S and, after 300yd, cross the North Fork of Blackwater River on an old RR bridge. Cross a natural gas line at 0.6mi, then pass the N and S switch of the Coketon RR spur. Cross SR27 at 0.9mi. (Allegheny Trail follows SR27 from Thomas and onto FS18 S of the community of Douglas.) Pass the Douglas Highwall #2 Project; it is a reclamation project to remove acid from strip mine drainage into the Blackwater River. At 2.0mi cross Long Run on a plate girder bridge.

From here the rugged remoteness is noticeable as the RR drops into the steep-walled canyon. Sounds of cascades can be heard, and sometimes seen in the wintertime. Tall oaks, maple, cherry, yellow poplar, hemlock and rhododendrons are dominant. The area is a black bear habitat. Some other wildlife are deer, squirrel, birds, and snakes. The canyon has a reputation of having a number of rattlesnake dens. Cross bridges with spectacular scenery of cascades over Tub Run at 4.8mi, Big Run at 5.9mi, and Flatrock Run at 7.4mi.

Segment 2: Junction with Limerock Trail (TR142) [C] (Map I-B-2) on your right, at 7.6mi. Cross Hickory Lick Run at 8.4mi. At 9.0mi are former RR double tracks. Wildflowers such as soapwort and jewelweed are common along the route. Reach the crossing of WV72 in Hendricks at 9.7mi. From here you will pass through residential areas of Hendricks and Hambleton to parallel the Dry Fork of the Cheat River. Cross Roaring Run near the junction of US219 and WV72 at 11.4mi. After 0.8mi is the entrance road to the Cheat Ranger District Office.

BOUNDARY TRAIL (TR116)   3.5mi(5.6km)
SCENERY: 2 (wooded)   NOTE: B,M,(1)
DIFFICULTY: II (moderate)   SKI-:   S2
CONDITION: B (average)   ELEV: 3300/3080
MAPS: USFS(A,B), Mozark Mountain, I-B-1 in this Guide
SEGMENTS: (1) FR18 E to Tub Run   1.3mi
          (2) Tub Run to FR18   2.2mi

Boundary Trail is an easy, moderate grade, well marked with red boundary blazes. There are sphagnum bogs, and abundant signs of beaver and deer. A number of open spaces are intermixed with dense forest. Camping is possible near the beaver ponds. In spring however the ground may be too wet at these sites. A loop hike is possible using FR18 (8mi total). The trail is suitable for ski-touring, except for the need to cross three strip mines. The woods are second growth. There has been no recent logging. The trail is shown and properly labeled on the Mozark topo.

Access: A sign at the W end [A] of the trail says "Tub Run 1.3mi. FR18 3.5mi". A sign is at the E end of the trail on FR18, 10yd inside the forest boundary posts.

Segment 1: Start from the sign at the W terminus. [A] Upon leaving the woods at the first strip mine the trail becomes hard to follow. Make a 10-20 degree turn left. Proceed on this course, dropping down the right side of an excavated pit (full of water in spring). Bear slightly right past this point for 75yd. Reaching the edge of the cinder bank you will see the trail into the woods below. The trail continues on to Tub Run [B] where there are a number of tent sites. Water from Tub Run is normally acidic.

Segment 2: Cross Tub Run and continue to the next strip mine. Proceed straight across it. Trees on the far side have red markers. Use extreme caution in climbing up the far side of this deep strip mine. The rocks and soil are unstable. The third crossing of a strip mine is easy. The remainder of the trail to FR18 is an easy walk, well marked with red blazes.

CANYON RIM TRAIL (TR117)   3.0mi(4.8km)
SCENERY: 1 (exceptional)   NOTE: B,M,(1)
DIFFICULTY: II (moderate)   SKI-:   S2
CONDITION: A (good)   ELEV: 3610/3090
MAPS: USFS(A,B), Mozark Mountain, I-B-1 and I-B-2 in this Guide
SEGMENTS: (1) Olson Tower E to FR18   3.0mi

    Canyon Rim Trail runs from near Olson Tower ⬚D (Map I-B-2) on
FR717 to Big Run ⬚G on FR18 where Big Run drops into Blackwater Canyon. The forest is varied, with lots of rhododendron. Big Run may be impossible to cross on foot in spring or after a heavy rain. Interesting rock formations, side trails, and several shelter caves are found along the trail. There is no water along the W end of the trail, and streams along the E end (except Big Run) are sometimes dry in summer and fall. The trail is not blazed, but is easy to follow. Big Run Overlook is worth a stop. It is 10yd from Canyon Rim Road, 0.2mi E on FR18 from the trailhead. It offers a great spot for photographs of Blackwater Canyon.
    Access: At the E trailhead ⬚G (Map I-B-1) on FR18 a sign says: "Olson Tower 3mi, US219 3mi (by road), Douglas 5mi (by road)". A pulloff area here offers parking space.
    Segment 1: At Olson Tower ⬚D are toilets, water pump, and an area big enough for 8-10 tents. One can have a nice view of the Allegheny Mountains from the top of Olson Tower. The E end of the trail ⬚G offers excellent views of Blackwater Canyon and Big Run Falls, particularly in late fall and early spring. Very close to Big Run is an established campsite on the trail. It would be ideal for late arrivals.

FANSLER TRAIL (TR118)   1.1mi(1.8km)
SCENERY: 2 (wooded)   NOTE: B,M (0)
DIFFICULTY: I (leisurely)   SKI-:   S2
CONDITION: A (good)   ELEV: 3660/2420
MAPS: USFS(A), Mozark Mountain, I-B-2 in this Guide
SEGMENTS: (1) FR717 to FR906   1.1mi

    Fansler Trail follows the ridge line of Backbone Mountain from Olson Tower Recreation Area SW before descending on private land to CO219/4.
    Access: The E trailhead ⬚D is in the picnic area near Olson Tower.
    Segment 1: Starting from ⬚D the blue-blazed trail begins among the boulders and passes first through rhododendron and later through an open hardwood forest of maple, ash and oaks. After a descent it reaches a grassy USFS logging road (FR906) at 1.1mi. A loop can be made by following the logging road NE to its gated entrance and junction with FR717 at 3mi. Another 0.6mi leads to Olson Tower Recreation Area ⬚D on FR717.

LIMEROCK TRAIL (TR142)   4.1mi(6.6km)
SCENERY: 1 (exceptional)   NOTE: M,(1)
DIFFICULTY: II (moderate)   SKI-:   S3
CONDITION: B (average)   ELEV: 3050/1800
MAPS: USFS(A,B), Mozark Mountain, I-B-1 and I-B-2 in this Guide
SEGMENTS: (1) FR18 [J] W to former CXS RR grade (TR115)   4.1mi

Limerock Trail follows an old RR grade for its entire length except its beginning on FR18, and is properly located and labeled on the Mozark topo. The trail is rarely steep. Big Run crossing [L] may be impassable after heavy rain. Four vistas (not always evident) overlook various points of interest in Blackwater Canyon. Water is available at several spots. Do not wear shorts in the summer when the trail becomes partially overgrown. Some parts of the trail are very rocky.

Access: The E trailhead [J] is on FR18 (Canyon Rim Road) 0.25mi W of Tub Run and 2 mi E of Big Run Overlook.

The W trailhead ([C] Map I-B-2) is on the former CSX RR grade, 2.1 mi E of Hendricks (WV72), at Limerock. A locked USFS gate is located near the trailhead. Reach Limerock by traveling E on the former CSX RR grade out of Hendricks (see TR115). This W trailhead [C] is signed 30yd into the woods.

Segment 1: Starting from the E, the section from FR18 to Big Run is blue-blazed. 0.2mi from FR18 is a vista on a 20ft rock ledge. Here the rapids of Tub Run can be heard. but the sound fades when the old RR grade trail turns W. At 1.6mi is a tributary where a RR trestle once bridged the deep ravine. After 130yd reach Big Run. Huge boulders are seen up and down the steep canyon. Unless the stream is at flood stage it can be rock-hopped to pass another tributary after 106yd. From Big Run [L] to Flat Rock Run the trail is not blazed but is obvious. The half-mile stretch E of Big Run [L] is rough, but maintenace is planned from results of the Olson Opportunity Analysis begun in 1991. Big Run [L] is somewhat scenic. At Flatrock Run, take time to follow this stream (easy cross-country) down to the 20ft waterfall which is almost to the RR grade. At 4.1mi is the former CSX (Western Maryland) RR which is now the Blackwater Canyon RR Grade Trail (TR115).

Raven Ridge in Northern Dolly Sods. Photo by Monika Vucic

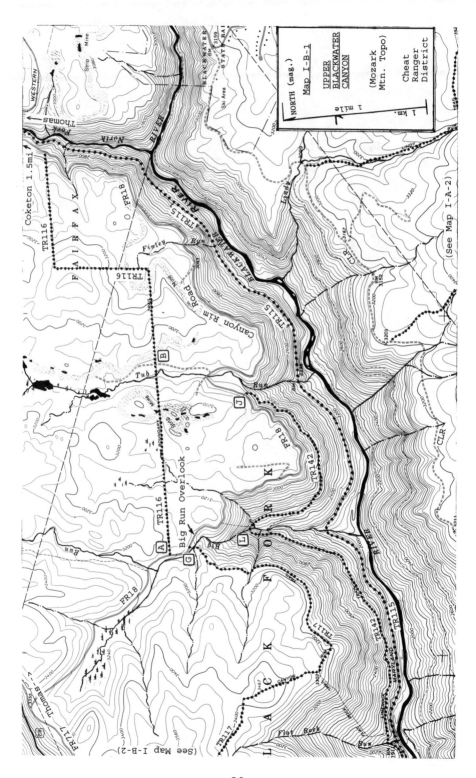

NORTH (mag.)

Map I-B-1

UPPER
BLACKWATER
CANYON

(Mozark
Mtn. Topo)

Cheat
Ranger
District

1 mile

1 Km.

(See Map I-A-2)

(See Map I-B-2)

Coketon 1.5mi

F A I R F A X

TR116

TR116

North Fork Thomas

FR18

STRIP MINE

BLACKWATER RIVER

Strip Mine

Ski Area

STATE PARK

BM 3159

Shady

CLR

BM 3162

BM 3152

Canyon Rim Road

Finley Run

TR115

Tub Run

Big Run Overlook

B L A C K W A T E R   R I V E R

B

J

A

G

L

FR18

TR142

CLR

Big Run

FR18

FR117

Thomas

FR117

TR117

TR117

Flat Rock

CANYON

Flat Rock

TR142

TR115

B L A C K   F O R K

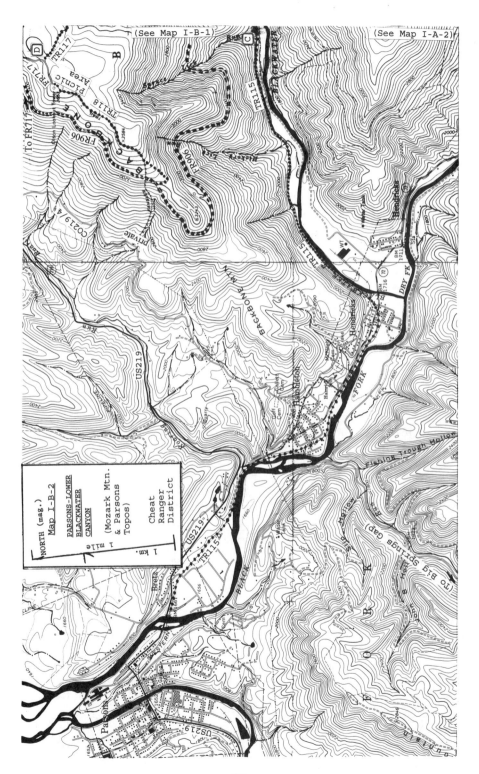

81

(I-C) PHEASANT MOUNTAIN AREA

This area lies immediately W of Parsons with US219 passing through its center, and with a major ridge trail on each side of US219. The N side has Pheasant Mountain Trail (TR120) (also called Pheasant Mountain Firebreak). It was extended in 1992 to follow a 1mi section of former Mail Route Trail and a new section through a clear-cut to a W terminus at Valley Fork Road (CO23). This trail will also serve as the route for the American Discovery Trail to connect with Shingletree Trail for a descent S to US219. (See American Discovery Trail, page 48.)

The other major ridge trail is South Haddix Trail, partially restored and extended 3.1mi S in 1992 after timber cuts in the late 1980s. Its N terminus is near the end of CO219/10 W of Moore, and its S terminus is on Pleasant Run Road (SR47). For its first 2.5mi it follows the crest of a ridge between Haddix Run (parallel to US219) and South Branch of Haddix Run. The trail then meanders along the boundary between Tucker and Randolph Counties on Cheat Mountain. Both it and Pheasant Mountain Trail have new signage.

PHEASANT MOUNTAIN TRAIL (TR120)   4.7mi(7.5km)

SCENERY: 2 (wooded)   NOTE: B,M,(1)
DIFFICULTY: I (leisurely)   SKI-: S2
CONDITION: A (good)   ELEV: 2600/1850
MAPS: USFS(A), Parsons, Montrose, I-C-1 in this Guide
SEGMENTS:
      (1) TR121(S) to TR121(N) (Shingletree Trail)   0.4mi
      (2) TR121(N) to TR124 (Clover Trail) [E]   1.8mi
      (3) TR124   to CO23 [H]   2.5mi

Pheasant Mountain Trail follows ridges W from its E trailhead at Shingletree Trail (TR121). The trail undulates on the ridge crest, switches to slopes, and dips to cross a stream near good campsites in Mail Route Hollow. It is used by hikers, bikers, skiers and hunters. Some illegal ATV use is also noticeable. In a hardwood forest of oaks, maple, beech, and birch, quiet hikers will likely see bear and deer, or signs of their presence. Although turkey and grouse may be seen, it is unlikely that pheasants, for which the ridge is named, will be observed.

Access: To reach the E trailhead [B] begin at either end (N or S) of the Shingletree Trail described later. (The former access to Pheasant Mountain Trail was at the top of the ridge on Mt. Zion Road (CO17), 1.7mi NW of Parsons. Although no longer maintained, the old route may be used by hikers for 0.8mi to Shingletree Trail.)

The W terminus [H] can be reached by continuing on Mt. Zion Road (CO17) and making a left turn [N] onto Clover Run Road (CO21) and then another left turn (SW) onto Valley Fork Road (CO23), and driving 0.2mi to a parking area for 4-5 cars on the left.

Segment 1: Starting from the E trailhead [B], Pheasant Mountain Trail and Shingletree Trail run N jointly for 0.4mi to a small sag [C]. Here Shingletree Trail (TR121-N) turns right, N, and descends to Clover Run Road, but Pheasant Mountain Trail continues on the ridgeline.

Segment 2: Soon after leaving Shingletree Trail [C], Pheasant Mountain Trail leaves the ridge and shifts to a W slope before returning to the ridge top. After 1.0mi from Shingletree Trail there is an old, faint trail to the right (N) [D] which descends to Clover Run Road (CO21). After crossing an old RR grade the trail meets Clover Trail (TR124) from the right [E] in a saddle at 2.2mi. Clover Trail descends to Clover Run Road (CO21). At this saddle, as at other flat places on Pheasant Mountain Trail, you may see bear tracks in the mud or soft soil.

Segment 3: At 2.3mi pass a junction with the former Ridge Trail (TR122) [F], now closed. Continuing W, the trail follows the ridge 0.2mi to the junction with the former Mail Route Trail (TR123) [G], now part of Pheasant Mountain Trail. (The fire ridge trail ahead dead-ends at a timber cut of the 1970s.) After turning right (N), Pheasant Mountain Trail passes an intermittent spring and campsite at 2.7mi. Here the trail joins an old road where the descent is between two ridges. At 3.5mi the trail curves right into Mail Route Hollow. (Space for campsites is found near the MNF boundary.)

After 90yd to a white oak on the left, the trail leaves the road, crosses a stream, and begins an ascent in a hardwood forest of black birch, oaks, maples, and curves in a watershed with ferns and wildflowers. After 0.4mi from the stream the trail joins a logging road cul-de-sac in a clear-cut at 3.9mi. It then follows the road on a gentle descent to a gate, crosses shallow Valley Fork, and reaches Valley Fork Road (CO23) [H] at 4.7mi.

SHINGLETREE TRAIL (S end) (TR121)   3.1mi(5.0km)
SCENERY: 2 (wooded)   NOTE: B,M,(0)
DIFFICULTY: I (leisurely)   SKI-:   S2
CONDITION: B (average)   ELEV: 2420/1760
MAPS: USFS(A), Parsons, I-C-1 in this Guide
SEGMENTS: (1) US219 to TR120 (Pheasant Mountain Trail)   3.1mi

The S portion of Shingletree Trail runs through a scenic forest. At first there are thick rhododendron thickets, then open hardwood and hemlock, and then all hardwoods at the N end of the trail. Although there is nothing spectacular, it is worth hiking.

Access: The S trailhead [I] is on US219 3.6mi S and W from the intersection of US219 and WV72 in Parsons. The trailhead offers parking for 4-5 cars. A trailhead sign indicates that it is 4.5mi to Clover Run Road (the total length of Shingletree Trail (TR121)).

Segment 1: From the S terminus [I] start up an old dirt road. In 100yd, just after crossing a small stream, turn sharp right. Note the small arrow sign. The trail starts up steeply for a short distance, then switchbacks for a gradual climb. (Note that the trail is on the E side of the run, not as shown on the topo.) The first portion of the trail cuts through rhododendrons. Several small, intermittent streams are passed. At 1.0mi the trail turns E around a small valley. A side trail [J] here looks overgrown. Apparently this is the trail shown on the topo as running along Hawk Run. At 1.1mi cross a small sag and soon encounter a small stream. For the next 0.25mi, good campsites are found in scenic areas.

At 1.2mi the trail enters a RR grade [K] which goes down the valley to the right (Sugarcamp Run). Do not go down Sugarcamp Run, but continue on Shingletree Trail. At 1.4mi the trail turns NW. Here is a fairly good view down Sugarcamp Run Valley. Continue generally NW as shown on the topo to Pheasant Mountain Trail (TR120) [B]. The logging road near TR120 [B] provides an opportunity to walk 1.5mi back down to US219 at the mouth of Goodwin Run.

SHINGLETREE TRAIL (N end) (TR121)

SCENERY: 2 (wooded)
DIFFICULTY: I (leisurely)
CONDITION: B (average)
MAPS: USFS(A), Parsons, I-C-1 in this Guide
SEGMENTS: (1) CO21 to TR120 (Pheasant Mountain Trail)   1.4mi

1.4mi(2.3km)
NOTE: B,M,(0)
SKI-:   S3
ELEV: 2450/1700

Shingletree Trail (N) runs S from Clover Run Road (CO21) [M] to Pheasant Mountain Trail (TR120) [C]. The topo map calls this Ridge Trail, but trail signs call it Shingletree Trail. This trail goes up a scenic valley with conifers, and is steep at times.

Access: The N trailhead [M] is on Clover Run Road (CO21) 0.5mi W of the intersection [N] with Mt. Zion Rd. (CO17) (See TR120).

Segment 1: Starting from the N [M], Shingletree Trail begins in a grove of white pines and follows a small stream for 0.2mi. At that point take the left fork of the stream and climb more steeply, reaching the first ridge top at 0.7mi. Contour along the E side of the steep hill on a trail somewhat eroded by trail bikes. Just before reaching the intersection [C] with TR120 the trail follows an old RR grade.

CLOVER TRAIL (TR124)

SCENERY: 1 (wooded)
DIFFICULTY: II (moderate)
CONDITION: A (good)
MAPS: USFS(A), Parsons, I-C-1 in this Guide
SEGMENTS: (1) TR120 (Pheasant Mountain Trail) to CO23   2.0mi

2.0mi(3.2km)
NOTE: B,M,(3)
SKI-:   S4
ELEV: 2245/1720

Clover Trail is one of two trails (Shingletree Trail being the other) which connects Clover Run Road (CO23) with Pheasant Mountain Trail (TR120). The trail is unique because it follows mainly an historic old RR grade where a train would pull into one switchback and go backward on the next switchback in order to cross the mountain. Part of the area was logged in 1990-91, so part of the trail was moved up onto FR937. The clearcut area offers nice vistas across the Clover drainage toward Mt. Zion. The trail is blazed with blue diamond markers and has signs at road/trail junctions.

Access: To get to the N trailhead, drive 0.4mi N on WV72 from the junction with US219 in Parsons. Turn left onto Mt. Zion Road (CO17) which leads to Clover Run Road (CO23). Along CO23 is a parking area [O] at the trailhead near an abandoned roadside park.

Segment 1: Starting from the N and CO21 [O], the trail passes a sign, crosses a small stream on stepping stones at 70yd, and ascends three switchbacks on a footpath to an old RR grade at 0.5mi. It follows the RR grade through a clearcut and at 0.7mi intersects a logging skid trail switchback to the right. At 0.8mi the trail switchbacks to the left on a log landing and joins with FR937. Follow FR937 to 1.8mi where it intersects again with the old RR grade. Turn right onto the RR grade. At 1.9mi, Clover Trail terminates at Pheasant Mountain Trail (TR120) [E].

SOUTH HADDIX TRAIL (TR126)   10.0mi(16.km)
SCENERY: 2 (wooded)   NOTE: B,M,(2)
DIFFICULTY: III (strenuous)   SKI-:   S4
CONDITION: B (average)   ELEV: 2650/1900
MAPS: USFS(A), Montrose, I-C-1 in this Guide
SEGMENTS: (1) FR116 to FR861   5.8mi
                (2) FR861 to SR47   4.2mi

Sections of South Haddix Trail have been restored and relocated since a timber cut in the late 1980s. Its main route follows the crests of mountain ridges, with occasional undulations. Its major features are: patches of hardwood forests, rhododendron "slicks" (dense tangles), and wildlife such as deer, bear, turkey, owls, hawks.

Access: The NE trailhead ⬜S⬜ is on FR116 which extends from the end of South Haddix Road (CO219/10), ⬜T⬜ 1.0mi from the community of Moore. There may be a problem with parking until the USFS constructs a parking area. Meanwhile, do not block gated FR116, the 4x4-wheel road across the South Branch of Haddix Run, or the nearby private driveways. Access to Moore is near Porterwood on US219, 3mi W of Parsons.

The S terminus is on Pleasant Run Road (SR47) 6.1mi S of Porterwood (2.8mi on Shavers Fork Road, SR39, and 3.3mi on Pleasant Run Road, SR47). The S terminus can also be reached from the W. Access is at the junction of US219 and Wilmoth Run Road (SR3) 1.1mi N of the community of Kerens. After 2mi on SR3 the road becomes SR47; it is 0.4mi farther to the 5-car parking area. (SR47 is off of Map I-C-1 to the S.)

Segment 1: Starting near the NE terminus at the gate ⬜T⬜ of FR116, the trail proceeds W, and after 0.4mi ⬜S⬜ turns right, sharply and steeply up the road embankment into a rhododendron thicket. For 0.2mi the trail is arbored with rhododendron; it then crosses the left (W) side of a wildlife food plot, and ascends to an old forest fire road where it turns right, N. After 0.2mi the trail turns left, W, off the road ⬜U⬜ and follows a footpath for the next 4mi.

Sounds of vehicular traffic from US219 can be heard from the N, but the sounds disappear when the trail curves S and approach a gas pipeline ⬜W⬜ at 3.9mi. Here are views to the W of Cherry Fork drainage and views to the E of the Haddix Run drainage. When the trail leaves the ridge at 5.2mi, it descends to join an old logging road where there are views of Pheasant Mountain to the SE (unrelated to Pheasant Mountain Trail, TR120). Dogwoods, blueberries, and trailing arbutus are prominent on the trailsides in the descent to the headwaters of Panther Run and grassy FR861 ⬜V⬜.

Segment 2: (Note: To the right, SW, on FR861 for 0.8mi and a footpath for 0.3mi is the old route of South Haddix Trail (ooo). It is still usable. Access to its S terminus is 1.6mi E from US219 on Cherry Fork Road (CO219/3), 1mi S of the community of Montrose.)

The extended trail segment proceeds left, SE, from Panther Run ⬜V⬜ on FR861. After 0.4mi the trail forks right in a curve to FR862 and follows it for the remaining 3.8mi (most of it not shown on Map I-C-1). Along the way the trail follows close to the ridgeline of Pheasant Mountain. It makes a horseshoe curve at 6.6mi; it passes logging roads at 7.3mi (FR861B), at 7.5mi (FR862B), and at 8.7mi (FR862A), all of which are on the E side of the mountain. Two other horseshoe curves are at 8.4mi and 9.6mi. From the latter the trail enters a cove and descends rapidly to SR47.

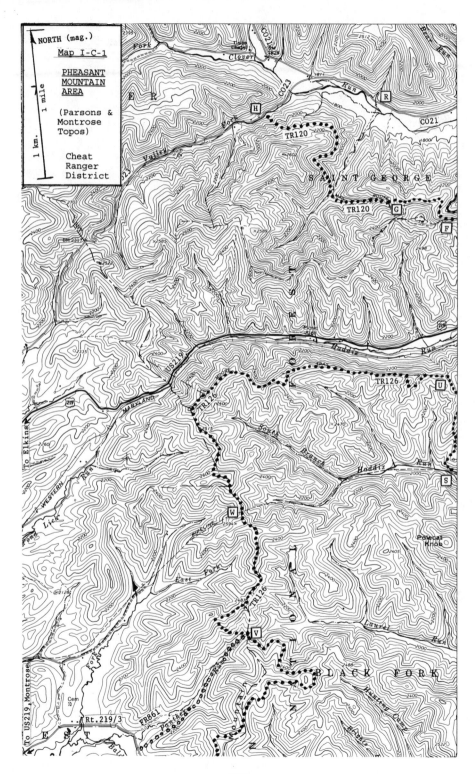

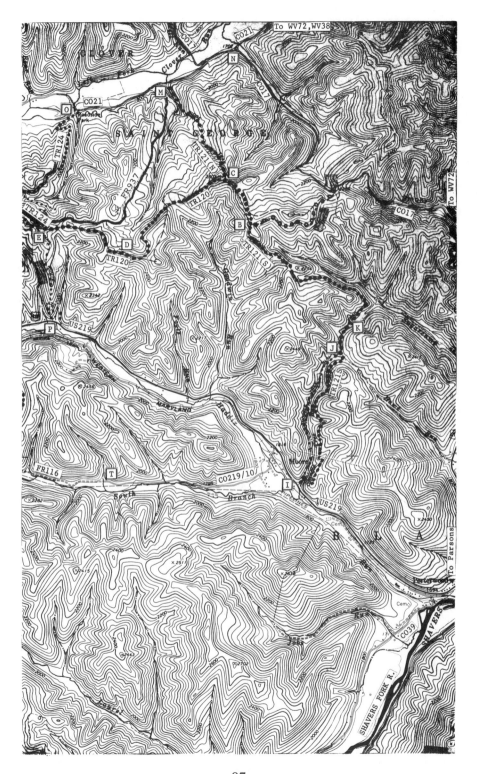

(I-D) HORSESHOE RUN AREA

The Horseshoe Run area is the most northern area of the MNF. Horseshoe Run drains from Close Mountain and Backbone Mountain on the E, and Stemple Ridge on the NW to its SW confluence with the Cheat River. The community of Lead Mine is the heart of the narrow Horseshoe Run valley. One mile S of Lead Mine is Horseshoe Run Recreation Area with picnic area and a group picnic shelter. Campground facilities include water and restrooms.

Hiking trails extend E and W of the recreation area, and one trail, McKinley Run Trail, connects to Allegheny Trail. There is also a 0.5mi Horseshoe Run Nature Trail near Horseshoe Run. Most trails are shown on Map I-D-1 in this Guide.

Access to the campground from Parsons is to drive N 6mi on WV72 to St. George. Turn SE onto CO1 and, after 3mi, turn left onto CO7. From here go 3.6mi to the campground. Another access is from US219 (N of the town of Thomas). Follow Lead Mine Mountain Road (SR9) for 5.6mi, and turn left, SW, in the community of Lead Mine onto CO7 and go another 1.6mi.

DORMAN RIDGE TRAIL (TR153)　　　　　　1.3mi(2.1km)
SCENERY:　　3 (pastoral)　　　　　　NOTE: B,H,M,(0)
DIFFICULTY: I (leisurely)　　　　　　SKI-:　S2
CONDITION: B (average)　　　　　　ELEV: 2540/2400
MAPS: USFS(A), St. George, Lead Mine, I-D-1 in this Guide
SEGMENTS:
(1) CO9 to TR155 (Losh Trail) and TR156 (Mike's Run Trail)　　1.3mi

Dorman Ridge Trail runs S from Hiles Run Road (CO9) [A] to an intersection [B] with Losh Trail (TR155) and Mike's Run Trail (TR156) at the head of the E fork of Mikes Run.

Access: The N end is at a steel-pipe gate beside Hile Run Road (CO9) 0.7 mi S along the road from its intersection with Location Road (CO5).

Segment 1: Starting from the pipe gate [A], follow the old farm road S through brushy and sometimes open fields for 0.8mi to a sharp W turn, at the edge of a large open field, near two lone apple trees. Travel S through the edge of the open field following a thick stand of autumn olive shrubs bordering the field. After passing through a white pine belt that divides the field in half, the trail cuts through the autumn olive border at 1.0mi and proceeds SE through the woods to TR155 and TR156. At this trails junction [B], camping is possible in the open woods or in an Adirondack shelter. Enroute to the shelter are a number of camping spots in and around the open field.

McKINLEY RUN TRAIL (TR154)　　　　　　1.0mi(1.6km)
SCENERY:　　2 (wooded)　　　　　　NOTE: B,M,(0)
DIFFICULTY: II (moderate)　　　　　　SKI-:　S4
CONDITION: B (average)　　　　　　ELEV: 2300/1720
MAPS: USFS(A), Lead Mine, I-D-1 in this Guide
SEGMENTS: (1) CO7 to FR903　　　　1.0mi

One can follow FR903 to Close Mountain Road (CO16) which can be followed down to CO7, 0.2mi E of the N end of the trail [E]. Allegheny Trail (yellow blazes) also follows Close Mtn. Road.

Access: McKinley Run Trail has its W terminus [C] on the S side of Horseshoe Run Road (CO7) where McKinley Run passes under the road before flowing through Horseshoe Recreation Area. The E terminus [D] is on FR903.

Segment 1: Starting from the W (CO7), ascend the rhododendron-covered slope on the N side of McKinley Run, reaching gently sloping benchland occupied by oak and pine at 0.1mi. Proceed SE through the oak-pine woods partially following an old woods road. At 0.4mi, cross an access road to a private tract. Continue ascending via three switchbacks to FR903 [D]. Backtrack or follow Close Mountain Road (CO16) for a 2.2mi loop.

LOSH TRAIL (TR155)   1.8mi(2.9km)

SCENERY: 2 (wooded)   NOTE: B,H,M,(2)
DIFFICULTY: III (strenuous)   SKI-: S4
CONDITION: B (average)   ELEV: 2450/1670
MAPS: USFS(A), Lead Mine, I-D-1 in this Guide
SEGMENTS:
(1) CO7 to TR156 (Mike's Run Tr.) and TR153 (Dorman Ridge Tr.)   1.8mi

Wildlife is likely to be seen along this blue-blazed trail which provides access to Dorman Ridge Trail (TR153) and Mikes Run Trail (TR156).

Access: The S terminus [F] of Losh Trail is off the road on the nature trail that parallels CO7 along the bank of Horseshoe Run between Horseshoe Recreation Area and YMCA Camp Horseshoe. Driving S on CO7, pass the village of Leadmine and park near the signboard at the entrance to the Horseshoe Recreation Area.

The N trailhead is marked by a sign saying, "Constructed by the Youth Conservation Corps 1978."

Segment 1: Starting from the S [F], follow the nature trail and turn right at the Losh Trail sign. Cross the arched footbridge over Horseshoe Run.

At 0.1mi is a comfortable camp site. Follow blue blazes to the right (E) of the camp site (away from the small run). The false trail that crosses the run dies out in either direction. Behind the campsite, the trail ascends steeply, curving W and staying N of Losh Run until crossing it [G].

In a forest of hemlock and yellow poplar, ascend steeply on switchbacks. Reach the top of the ridge at 1.1mi and join the old route of the trail at 1.5mi. Stay on the ridge to a saddle at 1.6mi where hemlock and white pine are prominent. Although there is an excellent campsite at the saddle, the trail shelter and water are only 0.2mi farther on.

The trail goes N through the saddle, crossing the head of Drift Run. After passing through the gap, the trail swings N through a mixed hemlock and hardwood stand before intersecting TR153 and TR156 [B] in a stately stand of white pine.

MIKE'S RUN TRAIL (TR156)   4.0mi(6.4km)

SCENERY: 2 (wooded)   NOTE: B,H,M,(15)
DIFFICULTY: III (strenuous)   SKI-: S4
CONDITION: C (poor)   ELEV: 2350/1620
MAPS: USFS(A), St. George, Lead Mine, I-D-1 in this Guide

SEGMENTS:
  (1) TR153 (Dorman Ridge Trail)/TR155 (Losh Trail) to CO7   4.0mi
    The lower 0.3mi between the Mikes Run-Horseshoe Run junction and CO7 crosses private land.
    Mikes Run Trail has its NE terminus [B] at the head of the E fork of Mike's Run in a stately white pine stand. It proceeds NW down the N side of the E fork to the main stem then proceeds SW down the main stem of Mikes Run to its junction [J] with Horseshoe Run.
    Access: The NE terminus [B] of Mike's Run Trail is at a junction with Losh Run Trail (TR155) and Dorman Ridge Trail (TR153). A 6-person, wooden shelter is on the bank of the run 100yd from the junction. The trail crosses the run in front of the shelter and, after 100yd, crosses a new gravel road (FR930) (not shown on Map I-D-1).
    Segment 1: Starting from the NE terminus [B], Mike's Run Trail almost immediately crosses to the N side of the E fork. At 0.1mi pass out of the white pine stand into mixed hardwood with a patchy rhododendron under-story. The trail descends along the N side of the stream, recrossing to the S side at 1.1mi, at a small opening suitable for camping. Continuing to descend on the N side of the main stem, pass through a hemlock stand suitable for camp spots. The trail continues to descend the E side of Mikes Run, passing through young mixed hardwood forest and variable-density rhododendron. A rock bench sits beside the trail at 1.5mi. The trail enters a small opening suit-able for campsites at 1.7mi. A small waterfall is below the trail at 1.8mi. The stream tumbles over numerous ledges at 2.1mi.
    The trail crosses Mikes Run to the W side at 2.4mi and passes across a very steep face before recrossing to the E side at 2.6mi. The descent contin-ues across the steep E side, reaching an old streamside road and recrossing to the W side of Mikes Run at 3.2mi. Follow the trail down the old road, re-crossing to the E side of Mikes Run at 3.4mi. Enter a large old field with scattered apple, hawthorn, and young white pine. The trail crosses to the W side of Mikes Run at 3.7mi, passes through a field, and descends through pri-vate property to the junction [J] of Mikes Run and Horseshoe Run at 4.0mi. Backtrack, or ford Horseshoe Run, to CO7 and turn left, NE, and go 2.0mi to Horseshoe Recreation Area. (Ask permission on private property.)

MAXWELL RUN TRAIL (TR157)   2.2mi(3.5km)
SCENERY: 1 (wooded)   NOTE: B,M,(5)
DIFFICULTY: II (moderate)   SKI-: S4
CONDITION: B (average)   ELEV: 2050/1680
MAPS: USFS(A), Lead Mine, I-D-1 in this Guide
SEGMENTS: (1) CO7 to Dead-end (FR03)   2.2mi
    Maxwell Run Trail follows Maxwell Run from its intersection [L] with CO7 E to its headwater forks [N].
    Access: Parking is found at Maxwell Run Bridge on CO7. The trail begins at the E end of the bridge, on the S side of CO7.
    Segment 1: Starting from CO7 [L], the trail begins on an old road but almost immediately ascends the road bank and passes through an old field into a white pine stand. Passing out of the pine, it descends back to the alluvial bottom and begins following Maxwell Run through hemlock and hardwood forest. At 0.3mi, the trail is cut into a steep ledge. At 0.4 mi is a K-dam in

Maxwell Run. Continuing upstream, the trail crosses to the S side at 0.5mi [M]. There is a second K-dam in Maxwell Run at this crossing.

A scenic four-foot waterfall is in the stream at 0.7mi, and 80yd above the waterfall is a large pool. At 0.8mi, the trail enters an open field, through which it passes for 260yd. Campsites are available in and around the field. After the trail reenters the woods, watch for a three-foot waterfall in the nearby stream. Continuing upstream, the trail crosses Maxwell Run to the N side at 1.0mi and then recrosses to the S side at 1.1mi. Generally following an old logging RR grade, the trail continues upstream, crossing back to the N side at 1.4mi then recrossing to S side at 1.7mi. Large rocks overhang the trail at 1.9mi, followed by two waterfalls. At 2.0mi cross the right fork of Maxwell Run, then after 75yd cross the left fork of Maxwell Run. Ascend Close Mountain in a NE direction to a switchback at 2.1mi. Follow the switchback in a SE direction and reach the end of FR903 at 2.2mi. (A loop can be made by walking 1.8mi on FR903 to McKinley Run Trail [TR154] and returning to the beginning of Maxwell Run Trail for a circuit of 6.0mi to 6.3mi depending on passage through the campground.)

Small knob on Cabin Mountain just west of Bald Knob, looking toward Weiss Knob. Photo by Barry Adams

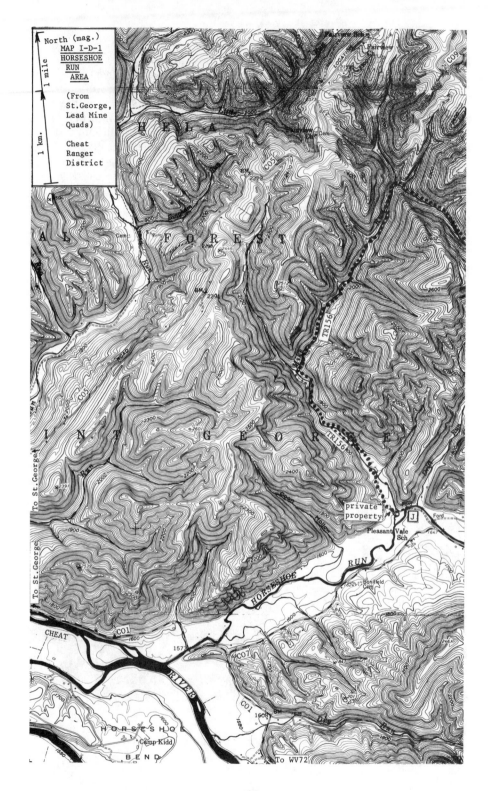

North (mag.)

MAP I-D-1
HORSESHOE
RUN
AREA

(From
St.George,
Lead Mine
Quads)

Cheat
Ranger
District

1 mile

1 km.

private
property

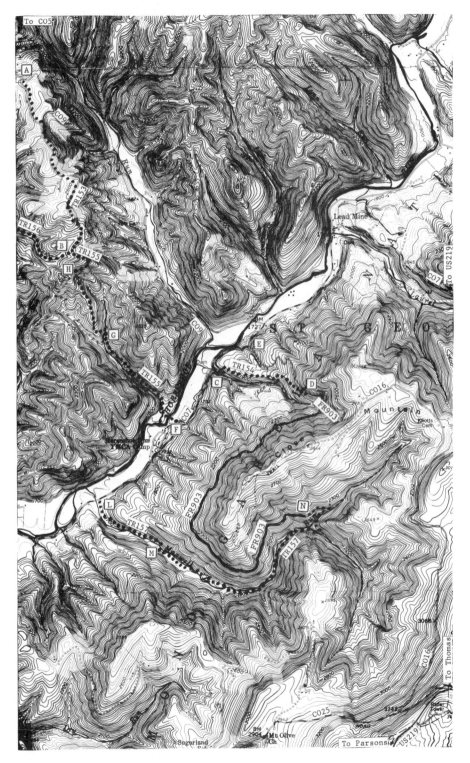

(I-E) OTTER CREEK AREA

Otter Creek Valley is an isolated drainage basin of 28.1sq.mi. The forest was thoroughly cut about 70 years ago, but once again covers the land in stands of great variety, many of which now approach impressive maturity. The basin contains no dwellings or permanent roads.

For 11 miles, Otter Creek itself forms the scenic heart of the area. From an elevation of 3050ft it is followed by an excellent trail as it drops over 1200ft, often running turbulently through mazes of boulders and ledges, down to the Dry Fork of the Cheat River. Parallel mountain ridges, rising as high as 3800ft, form an oval basin about 4mi wide, with a system of small streams draining into the main creek. Numerous bands of hard rock outcrops wind through the forests. Green Mountain closes off most of the N end of the basin. A rolling plateau slopes gently into the basin on its S side. It abruptly drops 1700ft on the N to Dry Fork of the Cheat River. To motorists on WV72 on the other side of Dry Fork canyon, it looms as an impressive forested wall.

The Otter Creek area is one of perhaps four areas in West Virginia wild and large enough to support a stable breeding population of black bear.

Maps on pages 108 and 110 show the trail system. On the map on page 96, elevations are shown at trail junctions and at high points along ridge trails.

Otter Creek Wilderness (20,000 acres) is one of the more used areas in the MNF, and has over-use problems on popular summer weekends. Before visiting Otter Creek Wilderness, please read the section "Wilderness Trails" on page 21 of this Guide. The MNF manages Wilderness in far different ways than it manages non-Wilderness. Wilderness visitors need to understand these differences, the reasons for them, and what Wilderness is all about. A Wilderness ranger has been assigned, during summertime, to answer questions about Wilderness, explain Wilderness policy, maintain trails to minimum standards, and provide basic law enforcement.

Trailhead parking is available at the following locations:

- Big Springs Gap on FR701 in Fernow Experimental Forest (space for 6 vehicles: often crowded). Access to Fernow is from downtown Parsons, E of Shavers Fork Bridge at a side street marked with an Otter Creek sign. Turn down the side street and, after 70yd, turn left at the first intersection (near a church) and follow signs for 5.6mi.
- Turkey Run (space for 6 vehicles, infrequently uses) is 0.5mi S of Big Springs Gap parking area on FR701;
- Dry Fork/Otter Creek (space for 20 vehicles in a parking lot between WV72 and the Dry Fork River) 2mi S of Hendricks along WV72;
- Condon Run (space for 20 vehicles, often crowded) is accessible on FR303, 0.6mi from FR91 and 1.3mi on FR91 from US33 at Alpena;
- Mylius by Glady Fork (space for 6 vehicles, infrequently used) is accessible on FR162, 0.1mi from Galdwin Road (CO12) which goes 4.7mi S to US33 and the Alpena Springs Lodge.
- FR324 provides access to Moore Run and Yellow Creek trailheads. FR324 is for 4WD only. It is not plowed in winter and could easily be inaccessible even for 4WD. It is open between August 15 and April 15.

Otter Creek Wilderness has been adversely affected by trailside camping. Because of this, and because structures are not allowed in Wilderness areas, and because campsites at trailheads and trail junctions impact the Wilderness experiences of others, the USFS is closing some campsites and

94

Access footbridge over Cheat River to Otter Creek Trail (TR131).
Photo by Allen de Hart

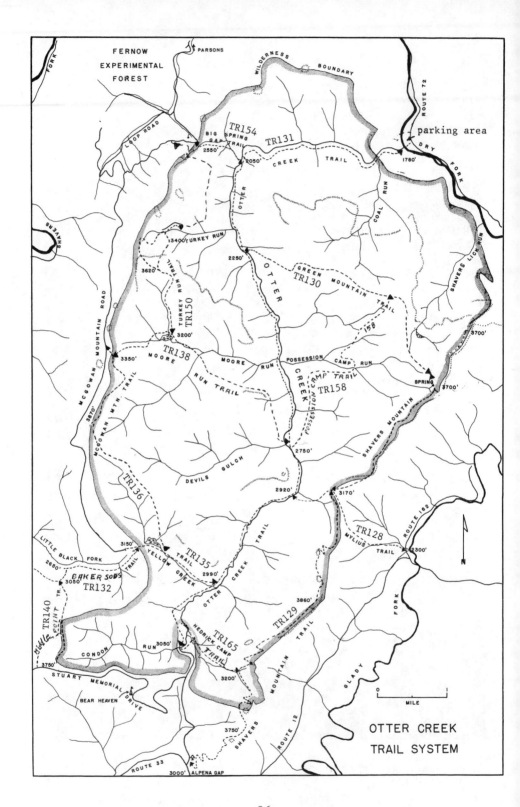

removing both trail shelters. For hikers who plan to access at the upstream entrance to Otter Creek Trail (Condon Run), and wish to have a developed campground with water and restroom facilities before going on the trail, both Bear Heaven and Stuart campgrounds are recommended nearby on FR91. Bear Heaven Campground offers good campsites, spectacular rocks, a magnificent view, a water pump and pit latrines.

MYLIUS TRAIL (TR128) 2.4mi(3.9km)

SCENERY: 2 (wooded)   NOTE: B,M,(1)
DIFFICULTY: II (moderate)   SKI-:   S4
CONDITION: A (good)   ELEV: 3170/2320
MAPS: USFS(A), Harman, Bowden, I-E-2 in this Guide
SEGMENTS:
　 (1) TR131 (Otter Creek Trail) to TR129 (Shaver's Mtn. Trail)   0.7mi
　 (2) TR129 to Glady Fork (FR162)   1.7mi
　 Mylius Trail is one of the "portals" to the trail systems of Otter Creek Wilderness. The trail itself, though largely outside the Wilderness boundary, offers as wild and scenic a setting as most of the trails within the Wilderness. The Glady Fork watershed is a pleasant, remote setting, ideal for exploratory hikes. FR162, for several miles N of the E trailhead of Mylius trail, offers a particularly pleasant leisurely walk on Allegheny Trail. It also offers ideal ski-touring. Glady Fork, adjacent to FR162, offers opportunities for swimming and views of beaver dams and hutches.
　 Access: The W trailhead [A] is at Otter Creek Trail (TR131).
　 The E trailhead [C] is on FR162, 0.1mi N of the junction of FR162 and CO12. This junction is 4.6mi N of US33 (Alpena) along CO12, a road which, in winter, could be treacherous (winding and steep in spots, with no guard rails). A trail register is located at the E trailhead. Nearby are good campsites in the grassy meadows along Glady Fork. Here is also a junction with Allegheny Trail (TR701).
　 Segment 1: Starting from the W [A], Mylius Trail, after crossing Otter Creek, begins its 0.7mi climb to the Shavers Mountain divide, passing through a forest clearing along the way. The junction [B] with Shavers Mountain Trail (TR129) is in a level area with large trees and little understory. Camping is not permitted at this trail junction for reasons mentioned above.
　 Segment 2: From the divide the trail drops 900ft down the mountain to FR162 on Glady Fork. For the final 0.3mi, the trail follows an old road down to the junction with FR162.

SHAVERS MOUNTAIN TRAIL (TR129) 10.0mi(16.1km)

SCENERY: 1 (exceptional)   NOTE: B,H,M,(0)
DIFFICULTY: III (strenuous)   SKI-:   S4
CONDITION: A (good)   ELEV: 3800/3030
MAPS: USFS(A), Harman, Bowden, Mozark Mtn., I-E-1 & -2 in this Guide
SEGMENTS: (1) Alpena Gap to TR165 (Hedrick Camp Trail)   3.0mi
　　　　　　 (2) TR165 to TR128 (Mylius Trail)   4.3mi
　　　　　　 (3) TR128 to Shavers Mtn. Shelter   2.2mi
　　　　　　 (4) Shelter to TR130 (Green Mountain Trail)   0.5mi

Shavers Mountain Trail is blazed, but blazes are infrequent, old and not maintained. It receives enough use that the route is normally clear.

Access: Shavers Mountain Trail has its S terminus [T](Map I-E-2) outside the Otter Creek drainage at the Alpena Gap junction of US33 and Stuart Memorial Drive (FR91). Water is available here and an information sign highlights the recreational opportunities of the district.

The official N terminus of the trail is at its junction [D](Map I-E-1) with Green Mountain Trail (TR130), although exploratory hikers could continue further N along Shavers Mountain Trail and enjoy some exceptional scenery.

Segment 1: Note that the first 1.8mi are outside the Wilderness boundary. Starting at the S end [T](Map I-E-2) of the trail, switchback up the mountain. The first section passes through relatively young second-growth timber that contrasts with the open, more mature forests of Otter Creek. Here the underbrush is heavier and the trail is, in places, a green tunnel through dense growth. Water is available at [V] and [W]. The surroundings improve steadily as you proceed N, and by the time Hedrick Camp Trail (TR165)[F] is reached, the forest has opened considerably.

Segment 2: From the junction with TR165, bear E and switch-back up the hill to the crest [G] of Shavers Mountain. Here is some scattered older growth with intermixed spruce. The last 0.5mi before Mylius Trail [B] is perhaps the most scenic, traversing rhododendron thickets above the stream.

Segment 3: From Mylius Gap N, the trail climbs steeply and steadily, gaining 400ft in elevation to regain the crest of Shavers Mountain. Older forest reappears in patches, and a small virgin stand of hemlock is encountered 0.5mi S of the former shelter site. These giants rise from a ground cover of rhododendron and ferns.

Shavers Mountain Shelter [I](Map I-E-1) is perched on the edge of the mountain crest. The USFS believes that the shelter may not be safe, so it will be removed by mid-1999. (Campers at this site should refrain from cutting any trees to enhance the view. This is a Wilderness area, and even if it were not, such cutting would not be permissible.) There is plenty of space for tents nearby. During wet periods a small stream runs directly in the trail 150yd N of the junction with the trail leading to the shelter. In drier weather a spring may be found by walking N of the trail junction 110 paces to a tree on the left side of the trail that is heavily blazed. A faint trail marked with small blazes leads 1000ft to a spring W of the trail. The spring is usually reliable.

Segment 4: The trail N of the former shelter is mostly level and traverses spruce, hemlock and hardwood forests. The trail ends 0.5mi N where it meets Green Mountain Trail (TR130) [D].

GREEN MOUNTAIN TRAIL (TR130)   4.0mi(6.4km)
SCENERY: 1 (exceptional)   NOTE: B,M,(0)
DIFFICULTY: II (moderate)   SKI-:   S3
CONDITION: A (good)   ELEV: 3580/2200
MAPS: USFS(A), Parsons, Mozark Mountain, I-E-1 in this Guide
SEGMENTS:
    (1) TR131 (Otter Creek Tr.) to TR158 (Possession Camp Tr.)2.7mi
    (2) TR158 to TR129   1.3mi
Green Mountain Trail, on the last 1.0mi of its N end, descends steeply through scenic maturing forest to Otter Creek. Its S portion offers interesting

walking through high-altitude bogs. Just before the start of the steep descent into Otter Creek Valley, the route gets confusing and blazes are infrequent, so stay on the descending route. Bear may be seen in the area, but they have never been known to create problems for hikers. The top 0.5mi of climb at the N end of the trail is steep and rocky, so good hiking boots are recommended. Rattlesnakes are more commonly seen here than anywhere else. They could be a problem.

Access: The N end of this trail [A] starts out from Otter Creek Trail (TR131), a short distance S of Turkey Run.

Segment 1: Starting from the N terminus, [A] Green Mountain Trail begins on an old grade, then joins an old skid trail right behind the old logging camp site known as "Camp 2". The skid trail climbs steeply up Green Mountain. At 1.2mi it reaches the top [B] and levels off. An outstanding vista of the central section of Otter Creek Wilderness may be obtained by leaving the trail at the edge [B] of the plateau and proceeding N along that edge for 200yd through open woods to a conglomerate outcropping. At 1.6mi [C] the trail turns right (E) where it joins an old RR grade, crosses a small stream, and continues E on this old grade. At 2.0mi the trail turns abruptly S onto a second old grade. The trail now winds through rhododendron thickets and young groves of conifers and northern hardwoods. At 2.7mi [E] Green Mountain Trail intersects Possession Camp Trail (TR158).

Segment 2: The junction with TR158 is in a small grassy opening, the remnant of an old logging campsite. A reliable spring is located in the rhododendron thicket near this junction. Green Mountain Trail leaves the old RR grade system here and winds uphill through carpets of ferns and thickets of rhododendron. At 3.25mi [F] a high point is reached (identified by a 2ft high pile of rocks on each side of the trail and the edge of a stand of spruce). The trail bears S, then E, staying in the woods around the S side of the open bog at the head of Shavers Lick. At 4.0mi [D] the trail ends at the junction with Shavers Mountain Trail (TR129) in open woods near the E side of Shavers Mountain.

OTTER CREEK TRAIL (TR131)   11.3mi(18.2km)
SCENERY: 1 (exceptional)   NOTE: B,M,S,(11)
DIFFICULTY: II (moderate)   SKI-:   S4
CONDITION: B (average)   ELEV: 3050/1780
MAPS: USFS(A), Bowden, Parsons, Mozark Mtn., I-E-1 & -2 in this Guide
SEGMENTS:

(1) WV72/Dry Fork R. to TR154 (Big Springs Gap Tr.)   2.5mi
(2) TR154 to TR130 (Green Mtn. Trail)   1.3mi
(3) TR130 to TR138/TR158 (Possession Camp Trail)   3.3mi
(4) TR138/TR158 to TR128 (Mylius Trail)   1.2mi
(5) TR128 to TR135 (Yellow Creek Trail)   1.8mi
(6) TR135 to FR91/TR165 (Hedrick Camp Trail)   1.2mi

Otter Creek Trail is central to the entire trail system, tracing through the heart of the Wilderness area from end to end. It passes through a mixture of hardwoods and conifers. Throughout its length, it is never more than a few feet from the stream's edge and affords surprises at every turn. Waterfalls, gushing limestone springs, small swimming holes, and continuous rapids delight the eye and fill the ear with the roar of white water.

The best stretch along Otter Creek is between Green Mountain Trail (TR130) [A](Map I-E-1) and Mylius Trail (TR128) [A](Map I-E-2). As with any streamside hike, upstream is the preferred direction of travel, since the best views are almost always to be had looking upstream. Waterfalls ranging up to ten feet in height are common from 3.6mi downstream of Condon Run to the mouth.

Throughout its length the trail follows an old RR grade. The spikes, rails and ties have vanished, but the rich humus, left behind, supports a lush carpet of moss. It also supports mushrooms of remarkable variety.

The trail crosses Otter Creek three times--3.6mi, 4.2mi, and 7.1mi from Condon entrance. One must also cross Otter Creek to get to Big Springs Gap Trail (TR154), Mylius Trail (TR128) and Moore Run Trail (TR138). In mid-summer the creek is often low enough and there are enough rocks in the stream bed that crossings are no problem. But in the spring, when runoff is considerably higher, or after heavy rain, it may be impossible to negotiate the crossings with dry feet. In heavy spring flood, the creek may be too high to cross safely.

Access: For the S access see Condon Run Access in the list of access points at the start of this section.

For the N access see the Dry Fork/Otter Creek Access in the list of access points at the start of this section.

Section 1: After crossing the swinging bridge over the Dry Fork of the Cheat River, Otter Creek Trail is a wide, shady, level old RR grade along Otter Creek. Several swimming holes are found along the way for hikes on hot summer days. Do not camp in this section. It is relatively untrammeled, and possible sites are too close to trails and Otter Creek.

Segment 2: There are no good campsites between the junction [G] (Map I-E-1) with Big Springs Gap Trail (TR154) and Green Mountain Trail (TR130) [A].

Segment 3: Just S of Green Mountain Trail, the trail crosses Otter Creek, and excellent stream-side campsites are on both sides of the stream. Another good site is on the W side of the trail, half-way between Green Mtn. Trail [A] and Moore Run Trail (TR138) [D](Map I-E-2). A nice swimming hole is below a waterfall in Otter Creek, 50yd downstream of Moore Run Trail.

Segment 4: Moore Run [J] (Map I-E-1) offers a complex of small waterfalls flanked by huge flat rock slabs, creating a fine scene. Just S of where this side stream crosses the trail is another primitive campsite (no facilities).

Segment 5: Another campsite [J] is midway between Mylius Trail (TR128) [A] and Yellow Creek Trail (TR135) [I] (1.0mi N of Yellow Creek) at the northernmost of the two stream crossings in this stretch. It can accommodate 3-4 persons. This campsite is useful when walking the circuit involving Turkey Run-, Moore Run-, McGowan Mountain- and Yellow Creek Trails.

Segment 6: Otter Creek Trail crosses Yellow Creek and proceeds through a boggy area before ascending to an old RR grade above Otter Creek. This grade can be followed 1.2mi to the S trailhead [S] where a system of limestone drums helps the W.Va. Department of Natural Resources maintain the pH (acidity) of Otter Creek. Condon Run parking lot and the W terminus of Hedrick Camp Trail (TR165) are also located here.

Small falls on Otter Creek (TR131). Photo by Roger Spencer

BAKER SODS TRAIL (TR132)   3.0mi(4.8km)
SCENERY: 2 (wooded)   NOTE: B,M,S,(1)
DIFFICULTY: II (moderate)   SKI-:   S4
CONDITION: B (average)   ELEV: 3150/?
MAPS: USFS(A), Bowden, I-E-2 in this Guide
SEGMENTS:
    (1) TR135 (Yellow Creek Tr.) to TR140 (Middle Point Tr.) 1.75mi
    (2) TR140 to Baker Sods   1.25mi

Baker Sods is a collection of small open fields with conifers planted in strips. The fields are mowed annually by the W.Va. DNR and managed for wildlife habitat. The trail offers wintertime views to the north, but there are no open overlooks. The trail is entirely outside the Wilderness boundary.

Access: Baker Sods Trail has its E terminus at the junction $\boxed{P}$ with Yellow Creek Trail (TR135) and McGowan Mtn. Road (FR324) near a 1-acre open boggy area.

The W terminus is at Baker Sods. There, FR798 leads 3.8mi to Shavers Fork Road (CO6).

Segment 1: Starting from the E, $\boxed{P}$ Baker Sods Trail goes 80yd SW and crosses Little Black Fork. It then descends to follow an old RR grade. At 0.5mi is the junction $\boxed{L}$ with Little Black Fork Trail (TR134) (abandoned, not shown). At 0.6mi the old RR grade forks. Continue W on the grade. (Heading E on the upper grade takes you back to Otter Creek Wilderness, 200yd SE of the starting point.) At 1.0mi traverse the E ridge of a side drain $\boxed{M}$. At 1.1mi the trail crosses the side drain. Nearby is a nice campsite on a ledge high above the Little Black Fork. This is the only good site between Yellow Creek Trail (TR135) and Middle Point Trail (TR140). From here the trail no longer follows the old RR grade. At 1.75mi is the junction $\boxed{N}$ with Middle Point Trail (TR140) at a low place of the ridge dividing Little Black Fork and Rattlesnake Run.

Segment 2: From $\boxed{N}$ TR140 follows an old skid trail W. Between miles 1.9 and 2.6 the trail goes NW along a truck road. On leaving the truck road the trail continues NW on an old skid road, through a narrow opening at 2.75mi, to Baker Sods at 3.0mi. Bears may have damaged signs.

YELLOW CREEK TRAIL (TR135)   1.3mi(2.1km)
SCENERY: 2 (wooded)   NOTE: B,M,(1)
DIFFICULTY: I (leisurely)   SKI-:   S1
CONDITION: A (good)   ELEV: 3150/2990
MAPS: USFS(A), Bowden, I-E-2 in this Guide
SEGMENTS:
    (1) TR131 (Otter Creek Tr.) to TR136 (McGowan Mtn. Tr.) 0.7mi
    (2) TR136 to TR132 & FR324   0.6mi

Access: The W terminus $\boxed{P}$ of Yellow Creek Trail is the end of Mc-Gowan Mtn. Road (FR324). There is a place just wide enough to turn a vehicle around here. Do not block it. Park at a turn-out 30yd up McGowan Mountain Road (FR324). This road is gated and locked in Fernow Experimental Forest from April 15 to August 15.

The E terminus $\boxed{I}$ is on Otter Creek Trail (TR131) 1.2mi N of the Condon Run parking lot.

Segment 1: Starting from the E [I], Yellow Creek Trail leaves Otter Creek Trail (TR131) in a stand of hemlocks on the N side of the mouth of Yellow Creek. At 0.7mi the trail meets McGowan Mountain Trail (TR136) [O] at the edge of a small opening.

Segment 2: Yellow Creek Trail continues straight ahead (W) to a slightly larger opening which was once a good campsite, surrounded by red pine. This site is rarely used now because beavers have killed the pines with backed-up water. The trail continues across a stream, leading out of this campsite and to another good campsite next to the trail.

At 0.8mi the trail crosses Yellow Creek and continues W through rhododendron and birch on the S side of a boggy area of Yellow Creek. Beaver dams on Yellow Creek sometime enlarge the size of the bog considerably, making passage through the area difficult. At a small opening you should see an "Otter Creek Wilderness" sign. At 1.2mi Baker Sods Trail (TR132) [P] meets Yellow Creek Trail from the SW and FR324.

McGOWAN MOUNTAIN TRAIL (TR136)   3.5mi(5.6km)

SCENERY: 1 (exceptional)   NOTE: B,M,(0)
DIFFICULTY: II (moderate)   SKI-: S3
CONDITION: A (good)   ELEV: 3900/3100
MAPS: USFS(A), Bowden, I-E-1 and I-E-2 in this Guide
SEGMENTS:

(1) TR138 (Moore Run Trail) to TR135 (Yellow Creek Trail)   3.5mi

Parts of McGowan Mountain Trail are closed in with rhododendron, spruce and hemlock. Some of the treadway is rocky and root-covered.

Access: The N terminus is at a marked junction [K] (Map I-E-1) with Moore Run Trail (TR138) 0.25mi from the McGowan Mountain Road (FR324) terminus of TR138. A metal USFS sign-in box is at this junction.

The S terminus [O] (Map I-E-2) is on Yellow Creek Trail (TR135), 0.1mi E of where TR135 crosses Yellow Creek.

Segment 1: Starting from the N [K] (Map I-E-1), McGowan Mountain Trail climbs moderately through a fine stand of cucumber magnolia. After a short distance the trail meets an abandoned primitive road which it follows for a few yards before resuming its S climb. At 0.1mi is a 60-degree change in direction from S to E. At 0.25mi is a rock outcrop on the mountain top. Here the trail winds between large boulders and turns SW along the mountain top. At 0.3mi is a hard-to-find view from a rocky overlook 15yd W of the main trail. At 0.9mi the trail passes through a few large boulders and the vegetation changes from birch-maple to red spruce and others, with rhododendron. At 1.0mi is a large, overhanging, hard-to-find rock 30yd W of the trail. It offers shelter for 3-5 people. Campsites and water are scarce along this section.

At 1.25mi [Q] (Map I-E-2) the trail direction changes from SW to SE near the high point on McGowan Mountain (el. 3912ft). After passing through dense rhododendron near the top of the mountain, the trail drops while passing through a naturally sculptured section of boulders. It then follows the ridge dividing Devils Gulch and Yellow Creek. The trail leaves the ridge on a foot trail and drops to an old logging RR grade bordered by spruce along a flat stretch near the stream at the head of Yellow Creek. At 2.3mi the trail leaves this flat and descends to an old logging skid trail along the E side of Yellow Creek. At 2.7mi this skid trail joins an old RR grade and follows it on the E side of Yellow Creek to its terminus [O] with Yellow Creek Trail (TR135) at 3.5mi at the SE end of a boggy, open area.

Note: In 1994 and in 1996, the headwaters of Yellow Creek were scoured by heavy rains and snow melt. As a result, the middle section of McGowan Mountain Trail (between [Q] and [O] or between elevations 3200ft and 3600ft) has become difficult to find. The USFS does not intend to reestablish the treadway in accordance with its policy of keeping Wilderness areas in a natural state and allowing natural processes to dominate as much as possible. Old blazes may be found on some trees. To get back to the established treadway continue on a generally downward trend on the E side of Yellow Creek and watch for the established treadway.

MOORE RUN TRAIL (TR138)   4.1mi(6.6km)
SCENERY: 1 (exceptional)   NOTE: B,M,(4)
DIFFICULTY: I (leisurely)   SKI-:   S3
CONDITION: A (good)   ELEV: 3350/2800
MAPS: USFS(A), Bowden, Parsons, I-E-1 and I-E-2 in this Guide
SEGMENTS:
    (1) TR131 (Otter Creek Trail) to TR150 (Turkey Run Trail)   2.9mi
    (2) TR150 to TR136 (McGowan Mtn. Trail)/FR324   1.2mi

Though Moore Run Trail links Otter Creek with the crest of McGowan Mountain, it is surprisingly gentle. In recent years, beavers have created dams in some low areas. So the trail's routing will be slightly changed in the future.

Access: The W terminus is on McGowan Mtn. Road, FR324, which is gated and locked in Fernow Experimental Forest from April 15 to August 15.

Segment 1: Start from the E by rock-hopping or wading across Otter Creek   [D] (Map I-E-2). The trail begins its slow climb up the flanks of McGowan Mountain. But because Otter Creek drops rapidly along its nearly parallel course, the valley soon recedes to an impressive depth below the trail. Along this stretch is a fine open hardwood forest. Though the timber stand is heavy, the lack of underbrush lets you see for surprising distances. There are no campsites in this section.

The junction [L](Map I-E-1) of Moore Run Trail and Turkey Run Trail (TR150) is near a complex boggy area of considerable interest. The trail approaches the bog from the E, following the old RR grade which crosses two main branches of Moore Run. These crossings make excellent rest stops. The water is often dark and slightly acidic from the bogs. Usually no water is available between Moore Run and Otter Creek.

At 0.1mi beyond the second crossing the trail makes an abrupt right turn away from the RR grade to circle the bog on the NE side behind a screen of low trees. Rocks and branches have been placed across the RR grade to mark this turn, but it is still easy to overlook the turnoff and continue straight ahead on the grade. Watch for the turn.

It is worthwhile to leave your pack at this turn and make a short side trip along the remains of the RR grade into the bog. This high-altitude bog is similar to Cranberry Glades in Gauley Ranger District or to Dolly Sods on Allegheny Front in Potomac Ranger District. The bogs are rich in flora of a more northerly clime, legacies of the cold climate that accompanied the advances of the great continental ice sheets 100 centuries ago or more. As a result, vegetation of these bogs are living relics of the Ice Ages. Fine vistas of the surrounding mountain slopes may be had as the trail skirts the perimeter of the bog. You may also see a beaver pond and dam here.

Segment 2: Shortly after leaving the bog (0.5mi W of Turkey Run Trail junction), the trail opens into a small opening in the forest. Here dead trees thrust out of a carpet of ferns. The trail here is weak and unsigned. Keep to the right (N) side of this fern meadow and look for the trail at the NW corner of the meadow. Now the trail skirts the S side of smaller bogs and is faint and wet in places. Rhododendron and laurel lining the bog are spectacular in season (typically mid-June to mid-July). The USFS plans to route the trail away from the upper bog in the summer of 1999 due to beaver activity. In the vicinity of the junction with McGowan Mountain Trail (TR136) [K] beware of several confusing unmarked junctions with other roads and trails.

MIDDLE POINT TRAIL (TR140) 1.6mi(2.6 km)
SCENERY: 2 (wooded)   NOTE: B,M,(0)
DIFFICULTY: II (moderate)   SKI-: S3
CONDITION: B (average)   ELEV: 3850/3040
MAPS: USFS(A), Bowden, I-E-2 in this Guide
SEGMENTS: (1) FR91 to TR132 (Baker Sods Trail)   1.6mi

Middle Point Trail lies outside Otter Creek Wilderness. It is an access route to the Wilderness. The trail is blue-blazed and well-defined. Note on Map I-E-2 that an old road leads 1.9mi from near the S terminus of Middle Point Trail to the parking area [S] at the mouth of Condon Run. It provides a 7.7mi loop route involving Otter Creek-, Yellow Creek-, Baker Sods- and Middle Point trails. This road is not maintained as a trail but is visible from either end.

Access: Middle Point Trail starts on Stuart Memorial Drive (FR91)[R] near a curve in the road under Stuart Knob (2.2mi W of Bear Heaven Campground). Parking is available for 3-4 cars.

Segment 1: Starting from the S, the trail heads N over rocky terrain. At 0.25mi it crosses the ridge between Stalnaker Run and Rattlesnake Run. Here the trail winds through large rocks. From here, contour along the W side of the ridge at the head of Condon Run. Bear ENE and then N and drop steeply down a spur ridge, leaving conifers and entering open hardwoods. The trail ends at the junction [N] with Baker Sods Trail (TR132) in a saddle on the ridge between Little Black Fork and Rattlesnake Run.

TURKEY RUN TRAIL (TR150) 4.0mi(6.4km)
SCENERY: 2 (wooded)   NOTE: B,M,(1)
DIFFICULTY: I (leisurely)   SKI-: S4
CONDITION: A (good)   ELEV: 3730/2630
MAPS: USFS(A), Parsons, I-E-1 in this Guide
SEGMENTS: (1) FR701 to TR138 (Moore Run Trail)   4.0mi

The trail is an easy, tree-shaded path (no views, and partially overgrown) along former Turkey Run Road. This road was gated and abandoned when Otter Creek became a Wilderness, and is now no more than a grassy lane through a middle-aged hardwood forest. A portion of this trail was rerouted in 1984, but in 1991 the USFS decided to return the trail to its original route to protect the wet, mossy plateau. Turkey Run Trail winds around, and then up and over McGowan Mountain, and down into Moore Run drainage.

Access: The N end $\boxed{\text{M}}$, is 0.5mi W of Big Springs Gap along Fernow Loop Road (FR701) which is accessible via Parsons.

Segment 1: Old Turkey Run Road (Trail) follows a sweeping curve of McGowan Mountain, with little change in elevation until, at 2.0mi, where the trail meets $\boxed{\text{N}}$ the original trail and the rerouted trail.

To follow the original trail, leave Turkey Run Road $\boxed{\text{N}}$ on a small woods road and descend to cross Turkey Run at 2.3mi in a grove of rhododendron. From here to the top of the mountain is a magnificent example of old-growth birch, beech, cherry, spruce and hemlock. Meet the rerouted trail $\boxed{\text{P}}$ at 3 mi and descend through a mixed forest of hardwoods and hemlocks to Moore Run Trail $\boxed{\text{L}}$ at 4mi (Just W of Moore Run are interesting bogs and meadows.)

BIG SPRINGS GAP TRAIL (TR154)   0.9mi(1.4km)

SCENERY: 2 (wooded)	NOTE: B,M,(1)
DIFFICULTY: I (leisurely)	SKI-: S4
CONDITION: A (good)	ELEV: 2450/2060

MAPS: USFS(A), Parsons, I-E-1 in this guide
SEGMENTS: (1) FR701 to TR131 (Otter Creek Trail)   0.9mi

Big Springs Gap Trail provides a starting point for hikes in the N part of Otter Creek Wilderness. But note that one must wade across Otter Creek to get to Otter Creek Trail (TR131). Big Springs Gap Trail partly follows an old wagon road that once led to an old homesite near a large spring.

Access: The W trailhead is along FR701 which is accessible via Parsons, as described in the introduction to this Section I-E.

Segment 1: Starting from Elklick Road (FR701) at Big Springs Gap, the trail makes two switchbacks and crosses Spring Run. It follows an old farm road until it bends left and joins Spring Run. At this point it was rerouted onto a path S along a bench on the W side of the run. It crosses a steeply banked, unnamed drain and continues around the hill before dropping back to the old trail location and crossing to the E bank of Spring Run. It follows the old farm road again down the drain, through a small meadow, and crosses to the W side of Spring Run. It then leaves the run and continues downhill to Otter Creek and across it to Otter Creek Trail (TR131) $\boxed{\text{G}}$.

Note: Near the W trailhead of TR154 is Zero Grade Trail (no number). It is a level, 0.25mi, loop trail that goes through several harvested areas in Fernow Experimental Forest. Along the way are signs explaining the reasoning behind each method of timber harvesting. It is accessible to visitors with disabilities. For more information contact Information Services, Northeast Forest Experiment Station, Timber and Watershed Laboratory Nursery Bottom, Parsons WV 26287 (Tel. 304-478-2000). Zero Grade Trail is not shown on Map I-E-1, nore are the switchbacks and the minor rerouting of TR154.

POSSESSION CAMP TRAIL (TR158)   3.3mi(5.3km)

SCENERY: 1 (exceptional)   NOTE: B,M,(2)
DIFFICULTY: II (moderate)   SKI-: S2
CONDITION: A (good)   ELEV: 3460/2780
MAPS: USFS(A), Bowden, Mozark Mtn., I-E-1 & I-E-2 in this Guide
SEGMENTS:
(1) TR130 (Green Mtn. Tr.) to TR131 (OCT)/TR138 (Moore Run Tr.)   3.3mi
   Possession Camp Trail lies on an old RR grade (a remnant of early 1900s logging operations). The grade was created as a USFS trail in 1977. It provides another loop hiking opportunity and a way to get back to Shavers Mountain when hikers get isolated due to high water in Otter Creek.
   Access: The N terminus [E] (Map I-E-1) is in a 0.3-acre opening on Green Mountain at its junction with Green Mtn. Trail (TR130).
   The S terminus [D] (Map I-E-2) is on Otter Creek Trail (TR131) near Moore Run Trail (TR138).
   Segment 1: Starting from the N, Possession Camp Trail leaves the opening heading SW through a tunnel of dense rhododendron. After crossing a drain and going around a point, the woods opens up. Here the terrain is nearly flat but rocky, and the trees are cherry, maple and birch. At 0.6mi is the North Fork of Possession Camp Run. Here the trail drops and winds through large sandstone boulders as it crosses the stream. The trail soon rejoins the RR grade and continues SW. At 0.75mi the trail runs along the edge of a steep drop to the W. At 1.1mi [Q] is the South Fork of Possession Camp Run. The stone foundation of an old RR bridge is still in place. The area between the two forks of Possession Camp Run is one of the more interesting areas in Otter Creek Wilderness. At 2.1mi [R] the trail crosses the ridge line dividing Possession Camp- and Otter Creek drainages. At 2.6mi the trail crosses a small side stream. A short distance before Otter Creek, the trail leaves the old RR grade. It then drops down to Otter Creek through scattered rhododendron. The mouth of Devil's Gulch is seen across Otter Creek from the junction [D] (Map I-E-2) with Otter Creek Trail (TR131). Moore Run Trail (TR138) starts nearby.

HEDRICK CAMP TRAIL (TR165)   1.0mi(1.6km)

SCENERY: 2 (wooded)   NOTE: B,M,(1)
DIFFICULTY: I (leisurely)   SKI-: S4
CONDITION: A (good)   ELEV: 3200/3000
MAPS: USFS(A), Bowden, I-E-2 in this Guide
SEGMENTS:
   (1) TR131 (Otter Creek Trail) to TR129 (Shaver's Mtn. Trail)   1.0mi
   This trail forms a 9.0mi loop with S sections of Otter Creek Trail (TR131), the W section of Mylius Trail (TR128) and the S section of Shavers Mountain Trail (TR129).
   Access: Hedrick Camp Trail begins near the N end of Condon Run Parking Lot [S]. (See description of Otter Creek access points above.)
   Segment 1: Starting from Condon Run [S], the trail heads E through rhododendron and spruce and hemlock. An open bog is on the S side of the trail. At 0.1mi cross Otter Creek (no foot bridge) The trail then proceeds SE on an old road paralleling the headwaters of Otter Creek. Hedrick Camp Trail ends at the junction [F] with Shavers Mountain Trail (TR129).

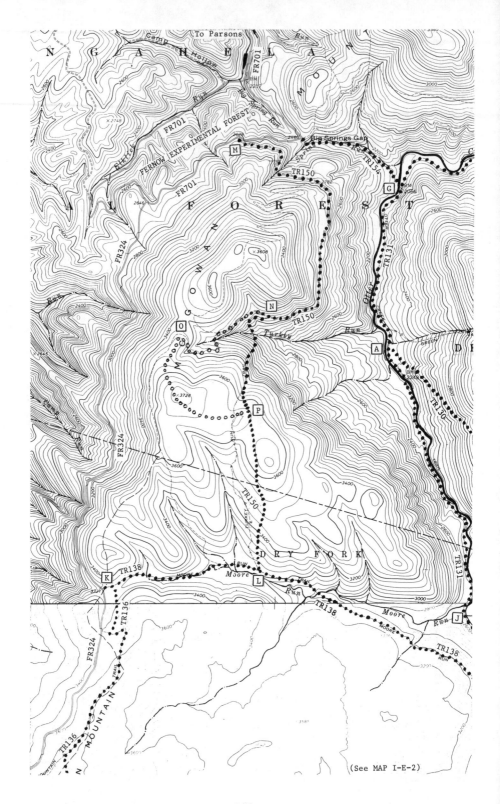

(See MAP I-E-2)

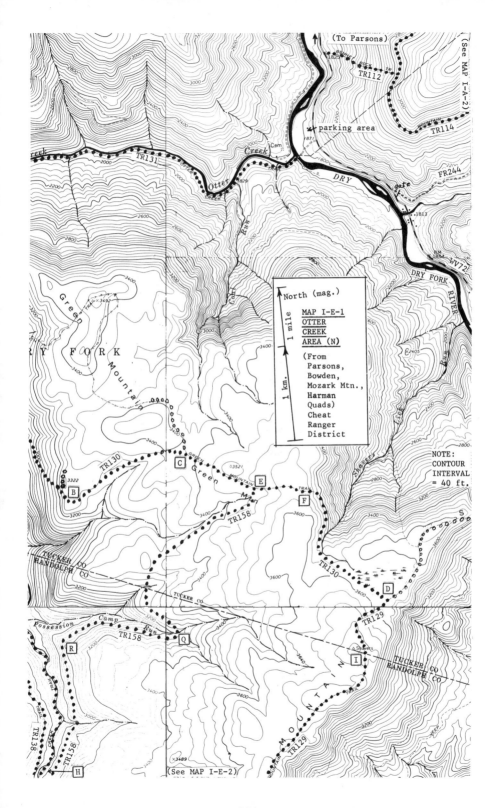

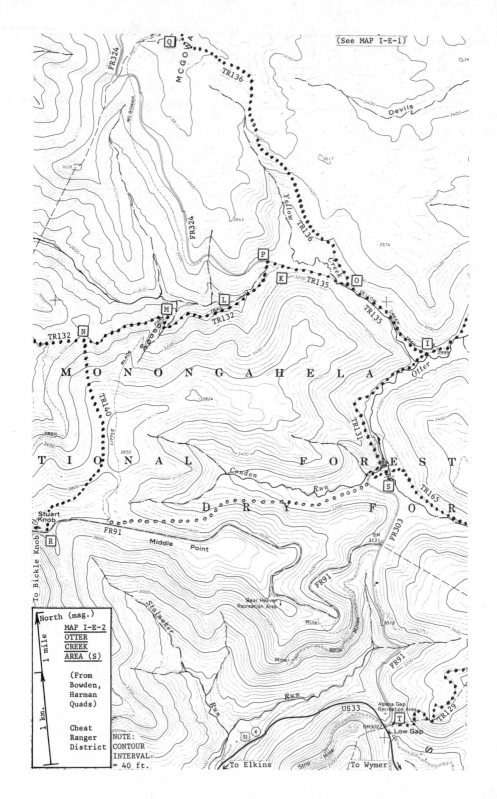

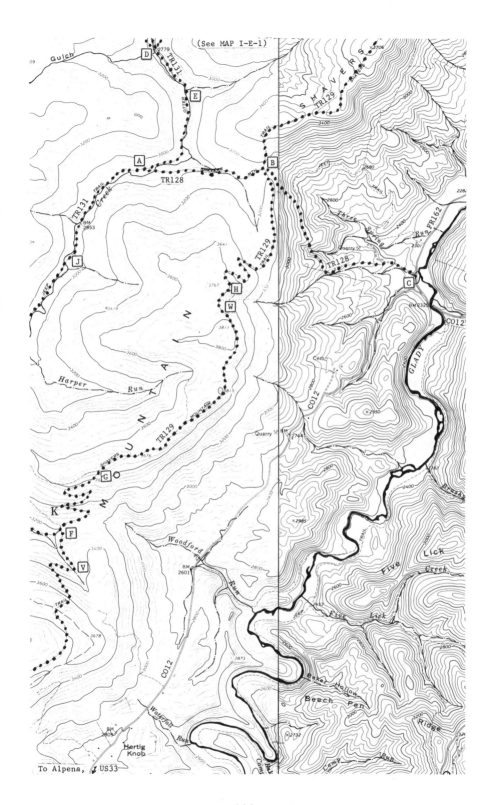

(See MAP I-E-1)

Waterfall and leaves on rock in Otter Creek (TR131).
Photo by Roger Spencer

GAULEY RANGER DISTRICT

Gauley Ranger District is in the SW corner of the MNF, and is contiguous with the W boundary of Marlinton Ranger District. Its N boundary is the Gauley Divide of the Gauley River. Although its S border extends to Cold Knob Mountain, its most southern trail is the E-W Fork Mountain Trail. Major streams in the area include Cranberry River, Williams River, Gauley River, and Middle Fork of the Williams River.

The heart of the district is the Cranberry Backcountry and Cranberry Wilderness, adjoining along a NW-SE border from near the confluence of Williams River and Middle Fork of the Williams River to Cranberry Glades. Other areas of significant interest to hikers in the Gauley District are:

- Cherry River area with connections to long distance trails such as Fork Mountain Trail and Pocahontas Trail;
- Cranberry Mountain Nature Center and nearby Cranberry Glades with a network of trails;
- Bishop Knob area between Gauley River and Cranberry River.

A stay in the district would not be complete without a visit to Summit Lake, Falls of Hills Creek Scenic Area, and Cranberry Glades Botanical Area. All are off of WV39 between Richwood and Mill Point. For the most spectacular views of both the Gauley and Marlinton ranger districts, drive along Highland Scenic Highway (WV150) from Cranberry Mountain Nature Center N to US219 near Slaty Fork.

District ranger offices are in Richwood (26261), 2.0mi E of Richwood on WV39 (Tel: 304-846-2695). A free "Recreation Guide for the Gauley District" is available upon request. It describes the activities of the district, with guidelines for camping, picnicking, backpacking, horseback riding, bicycling, kayaking, canoeing, hunting, fishing, trapping, and cross-country skiing. The Guide also has information on Cranberry Wilderness and Cranberry Backcountry. Additional information is available on the W section of Marlinton Ranger District. One of the most helpful features of the Guide is a map of all the trails, their USFS numbers, and the state- and forest roads.

Four campgrounds and two picnic areas are located in the district. They are usually open from mid-March to at least the first week of December. Small fees are charged at all campgrounds, but picnic areas are free. Also free are the single campsites without facilities along Cranberry River W of Cranberry Campground. Shelters for hikers are found along Cranberry River between Cranberry River Campground and E to Cranberry Glades. The campgrounds (CG) and picnic areas are:

- Big Rock CG: (5 sites) picnic table, water, toilets
- Bishop Knob CG: (63 sites) picnic table, water, toilets
- Cranberry CG: (30 sites) picnic table, water, toilets
- Summit Lake CG: (33 sites) picnic table, water, toilets
- Cranberry Mountain Nature Center: picnic tables (Water and toilets are in the Nature center.)
- North Bend Picnic Area: picnic tables, water, toilets
- Woodbine Picnic Area: picnic tables, grills, group shelter, toilets

Tea Creek Campground, (on the NE side of Williams River, 1.0mi W of Highland Scenic Highway on FR86) is in Marlinton Ranger District, but is close to Gauley Ranger District. This campground has 29 sites (with facilities

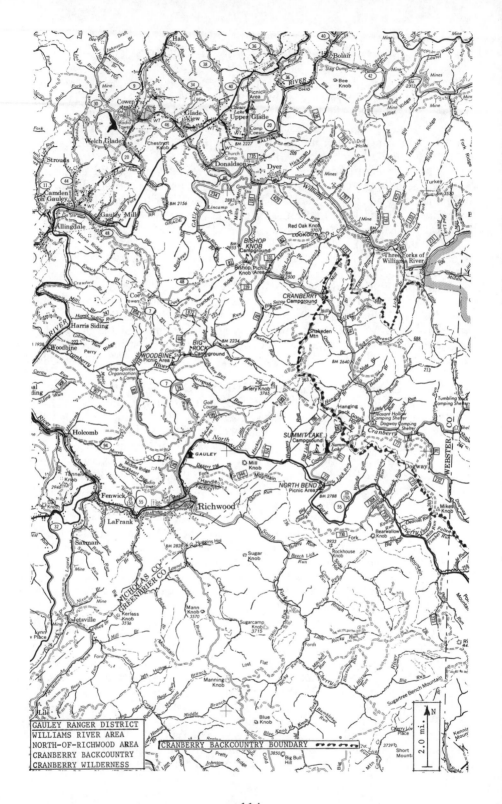

GAULEY RANGER DISTRICT
WILLIAMS RIVER AREA
NORTH-OF-RICHWOOD AREA
CRANBERRY BACKCOUNTRY
CRANBERRY WILDERNESS

CRANBERRY BACKCOUNTRY BOUNDARY

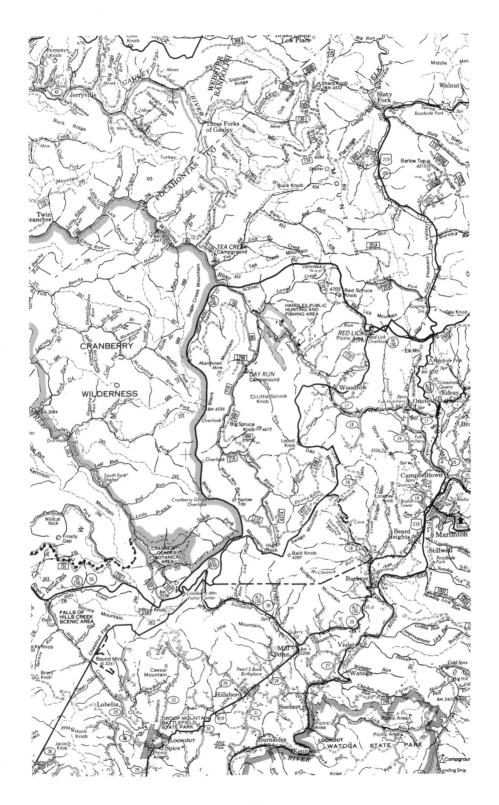

like those in Gauley Ranger District), and is open from mid-April through the first week of December.

Hikers will see a combination of blue plastic diamond-shaped blazes and older blue paint rectangular blazes. The district is in the process of phasing out the painted-blaze system. Some trail routes may be confusing in this transfer because two markers are not installed at trail turns. Also, bears have torn the plastic markers loose from their light nail moorings. There are also some white plastic diamond-shaped blazes. Examples are on some of the trails for cross-country skiing and at the Cranberry Volkswalk trail system.

Ski-touring in Gauley Ranger District

The Gauley District offers a wide variety of nordic ski-touring and snowshoeing opportunities for a wide range of skill levels. A free map highlighting these opportunities is available from the Gauley District by writing to them at P.O. Box 110, Richwood WV 26261, or call them at Tel. 304-846-2695.

Some USFS roads in the Gauley (and W Marlinton) districts are normally unplowed in winter. These roads offer opportunities for ski-touring.

Cranberry Backcountry (II-A & B)

FR102   from WV39 and Cranberry Mountain Nature Center N to FR76 & TR272 (7mi)

FR232   from WV39 near Cranberry Mountain Nature Center NW to WV39 near North Bend Recreation Site (13mi)

Highlands Scenic Highway Area

FR24	from US219 N to a dead-end	11mi
FR76	from FR86 W to WV150 *	4mi
FR86	from WV150 S to FR216 *	3mi
FR216	from WV150 N to FR86 *	8mi
FR251	from US219 W to a dead-end *	2mi
FR999	from FR216 S to a dead-end *	3mi
WV150	from WV39 N to Red Lick Overlook	20mi

* Exclusively in Marlinton Ranger District

Bishop Knob Area   (II-D)

FR82	from FR76 E to Red Oak Knob	2mi
FR101	from FR234 S to FR82	2mi
FR234	from FR101 E to a dead-end	5mi

CRANBERRY BACKCOUNTRY AND CRANBERRY WILDERNESS

This is the best-known area in the S half of the MNF. It is a favorite of fishermen and hikers in particular. A number of wilderness-type restrictions have been imposed in order to protect the tranquility and primitive characteristics of the areas. For more than 50 years about 53,000 acres (80sq.mi) have been known as the Cranberry Backcountry, but under terms of the 1964 Wilderness Act it was divided, and the E section (55.5sq.mi) became the Cranberry Wilderness in January, 1983. It was the result of efforts begun in the early 1970s, and led by West Virginia Senator Robert C. Byrd.

Cranberry Backcountry includes the South Fork of the Cranberry River and the Cranberry River from the N edge of Cranberry Glades, downstream to Cranberry Campground. It also includes a section E of Cranberry River near Birchlog Trail (TR250) and Little Fork Trail (TR242).

116

Cranberry Wilderness is on the NE border of the Backcountry. It is N of Cranberry Glades, W of Highland Scenic Highway (WV150) from near the Glades N to Williams River, and is S of Williams River from WV150 to the N terminus of Middle Fork Trail (TR271) and Little Fork Trail (TR242). The Cranberry Wilderness boundaries are shown on page 114.

Although usage and restrictions are similar, some major differences exist between the Backcountry and the Wilderness:

- Activities such as timber harvesting, road construction, wildlife control, and mineral explorations are authorized in the Backcountry, but not in the Wilderness;
- All motorized vehicle use is prohibited in the Wilderness, but in the Backcountry gated forest roads are used by the USFS;
- Trails are paint- or plastic blazed in the Backcountry, but blazes are being phased out in the Wilderness;
- Trail shelters are found in the Backcountry, but not in the Wilderness.

Bicycles, hand-drawn carts and wagons are allowed only in Backcountry areas.

Cranberry Wilderness has about 60mi of hiking trails; Cranberry Backcountry has about 75mi. Permits are not required in either area, but the USFS recommends that overnight backpackers register at the Cranberry Mountain Nature Center, Gauley Ranger Station, or at a trailhead. It also recommends that party size not exceed 10 backpackers in the Wilderness. "No Trace Camping" is encouraged in both the Backcountry and the Wilderness.

The Backcountry and Wilderness are open all year, and an enjoyable visit is possible any time. Most visitors are fishermen who come when fishing is best--in late spring and to a lesser extent, in the fall. All seven shelters in the backcountry are likely to be occupied then. Use is particularly heavy in June after school is out. Trails receive heaviest use during the deer (gun) season. People who do not come to hunt or fish may wish to plan visits at other times, especially if they seek solitude. However, except during the two-week deer (gun) season, this is easily solved by avoiding Cranberry River Road below the Forks, and the Glades Road.

Cranberry Backcountry offers an illuminating case history of the relation between hunters and fishermen and roads. All roads in this 80sq.mi area are closed to public vehicular access. Yet the USFS has found overwhelming public support from residents of the region for its closure of the roads, even though the vast majority of Backcountry users are hunters and fishermen. The Cranberry River running through the Backcountry has a popularity rating in the top three of West Virginia's fishing streams, and in the top 20 nation-wide.

The Backcountry and Wilderness offer excellent ski-touring because of its altitude, scenery and trails. The temperature frequently falls below zero on the high ridges. The Highland Scenic Highway (WV150) is not plowed in winter and frequently will be impassable to conventional vehicles. Other roads leading to the Backcountry and Wilderness boundaries may be closed to automobiles by snow unless they are regularly used by logging trucks or other authorized vehicles. (Check with the Gauley District Ranger Station, Tel. 304-846-2695, before making definite plans on a route.) Be prepared for cold weather and snow. Wading rivers in winter is a cold, dangerous ordeal. Snowfall averages 90 inches annually.

Water is abundant along roads and trails except on the tops of ridges. Rainfall averages over 60 inches annually. There are no dangerous animals.

Few poisonous snakes are found in the area, except on the W edge. The area is one of the few good black bear habitats in West Virginia. and has been designated as a sanctuary for black bear. Bears of the region are shy, and not often seen. The area is relatively free of mosquitoes, but from late spring to late summer, black gnats ("no-see-ums") can be troublesome.

Three Forks of the Williams River

This large, open meadow marks the junction of Middle Fork and Little Fork of the Williams River with its main branch. In the early 1930s this was the site of a small logging community. Three designated campsites are found in the vicinity, with several more along FR86. There are also plenty of secluded campsites for backpackers. A chain of beaver ponds runs along the meadow's S edge.

Cranberry Mountain Nature Center

This center is 23mi E of Richwood on Highland Scenic Highway (WV39/150) at the intersection with WV55. It contains exhibits on forestry, mining, local history, wildlife and plants in the MNF, particularly Cranberry Glades which is nearby. Short, educational movies and slide shows are shown frequently in the auditorium. Large picture windows offer views of nearby mountain scenery. Outside the Center is an interpretive trail. Guided tours of the Cranberry Glades Botanical Area boardwalk are also available. Nearby is Falls of Hills Creek Scenic Area. Maps and other literature are available at the desk, and a naturalist is on hand to answer questions. Cranberry Mountain Nature Center is open daily during summer from Memorial Day to Labor Day, and is open on weekends during spring, fall and winter (closed in December). The telephone number is 304-653-4826.

Cranberry Glades Botanical Area

This special area of 1.2sq.mi was established by the USFS in 1965. It includes fascinating sphagnum bogs, or muskegs, reminiscent of Arctic tundra. Certain plants and animals characteristic of more northern climates reach their southernmost distribution here. A 0.5mi boardwalk and interpretive trail leads into Flag Glade. Visitors are not permitted to leave the boardwalk without permission of the Gauley District Ranger. During the summer, Cranberry Mountain Nature Center naturalists conduct guided nature walks in the Glades.

Shelters

Seven shelters are found in the Backcountry along FR102 and FR76. All shelters are open-front, three-sided Adirondack buildings with overhanging eaves and wooden floors raised above the ground. They do not have bunks. Each accommodates six to ten people. They are provided with a fireplace with a grate and a wooden picnic table. Some have pit toilets but most do not. All have a permanent source of water. They are available on a first-come-first-served basis. It is never safe to assume they will be unoccupied, except perhaps in mid-winter.

General Notes on Trails

Cranberry Backcountry and Cranberry Wilderness Area offers over 130mi of hiking trails that present a wide choice of routes for one-day hikes, multi-day backpacking trips. The topography is rugged; trips should be planned that cover under 6-8 miles per day for time to enjoy your surroundings to the fullest. Most USFS trails (3-digit numbers) are blue-paint blazed with blue plastic diamond-shaped blazes, and signed at most trail junctions. The Backcountry has a fairly well-marked and maintained trail systems.

If you see motor vehicles in the Backcountry that do not seem to belong to the USFS or to a logging company, report the license number to the Gauley District Ranger, Richwood, WV 26261.

For up-to-date information on roads and trails in the MNF and local weather conditions, contact the Cranberry Mountain Nature Center when it is open. (See the paragraph above, titled "Cranberry Mountain Nature Center", for Nature Center hours.) At other times, ask at the Gauley District Ranger Station located on WV39 2mi E of the main part of the Richwood. (Zip Code 25261; Tel. 304-846-2695.). It is open 8 A.M. to 5 P.M. on week days only.

FR76 and FR102

Along the gated portions of FR76 and FR102 are seven trail shelters and the trailheads of numerous trails of Cranberry Backcountry and Cranberry Wilderness. It is highly probable that you will use these roads for some part of almost any trip you take in the region. To help you in planning these trips, the table below gives distances between points of interest along these routes.

Landmark		Distance in miles to:			
	Map No.	Forest Road	Lower Gate	Next landmark	Upper gate
Lower Gate on FR76	II-A-1	FR76	0.0	0.1	15.9
North-South Trail (TR688)	II-A-1	FR76	0.1	2.1	15.8
Lick Branch Trail (TR212) and Queer Branch Shelter	II-A-4	FR76	2.2	2.4	13.7
Rough Run Trail (TR213)	II-A-5	FR76	4.6	0.3	11.3
Fisherman Trail (TR231)	II-A-5	FR76	4.9	0.1	11.0
Pheasant Hollow Shelter	II-A-5	FR76	5.0	1.7	10.9
Dogway Shelter	II-A-5	FR76	6.7	1.7	9.2
Houselog Run Shelter	II-A-5	FR76	8.4	0.8	7.5
Birchlog Run Trail (TR250)	II-A-5	FR76	9.2	0.4	6.7
Tumbling Rock Shelter	II-A-5	FR76	9.6	0.1	6.3
Tumbling Rock Trail (TR272)	II-A-5	FR76	9.7	1.6	6.2
North Fork Shelter	II-A-5	FR76	11.3	0.1	4.6
North Fork Trail (TR272) and Forks of Cranberry Trail (TR245)	II-A-5	FR102	11.4	2.2	4.5
South Fork Shelter	II-A-8	FR102	13.6	2.0	2.3
Cow Pasture Trail (TR253) and South Fork Trail (TR243)	II-A-8	FR102	15.6	0.3	0.3
Upper Gate on FR102	II-A-8	FR102	15.9	0.0	0.0

Cow Pasture Trail (TR253). Photo by Jackie Hallinan

(II-A) SOUTHERN CRANBERRY BACKCOUNTRY AND

CRANBERRY WILDERNESS AREA

Trails in this section are all off WV39 (between Cranberry Mountain Nature Center and Richwood) or the S end of Highland Scenic Highway (WV150). Strictly speaking, some of these trails are not within the Backcountry or Wilderness, but are a short distance S of Cranberry Backcountry. Because of their proximity they are described together in this section. Only Forks of Cranberry Trail (TR245) is within Cranberry Wilderness. Wilderness trails are described mainly in Section II-B.

SUMMIT LAKE TRAIL (No. #)   1.8mi(2.9km)
SCENERY: 1 (exceptional)   NOTE: M, (2)
DIFFICULTY: I (leisurely)   SKI-:   S4
CONDITION: A (good)   ELEV: 3440/3340
MAPS: USFS (A), Webster Springs SW, Fork Mountain, II-A-4 in this
      Guide
SEGMENTS: (1) parking area or campground & return   1.8mi
This pleasant, easy loop trail circles 42-acre Summit Lake and, in the process, crosses two tributaries of Coats Run. The trail passes through hardwoods, rhododendron and ferns. Summit Lake is stocked with trout, but there are also bass and pan fish. Swimming in the lake is prohibited. The fee campground has 33 sites with water and restrooms, and is a good base camp for access to Pocahontas Trail (TR263).

Access: Walking access is from the campground or the lake parking area which is on WV39/5 (FR77 on Map II-A-4). To get there, turn off WV39 onto FR77 6.6mi E of Richwood and drive 2.0mi on FR77.

FISHERMAN'S TRAIL (TR231)   1.5mi(2.4km)
SCENERY: 2 (wooded)   NOTE: B,H,M,(1)
DIFFICULTY: II (moderate)   SKI-:   S4
CONDITION: B (average)   ELEV: 3640/2800
MAPS: USFS(A), Webster Springs SW, II-A-4, -5 in this Guide
SEGMENTS: (1) FR77/FR99 to FR76 (TR272)   1.5mi
This well-marked, well-maintained trail provides another good access to Cranberry River.

Access: The SW terminus [D](Map II-A-4) of Fisherman's Trail (formerly Pheasant Hollow Trail) is at the junction of FR77 and FR99 (Pocahontas Road), near the gate N of Summit Lake. There is a gate here, along with a picnic table and trash can. The NE terminus [S](Map II-A-5) is at Cranberry River and Cranberry River Road on the opposite side of the river. Pheasant Hollow Shelter is 50yd up-river from this terminus. The trail is signed at both ends.

Segment 1: Starting from the SW [D](Map II-A-4), follow the path leading down through the center of the clear-cut area that the USFS has signed as a demonstration plot. After 0.2mi cross a logging road that looks worth exploring. From here the trail is pleasant and easy to follow, following a stream down through unlogged woods. About 500yd from the NE terminus

121

(Map II-A-5) the trail makes an abrupt left turn, crosses Pheasant Hollow Creek-bed, and runs along the narrow divide between Pheasant Hollow and Goose Hollow. No bridge crosses Cranberry River at the NE end of the trail. The river is wadeable normally, but it could be dangerous during high water.

FORK MOUNTAIN TRAIL (TR236)   21.4mi(34.2km)

SCENERY: 1 (exceptional)   NOTE: B,M,(4)
DIFFICULTY: III (strenuous)   SKI-:   S3/4
CONDITION: B-C (average-poor)   ELEV: 4310/2340
MAPS: USFS (A), Richwood, Fork Mountain, Lobelia, II-A-4, II-A-7,
    II-A-8, & II-A-9 in this Guide
SEGMENTS: (1) WV39 to North Bend Trail   6.0mi
               (2) North Bend Trail to TR237 (Big Run Trail)   4.8mi
               (3) TR237 to FR223   5.2mi
               (4) FR223 to Falls of Hills Creek   2.4mi
               (5) Falls of Hills Cr. to TR263 (Pocahontas Trail) 2.7mi

Fork Mountain Trail has received additional relocations in the early 1990s to keep it away from timber harvesting and private property, and for more convenient cross-country skiing in some sections. It remains, however, less frequently used than the district's other two long trails (North-South and Pocahontas). With the addition of North Bend Trail access, usage is expected to increase, particularly for ski tours from W to E to descend on North Bend Trail. Extensive relocation has been completed at Falls of Hills Creek Scenic Area and on the N slope of Spruce Mountain. With a relocation to the N slope of Rocky Knob, the trail's length has been slightly reduced. Water is available near each end area of the trail, but the long high central section does not have streams.

Access: Access points are found at:
- WV39 [E](Map II-A-4) 2.0mi E of Richwood (at the first bridge over North Fork of Cherry River);
- North Bend Trail at North Bend Picnic Area on WV39;
- Big Run Trail (TR237) [D](Map II-A-7);
- Bear Run Road (FR223);
- Falls of Hills Creek Scenic Area parking area [B]; and
- Pocahontas Trail (TR263) [A](Map V-A-8) near Spruce Mtn.

Segment 1: Starting from the W [E](Map II-A-4), Fork Mountain Trail follows the S bank of Cherry River W (downstream) for 0.9mi, and curves left [F]. It follows an old RR grade in an ascent by Desert Branch to cross FR946 (not shown on Map II-A-4 or -9) and reaches the ridge-top above the headwaters of Shiros Run (Map II-A-9). It then follows the top of Fork Mountain E to the junction with North Bend Trail at 6.0mi.

Segment 2: At 10.6mi it meets Big Run Trail (TR237) [D](Map II-A-7). Along the trail are rocky sections, seepage, mossy patches, wildflowers, hardwoods, rhododendrons, and evidence of deer and wild turkey.

Segment 3: The trail crosses Bear Run Road (FR223) (off Map II-A-7 to the S), an access to WV39 at 16.0mi.

Segment 4: Ahead it goes E to skirt the N slope of Rocky Knob (the ridge's highest point), after which it turns NE in a rapid descent to Falls of Hills Creek Scenic Area [B].

Segment 5: After crossing Hills Creek it ascends on the N slope of Spruce Mountain in a rocky area with conifers to meet Pocahontas Trail (TR263) [A] (Map II-A-8) at 21.4mi, and 4.2mi W of Cranberry Mountain Nature Center [J]. To the left (N) on Pocahontas Trail it is 1.4mi to WV39.

NORTH BEND TRAIL (TR225)   2.4mi(3.8km)
SCENERY: I (exceptional)   NOTE: B, M (1)
DIFFICULTY: II (moderate)   SKI-: S2
CONDITION: A (good)   ELEV: 3680/2780
MAPS: USFS(A) Fork Mountain, II-A-9 in this Guide
SEGMENTS: (1) WV39 to TR236 (Fork Mountain Trail)   2.4mi

This wide trail was completed and opened to the public in 1991, and it serves as a major access to Fork Mountain Trail (TR236) from WV39. It mainly follows old logging roads, but switchbacks through an open forest with wildflowers in its lower elevations. Blue plastic diamond-shaped blazes mark the trail.

Access: Access along WV39 is at North Bend Picnic Area, 6.6mi E of Richwood.

Segment 1: From North Bend Picnic Area, the trail begins at the high footbridge over North Fork of Cherry River. It follows downstream 0.3mi before ascending on five switchbacks to a more gradual ascent on a logging road. On the switchbacks are poplar, maple, cherry, and birch with rich beds of trillium, ferns, ramps, and foamflowers. After 1.1mi, at junction with FR730 (not shown on Map II-A-9), the trail turns left and goes 75yd before turning right. On a narrow logging road the trail ascends through a clear-cut dense with blackberries. The trail meets Fork Mountain Trail (TR236) on a flat ridge crest of Fork Mountain.

BIG RUN TRAIL (TR237)   1.0mi(1.6km)
SCENERY: 2 (wooded)   NOTE: B,M,(1)
DIFFICULTY: II (moderate)   SKI-: S4
CONDITION: B (average)   ELEV: 3930/3050
MAPS: USFS(A), Fork Mountain, II-A-7 in this Guide
SEGMENTS: (1) WV39 to TR236 (Fork Mountain Trail)   1.0mi

Big Run Trail (formerly part of Fork Mountain Trail) provides access to Fork Mountain Trail (TR236) from WV39.

Access: The E trailhead [E] is on the S side of WV39, 12mi E of Richwood and 9.3mi W of Cranberry Mountain Nature Center.

Segment 1: From WV39 [E] the trail starts on the W side of Big Run and, after 220yd, crosses the stream. Its junction with TR236 [D] is just S of Bearwallow Knob. The location shown on the Fork Mountain Topo is more accurate than on the MNF Recreation Map (USFS(A)).

EAGLE CAMP TRAIL (TR259)   1.0mi(1.6km)
SCENERY: 2 (wooded)   NOTE: B,M,(1)
DIFFICULTY: II (moderate)   SKI-: S4
CONDITION: B (average)   ELEV: 3600/3310
MAPS: USFS(A), Lobelia, II-A-7 in this Guide

SEGMENTS: (1) WV39 to TR263 (Pocahontas Trail)   1.0mi

This trail serves as an access route between Pocahontas Trail (TR263) and WV39 [H]. From the highway parking area, which is 10.1mi E of Summit Lake Campground, pass through a short field to cross a foot bridge over the North Fork of Cherry River. It ascends gradually on the W side of Left Branch to meet Pocahontas Trail [G] after 1.0mi.

POCAHONTAS TRAIL (TR263)   20.2mi(32.5km)
SCENERY: 1 (exceptional)   NOTE: B,M,(4)
DIFFICULTY: III (strenuous)   SKI-:   S3
CONDITION: B (average)   ELEV: 4100/3420
MAPS: USFS(A), Lobelia, Webster Springs SW, II-A-4, II-A-5, II-A-7
        and II-A-8 in this Guide
SEGMENTS:
(1) WV39/150(Nature Ctr.) to TR244 (Kennison Mtn. Trail)   2.5mi
(2) TR244   to TR236 (Fork Mtn. Trail)   1.6mi
(3) TR236   to WV39/150   1.4mi
(4) WV39/150 to TR259 (Eagle Camp Trail)   2.3mi
(5) TR259   to TR235 (Frosty Gap Trail)   1.3mi
(6) TR235   to Mike's Knob   1.5mi
(7) M. Knob to TR231 (Fisherman Trail)/FR77   5.4mi
(8) TR231/FR77 to Hanging Rock   1.6mi
(9) Hanging Rock to FR99   2.6mi

Pocahontas Trail is easy to follow. It goes through beautiful hardwood forests and here and there are huge birch and other trees rejected by early loggers. The trail follows the route of a branch of the Seneca Indian Trail (now US219). It was also used by pioneers before the Civil War. The route was retraced in the early 1950s by Howard Deitz and others in Richwood. Some years later the USFS designated it a system trail. Footbridges span Hills Creek and Left Branch of the North Fork of Cherry River.

Access: The E trailhead [J] (Map II-A-8) is at Cranberry Mountain Nature Center along WV39.

The W terminus [B](Map II-A-4), on FR99, is closed to private cars, but it is only 0.7mi along FR99 to a point of vehicle access.

Segment 1: Starting from the E [J] (Map II-A-8), the first 2.5mi section of trail (to Blue Knob) is well maintained, with easy grades through an attractive forest. About 1.0mi from the Nature Center the trail joins an old wagon road. At Blue Knob, Kennison Mountain Trail (TR244) [E] leaves Pocahontas Trail to the N at two places--SE for a spur trail and S for the main trail.

Segment 2: From Blue Knob, Pocahontas Trail continues W and meets Fork Mountain Trail (TR236) [A] in 1.6mi.

Segment 3: The trail crosses WV39/150 [F](Map II-A-7) 3.0mi W of Blue Knob. This three-mile section offers old logging artifacts and rare orchids to the observant eye.

Segment 4: From WV39/150 [F] the trail heads NW. Two miles from WV39/150 is a good campsite near where Eagle Camp Trail (TR259) [G] comes up from the S.

Segment 5: From TR259 proceed 3mi NW to [J], the W end of Frosty Gap Trail (TR235).

Segment 6: From Frosty Gap Trail Pocahontas Trail proceeds 1.5mi NW to Mike's Knob area [A]. Directly below the former site of a fire tower the trail skirts the upper edge of an open meadow (game food plot) with a pond at its lower end. For an excellent view of the surrounding country, follow the jeep trail leading up from the meadow to FR77.

Segment 7: West of Mike's Knob [A] the trail follows the ridge top NW to near the intersection [D](Map II-A-4) of FR99, FR77, and Fisherman's Trail (TR231) just E of Summit Lake Campground.

Segment 8: From TR231 the trail continues N for 1.6mi to Hanging Rock [G], crossing FR99 [H] once. This section of trail is in good condition.

Segment 9: From Hanging Rock [G] the trail goes NW 2.6mi to its W terminus [B] on FR99, 0.6mi SE of the E terminus [A] of Barrenshe Trail (TR256) and 0.7mi SE of Briery Knob. This last stretch of Pocahontas Trail contains at least one logged area. Since FR99 is closed to private cars, one has two options:

(A) Walk 0.6mi N on FR99 to Barrenshe Trail (TR256) and walk another 4.5mi on TR256 to FR76 or,

(B) Walk S on FR99 for 0.7mi to an access road at the gate that has vehicle access to Richwood via FR99, CO76-1 and CO76, a total of 6.1mi.

SOUTH FORK TRAIL (TR243)   1.6mi(2.6km)
SCENERY: 1 (Exceptional)   NOTE: B,M,(0)
DIFFICULTY: I (Easy)   SKI: S3
CONDITION: A (good)   ELEV: 4440/3370
MAPS: USFS(A), Lobelia, II-A-8 in this Guide
SEGMENTS:

    (1) TR244 (Kennison Mtn. Trail) to TR253 (Cow Pasture Trail) 1.6mi
    South Fork Trail is a grassy old timber road.

Segment 1: Starting from the SW [K] descend to a switchback to the right at 0.6mi, and then to a switchback to the left. From here descend to Cranberry River Road (FR102) [H] at 1.6mi. Here it makes a juncture with Cow Pasture Trail (TR253). To the right, upstream, it is 0.2mi to a forest road gate, and another 0.9mi to Cranberry River Road parking lot at the Cranberry Glades Botanical Area.

KENNISON MOUNTAIN TRAIL (TR244)   9.7mi(15.5km)
SCENERY: 1 (exceptional)   NOTE: B,M,(1)
DIFFICULTY: II (moderate)   SKI-:   S3
CONDITION: B (average)   ELEV: 4440/2980
MAPS: USFS(A), Webster Springs SE, Lobelia, II-A-5, II-A-7 and II-A-8
       in this Guide
SEGMENTS:

    (1) TR263 (Pocahontas Trail) to WV39/WV150   1.0mi
    (2) WV39/150 to TR243 (South Fork Trail)   0.4mi
    (3) TR243 to TR235 (Frosty Gap Trail)   1.3mi
    (4) TR235 to FR76/TR272 (North Fork Trail)   7.0mi

Kennison Mountain Trail passes through the most beautiful spruce forest in the area. Along the way are clearings at the edge of the forest which allow excellent overlooks into the canyon of the South Fork of Cranberry

Footbridge over North Fork of Cherry River at the north trailhead of North
Bend Trail (TR225). Photo by Allen de Hart

River. Mostly the trail sticks to the ridge line, making a path that is essentially level. Some sections are overgrown. The few sections of uneven terrain are short and gradual. The most difficult stretch of the trail comes where the trail descends Kennison Mountain to Cranberry River. For over a mile the trail drops consistently and sharply from the summit to the S bank of Cranberry River. During prolonged dry spells no water is available along Kennison Mountain. Usually water can be found in seeps and rivulets alongside the trail. Tent sites are convenient on the ridge and along Cranberry River, including several good sites before one fords the river at the end of the trail.

Access: The S trailhead E (Map II-A-8) is atop Kennison Mountain along Pocahontas Trail (TR263) just S of Blue Knob and 2.5mi W of Cranberry Mountain Nature Center J (via TR263). A spur route of 0.7mi is SE of Blue Knob where it leaves TR263 to ascend NE of the mountain. It rejoins Kennison Mountain Trail 0.5mi W of WV39/150. A more convenient access point is D where Kennison Mtn. Trail crosses WV39/150, 2.0mi W of Cranberry Mountain Nature Center J .

At the N terminus T (Map II-A-5) one must ford Cranberry River to get to FR76. During low water the river is knee-deep here. In high water it would be impassable.

Segment 1: Starting from the S E (Map II-A-8), 0.2mi W of the spur trail, ascend the W side of Blue Knob. This portion of the trail is well-marked, although wet in some areas. Cross WV39/150 after 1.0mi D.

Segment 2: At 0.4mi N of WV39/150, the trail emerges into an old clear-cut and logging road network. Briars are sometimes a problem here, but the trail is blue-blazed and the tread is clear. To the right (N) is South Fork Trail (TR243) K that follows an old timber road.

Segment 3: Kennison Mountain Trail meets Frosty Gap Trail (TR235) after another 0.7mi. This junction B is marked with overhead signs hanging from trees. Frosty Gap Trail goes straight ahead, while Kennison Mountain Trail turns sharply right.

Segment 4: From Frosty Gap Trail B there is no difficulty in keeping on the blazed, clear trail N and NW along the top of Kennison Mountain to Cranberry River T (Map II-A-5).

FROSTY GAP TRAIL (TR235)   5.2mi(8.3km)
SCENERY: 2 (wooded)   NOTE: B,M,(2)
DIFFICULTY: II (moderate)   SKI-:   S1
CONDITION: A (good)   ELEV: 4400/3980
MAPS: USFS(A), Lobelia, II-A-7 & II-A-8 in this Guide
SEGMENTS: (1) TR244 (Kennison Mtn. Trail) to FR232   0.6mi
                 (2) FR232 to TR263 (Pocahontas Trail)   4.6mi

Most of the original Frosty Gap Trail has been replaced by Frosty Gap Road (FR731), a logging road constructed in the late 1980s. But a more scenic relocation near large rock formations is planned by the USFS from FR232 to the Frosty Gap area N of Left Branch. Meanwhile, nearly 4.0mi on FR731 serves as both a pleasant hiking trail and ski touring trail through hardwoods and conifers.

Access: The E access ⃞B (Map II-A-8) is from a knob on Kennison Mountain Trail (TR244). (A 1.0mi hike from WV39 on Kennison Mountain Trail (TR244) is necessary.)

A road access near the E end of Frosty Gap Trail is on Dogway Road (FR232) ⃞C from WV39.

Segment 1: Starting from the E ⃞B (Map II-A-8) on an easy descent, the original Frosty Gap Trail leads 0.6mi to a crossing ⃞C of Dogway Road (FR232).

Segment 2: From FR232 Frosty Gap Trail follows FR731 on the S side of the ridge for 2.0mi before turning N to cross two tributaries of Left Branch, and to a dead-end of FR731. Its last 0.5mi is on the original trail, which meets Pocahontas Trail (TR263) in a saddle ⃞J (Map II-A-7) between two knobs, both over 4,000ft in elevation.

CRANBERRY VOLKSWALK (No #.)   6.0mi(9.6km)

SCENERY: 1 (exceptional)   NOTE: M,(3)
DIFFICULTY: I (leisurely)   SKI-:   S1
CONDITION: A (good)   ELEV: 3640/3380
MAPS: USFS(A), Lobelia, II-A-8 in this Guide
SEGMENTS: (1) Nature Center to Cranberry Glades   2.4mi
                 (2) Cranberry Glades to Nature Center   3.6mi

In 1991 Gauley Ranger District opened the Cranberry Volkswalk, a series of interconnecting loop trails between Cranberry Mountain Nature Center and Cranberry Glades Botanical Area. The series also includes the 0.5mi boardwalk loop in the Glades. Through forests and flowering meadows, the loops are marked with plastic white diamonds to the Cranberry Glades, and by plastic white diamonds with black insets on the return route. A directional map is available at the Nature Center.

Access: To approach the trailhead, park at the Nature Center and walk to the NW corner of the intersection of WV39 and WV150 ⃞M.

Segment 1: Follow a wide trail in a forest of cherry, maple, hemlock and red spruce 0.4mi before turning right. Ferns in this area make a dense ground cover. At 0.7mi turn left, cross Charles Creek, and follow an old gravel road through the historic site of Millpoint Federal Prison (active from 1938 to 1959). After passing natural gardens of willows and crown vetch, reach FR102 at 1.5mi ⃞N. Turn right and follow FR102 to the parking area at Cranberry Glades Botanical Area (0.1mi N of ⃞L) at 2.4mi.

Segment 2: After a visit into Cranberry Glades on the boardwalk, the route returns S 0.1mi to Cow Pasture Trail (TR253) ⃞L. Turn left onto TR253 and go 0.5mi to where Cranberry Volkswalk Trail turns right, off of TR253, near a stream. The trail passes cascades in a forest of hemlock, ascends to a grassy meadow, and reaches FR102 ⃞O after another 0.9mi. From here the trail follows S along paved FR102 for 0.6mi to WV39 ⃞P. (A short-cut trail from ⃞P along the N side of WV39 returns to the trail's origin.) For the remaining 1.1mi, the trail crosses WV39 and proceeds SE to Pocahontas Trail (TR263) ⃞Q. Here it turns left onto Pocahontas Trail and returns to the Nature Center ⃞J.

COW PASTURE TRAIL (TR253)   5.5mi(8.8km)
SCENERY: 1 (exceptional)   NOTE:M,(4)
DIFFICULTY: II (moderate)   SKI-:S4
CONDITION: B (average)   ELEV:3520/3350
MAPS: USFS(A), Hillsboro, Lobelia, II-A-8 in this Guide
SEGMENTS: (1) FR102 to FR102   5.5mi

Cow Pasture Trail (formerly South Fork Trail) circles the Cranberry Glades. A well-marked and signed loop trail offers excellent views of the Glades and surrounding country. (No one is allowed into Cranberry Glades [other than on the boardwalk] without written permission due to the fragile character of the area.) Parts of the trail can be muddy during wet periods.

Access: The best place to start is at the gate [L] just off Cranberry Glades Road (FR102) at the S end of the Cranberry Glades. A parking area for this trail and for the Cranberry Glades boardwalk trail is 0.2mi N of this gate.

The NW terminus [H] is also along FR102, 0.2mi NW of the gate (shown on the topo map) across FR102, and 1.3mi NW of [L].

FORKS OF CRANBERRY TRAIL (TR245)   5.7mi(9.1km)
SCENERY: 1 (exceptional)   NOTE: B,M,(0)
DIFFICULTY: II (moderate)   SKI-:   S4
CONDITION: B (average)   ELEV: 4570/3160
MAPS: USFS(A), Lobelia, Hillsboro, Webster Springs SE, II-A-5, II-A-6,
      and II-A-8 in this Guide
SEGMENTS: (1) WV150 to Cranberry Glades overlook   0.2mi
          (2) Overlook to spring, rock outcrop   2.0mi
          (3) Spring to Elephant Rock   1.1mi
          (4) Elephant Rock to FR102 (Glades Road)   2.4mi

Forks of Cranberry Trail was once known as Black Mountain Trail. The Webster Springs SE topo shows the route. The first 2.5mi of this trail pass through an area that was burned practically to bare rock in the 1937 Black Mountain Fire. The trail is easy to follow.

Access: The E trailhead [G](Map II-A-8) is along the Highland Scenic Highway (WV150). A sign here says "Cranberry River 6." Five cars can park here.

The W trailhead [I] (Map II-A-5) is on FR102 along Cranberry River, 200yd upstream from the Forks of Cranberry [H]. This trailhead is also signed.

Segment 1: There is a fine view at the E trailhead [G](Map II-A-8) and another 0.5mi down the trail. Shortly after that is a spectacular view to the S, and an intriguing rock slide. However some off-trail bushwhacking is needed for these. Watch carefully to determine where to leave the trail.

Segment 2: At 0.3mi the trail enters a large field and takes an immediate right turn to leave the field. It is easy to enter the field and lose the trail here. Watch for rock piles (cairns). The mile of trail after the field is rocky and runs through young growth and burnt-out stumps from the 1937 fire. The area is also full of ferns, mosses, conifers, blackberries, blueberries, rhododendron, laurel and mushrooms. At 2.2mi is a seasonal spring (the headwater of Red Run) and a campsite large enough for a few tents.

Segment 3: At 3.3mi is Elephant Rocks [L](Map II-A-6) that can be climbed to obtain a view of the S fork of Cranberry Valley. The views are best when the leaves are off the trees. Unwary hikers might miss Elephant Rocks.

Segment 4: A spring (seasonal) [M] is 0.3mi beyond Elephant Rocks. The descent to FR102 is steep, a bit overgrown, not overly difficult, and has several switchbacks. Several campsites are along Cranberry River in the vicinity of the W trailhead. [I] (Map II-A-5) Two shelters, one downstream [H] and one upstream are on FR102 near this trailhead. It is an easy 4.2mi walk on FR102 to the lower parking lot of Cranberry Glades. (See Map II-A-8.) Along FR102 are many wildflowers, blackberries and large trees.

Pocahontas Trail (TR263). Photo by Allen de Hart

(II-B) NORTHERN CRANBERRY BACKCOUNTRY AND CRANBERRY WILDERNESS AREA

Trails described in this section II-B are within Cranberry Wilderness (mainly) or Cranberry Backcountry or both. They are accessed from Highland Scenic Highway (WV150) and FR86 (off WV150). WV150 forms the E border of Cranberry Wilderness, and FR86 forms the N border. Cranberry Backcountry is immediately SW of Cranberry Wilderness.

NORTH-SOUTH TRAIL (TR688)

15.1mi(24.2km)

SCENERY: 2 (wooded)   NOTE: B,M,(0)
DIFFICULTY: III (strenuous)   SKI-: S4
CONDITION: B (average)   ELEV: 4460/2530
MAPS: USFS(A), Woodrow, Webster Springs SE & SW, II-A-1, II-A-2,
       II-A-5, II-A-6 & IV-D-1 in this Guide
SEGMENTS:

- (1) TR271 (Middle Fork Trail) to TR272 (North Fork Trail)   0.4mi
- (2) TR272 to TR214 (Tumbling Rock Trail)   4.5mi
- (3) TR214 to TR267 (Laurelly Br.Tr.)/TR250 (Birch Log Trail)   2.9mi
- (4) TR267/TR250 to TR213 (Rough Run Trail)   0.9mi
- (5) TR213 to TR242 (Little Fork Trail)   0.5mi
- (6) TR242 to TR212 (Lick Branch Trail)   1.2mi
- (7) TR212 to Cranberry Campground/FR76   4.7mi

The name and number of North-South Trail is retained only on Gauley Ranger District where much of it was formerly called Red and Black Trail. Above the 4000-foot level the trail passes through thick stands of young spruce and hemlock carpeted with moss. At lower elevations hardwoods interspersed with hemlock take over. There are no views of note anywhere along the trail. Do not depend on finding water along the trail, although you will find seeps along it in wet weather. Water can be located a few hundred feet off the trail at the headwaters of some of the major streams. The trail is easy to follow.

Access: The W terminus [R](Map II-A-1) of the trail is at the locked gate on FR76 at Cranberry Campground.

The E terminus [A](Map IV-D-1) is off Highlands Scenic Highway (WV150), 0.3mi N of Little Spruce Overlook.

Segment 1: From a parking area on Highlands Scenic Highway (WV150), 0.3mi N of Little Spruce Overlook, enter a dense forest of red spruce. After 0.4mi arrive at an intersection with North Fork Trail (TR272) right and left on Old FR76. The North-South Trail continues ahead.

Segment 2: The North-South Trail follows the ridge dividing the watersheds of Cranberry River and Williams River. At 4.9mi W of Highland Scenic Highway is the junction [K](Map II-A-5) with Tumbling Rock Trail (TR214) which drops S off the ridge.

Segment 3: At 2.9mi farther, Laurelly Branch Trail (TR267) [L] comes up from the N and Birchlog Trail (TR250) [M] comes up from the S.

Segment 4: After another 0.9mi W of the junction with TR267 and TR250, Rough Run Trail (TR213) [O] comes up from the S.

Cranberry River near Tumbling Rock Trail (TR214). Photo by Allen de Hart

Segment 5: With an additional 0.5mi is the junction P with Little Fork Trail (TR242) coming up from the N.

Segment 6: Continuing W from TR242, the junction Q with Lick Branch Trail (TR212) is reached after another 1.2mi in a total of 10.4mi. Between the junctions of Little Fork Trail and Lick Branch Trail is an interesting large sandstone outcropping. Some large trees (some are birch) are scattered along it near the top of Lick Branch Trail. They were probably left over from the original virgin forest because they were unsuitable as lumber. About 0.5mi W of this last intersection there has been extensive "timber-stand improvements" where trees judged undesirable have been girdled, resulting in considerable undergrowth.

Segment 7: From the junction with Lick Branch Trail (TR212) the trail leads W, crosses FR272, and drops down to Cranberry Campground R (Map II-A-1) along FR76, 4.7mi from Lick Branch Trail (TR212). This is the W trailhead of North-South Trail at 15.1mi. Several campsites are evident on the ridge W of Lick Branch Trail.

COUNTY LINE TRAIL (TR206)   9.2mi(14.7km)

SCENERY: 2 (wooded)   NOTE: B,M,(2)
DIFFICULTY: III (strenuous)   SKI-:   S4
CONDITION: B-C (average-poor)   ELEV: 3960/2390
MAPS: USFS(A), Webster Springs SE, Bergoo, II-A-2, II-A-3 & IV-D-3
        in this Guide
SEGMENTS:
   (1) Three Forks/TR271 (Mid.Fork Tr.) to TR248 (Dist.Line Trail) 7.0mi
   (2) TR248 to FR86, Williams River   2.2mi

County Line Trail is an up-and-over route from Middle Fork of Williams River to Williams River. The trail is well blazed, little used, but easy to follow.

Access: The W terminus B (Map II-A-2) is near the trench barrier across Middle Fork Trail (TR271) at Three Forks parking area off FR86. Park outside the barrier. FR86 is in excellent condition.

Segment 1: Starting from the W B, the narrow trail climbs steeply (no switchbacks) for 1.2mi up the hill to the left as you face the trench barrier from the road side (facing SE). Look for blue blazes. After the climb to the ridge top, numerous flat spots offer good campsites. At 2.0mi, is an outcropping of large rocks to the left of the trail (facing E) which might also make a good site. Among these rocks are several large overhangs offering shelter, almost like caves. At 3.0mi and 3.8mi cross small streams. Along the ridge to District Line Trail (TR248) the trail climbs slowly but continuously over terrain that is often rocky and over-grown. The area is densely wooded with beautiful hardwood forest. (These woods have been unmolested since early in this century.) There are no views anywhere along this ridge, but you can hear the rapids of Williams River. Water is scarce in this segment.

Segment 2: At the junction I (Map II-A-3) with District Line Trail (TR248) at 7.0mi, all signs have been torn down or badly chewed by bears. Here County Line Trail turns N and makes a long descent to Williams River. The last 0.5mi of descent is steep, rocky, and slippery when wet. Exit the trail at FR86 along Williams River, just opposite the mouth of Lower Bannock Shoals Run J.

BIG BEECHY TRAIL (TR207)   5.4mi(8.7km)
SCENERY: 2 (wooded)   NOTE: B,M,(0)
DIFFICULTY: II (moderate)   SKI-:   S4
CONDITION: B (average)   ELEV: 4440/2620
MAPS: USFS(A), Webster Springs SE, II-A-2, II-A-3 & IV-D-1 in this
      Guide
SEGMENTS:
    (1) TR271 (Middle Fork Tr.) to TR248 (Dist. Line Trail)   4.5mi
    (2) TR248 to former TR688 (North-South Trail)   0.9mi
    Access: The W terminus [C](Map II-A-2) of Big Beechy Trail is on
Middle Fork Trail (TR271), just upstream from Big Beechy Run.
    Segment 1: From the W terminus [C], the trail angles uphill, away
from the Big Beechy Run creek bed, and climbs to the top of the ridge dividing the watersheds of Big Beechy Run and the Middle Fork. Except for one
portion 3/4 of the way to the top of the ridge, the trail does not follow any old
RR grades. Near the junction [H](Map II-A-3) with District Line Trail
(TR248) is a stand of large spruce, possibly virgin. Westbound hikers should
note that the trail does not drop abruptly from the ridgetop to the Big Beechy
streambed. (There are some impressive rhododendron thickets down there!)
Eastbound hikers should note that the trail climbs steadily except where it follows an abandoned RR grade for a short distance.
    Segment 2: The trail continues E beyond the junction [H] of District
Line Trail (TR248) 0.9mi to the former North-South Trail (TR688). [G](Map
IV-D-1) This section is mostly dense hemlock and has no views, water, or
level campsites. Backtrack.

LICK BRANCH TRAIL (TR212)   2.1mi(3.4km)
SCENERY: 1 (exceptional)   NOTE: B,M,(1)
DIFFICULTY: II (moderate)   SKI-:   S4
CONDITION: B (average)   ELEV: 3670/2610
MAPS: USFS(A), Webster Springs SW, II-A-4 & -5 in this Guide
SEGMENTS: (1) FR76 to TR688 (North-South Trail)   2.1mi
    The lower (W) section of Lick Branch Trail is particularly appealing,
with small waterfalls and cascades between moss-covered rocks, all shaded by
large hemlocks. The middle section follows a logging road seeded for game
food. The trail is well-marked but some parts are rocky.
    Access: The W terminus [C](Map II-A-4) of Lick Branch Trail is on
Cranberry River Road (FR76) just S of Lick Branch and 2.8mi upstream of
the lower gate at Cranberry Campground. The W terminus is signed.
    The E terminus [Q](Map II-A-5) at the junction with TR688 is 1.0mi
NW of the junction [P] of TR688 and Little Fork Trail (TR242). The E terminus is not signed.
    Segment 1: From the W terminus [C] (Map II-A-4), Lick Branch Trail
ascends E to the ridge line where it junctures with North-South Trail (TR688).
The trail's lower (W) section is steep (30% grade). At 0.6mi it joins, and
turns left onto, an old logging road.

ROUGH RUN TRAIL (TR213)   3.0mi(4.8km)

SCENERY: 1 (exceptional)   NOTE: B,M,(6)
DIFFICULTY: II (moderate)   SKI-: S4
CONDITION: B (average)   ELEV: 3680/2785
MAPS: USFS(A), Webster Springs SW, Webster Springs SE, II-A-5 in this
      Guide
SEGMENTS: (1) FR76 to TR688 (North-South Trail)   3.0mi

Rough Run Trail is interesting because of the variety of forest types it
passes through, including young hardwoods, rhododendron thickets, and a
dense stand of young hemlocks. You may discover the site of an old logging
camp. It follows an abandoned RR grade most of the way. It is marked with
standard USFS blaze and is easy to follow.

Access: The W terminus [R] is on Cranberry River Road (FR76) near
the bridge and S of Rough Run.

The E terminus [O] is on North-South Trail (TR688), 0.2mi W of the
junction [M] of TR688 and Birchlog Trail (TR250).

Segment 1: From the W terminus [R] Rough Run Trail ascends NE
along the S bank of Rough Run to the ridge line where it junctures with
North-South Trail (TR688). [O] The trail crosses many small feeder streams
and one major tributary. One good campsite (2 tents) is 0.3-0.4mi uphill from
the major tributary.

TUMBLING ROCK TRAIL (TR214)   2.5mi(4.0km)

SCENERY: 2 (wooded)   NOTE: B,H,M,(2)
DIFFICULTY: II (moderate)   SKI-: S3
CONDITION: A (good)   ELEV: 3880/3080
MAPS: USFS(A), Webster Springs SE, II-A-5 in this Guide
SEGMENTS: (1) FR76 to TR688 (North-South Trail)   2.5mi

Tumbling Rock Trail follows an old RR grade most of the way. Trailside scenery is a pleasing mixture of mixed hardwoods and conifers. The trail
is well-maintained and marked.

Access: The SW terminus [J] of this trail is Cranberry River Road
(FR76) 0.1mi E of Tumbling Rock Shelter.

Segment 1: From the SW terminus [J], Tumbling Rock Trail ascends
NE to the ridge line and junctures with North-South Trail (TR688) [K]. An
unmarked branch, forking off to the W not far from the SW terminus, leads
0.8mi to an abandoned mine where coal was obtained for logging trains in the
first quarter of the 20th century. It is easy to mistake the side trail to the
abandoned coal mine for the main trail. This side trail is 0.2mi N of the SW
terminus.

LITTLE FORK TRAIL (TR242)   3.5mi(5.6km)

SCENERY: 1 (exceptional)   NOTE: B,M,(2)
DIFFICULTY: II (moderate)   SKI-: S3
CONDITION: A (good)   ELEV: 3650/2390
MAPS: USFS(A), Webster Springs SE, Webster Springs SW, II-A-2,
      II-A-5 in this Guide
SEGMENTS:
(1) TR271 (Mid.Fork Tr.)/TR206 (County L.Tr.) to TR688 (N-S Tr.)   3.5mi

The central part of Little Fork Trail has a great deal of appeal. It parallels a large stream which tumbles down the mountain under a tight canopy of trees and laurel. The trail offers no views or obvious campsites. The S end of the trail is steep.

Access: The N trailhead B (Map II-A-2) is near the junction of Middle Fork Trail (TR271) and County Line Trail (TR206), across a hummock at the Three Forks parking area. The trailhead is signed. Numerous campsites are found in the vicinity.

The S terminus P (Map II-A-5), where it intersects North-South Trail (TR688), is in a dense grove of spruce.

Segment 1: Starting from the N B (Map II-A-2) Little Fork Trail begins as a narrow but obvious trail through high brush. Wade or rock-hop across Middle Fork. Blue blazes begin after the brush. Follow a low area before beginning the steep climb to the top of the ridge. North-bound hikers should watch for a spot where the old RR grade that the trail has been following continues on straight, while the trail turns right and drops steeply. The trail meets North-South Trail P (Map II-A-5) 0.5mi NW of the junction O with Big Rough Trail (TR213).

DISTRICT LINE TRAIL (TR248)   2.8mi(4.5km)
SCENERY: 2 (wooded)   NOTE: B,M,(0)
DIFFICULTY: II (moderate)   SKI-:   S2
CONDITION: A (good)   ELEV: 4420/3960
MAPS: USFS(A), Webster Springs SE, II-A-3 in this Guide
SEGMENTS:
(1) TR206 (County Line Trail) to TR207 (Big Beechy Trail)   2.8mi

District Line Trail climbs slowly over rough terrain through alternating hemlock and hardwood forests along the ridgetop dividing the main fork and Middle Fork of the Williams River. There are no views, no good campsites and no dependable water anywhere along this trail. The main feature to note is that almost every hilltop is capped with a spectacular hemlock forest growing from what appears to be a rocky bed of deep green moss. It is so thick, it is like a carpet and makes a great rest stop. Though well blazed, this trail is rough, rocky and overgrown.

Access: No car access.

Segment 1: Starting from the N I at County Line Trail (TR206), District Line Trail proceeds S through dense laurel and rhododendron thickets that grow completely across the trail. It is hard going for about 0.5mi before the underbrush subsides. Near its S terminus H with Big Beechy Trail (TR207), the trail is a fast path through a lovely spruce-hardwoods forest carpeted with dense ferns and moss.

BIRCH LOG TRAIL (TR250)   3.0mi(4.8km)
SCENERY: 2 (wooded)   NOTE: B,M,(3)
DIFFICULTY: II (moderate)   SKI-:   S4
CONDITION: A (good)   ELEV: 3760/3070
MAPS: USFS(A), Webster Springs SE, II-A-5 in this Guide
SEGMENTS: (1) FR76 to TR688 (North-South Trail)   3.0mi

Birch Log Trail follows an abandoned logging road used in making selective timber cuts in the late 1950s. This road apparently replaced the former route of the trail. It is well-marked and signed.

Access: The S end $\boxed{N}$ of this trail is along Cranberry River Road (FR76) 0.5mi W of the S end $\boxed{J}$ of Tumbling Rock Trail (TR214).

Segment 1: From Cranberry River Road, FR76, the trail ascends N to the ridge line where it intersects North-South Trail (TR688) $\boxed{M}$. One confusing point $\boxed{U}$ occurs 0.5mi N of FR76 where the trail turns uphill (right) at a side-valley of Birchlog Run. (Another unmarked trail continues up Birch Log Run.)

LAURELLY BRANCH TRAIL (TR267) 3.4mi(5.5km)

SCENERY: 2 (wooded) NOTE: B,M,(1)
DIFFICULTY: II (moderate) SKI-: S4
CONDITION: C (poor) ELEV: 3920/2830
MAPS: USFS(A), Webster Springs SE, II-A-2, II-A-5 in this Guide
SEGMENTS:
(1) TR271 (Middle Fork Trail) to TR688 (North-South Trail) 3.4mi

Laurelly Branch Trail serves as a vital connector between two long, popular, parallel trails (North-South Trail, TR688, and Middle Fork Trail, TR271). The trail offers nice views in spring and fall. A small, but nice, campsite is just above the last stream crossing near the top (S) end of the trail.

Access: The top (S) end $\boxed{L}$ (Map II-A-5) of the trail is signed.

The N trailhead $\boxed{D}$ (Map II-A-2) is on Middle Fork Trail (TR271), halfway between the mouth of Laurelly Branch and the mouth of Hell-for-Certain Branch.

Segment 1: A crossing of Middle Fork of the Williams River is required to get from TR271 to this trail from the N, but is normally a rock-hop if the water is low. Crossing would be dangerous or impossible during high water. The trail (an old RR grade) climbs continuously from the Middle Fork of the Williams River.

MIDDLE FORK TRAIL (TR271) 10.0mi(16.1km)

SCENERY: 1 (exeptional) NOTE: B,M,S,(8)
DIFFICULTY: II (moderate) SKI-: S4
CONDITION: A (good) ELEV: 4180/2390
MAPS: USFS(A), Webster Springs SE, Woodrow, II-A-2, II-A-3 & II-A-6
    in this Guide
SEGMENTS:
(1) TR688 (N-S Tr.) to TR267 (Laurelly Br. Trail) 6.2mi
(2) TR267 to TR207 (Big Beechy Trail) 1.3mi
(3) TR207 to TR242 (Little Fork Tr.)/Three Forks 2.5mi

Until the E part of Cranberry Backcountry received its Wilderness designation in 1983, this trail was a USFS road (FR108). It is now closed and has become sufficiently eroded along the Middle Fork of the Williams as to make it impassable for vehicles. This trail fords the river several times during its length and, except during high water, many of these fords can be made by careful rock-hopping. Wading should not be ruled out, so winter hikers

Hikers on North Fork Mountain Trail (TR501) north of Landis Trail (TR502). Photo by Allen de Hart

beware. There is abundant evidence of severe flooding all along this valley, so avoid this area during heavy rains or snow-melt periods.

Besides the pleasant views, the trail offers opportunities to enjoy small waterfalls, cascades, and boulder-strewn pools along the river. There are numerous deep swimming "tubs" worn in the rock slabs that frequently make up the bottom. The forests in this watershed are mostly hardwood and have been left untouched since the early 1900s.

Primitive campsites exist all along the trail and water is available everywhere. There are no steep grades or difficulties with staying on the trail. The mouths of the various runs draining into Middle Fork of the Williams River are marked by signs giving the names of the runs. So hikers with a topo can locate themselves.

Access: The E terminus [I] (Map II-A-6) of this trail is off TR272 1.2mi S of the barricade across old FR76 at WV150 (Highland Scenic Highway) (near [H]). This gate is a good place to leave your car. This short segment of former FR76 is now part of North Fork Trail (TR272).

The W trailhead [B](Map II-A-2) is at the Three Forks of the Williams River on FR86. A barrier crosses TR271 here. Outside the barrier are usually camping vehicles and tents. The W terminus of County Line Trail (TR206) and the N terminus of Little Fork Trail (TR242) are nearby. There is plenty of room for trailhead parking. FR86 is in excellent shape.

Segment 1: Starting from the E car access [H](Map II-A-6), follow North Fork Trail S for 1.2mi to the E terminus [I] of TR271. Chemically untreated signs usually mark this junction of TR272 and TR271. Leave TR272 here and follow TR271 downhill to the far upper reaches of the Middle Fork of Williams River. The remainder of the trail follows this stream.

Rock formations are found at Middle Fork Falls where Slick Rock Run enters the Middle Fork, and at the mouth of Sheets-Gordon Run Hollow. The junction with Laurelly Branch Trail (TR267) [D](Map II-A-2) is encountered 0.5mi NW of the mouth of Hell-for-Certain Branch.

Segment 2: The mouth of Big Beechy Run [C] where Big Beechy Trail (TR207) has its W terminus is scenic. Middle Fork has a waterfall, 8ft high, and a small swimming hole directly below it. A campsite is above and next to it. Other campsites are nearby.

Segment 3: The final 2.5mi to Three Forks of Williams River and FR86 are scenic and easy to follow.

NORTH FORK TRAIL (TR272)   8.9mi(14.2km)

SCENERY: 1 (exeptional)   NOTE: B,M,S,(4)
DIFFICULTY: II (moderate)   SKI-:   S2
CONDITION: A (good)   ELEV: 4470/3190
MAPS: USFS(A), Webster Springs SE, Woodrow, II-A-5 & II-A-6 in this
      Guide
SEGMENTS: (1) FR76/102 to WV150   8.9mi

North Fork of Cranberry River Road (FR76) was closed to motor vehicle access when the Cranberry Wilderness was established in January, 1983. A 6.5mi portion of FR76 within the Wilderness (from the intersection of FR76 and FR102 to the trail's connection with North-South Trail (TR688)) was renamed North Fork Trail (TR272). Its character and scenic attributes are changing from that of a maintained USFS road to one of forest encroachment.

A major feature of the trail is its potential for forming loop routes using trails between North-South Trail on the ridge line and FR76, which parallels Cranberry River. Shelters along the river and FR76 (both of which are outside the Wilderness) add to the options of where to camp. Note that FR76, shelter sites (Tumbling Rocks [J], Houselog, Dogway [V], Pheasant Hollow [S], and Queer Branch) and connecting trails (TR214 [J], TR250 [N], TR244 [T], TR231 [S], TR213 [R], TR212 [C](Map II-A-4) and TR688 [R](Map II-A-1)) are shown on Maps II-A-5, II-A-4 and II-A-1. Water, campsites and swimming holes are common along the trail.

Access: The E trailhead [J] (Map II-A-6) is off Highlands Scenic Highway (WV150) at a parking area with a registration box.

The W trailhead [H] is at the confluence of Cranberry River and North Fork where FR76 and FR102 meet. The nearest access to this point is at the Cranberry Glades parking area, 4.3mi upstream on FR102. Downstream on FR76 it is 11mi to Cranberry Campground [R]. Motor vehicle traffic (except by USFS personnel) is prohibited on both FR102 and FR76.

Segment 1: From the parking area off Highlands Scenic Highway (WV150) follow through a low gap and follow old FR76 (former North-South Trail, TR688) mainly through a spruce forest. At 1.2mi pass a juncture, right, with Middle Fork Trail (TR271). Continue S for another 1.2mi on old FR76 among seedlings and new-growth spruce. At 2.4mi arrive at an intersection with North-South Trail (TR688) right and left. (To the left, North-South Trail goes 0.4mi to its E terminus at a parking area on Highlands Scenic Highway, 0.3mi N of Little Spruce Overlook).

Segment 2: Starting from the E at North-South Trail, the trail crosses Left Fork at 2.5mi and North Fork at 4.4mi. Young red spruce form a dense border along the trail at higher elevations, and young oak, maple, and birch are more prominent besides the cascading stream in lower elevations. White snakeroot, ferns, and mosses are found in frequent patches. Campsites are more desirable along the last mile of the trail. At 8.9mi reach FR102.

(II-C) WILLIAMS RIVER AREA

Twin Branch Trail (TR205) and Turkey Mountain Trail (TR209) (described in the previous edition of this guide) have been abandoned for lack of maintenance, blazing and usage.

(II-D) BISHOP KNOB AREA

Bishop Knob Recreation Area is 12mi N of Richwood (on CO76, FR76, and FR81), and 3mi S of Dyer (on FR101). High on Cranberry Ridge, it has the district's largest developed campground. There are two camping loops with 49 individual sites and six double sites. The campground area is an ideal base camp for fishing, kayaking and rafting in the Gauley and Cranberry rivers. Other outdoor activities in the area are hunting, hiking, biking and cross-country skiing. Nearby are scenic Red Oak Knob (el. 3707ft), Woodbine Picnic area, Big Rock Campground, Cranberry Campground, and Glade Run Pond. Trails in the area have low traffic volume, and there are logging roads available for exploring.

HINKLE BRANCH TRAIL (TR219)   1.2mi(1.9km)

SCENERY: 1 (exceptional)   NOTE: B (1)
DIFFICULTY: II (moderate)   SKI-:   S4
CONDITION: B (average)   ELEV: 2560/2080
MAPS: USFS(A), Camden-on-Gauley
SEGMENTS: (1) CO7 to Cranberry River   1.2mi

Hinkle Branch Trail is on the S slope of Perry Ridge, 2.0mi NW of Big Rock Camping Area. The trail is a delightful walk among virgin hemlocks along a creek typical of the Cranberry region. The stream has several small rapids. A profusion of lower-elevation wildflowers carpets the forest floor from early April until late October. Primitive camping is available at several spots off the trail. Along the trail itself there is not enough cleared ground until Cranberry River. Hinkle Branch should not be considered safe to drink.

Access: To get to the C07 terminus from Big Rock, proceed 0.7mi NW on FR81, a gravelled, well-graded dirt road, to a junction with CO7 from the left. The trailhead for TR219 lies 1.2mi along CO7; CO7 is not identified as such on the USFS sign placed opposite the beginning of the road. The sign states: "Coe- 4 mi." and "Camden- 7 mi.".

CRANBERRY RIDGE TRAIL (TR223)   5.8mi(9.3km)

SCENERY: 2 (wooded)   NOTE: B,H,M,(2)
DIFFICULTY: II (moderate)   SKI-:   S2
CONDITION: B (average)   ELEV: 3100/2700
MAPS: USFS(A), Camden-on-Gauley, Webster Springs SW, II-A-1 in this
     Guide
SEGMENTS: (1) CO7 to FR81   2.0mi
              (2) FR81 to FR81 near Bishop Knob Campground   3.8mi

Segment 1: Cranberry Ridge Trail begins on CO7 near the top of the ridge between the Cranberry- and Williams River drainages. It goes through the head of Hinkle Branch, and crosses FR81 (2.0mi N of Big Rock Campground) at 1.9mi. (Not shown on Map II-A-1.)

Segment 2: After crossing FR81, the trail crosses a ridge and descends to cross Glade Run below the dam of Glade Run Pond. At the E edge of the pond it turns N at 3.3mi. At 5.0mi it joins Bishop Knob Trail, turns left and runs jointly for 0.6mi. It turns left again and ends at FR81, opposite the road from Adkins Rockhouse Trail (TR228) [B].

BISHOP KNOB TRAIL (NO #)   2.5mi(4.2km)

SCENERY: 2 (wooded)   NOTE: B,M,(1)
DIFFICULTY: I (easy)   SKI-:   S1
CONDITION: A (good)   ELEV: 3120/3000
MAPS: USFS(A), Webster Springs SW, II-A-4 in this Guide
SEGMENTS: (1) Loop from Campground entrance   2.5mi

Bishop Knob Trail, completed in 1992, is a loop around the Bishop Knob Campground. It stays completely on Cranberry Ridge, and extends to the ridge edge only on the SE where the ridge base is at the Cranberry River. The trail is well-maintained, follows a generally level contour, passes between two campground ponds, and serves as a connector trail to Adkins Rockhouse

Trail (TR228) and Cranberry Ridge Trail (TR223). The forest is all hard-wood with scattered conifers, ferns and wildflowers throughout.

Access: From FR101 and the campground gates, the trail crosses the entrance road E and W.

Segment 1: If following the trail W, it goes between two small ponds, and after 0.3mi, meets Cranberry Ridge Trail (TR223), where it runs jointly for 0.6mi. It then turns NE to make a horseshoe bend on Cranberry Ridge before returning to the campground entrance road.

ADKINS ROCKHOUSE TRAIL (TR228)   2.1mi(3.4km)

SCENERY: 2 (wooded)   NOTE: B,M,(1)
DIFFICULTY: II (moderate)   SKI-:   S2
CONDITION: B (average)   ELEV: 3060/2120
MAPS: USFS(A), Camden-On-Gauley, II-A-1 in this Guide
SEGMENTS: (1) FR81 to FR234   2.1mi

Adkins Rockhouse Trail is paint-blazed. It is on the NE side of Adkins Rockhouse Run. The trail follows an old RR grade for most of its length.

Access: To get to the SE trailhead, drive to the intersection of FR81 and FR101 [D] and then SW along FR81 for 0.3mi to Bishop Knob Black Cherry Seed Orchard. Follow the fence around the S side of the orchard to where it turns NW. A sign marking the SE trailhead can be seen at the S edge of the orchard.

The W terminus [F] is on Gauley River Road (FR234).

Segment 1: Starting from FR81 [B], Adkins Rockhouse Trail crosses a logging road at 0.6mi and, later, several RR grades.

BARRENSHE TRAIL (TR256)   4.5mi(7.2km)

SCENERY: 2 (wooded)   NOTE: B,M,(0)
DIFFICULTY: II (moderate)   SKI-:   S4
CONDITION: C (poor)   ELEV: 3780/2100
MAPS: USFS(A), Camden-On-Gauley, Webster Springs SW, II-A-4 in this
        Guide
SEGMENTS: (1) FR76 to FR99 (near TR263 (Pocahontas Trail)   4.5mi

Barrenshe Trail is useful for backpackers wanting to use Pocahontas Trail (TR263) and as a W trailhead accessible by car. The trail is blue-blazed. Some hikers get sidetracked onto (abandoned) Bee Run Trail which leads, via Cranberry River Road, to the W terminus of TR256.

Access: The W end of Barrenshe Trail is on Cranberry River Road (FR76), 1.0mi S of Woodbine Picnic Area. (Not shown on Map II-A-4)

The E trailhead [A] is on FR99, 1.0mi outside the W boundary of Cran-berry Backcountry and 0.6mi N of the W terminus of Pocahontas Trail (TR263) [B].

North Fork of the South Branch of the Potomac River near Seneca Rocks.
Photo by Allen de Hart

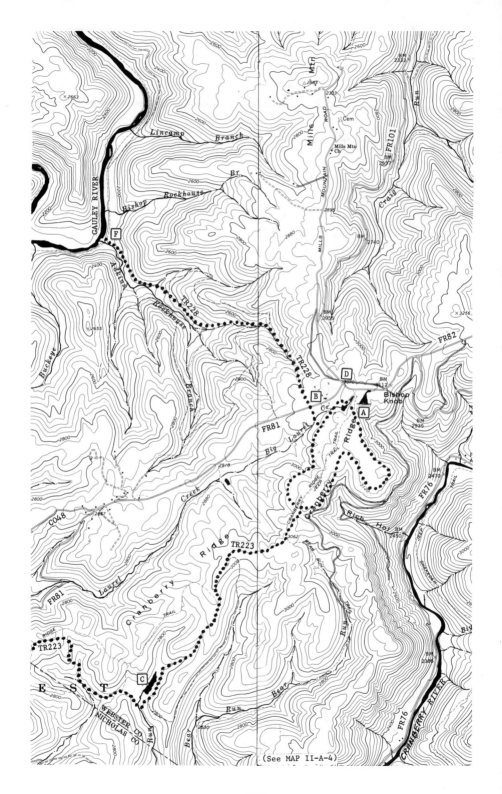

(See MAP II-A-4)

144

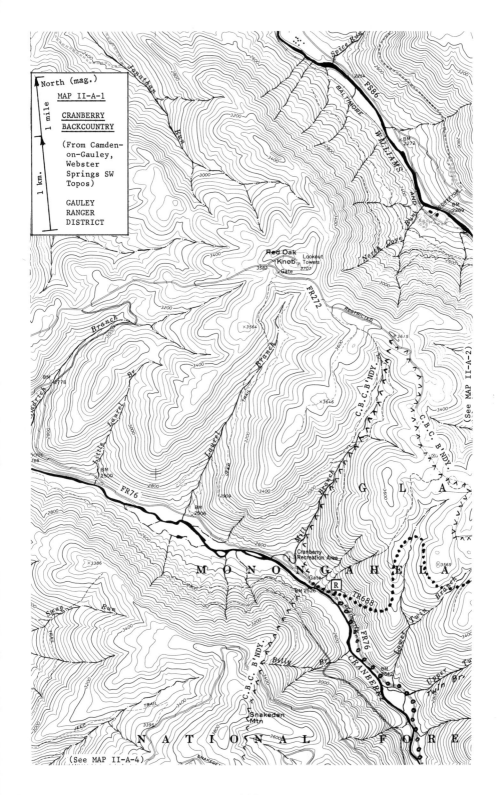

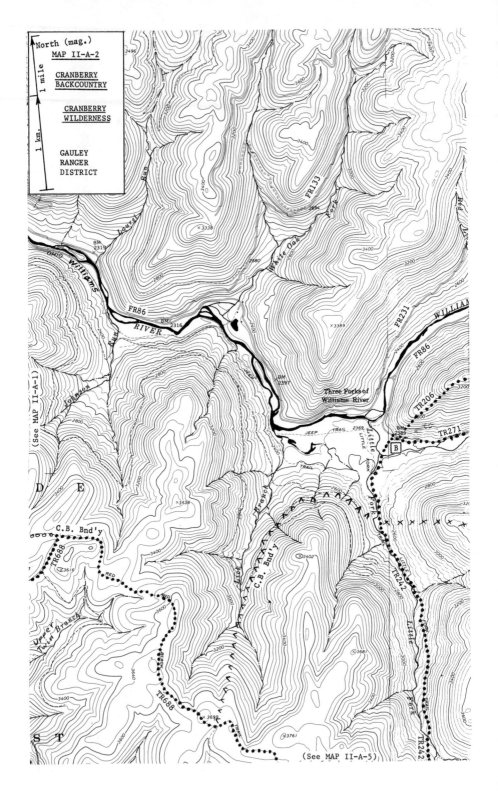

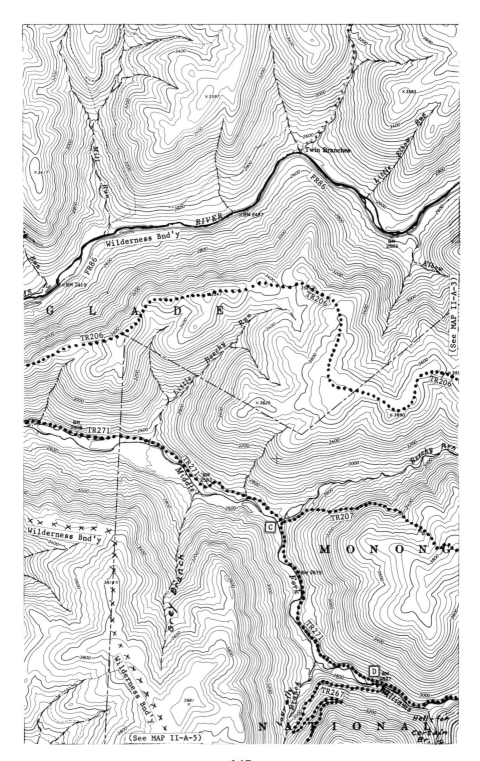

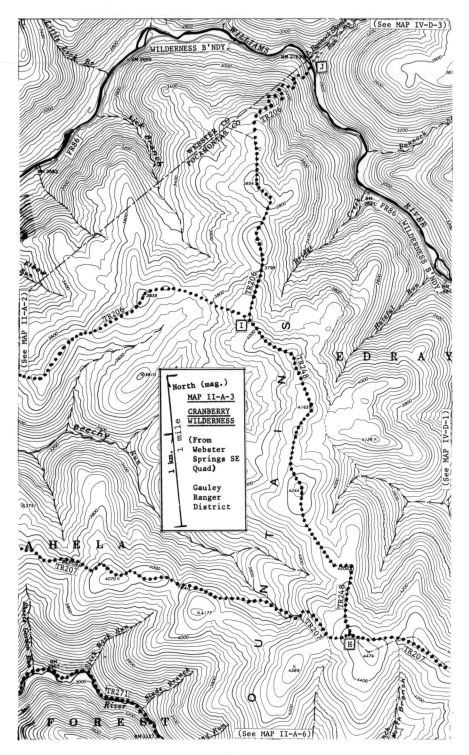

Overlook at Bear Rocks (looking east) in Dolly Sods Scenic Area.
Photo by Steve Swingenstein and Dee Ashliman

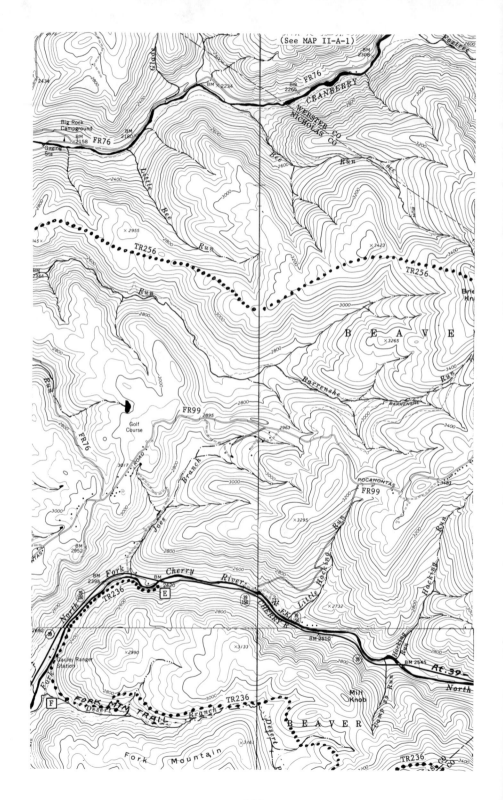

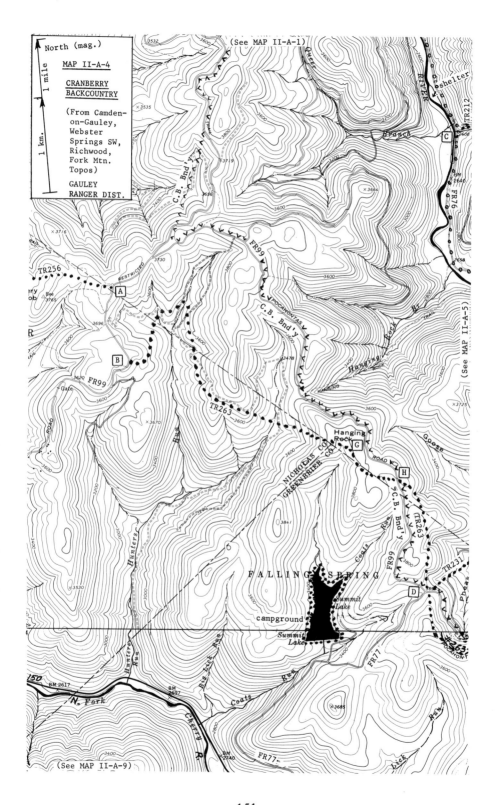

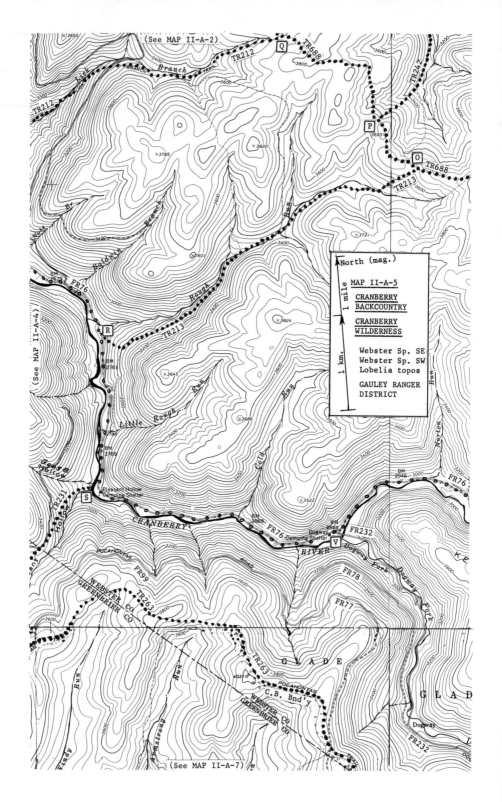

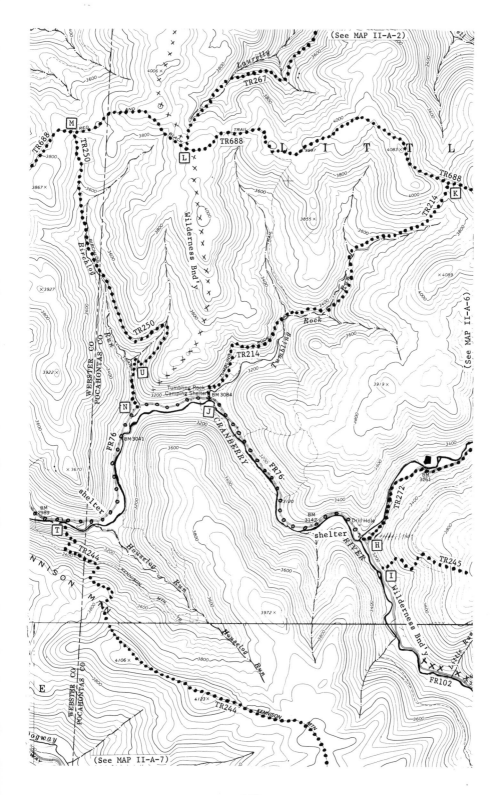

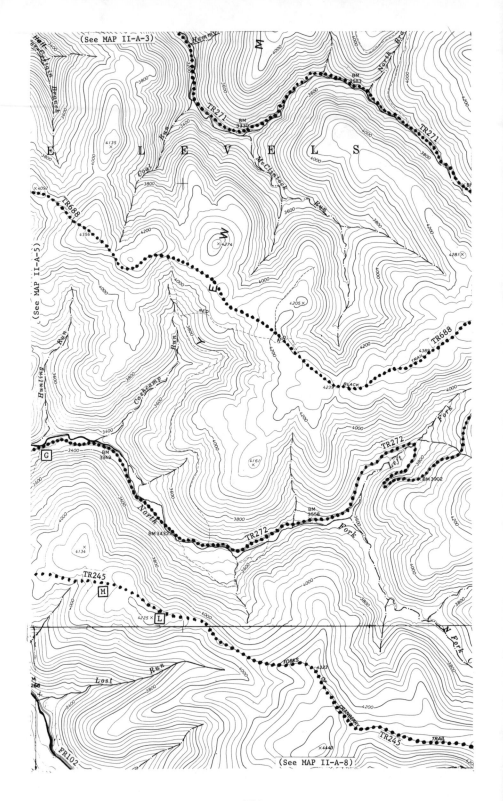

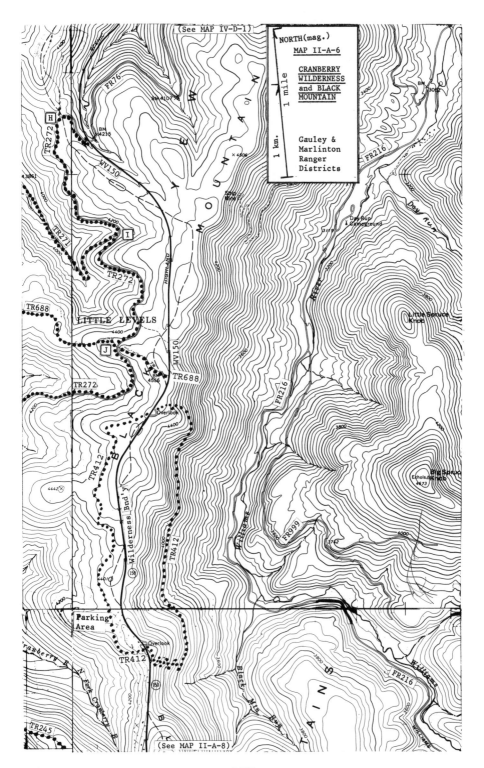

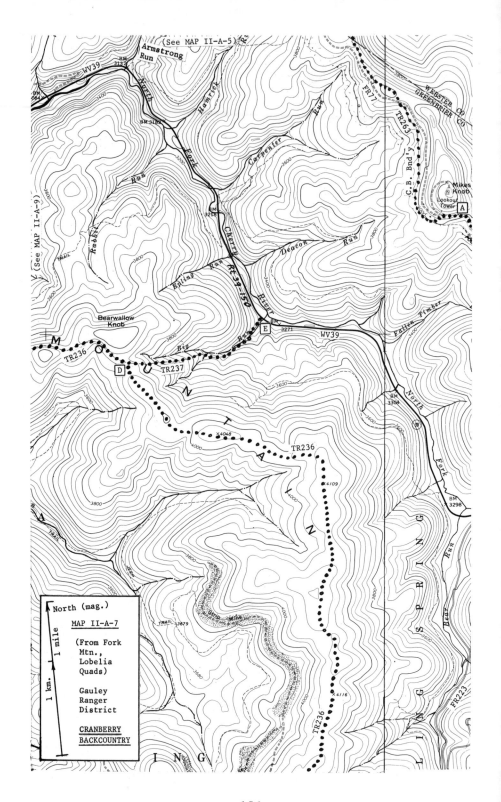

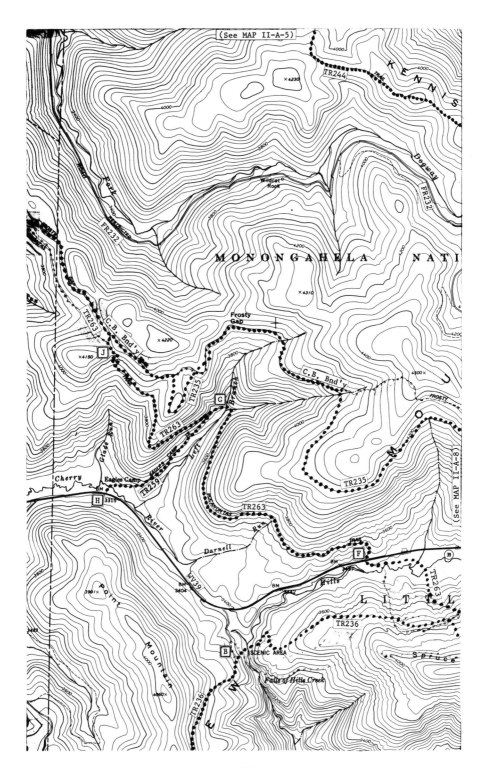

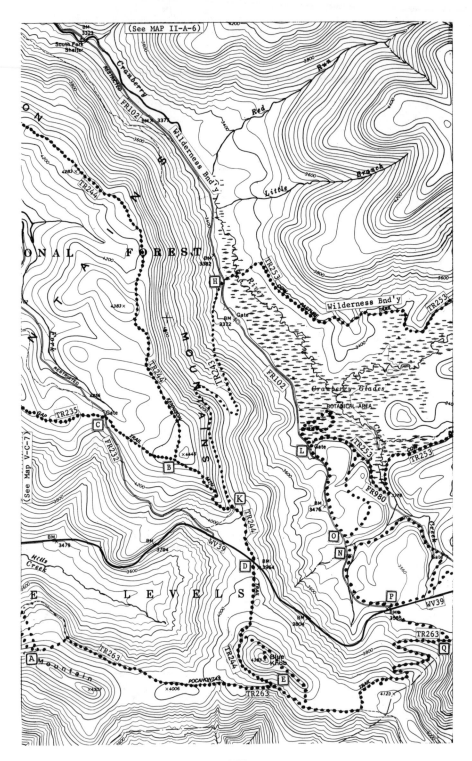

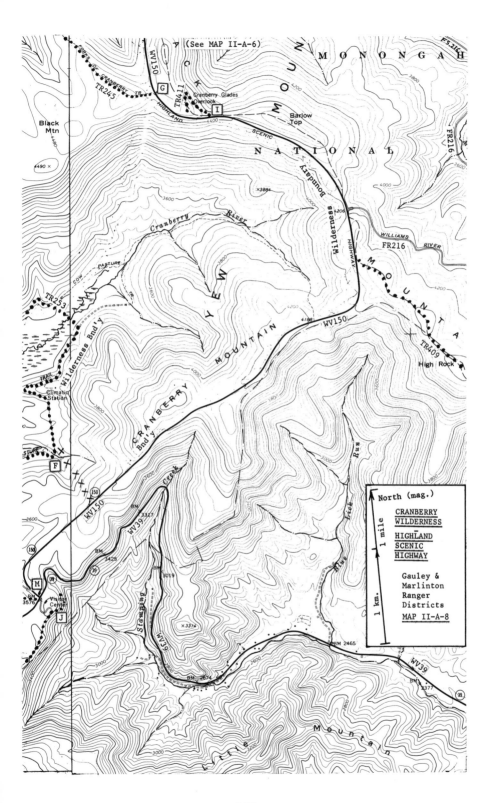

(See MAP II-A-6)

CRANBERRY
WILDERNESS

HIGHLAND
SCENIC
HIGHWAY

Gauley &
Marlinton
Ranger
Districts
MAP II-A-8

North (mag.)

159

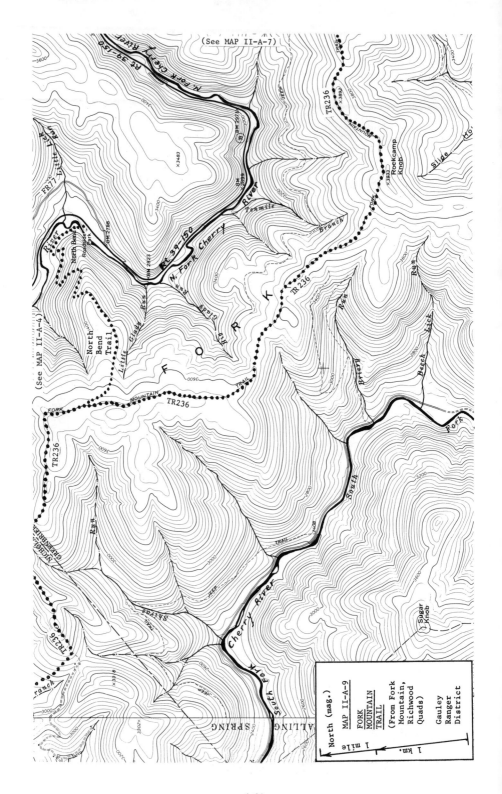

(See MAP II-A-7)

MAP II-A-9

FORK
MOUNTAIN
TRAIL

(From Fork
Mountain,
Richwood
Quads)

Gauley
Ranger
District

North (mag.)

1 mile

1 Km.

Cabin Mountain/Raven-Ridge Area in northern Dolly Sods. Photo by Steve Swingenstein

GREENBRIER RANGER DISTRICT

Greenbrier Ranger District is in the north-central portion of the MNF, immediately SW of Potomac Ranger District. The area is drained by Shavers Fork, Dry Fork, Laurel Fork and Glady Fork, all of which drain N into the Cheat. Being such a source of headwaters, the area is frequently called "the birthplace of rivers". A long, privately-owned strip of land along the Dry Fork River and Rich Mountain separates the Spruce Knob Area of Potomac Ranger District from the Middle Mountain area of Greenbrier Ranger District. The Shavers Fork area extends from US250 N almost to Bemis along the Shavers Fork drainage. In a N-S parallel to that is Middle Mountain which extends from US250 N to US33. These areas, plus the 63.8sq.mi Mower Tract S of US250, may not be as well known as some of the sections of the Cheat and Potomac ranger districts, but hikers will find many remote trails of equal significance.

Weaving its way through the district is nearly 60mi of the Allegheny Trail. It follows some of the most secluded mountain ridges and crosses mountain streams void of human habitation. Wildlife and wildflowers are prominent throughout its route. Another long trail is the 25.5mi West Fork Trail, which mainly follows the West Fork of Greenbrier River. Other challenging and unmarked trails are in the North Laurel Fork and South Laurel Fork Wilderness Areas.

The district is known for the largest black bear breeding areas left in the state. Because black bears breed only in large roadless areas, Wildlife specialists and conservationists are concerned that the USFS and the West Virginia Department of Natural Resources may plan more roads near FR92, endangering the bear habitat.

A major district land acquisition was in 1986 when the U.S. Congress approved the purchase of the 63.8 sq.mi. Mower Tract. Formerly owned by Mower Lumber Company, the 40,827 acres (63.8sq.mi) were purchased by the USFS for $20,000,000. The tract is mainly on the Shavers and Cheat Mountain ranges in Randolph and Pocahontas counties. U.S. Senator Robert C. Byrd (D-WV) was influential in the purchase, and said the purchase "is a unique Wilderness Preserve, and it will be a valuable addition to our (Monongahela) National Forest."

The purchase was in three phases, beginning in July, 1987, and ending in March, 1988 (though the option was until 1994). There were two reservations on the deed: the first was for 31,000,000 board ft. of timber (of which nearly 27 million was spruce), all of which was harvested by the fall of 1988. (The USFS has agreed to not cut additional timber within the next 10 years.) The second reservation allows for deep coal mining until February, 2035.

The first phase of 23,941 acres (37.4sq.mi) extended from the Cheat Bridge area at US250 S to Cass Scenic Railroad State Park, NE of Snowshoe Ski Resort, and E on Back Allegheny Mountain toward highway CO1. The second phase, of which 3,300 acres were purchased in December, 1987, is W of Shavers Fork and S of US250; it includes Barton Knob (el.4434ft). The third phase included 13,586 acres purchased in March of 1988. This pristine location extends from W of Shavers Fork to the high ridgeline of Cheat Mountain, known for its high knobs such as Crouch (4,529ft), Snyder (4,700ft), Ward (4,545ft), Beech Flat (4,682ft), and Rocky (4,743ft).

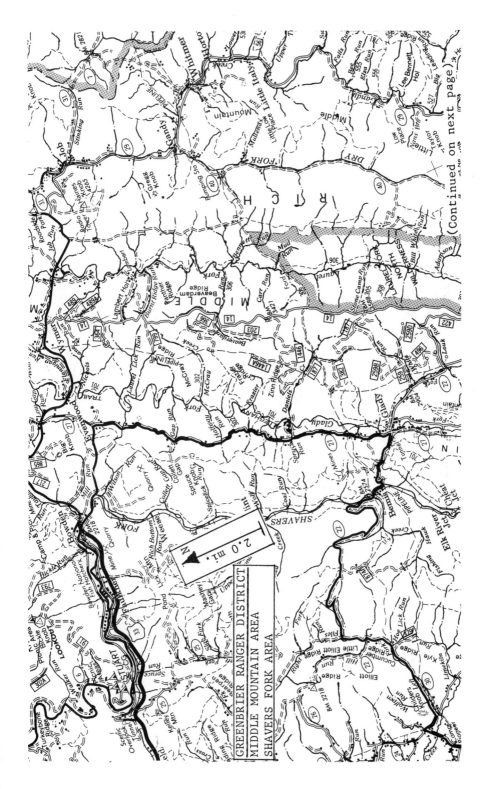

GREENBRIER RANGER DISTRICT
MIDDLE MOUNTAIN AREA
SHAVERS FORK AREA

N
2.0 mi.

(Continued on next page)

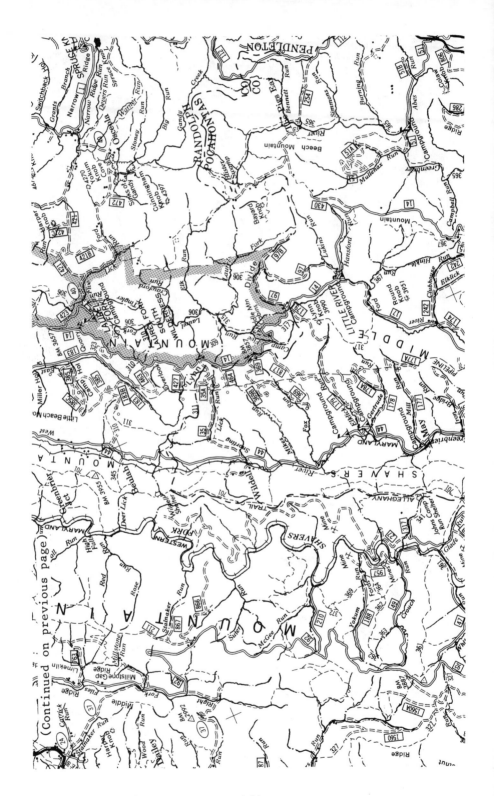

(Continued on previous Page)

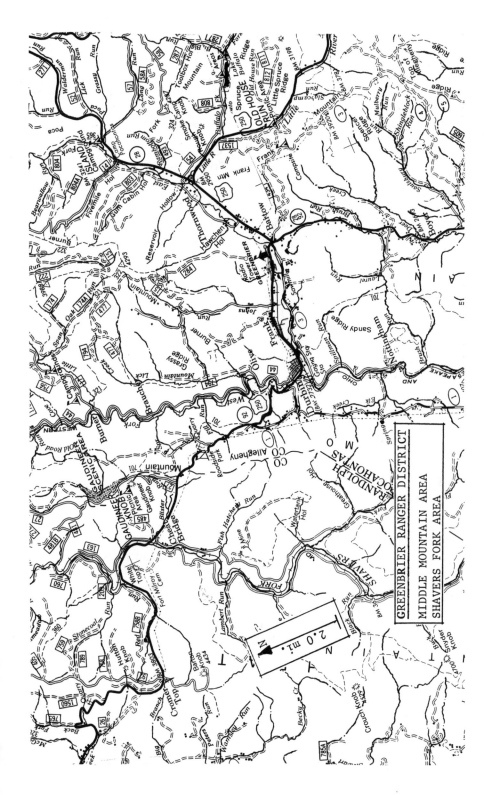

GREENBRIER RANGER DISTRICT

MIDDLE MOUNTAIN AREA

SHAVERS FORK AREA

Described as the Old Spruce Recreation Area, the USFS has begun to designate gated old roads for hiking, hunting, and other limited access recreation under semi-primitive and non-motorized use management. A detailed access map may be obtained from the district ranger's office, P.O. Box 67, Bartow, WV 24920, Tel. 304-456-3335.

Also in early 1986, another major land acquisition expanded the recreation opportunities for the district. This purchase was of the abandoned Western Maryland RR right-of-way from Cheat Junction on Shavers Fork E to Glady and S to Durbin. The right-of-way is now the non-motorized West Fork Trail, which for 18 of the 25.5mi, follows the West Fork of Greenbrier River, a scenic and popular trout stream.

Ski-Touring in Greenbrier Ranger District

Some USFS roads in the Greenbrier Ranger District are normally unplowed in winter and offer opportunities for ski-touring. These are:
Peters Mountain Area (III-A)
(none)
Middle Mountain Area (III-B)

- FR14	from 3mi S of Wymer S to FR17	16mi .
- FR17	from FR14 SW to FR44	6mi
- FR35	from FR14 W to FR44	4mi
- FR44	from FR17 N to FR35	7mi
- FR51	from WV28 NW to dead-end	4mi
- FR52	from WV28 E to FR106	2.5mi
- FR54	from WV28 SE to FR106	5mi
- FR57	from WV28 SE to FR106	3mi
- FR106	from FR54 N to FR52	5mi

Shavers Fork Area (III-C)

- FR47	from FR92 E to Shavers Fork River	3mi
- FR92	from US150 N to CO37	12mi

- Old Spruce Recreation Area on Cheat Mountain S of US250 (Contact the District Ranger's office [address above] for details on roads.)

(III-A) PETERS MOUNTAIN AREA

The Peters Mountain area is the district's most southern; it borders Marlinton Ranger District. It is almost surrounded by streams--Deer Creek on the N, Moore Creek on the E, and Sitlington Creek on the S, all of which flow W to Greenbrier River. The interior area is roadless, with Peters Mountain Trail (TR359) following the ridgeline from WV28/92 to WV7 near Cass. Secluded and rarely visited hollows, named by pioneer settlers such as Kline, Smith, Clay and Campbell, have small, clear streams. In a hardwood forest, wildlife and wildflowers are prominent. One of the areas most unique characteristics is an unnamed peak (2,855ft) nearly encircled by Deer Creek. The peak can be seen from WV7 from a rocky bluff, and from Peters Mountain Trail in winter. Although camping is convenient on the trail route, the nearest developed campground is Whittaker Camping Area, 2mi SW of Cass.

Other nearby features are Seneca State Forest to the S, the National Radio Astronomy Observatory to the NE, Cass Scenic Railroad State Park to the NW, and Greenbrier River Trail to the W. Also, Allegheny Trail passes through this area.

LITTLE MOUNTAIN TRAIL (TR332)   2.5mi(4.0km)

SCENERY: 2 (wooded)   NOTE: B
DIFFICULTY: II (moderate)   SKI-:   S4
CONDITION: B (average)   ELEV: 3200/2556
MAPS: USFS(A), Cass, III-A-3 in this guide
SEGMENTS: (1) WV7 to TR701 (Allegheny Trail)   2.5mi

This trail is part of an old jeep road that ascends the ridge of Little Mountain and descends to a residential road near Greenbrier River. The part that was on private land has been changed to provide a route to the Allegheny Trail completely on national forest property.

Access: From Cass drive E on WV7 3.0mi to a small parking space on the S side of WV7 near Deer Creek. If accessing from the E, turn off WV28/92 on WV7 and drive 2.3mi to the parking space P on the S side of the road. There is a trail sign on the N side of the highway.

Segment 1: From the trail sign ascend 45yd and turn left. Ascend gradually on an old, narrow path for 0.8mi to a streamlet S that may be dry in summer. Twenty feet beyond, turn sharply right off of the old road and ascend in a rocky area. Blazes may be infrequent. At 1.2mi reach the top of Little Mountain Ridge in a hardwood forest. Make a sharp right turn and begin a descent at 1.6mi. Undulate for the next 0.4mi, and, at 2.0mi, begin a steep descent on switchbacks into a hollow. At 2.5mi intersect Allegheny Trail A, right and left, in a dense grove of hemlocks and rhododendron. Backtrack, or follow Allegheny Trail left 3.0mi to the bridge over the Greenbrier River in Cass.

HOSTERMAN TRAIL (TR337)   5.2mi(8.3km)

SCENERY: 2 (wooded)   NOTE: B
DIFFICULTY: I (easy)   SKI-:   S2
CONDITION: A (good)   ELEV: 2960/2565
MAPS: USFS(A), Green Bank, Map III-A-2 in this guide
SEGMENTS: (1) CO-1/24 to TR701 (Allegheny Trail)   2.6mi
                (2) TR701 to CO-1/24   2.6mi

This trail follows Hosterman Road that is now closed to vehicular traffic. Although passage on foot is permitted with permission from the National Radio Astronomy Observatory, the description here is confined to property within the MNF as a backtracking route. It is a popular trail with hunters, and Greenbrier River, over which the trail crosses, is popular with fishermen. Rosebay rhododendron are colorful in late June.

Access: To get to the N trailhead from Durbin, go W on US250. Cross the bridge and turn left onto Grant Vanderventer Road (CO250/11). After 1.0mi turn left onto Back Mountain Road (CO1). Go 6.8mi and turn left onto Hosterman Road (CO1/24). Descend 1.2mi, turn right, cross old RR ties and through a rutted meadow for 0.2mi to the bank of Greenbrier River on your left. Another approach is from Cass off WV7 on CO1 for 6.2mi to Hosterman Road on your right.

Segment 1: Starting from the N, walk across the 69yd swinging footbridge. The high bridge was built to be above all flood water levels, but in 1996 a flood rose to the top of the guard rails. After following a rocky path through dense rhododendron and hemlock, exit onto an old and wide road at 0.3mi. Turn left. (There may not be any blue blazes on this trail.)

Ascend a gentle grade among a mixture of hardwoods and evergreens. The road is in generally good condition. It is spacious enough for a feeling of botanical garden-like atmosphere. There are plenty of songbirds, wildflowers, and wildlife sch as fox, deer, and owls. Sounds of ther Greenbrier River can be heard at 1.3mi. At 1.8mi is an open field. Cross a washed-out culvert rocky stream at 1.9mi. Ascend to a junction [B] with Allegheny Trail (TR701), right and ahead, at 2.6mi. After 60yd the trail ends at gated Slavin Hollow Road (boundary of National Radio Astronomy Observatory).

Segment 2: Backtrack. If you plan to hike Allegheny Trail, it is 10mi N to Durbin, and 7.2mi S to Cass.

PETERS MOUNTAIN TRAIL (TR359)   5.5mi(8.8km)

SCENERY: 1 (exceptional)   NOTE: B (2)
DIFFICULTY: II (moderate)   SKI-: S4
CONDITION: B (average)   ELEV: 3180/2425
MAPS: USFS(A), Cass, Green Bank, Clover Lick, III-A-1 in this Guide
SEGMENTS: (1) WV28/92 to TR370 (Bar Ford Trail)2.7mi
          (2) TR370 to WV7   2.8mi

The trail is named for the mountain ridge it follows from Moore Run in the E to near the confluence of Deer Creek and Greenbrier River on the W. Exclusively on the ridge, the trail crosses water only at its descent to Deer Creek, where wading is necessary.

Access: The E terminus [A] on WV28/92 is 2.9mi N of Dunmore and 0.6mi S of the junction with WV7. Parking is on the E side of the highway. The W terminus [G] is 0.6mi E of the Greenbrier River bridge in Cass on WV7. Parking is difficult here.

Segment 1: Starting from the E [A], ascend on a blue-blazed trail, W of the highway. After reaching the crest of the ridge, follow W on mild undulations. Wildflowers are a major feature in the springtime. After 2.7mi the trail forks, where Bar Ford Trail (TR370) goes right [C]. (Bar Ford Trail is a 1.5mi appendage trail from Peters Mountain Trail to WV7. It descends to Clay Hollow, follows Deer Creek briefly before crossing it [D] for a steep climb on a rocky bluff to WV7. Deer Creek must be waded. Roadside parking is difficult and limited.)

Segment 2: At 5.4mi Peters Mountain Trail crosses Deer Creek, where wading is necessary, and ascends gently on an old, narrow road to a curve at WV7 [G].

ALLEGHENY TRAIL (TR701)   21.8mi(34.9km)

SCENERY: 1 (exceptional)   NOTE: B,M,S (8)
DIFFICULTY: III (strenuous)   SKI-: S4
CONDITION: A (good)   ELEV: 3478/2365
MAPS: USFS(A), Cass, Clover Lick, Durbin, Green Bank, III-A-1 in this Guide
SEGMENTS: (1) CO12 to WV7   3.5mi
          (2) WV7   to TR337 (Hosterman Trail) 7.2mi
          (3) TR337 to US250   11.1mi

This section of Allegheny Trail (TR701) is one of three described in Greenbrier Ranger District. From S to N it begins at Siglington and ends in

Durbin. It follows jointly with Greenbrier River Trail to Cass, after which it ascends to Little Mountain, descends to Laurel Run, ascends to Sandy Ridge and descends to East Fork of the Greenbrier River at Durbin. Along the way it follows 6.5mi of the old Little Mountain Trail (TR349). Because vehicle access is nonexistent on Little Mountain and in Laurel Run Gorge, there are frequent sightings of wildlife.

Access: The Sitlington Road (CO12) terminus is 3.1mi W of Dumore. The Durbin access is at the junction of US250 and River Road (CO250/2) near the historic RR depot. Durbin has stores, a restaurant, laundry, post office, and telephone. (See Marlinton and White Sulphur ranger districts for segments of Allegheny Trail further S.)

Segment 1: Proceed upstream on the old RR grade jointly with Greenbrier River Trail (a 75-mile multiple-use state park trail from Caldwell N to Cass) for 3.5mi to the historic RR town of Cass and WV7. Here is the train station of Cass Scenic Railroad State Park, with steam-powered trains to transport visitors to the top of Back Allegheny Mountain in an elevation climb of over 2100ft. Here also are stores, post office, and a developed campground.

Segment 2: Cross Greenbrier River Bridge on WV7, and immediately turn left onto a gravel road. Go upstream 1.5mi before entering the MNF at 5mi. After 1.0mi on an old RR grade, cross a small stream and follow it for 0.5mi before reaching the crest of Little Mountain at 7.4mi. On the ascent pass the N terminus of Little Mountain Trail (TR332), right, at 7.2mi. From here to the N end of Little Mountain, the trail undulates from saddles and knobs, on slopes, and drops 700ft in elevation to Laurel Run. On a scenic and pleasant ridge a few sections follow old logging roads and a 6.5mi section on the old Little Mountain Trail (TR349) from Slavin Hollow Gap to S of Brush Run. This accounts for occasionally seeing blue blazes with the Allegheny Trail's yellow blazes. Less than 1mi of the trail passes through the irregular and private W boundaries of the National Radio Astronomy Observatory (NRAO). Views of the NRAO and Deer Creek Valley with Green Bank and Arborville are outstanding. Campsites are more prominent for about 1.0mi under tall trees along Laurel Run. At 10.7mi cross gated Slavin Hollow-Hosterman Road. A few yd. before the gate is a junction with old Hosterman Road. (It is now Hosterman Trail [TR337] and descends to cross a swinging bridge over the Greenbrier River after 2.6mi.)

Segment 3: The trail begins to descend at 12mi and, after about 0.5mi, crosses Laurel Run. Campsites are found near the stream in a scenic area of tall trees. After leaving the stream, begin an ascent to Twin Knobs, the highest points (3425ft and 3478ft) on this section of trail at 13.9mi and 14.3mi. The trail leaves Little Mountain at 17.2mi to descend steeply to a crossing of Brush Run at 18.7mi. It then ascends to follow the E slope of Sandy Ridge before crossing Spillman Run at 19.8mi. After crossing a saddle in a ridge, the trail intersects River Road (CO250/2), crosses a bridge of the East Fork of Greenbrier River, and intersects US250 in Durbin.

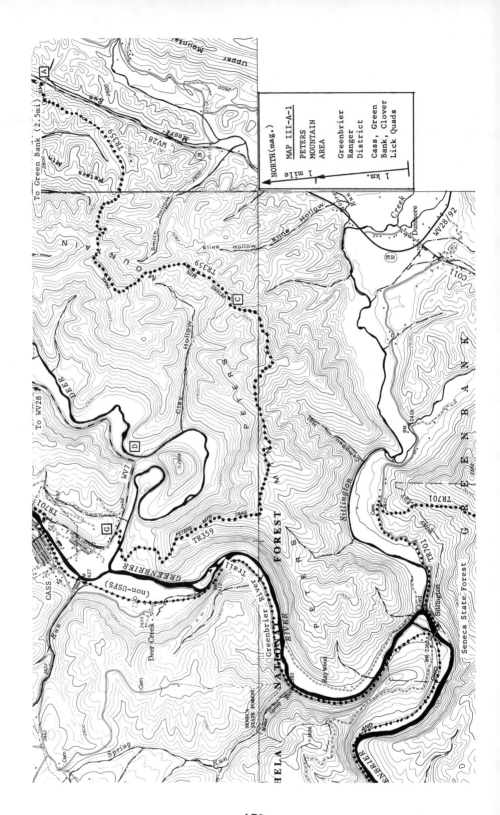

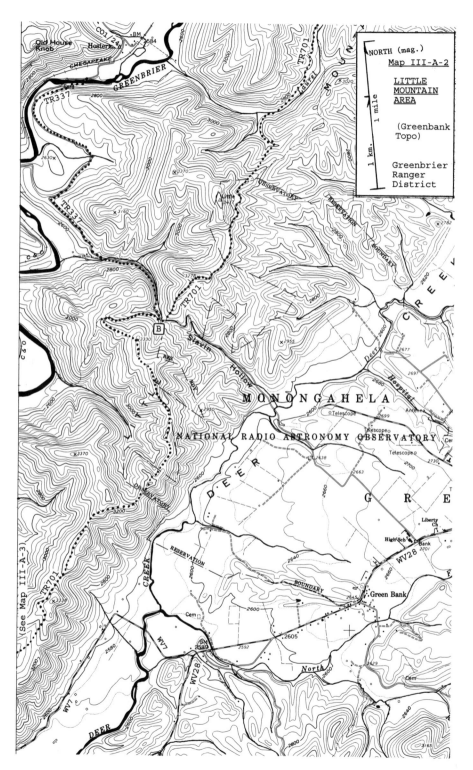

NORTH (mag.)

Map III-A-2

LITTLE
MOUNTAIN
AREA

(Greenbank
Topo)

Greenbrier
Ranger
District

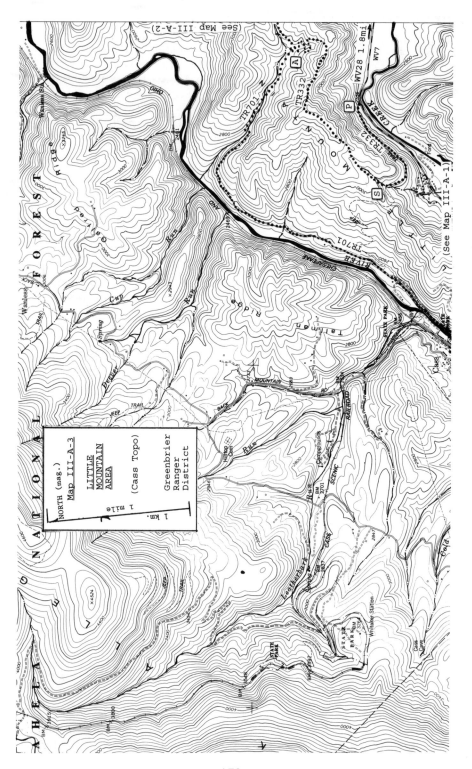

(III-B) MIDDLE MOUNTAIN AREA

The area has irregular terrain, with elevations ranging from nearly 4000ft at Lynn Knob to under 2800ft. The woods are largely intact second growth, with little evidence of recent logging operations. Many fishermen line the W fork of the Greenbrier in the summer, and hunters are numerous in the fall. Streams are generally paralleled by old RR grades which make excellent and attractive trails. Two Wilderness areas are located in this area-- the Laurel Fork North Wilderness and the Laurel Fork South Wilderness. (See TR306.)

The N portion of the area has many natural gas storage wells. These wells are not located along major trails, and the lines (swaths) connecting the wells are generally unobtrusive. Access roads to wells are, for the most part, closed to traffic. Some of these roads make excellent summer hikes because they are kept open by vehicular traffic. They offer excellent ski touring, although many are plowed for winter maintenance. Grades on roads are not excessive, but pipelines are steep in places. A wide variety of interesting routes are available.

Access Roads in the Middle Mountain Area:

- FR14 (Middle Mountain Road) goes from Wymer on US33 to Camp Pocahontas on WV28. It is a two-lane gravel road in good condition. Only the N 5-6 miles are plowed in winter.
- CO27 from Alpena on US33 to Glady is a two-lane asphalt road in good condition, but has many sharp curves. It is plowed in winter.
- FR44 from Glady S to Durbin is a two-lane gravel road in excellent condition. It is not plowed in winter.
- FR422 (Glady to FR14) and FR423 (FR14 to Laurel Fork Campground) are two-lane gravel roads in good condition. They are plowed. (Some old USFS maps show these two roads as FR1 and WV22.)
- FR35 between FR14 and FR44 is a two-lane dirt road in fair condition. It is passable by passenger cars, but has steep grades and sharp switchbacks.
- FR17 between FR14 and FR44 is a two-lane gravel road in good condition.
- FR15 from FR14 on Burner Mountain to US250 at Frank is a narrow dirt road with sharp curves and steep grades. It is one lane in most places and is poorly maintained.
- FR423/CO40 from Spruce Knob/Sinks of Gandy is a good two-lane gravel road over the FR423 portion (formerly FR1). CO40 is one-lane and primitive.

Camping

The only developed campground in the area is Laurel Fork. It is a typical USFS campground, with fire places, tables, a well, latrines, and 14 sites. In addition to the campground, plenty of open space is adjacent to the campground and across Laurel Fork. Just to the N of this campground is the Laurel Fork North Wilderness. Just to the S is the Laurel Fork South Wilderness. All blazes have been removed from trails in the Wilderness areas. Hikers should take topo maps or this guidebook with them when hiking. Some of the signs may be in the process of repair by the USFS.

A small, undeveloped, dispersed campsite area is at the junction of FR14 and FR17. Numerous single sites without facilities are seen all along all

USFS roads in the area. In summer, sites along FR44, though undeveloped, are over-run with fishermen, but other areas have plenty of space. For solitude try FR15, but water is scarce there. The map of Greenbrier Ranger District on pages 163-165 shows about ten campgrounds in the Middle Mountain area. (But they are actually undeveloped, dispersed campsite areas.)

McCRAY RUN TRAIL (TR302)

McCRAY RUN TRAIL (TR302)	4.7mi(7.6km)
SCENERY: 2 (wooded)	NOTE: B,M,W,(1)
DIFFICULTY: II (moderate)	SKI-: S2
CONDITION: A (good)	ELEV: 3010/2780

MAPS: USFS(A,B), Glady, III-B-1 in this Guide
SEGMENTS:
    (1) FR14/TR306 (Laurel River Trail) to TR701   3.4mi
    (2) TR701 (Allegheny Trail) to CO27   1.3mi

    McCray Run Trail is sometimes referred to as McCray Ridge and McCray Creek Trail. The trail provides access to Allegheny Trail (TR701) from FR14 and CO27. The middle section of McCray Run Trail has been moved from the N bank to the S bank of McCray Creek. The E end cuts S to Beaver Dam Run and joins FR14 there. On the W end (W of Glady Fork) the trail runs up the valley paralleling Halfway Run 0.4mi to the S. (The topo shows it running up a valley to the N of Halfway Run.) This trail is a combination of old roads, RR grades and foot trails. The section E of Glady Fork is suitable for ski touring. Do not drink from McCray Creek or Glady Fork without treatment.

    Access: To get to the E trailhead, drive 5.0mi S from Wymer on FR14. Begin at a gated side road [A] 100yd N of Beaver Dam Run.

    To get to the W trailhead on CO27, drive 5.1mi S from Alpena on CO27. The trailhead [H] (signed) is on the E side of CO27 on a sharp bend, 4.3mi N of Glady. There is parking for 4-6 cars.

    Segment 1: Starting at the E end [A], a USFS sign says: "McCray Run Trail, Glady Fork Trail 4mi, Glady-Alpena Road 5mi". Another sign says "Storage Well 7426". At 0.5mi beaver dams can usually be seen on the left, along Beaver Dam Run and its tributaries. At 1.1mi is the junction with an old road to the N. Turn right, off the road, and follow an old woods road. A sign reads "McCray Run Trail, Middle Mountain Road 1mi, Glady Fork 3mi, Glady-Alpena Road 4mi". A second sign points W along the main road to Atlantic Seaboard Corp. Well #7218. Walk N on the old road trace along the E bank of a small creek through rhododendrons. At 2.0mi reach McCray Creek [C]. Shortly before reaching the creek is a shortcut marked with arrows for reaching the trail heading W.

    Proceed W along McCray Creek for 0.5mi to a gas pipeline. From this pipeline you may see an abandoned trail near an old creek bed. The current trail runs along the S side of the creek. Turn left on the pipeline and walk 20yd to where the trail turns right (W). Follow this trail along the creek to Glady Fork [E]. The trail runs through fairly mature forest (hemlock predominantly) with lots of rhododendrons and ferns. In the Glady Fork junction area are a number of old RR grades. A few hundred yds. downstream along Glady Fork is at least one swimming hole.

    Segment 2: The trail picks up an old RR grade where it joins the Allegheny Trail (TR701), and proceeds upstream along the E bank of Glady

Fork. After 0.45mi leave TR701 and descend a steep bank to a ford ⬚F⬚ marked with arrows. The Glady here is 1-2ft deep and 20yd wide. It may be impassable in spring when it is deeper, wider and faster. Cross Glady Fork and follow along the W bank 0.5mi to a tributary coming in from the W. Follow this tributary W along its N bank. The W trailhead ⬚H⬚ along CO27 is 0.5mi from Glady Fork along this stream.

STONE CAMP RUN TRAIL (TR305)   1.5mi(2.4km)
SCENERY: 2 (wooded)   NOTE: B,M,(3)
DIFFICULTY: II (moderate)   SKI-:   S4
CONDITION: B (average)   ELEV: 3600/2950
MAPS: USFS(A), Glady, III-B-2 in this Guide
SEGMENTS: (1) FR14 to TR306 (Laurel River Trail)   1.5mi
   Stone Camp Run Trail connects FR14 with Laurel River Trail (TR306)(N). It descends 650ft through an open hardwood forest and a wet hollow to a wildflower meadow along the Laurel River. The trail is entirely within Laurel Fork North Wilderness.
   Access: The NW trailhead ⬚A⬚ is 9.3mi S of Wymer on FR14, 3mi N of the FR14 junction with FR1 (5mi N of Laurel Fork Campground). The FR14 trailhead (signed) has space for 6 cars.
   Segment 1: Starting from the NW ⬚A⬚, descend 0.3mi in a hardwood forest of exceptionally tall birch, beech, maple and cherry. In a deep hollow follow the trail on an old RR grade that weaves back and forth over Stone Camp Run. Black cohosh and ferns are prominent. On the approach to Laurel River, pass through a grassy meadow of asters and golden Alexander. Wade the Laurel Fork to get to the junction ⬚H⬚ with Laurel River Trail (TR306).

LAUREL RIVER TRAIL (TR306) (N)   9.6mi(15.4km)
   (N of Laurel Fork Campground)
SCENERY: 2 (wooded)   NOTE: B,M,S,(9)
DIFFICULTY: II (moderate)   SKI-:   S1
CONDITION: B (average)   ELEV: 3090/2820
MAPS: USFS(A), Glady, Sinks of Gandy, III-B-1, -B-2, -B-3 in this Guide
SEGMENTS:
   (1) Campground to TR307 (Middle Mtn. Trail)   1.6mi
   (2) TR307 to TR305 (Stone Camp Trail)   2.7mi
   (3) TR305 to FR14/TR302 (McCray Run Trail)   5.3mi
   Laurel River Trail follows close to the Laurel Fork, except for the N connection (Beaverdam Run) to Middle Mountain Road (FR14). (All former blue blazes have been removed.) The bulk of the trail runs through the Laurel Fork North Wilderness. It is a combination of old wood roads, an old RR grade, and foot paths. Many excellent camp sites are found along the trail. The area is quite undeveloped and should remain that way as a result of the Wilderness designation. Signs of beaver and deer are abundant and there are many small clearings. Except for the N connection (away from Laurel Fork) the trail offers excellent ski-touring. Water should not be drunk directly from the main stream. The forest is second-growth hardwoods (yellow birch, maple, beech, hemlock).

Greenbrier River Footbridge to Hosterman Trail (TR337).
Photo by Allen de Hart

Access: To get to the S trailhead drive 12.1mi S on FR14 from Wymer to CO40. The intersection [C](Map III-B-2) is marked with USFS signs pointing to Laurel Fork Campground. Drive E on CO40 1.4mi to Laurel Fork. There you should see a standard USFS trail sign with name and number on the N side of CO40 in front of the "Beaver Dam Wildlife Cooperative Management Area" ranger cabin on the W side of Laurel Fork. The trailhead is at Five Lick Run [D] (Map III-B-3), 0.4mi further E on CO40. The trailhead is on the N side of the road where posts in the ground block the old road which is the trail. A USFS sign says "Seeded to Game Food, Foot Travel Only". At the trailhead on Laurel Fork is unlimited parking, and the campground is adjacent. At Five Lick Run is adequate parking, several picnic tables, and camp sites adjacent to the trailhead.

To get to the N (FR14) trailhead by car drive S 5.1mi from Wymer on FR14. The trailhead [M](Map III-B-1) is 0.1mi S of the TR302 trailhead and 100yd S of Beaver Dam Run (signed). On the E side of FR14 is a sign "Laurel Fork Trail, Laurel Fork River 1.5mi, Osceola 11mi". Because of the narrow space here, park near the TR302 trailhead.

Segment 1: Starting from the S and the Five Lick Run trailhead [D] (Map III-B-3), follow the old road and, after 200yd, enter a field. Continue to follow the road, parallel to Laurel Fork on the E bank. Cross Five Lick shortly after the N end of the field. At the next small clearing the RR grade continues along the bed of Laurel Fork and the road bears off to the right. From here on there are two routes: the RR grade which generally stays at the level of Laurel Fork, and the road 200yd E and 50ft above the level of the RR grade. The road is easy walking, and is a reasonably pleasant trail. The RR grade is somewhat overgrown and washed out periodically. At 1.6mi is the junction [F] (Map III-B-2) with Middle Mountain Trail (TR307).

Segment 2: For the next 1.0mi follow the trail (road) NE. There are fine views to W of Middle Mountain and Laurel Fork. At 2.5mi cross Adamson Run (signed). Nearby is a large meadow with apple trees (excellent campsite). At 3.2 miles cross Bill White Run. Here the RR continues straight and the road bears slightly right and enters a small field. For the next 0.5mi note signs of beaver cuttings along Laurel Fork. It is somewhat swampy here due to beavers. At 3.7mi cross "Shine Run" (signed). About 75yd upstream of Shine Run is a large rock outcrop which could serve as a shelter. (The old topo shows a trail up Shine Run.)

At 4.3mi cross Three Bear Run (signed). Enter a field N of the stream. TR305 (Stone Camp Run Trail) [H] enters this field from the W. It leaves the field to the E.

Segment 3: For the next 0.7mi follow the road trail through a stand of hemlocks. At 5.0mi cross "Scale Lot Run" (signed). At 5.5mi cross "Stone Camp Run" (signed) (Note that there are two Stone Camp Runs in this area, both tributaries of Laurel Fork.) There are many beaver dams to the W along Laurel Fork at this point. For the next 1.0mi ascend gradually, passing through rhododendrons and laurel, to the trail crest. Descend gradually to a pipeline trace [J] at 6.6mi. For the next 0.2mi follow the road/trail along the pipeline trace. At 6.8mi cross Mud Run. Leave the pipeline and follow the road/trail down the right bank of Mud Run. There are excellent views from the pipeline trace to the E of Mud Run.

At 7.8mi enter a field where an old USFS sign reads "Middle Mtn. Road, 2 miles". The overgrown RR grade leaves the field to the NE. After

0.2mi cross Laurel Fork [L]. This could be difficult or impossible in spring runoffs. For the next 0.25mi follow the trail on the W bank of Laurel Fork through spruce, yellow birch, then turn sharply to the W, up the right side of a small creek [N] (Beaverdam Run). Several large boulders to the W of the trail mark this turn. The trail route is obvious. For the next 0.6mi the trail goes through a spruce forest. Keep steadily uphill along the creek, crossing two small tributaries. The last 0.5mi before reaching FR14 [M] (Map III-B-1) has excellent views of Laurel Fork Valley.

LAUREL RIVER TRAIL (TR306) (S)   7.6mi(12.2km)
(South of Laurel Fork Campground)

SCENERY: 1 (exceptional)   NOTE: B,M,S,(8)
DIFFICULTY: II (moderate)   SKI-:   S4
CONDITION: B (average)   ELEV: 3760/3100
MAPS: USFS(A), Sinks of Gandy, III-B-3 in this Guide
SEGMENTS: (1) Campground to TR323 (Forks Trail)0.6mi
                    (2) TR323 to TR310 (Beulah Trail)   0.9mi
                    (3) TR310 to TR315 (Camp Five Trail) 2.6mi
                    (4) TR315 to FR14   3.5mi

Laurel River Trail (S) is a major trail in the Middle Mountain area. Except for the last 2.0mi in the S, the trail follows long-abandoned logging RR grades along the scenic valley of the Laurel Fork, and, in most places, is within 100yd of the stream. The trail has a gentle grade and is easy to hike. One sees numerous pleasant vistas of surrounding mountains and the Laurel Fork. Active beaver dams and a virgin spruce patch are found along the trail. The majority of the growth is yellow birch, beech, hemlock, pine, spruce, alder, and ground cedar. Signs of bear, beaver, deer, and ducks are common. The trail is not blazed, but is easy to follow. It is entirely within the Laurel Fork South Wilderness.

Access: For the N trailhead [E] (Map III-B-3) follow the directions for getting to the ranger cabin mentioned for TR306 (N).

To get to the S trailhead [N] drive 19.9mi S from Wymer (US33) on FR14 to the *first* junction with FR97. This point is marked with a standard USFS trail sign. FR97/TR306 heads E from FR14 and is gated and closed to all motorized vehicles. To get to this trailhead from the S (Camp Pocahontas on WV28--NE of Bartow) drive 10.5mi N on FR14 to the *second* junction with FR97. At the junction with FR14 a USFS sign reads "Laurel River Trail, 8 miles to Osceola Rd., 19 miles to Middle Mountain Road". FR97 is blocked by a locked gate. Parking space is plentiful.

Segment 1: From the N terminus [E], the trail starts out as a road through the campground on the left (E) bank of Laurel Fork. Within 100yd is a USFS gate and sign saying "Seeded to Game Food--Foot Travel Only". After 0.1mi is a spring coming from a pipe 20yd W of the trail behind a "cellar hole". At 0.6mi is the junction with Forks Trail (TR323) [G] . A USFS sign says: "Forks Trail, Middle Mtn. Rd. 2".

Segment 2: Immediately after this junction enter a field (75x150yd). The trail picks up the old RR grade at the S end of the field. (Note: when traveling N here it is easy to continue on the RR grade rather than the trail skirting the edge of the field.) At 1.3mi the trail is 70-80ft above Laurel Fork. Watch for excellent views of the pools and rapids. The trail remains on the left bank and does not cross Laurel Fork as the topo indicates. At 1.6mi is the junction [I] with Beulah Trail (TR310). A USFS sign says "Beulah Trail, 1 mile to Middle Mtn. Rd., 1.5mi to East Fork Glady Rd., TR310".

Segment 3: At 0.4mi beyond TR310 the trail is 50 ft. above Laurel Fork. Note that the trail remains on the left bank, contrary to the topo. At 0.75mi from TR310 a tributary (Crawford Run) enters Laurel Fork from the E. Good views of Laurel Fork and beaver dams are common. At 1.5mi from TR310 is a spruce thicket between the trail and Laurel Fork. Half a mile farther is a virgin spruce patch where the forest floor is covered with moss. After 2.6mi from TR310 enter a semi-open field and cross a stream to the junction [K] with Camp Five Trail (TR315) at 4.1mi. (Chaffey Trail (TR320) just N of TR315 was abandoned by the USFS.)

Segment 4: The trail then goes through a spruce- and pine thicket and, after 100yd, rejoins the RR grade. Cross Laurel Fork on an old beaver dam to the right bank (for the first time). At 0.4mi beyond TR315 is a large blackberry patch and fine views of meadows and beaver dams. The trail follows an overgrown road. Several small trails lead down to Laurel Fork. At 0.7mi beyond TR315 a survey line crosses the road/trail. After 30yd farther, the trail leaves the road and goes down toward Laurel Fork. (Note: when traveling S it is easy to continue on the road which is the "obvious route".) Soon the trail takes a 90-degree turn in a meadow and follows an old road. (The trail does not cross Laurel Fork as the topo indicates.) The meadow here is 200-300yd wide and covers the entire valley floor. Good views, blackberries, and campsites are here.

The trail continues from here on an old road through a pitch pine thicket, and out to a meadow along Laurel Fork. Because of the beaver dams the trail is obscure in the meadow. Cross Laurel Fork (wading may be necessary) [L] and locate an old jeep road. Turn left and follow the old jeep road through the forest to join FR97 [M] at 6.3mi (2.2mi from Camp Five Trail). Follow seeded FR97 for 1.3mi to its junction with FR14 and the S trailhead [N].

MIDDLE MOUNTAIN TRAIL (TR307)   1.2mi(1.9km)

SCENERY: 2 (wooded)   NOTE:B,M,(2)
DIFFICULTY: II (moderate)   SKI-:S4
CONDITION: A (good)   ELEV:3650/3020
MAPS: USFS(A), Glady, III-B-2 in this Guide
SEGMENTS: (1) FR14 to TR306 (Laurel River Trail)   1.2mi

Middle Mountain Trail provides excellent access to Laurel Fork and TR306. It is steep, following an unnamed tributary of Laurel Fork. The forest in this area is second-growth hardwood. The trail is within Laurel Fork North Wilderness.

Access: To get to the W (FR14) trailhead [B] drive S from Wymer on FR14 for 11.5mi. The trailhead is 0.2mi N of the junction of FR14 and FR1. A sign on the E side of FR14 says "Middle Mtn. Trail, Laurel Fork 1mi, Laurel River Trail (TR306) 1mi". Two cars could park on the road-side 200ft from the trail. Better parking is at the junction of FR14 and FR1.

Segment 1: Starting from FR14 [B], Middle Mountain Trail begins on the N bank of the tributary. Before reaching Laurel Fork the trail crosses to the S bank. The ford at Laurel Fork is 20ft wide and 0.5ft deep normally. In the spring it could be several times this depth. On the E side of Laurel Fork enter a small clearing with apple trees. Cross an old RR grade and ascend 70yd (steep) to TR306 [F].

BEULAH TRAIL (TR310) (E)   0.9mi(1.4km)
SCENERY: 2 (wooded)   NOTE: B,M,(1)
DIFFICULTY: II (moderate)   SKI-: S4
CONDITION: A (good)   ELEV: 3610/3200
MAPS: USFS(A,B), Sinks of Gandy, III-B-3 in this Guide
SEGMENTS: (1) FR14 to TR306 (Laurel River Trail)   0.9mi
The E section of Beulah Trail connects FR14 and Laurel River Trail (TR306). The trail is easy to follow, and runs through mixed hardwoods (yellow birch, beech, black cherry, and ash). It is within Laurel Fork South Wilderness.

Access: To get to the FR14 trailhead [P] drive S on FR14 from Wymer for 14.7mi. TR310 crosses FR14 here. A trail sign pointing W reads: "East Fork, Glady Road 1/2 Mile". A sign pointing E reads: "Laurel Fork Trail (TR306) 1 Mile". Parking space is plentiful.

Segment 1: Heading E, the trail descends steadily, and after 0.3mi, follows the left bank of a stream. After a short distance cross to the right bank and proceed on to TR306 [I]. The junction is unsigned.

BEULAH TRAIL (TR310) (W)   3.3mi(5.3km)
SCENERY: 2-3 (wooded-developed)   NOTE: B,M,(4)
DIFFICULTY: II (moderate)   SKI-: S2
CONDITION: A (good)   ELEV: 3420/3000
MAPS: USFS(A,B), Glady, Sinks of Gandy, III-B-3 & III-C-1 in this Guide
SEGMENTS: (1) FR14 to FR183   0.6mi
          (2) FR183 to TR311 (County Line Trail)1.5mi
          (3) TR311 to FR44   1.2mi
The W section of Beulah Trail is an excellent connector route from the Middle Mountain area to the Shavers Mountain area when used in conjunction with High Falls Trail (TR345). The trails, roads and gas lines branching from FR183 and FR14 in this area offer possibilities for ski-touring. The trail is blue-blazed and easy to follow.

Access: To get to the SE trailhead on FR14 [P](Map III-B-3), refer to the TR310(E) notes.

To get to the NW (FR44) trailhead [V](Map III-C-1) drive S on FR44 for 3.4mi from Glady. The trailhead on the E side of the road is marked with a USFS sign reading "Beulah Trail, TR310, East Fork of Glady Road 3 Miles, Middle Mtn. Rd. 4 Miles". The trailhead is actually 0.1mi N on FR44. The Spruce Knob NW topo is correct. Parking space is plentiful at the NW trailhead.

Segment 1: From FR14 [P] (Map III-B-3) the trail descends steeply along the SW bank of a small stream. After 0.6mi is the junction [Q] with FR183. A trail sign reads "Beulah Trail TR310, Middle Mtn. Rd. 1/2 Mile, Laurel Fork Trail 1.5 Miles (E), West Fork of Glady Road 3 Miles (W)".

Camp Five Run (TR315) in the Middle Mountain area. Photo by by Robert Gebhardt

Segment 2: The trail follows the road up the S bank of the East Fork of the Glady. After 0.25mi the road/trail crosses the East Fork of the Glady. over 2 large culverts. From here the road/trail leaves the stream to the NW and after 0.8mi, comes to a switch-back at a gas well. At 1.1mi from the East Fork of the Glady [W] (Map III-C-1) the trail leaves this road at a sign reading: "Beulah Trail, East Fork Glady, 1 Mile (E), West Fork of the Glady 1.5 Miles (W)". Another sign reads: "County Line Trail (TR311), Snorting Lick Road 5 Miles". This is the N end of TR311 which continues to follow the road.

Segment 3: Beulah Trail descends steadily from this point, passing through second-growth hardwoods. For most of the 1.2mi to FR44 [V] the trail parallels a small stream. The last 0.25mi follows an overgrown logging road.

COUNTY LINE TRAIL (TR311)   4.1mi(6.6km)
SCENERY: 2 (wooded)   NOTE: B,M,(0)
DIFFICULTY: II (moderate)   SKI-:   S2
CONDITION: A (good)   ELEV: 3720/3380
MAPS: USFS(A), Sinks of Gandy, Wildell, III-B-3 and III-C-1 in this Guide
SEGMENTS: (1) FR35 to TR310 (Beulah Trail)   4.1mi

Access: The S end of County Line Trail is on FR35 0.7mi W of the junction [R](Map III-B-3) of FR35 and FR14 and 3.2mi E of the junction of FR35 and FR44. The trailhead is on the N side of the road at a sharp bend in the road. A USFS sign reads: "County Line Trail, Beulah Trail, TR311". Parking space is plentiful.

Segment 1: County Line Trail starts out from the S on FR35 as a gas-storage-well access road. After 0.4mi, at the well-head, the trail continues alone at the far side of the clearing. From here the trail follows the ridge through open hardwood forest. At 1.5mi [A](Map III-C-1) cross an old RR grade in a saddle. (This old RR grade is probably the branch of TR311 shown on the USFS map as going to FR44. It is not marked and apparently abandoned.)

Here you find a spring on the E side of the trail and a good site for several tents. The trail continues to be blue-blazed and marked with wood arrow signs in this area, and ascends to the top of the ridge at 2.8mi. At 3.6mi enter a clearing for gas storage well #7445. From here follow the gas storage well access road to the junction with Beulah Trail (TR310) [W].

CAMP FIVE TRAIL (TR315)   1.6mi(2.6km)
SCENERY: 2 (wooded)   NOTE: B,M,(2)
DIFFICULTY: II (moderate)   SKI-:   S1
CONDITION: A (good)   ELEV: 3620/3350
MAPS: USFS(A), Sinks of Gandy, III-B-3 in this Guide
SEGMENTS: (1) FR14 to TR306 (Laurel River Trail (S))   1.6mi

Camp Five Trail follows abandoned roads and RR grades and offers pleasant hiking. It is within Laurel Fork S Wilderness.

Access: To get to the SW trailhead [T] drive S from Wymer on FR14 for 18.7mi. Or drive N on FR14 for 11.9mi from Camp Pocahontas on

WV28. The trailhead on the NE side of the road is marked with a sign reading: "Camp Five Trail, Laurel River Trail (TR306) 1.5 Miles TR315". Another sign reads: "MNF Middle Mtn. Guard Station". A locked gate blocks the road/trail. Parking space is plentiful, but do not block the road used to reach the "Guard Station". (The cabins at the "Guard Station" are available for public rental from April through October.)

Segment 1: Camp Five Trail starts out from FR14 [T] on a gravel road. It jointly follows Spring Box Loop Trail (TR336) for the first 0.1mi to Middle Mountain Guard Station. It also parallels Camp Five Run that empties into Laurel Fork. At 0.6mi cross to the NW bank of the stream immediately before a tributary enters from the right (E). After crossing the stream the trail follows an old RR grade. At 1.2mi enter a meadow near an old beaver dam on the stream. At 1.3mi is the junction [V] with Chaffey Trail (abandoned). One sign reads: "Camp Five Trail, Middle Mtn. Rd. 1.5". The trail continues along the SE bank of the stream 50yd above it. There are good views to the N and W. The junction [K] with Laurel River Trail (TR306)(S) along the W bank of the Laurel Fork is the E terminus of Camp Five Trail.

LYNN KNOB TRAIL (TR317)   3.1mi(4.9km)
SCENERY: 1 (exceptional)   NOTE: B,M,(0)
DIFFICULTY: II (moderate)   SKI-:   S3
CONDITION: A (good)   ELEV: 3990/3150
MAPS: USFS(A), Sinks of Gandy, Wildell, III-B-3 and -4 in this Guide
SEGMENTS: (1) FR179 to TR367 (Hinkle Run Trail) & FR17   3.1mi

Lynn Knob Trail's N entrance begins at a parking area on Elklick Run Road (FR179), 0.6mi W of FR14. Through a forest of beech and cherry it ascends to Lynn Knob (3900ft) after 0.4mi. Its descent is through sections of beautiful maple. The trail is well-drained, blue-blazed, and easy to follow. (There is a 0.5mi connector trail from Spring Box Loop Trail (TR336) to the N entrance.)

Access: To get to the N (FR14) trailhead [X](Map III-B-3) drive S on FR14 for 19.7mi from Wymer. From WV28 at Camp Pocahontas drive N of FR14 for 10.5mi. [N] (Map III-B-3). (Drive SW on FR179 for 0.6mi to another junction [A](Map III-B-4) with Lynn Knob Trail.)

Segment 1: Proceed S from FR179. Turkey are common in the area. At 0.4mi from FR179 cross Lynn Knob. Beyond this point descend steeply to a saddle [C] at 1.7mi and an old logging road at 2.2mi. Here the trail turns left (E) and descends to TR367 and FR17 [E], 1.4mi W of Middle Mountain Road (FR14).

HINKLE RUN TRAIL (TR367)   3.7mi(6.0km)
SCENERY: 2 (wooded)   NOTE: B,M,(5)
DIFFICULTY: II (moderate)   SKI-:   S2
CONDITION: A (good)   ELEV: 3850/3150
MAPS: USFS(A), Thornwood, Sinks of Gandy, Wildell, III-B-4 and III-B-5 in this Guide
SEGMENTS: (1) FR14/FR15 to FR17/TR317 (Lynn Knob Trail)   3.7mi

Hinkle Run Trail is shown as May Burner Trail (TR316) on old USGS maps. The trail is blue-blazed and easy to follow. It follows abandoned log ging roads and offers pleasant hiking. There are meadows and beaver ponds along the trail. For most of its length the trail follows Little River and Hinkle Run.

Access: The N trailhead is at FR17 [E] (Map III-B-4) 1.4mi W of the junction of FR17 and FR14 [M]. A sign on the N side of the road reads "Lynn Knob Trail (#317), Elklick Run Road (FR179) 3mi". Several cars can park here.

The S end of TR367 is on FR14 at the junction with FR15 [A] (Map III-B-5). From Camp Pocahontas [P] on WV28 drive N on FR14 3.8mi to the trailhead. From Wymer, drive S on FR14 for 26.6mi. The trailhead is on the W side of the road in a pine forest. The trail is gated and a USFS sign reads: "Seeded to Game Food, Foot Travel Only". Several cars can park there.

Segment 1: Beginning from the N at FR17 [E], descend gently on an old grassy road to wade or rock-hop across Little River at 0.1mi. At 0.2mi is a meadow seeded to grass (good camp site) and a small waterfalls. At 0.4mi the trail crosses Little River [G]. Avoid this crossing by staying on the S bank and following an old trail that regains the blue-blazed trail at 0.6mi. This alternative has good views of the stream below and is dry. At 0.6mi leave Little River and start up the S bank of Hinkle Run. There are potential campsites in a grassy meadow at 1.4mi. At 2.3mi turn sharply left off the old grassy road and rock-hop the tributary on another old road. Immediately turn right off the road and join another old road. Pass through a stand of hemlock at 3.0mi. Continue ascending and pass S of a large grassy field. Curve left at 3.2mi where the road becomes level on top of Burner Mountain. Pass through a beautiful red pine plantation and exit at the juncture of FR14 and FR15 [A] (Map III-B-5).

SPAN OAK TRAIL (TR321)   3.7mi(6.0km)

SCENERY: 2 (wooded)   NOTE: B,M,(0)
DIFFICULTY: II (moderate)   SKI-:   S3
CONDITION: A (good)   ELEV: 4100/2950
MAPS: USFS(A), Durbin, III-B-5 in this Guide
SEGMENTS: (1) FR17 to FR15   3.7mi

Span Oak Trail is blue-blazed and easy to follow.

Access: To get to the W trailhead [B] from Glady, drive 16.2mi S on FR44. From the junction of FR44 and US250 at Durbin, drive 6.9mi N on FR44. The trailhead is on the E side of FR44 at the S end of a concrete bridge over Little River.

To get to the E trailhead [E] from US250 at Frank, drive 5.7mi N on FR15. From the junction [A] of FR14 and FR15, drive 4.7mi W on FR15. The trailhead is on the W side of FR15, a narrow, one lane, poorly maintained road.

Segment 1: Starting from FR44 [B], Span Oak Trail starts out as an old logging road along the Little River. Pass through several game food plots.

BURNER MOUNTAIN TRAIL (TR322)   3.6mi(5.8km)

SCENERY: 2 (wooded)   NOTE: B,M,(0)
DIFFICULTY: II (moderate)   SKI-:   S2
CONDITION: B (average)   ELEV: 4280/3850
MAPS: USFS(A), Thornwood, Durbin, III-B-5 in this Guide
SEGMENTS: (1) FR15 to FR14/TR367 (Hinkle Run Trail)   3.6mi

The W portion of Burner Mountain Trail follows an overgrown road through open areas and second-growth hardwoods. It is on generally level ground except for a steep grade at the E trailhead. The trail is blue-blazed. The USFS plans to relocate this trail, so contact the district ranger's office for an update before your trip.

Access: To get to the E (FR14) trailhead [K] from Wymer, drive 27.8mi S on FR14. From Camp Pocahontas [P] on WV28 drive 2.9mi N on FR14. The trailhead is on the W side of FR14 and is marked with a USFS sign reading: "Burner Mtn. Trail, 4 Miles to Burner Mtn. Road, TR322". Parking space is plentiful.

To get to the W (FR15) trailhead [G] from US250 at Frank, drive 6.3mi N on FR15. To get there from the junction [A] of FR14 and FR15 drive 3.8mi SW on FR15. The W trailhead is marked with a sign reading: "Burner Mtn. Trail, 4 Miles to Middle Mtn. Road". Plenty of parking and good tent sites are available at this trailhead. See TR321 Notes for comment on FR15.

FORKS TRAIL (TR323)   1.1mi(1.8km)

SCENERY: 2 (wooded)   NOTE: B,M,(0)
DIFFICULTY: II (moderate)   SKI-:   S4
CONDITION: A-B (good-average)   ELEV: 3420/3150
MAPS: USFS(A), Sinks of Gandy, III-B-3 in this Guide
SEGMENTS: (1) FR183 to FR14   0.5mi
              (2) FR14 to TR306 (Laurel River Trail)0.6mi

The W portion of Forks Trail (NW of FR14) is overgrown, but can be followed as a connector trail to FR183. The trail is blue-blazed and easy to follow.

Access: From Wymer drive 13.7mi S on FR14 to the middle trailhead [Z]. Forks Trail crosses the road here. The E section of TR323 joins TR306 [G], and the W section goes to East Fork of the Glady Road (FR183). The trailhead sign on FR14 says: "Forks Trail, Laurel River Trail, 2 Miles to Laurel Fork" (0.6mi is correct.) Parking space is plentiful.
See TR306 for information on the SE trailhead.

Segment 1: The NW portion of the trail from FR14 to FR183 is steep, and passes close to a gas well. After 0.5mi it reaches FR183 where a sign reads: "Forks Trail, 1 Mile to Middle Mtn. Road".

Segment 2: Going SE from FR14 [Z], Forks Trail drops down to Laurel River Trail (TR306) at 0.6mi.

SMOKE CAMP TRAIL (TR324)   1.8mi(2.9km)

SCENERY: 1 (exceptional)   NOTE: (1)
DIFFICULTY: II (moderate)   SKI-:   S4
CONDITION: A (good)   ELEV: 4190/2900
MAPS: USFS(A), Thornwood

SEGMENTS: (1) WV28 to FR58   1.8mi

Smoke Camp Trail is steep, averaging 20% in most places. The trail does not run directly into the dead-end of FR58 as the MNF map suggests.

Access: Smoke Camp Trail joins FR58 just below 4218ft Smoke Camp Knob, a former location of a USFS fire lookout station.

Segment 1: The trail starts 100yd N of the junction of WV28 and Buffalo Fork Road (FR54), 2.0mi N of Bartow. The trail leaves WV28 and starts uphill, passing through the Rothkugel Plantation from 0.1mi to 0.6mi. This area was seeded to Norway Spruce and European Larch by German forester Max Rothkugel in 1907 after it was logged. An informative sign on the history of the area is located 100yd N of the trail along WV28. Continuing uphill, the trail passes several springs at 0.8mi. The trail enters a truck road and turns left at 1.6mi and intersects Smoke Camp Road (FR58) at 1.8mi. Backtrack for a 3.6mi round-trip.

EAST FORK TRAIL (TR365)   8.0mi(12.8km)

SCENERY: 1 (exceptional)   NOTE: B,M,(4)
DIFFICULTY: II (moderate)   SKI-:   S2-S4
CONDITION: A (good)   ELEV: 3550/3000
MAPS: USFS(A), Thornwood, Sinks of Gandy, III-B-6 in this Guide
SEGMENTS: (1) WV28 to FR51   5.0mi
          (2) FR51 to FR254   3.0mi

East Fork Trail is in neither the Middle Mountain Area nor the Shavers Fork Area, but it is close enough to Middle Mountain to be considered as part of that system. It parallels the East Fork of Greenbrier River from Island Campground (1.0mi E of Camp Pocahontas on WV28) to Pig's Ear Road (FR254). The campground has pit toilets but no drinking water. It passes three pine plantations for most of the way. (Do not drink East Fork water because of livestock at Pig's Ear and campers at Abe's Run.) The trail is in good condition, although somewhat overgrown N of Abe's Run [E]. The trail is exceptional when serviceberries are in bloom or in fruit. The trail has heavy bracken fern where the pine plantations are not very thick, and gives a good view of the plantations along the trail. Overall, the trail is scenic, easy, and offers a good deal of variety, but is wet in sections near the river. The W. Va. Sierra Club has built a high-water route 0.5mi N of Island Campground.

Access: At the N terminus [G], parking is available for 2-3 cars along Pig's Ear Road (FR254) 3.5mi W from WV28.
The S (WV28) terminus of East Fork Trail is along Island Campground Road at the East Fork Trail sign [A] at a wildlife road (old RR grade).

Segment 1: Starting from the S (WV28) [A], East Fork Trail proceeds N 0.3mi until it parallels East Fork. The trail follows the East Fork closely for 2.0mi and crosses a thick field. The trail may be hard to see here. Proceed along the uphill (E) edge of the field until the trail is again encountered at the far edge. Wild strawberries are numerous at the N end of this field. The fords indicated by the blazes and topo at Mile 2.5 [C] are not necessary. Instead, follow the stream along its E bank to regain the trail within 300yd. Small water falls are found at 3.9mi. At 4.0mi is a stand of hemlock on level ground free of underbrush--a good campsite. Another small falls and a beaver dam lie just upstream. The trail then climbs steeply and goes around the mountainside 0.5mi before descending into two small fields and a pine plan

Hosterman Trail (TR337). Photo by Allen de Hart

tation. Proceed on to Abe's Run [E] on Abe's Run Road (FR51) at 5.0mi where there are campsites.

Segment 2: Ford Abe's Run and cross the road to find the trail continuing along the same (E) side of East Fork. At 6.2mi the trail goes through another stand of hemlock, also suitable for small tents. The trail then fords a tributary and climbs gradually through more young stands of hemlock and rocky clearings. The stream can be heard below but is no longer visible. Pig's Ear Road (FR254) [G] is met at 8.0mi after passing through an open stand of young pine.

POCA RUN TRAIL (TR335)   2.5mi(4.0km)

SCENERY: 1 (exceptional)   NOTE: B,M,(0)
DIFFICULTY: I (leisurely)   SKI-:   S1
CONDITION: A (good)   ELEV: 4020/3281
MAPS: USFS(A), Thornwood, III-B-6 in this Guide
SEGMENTS: (1) WV28(S) to WV28(N)   2.5mi

Poca Run Trail gently ascends to the headwaters of Poca Run and crosses a ridge between Colow Knob in West Virginia and near the Highland County line in Virginia. It begins and ends on WV28.

Access: The W trailhead [N] is on the N side of WV28 and on the E side of Poca Run, 4.1mi NE of the junction with US250 at Thornwood.

The E trailhead [S] is 2.3mi from Poca Run at the WV28 junction with FR806. (FR806 is not shown on Map III-B-6.)

Segment 1: Beginning at Poca Run [N], follow a blue-blazed old woods road on the E side of the stream, 0.6mi to a right curve. (Down an embankment, across the stream, and upstream to FR286 is an unnamed 1.8mi blue-blazed trail to the top of Poca Ridge.) At 1.2mi is a red cedar forest [P] near the headwaters of Poca Run. From here the trail follows FR271A 0.5mi to FR806, which it follows down a ridge to a gate [S] at WV28. Forest vegetation includes cherry, yellow birch, basswood, sweet cicely, ferns and blue cohosh.

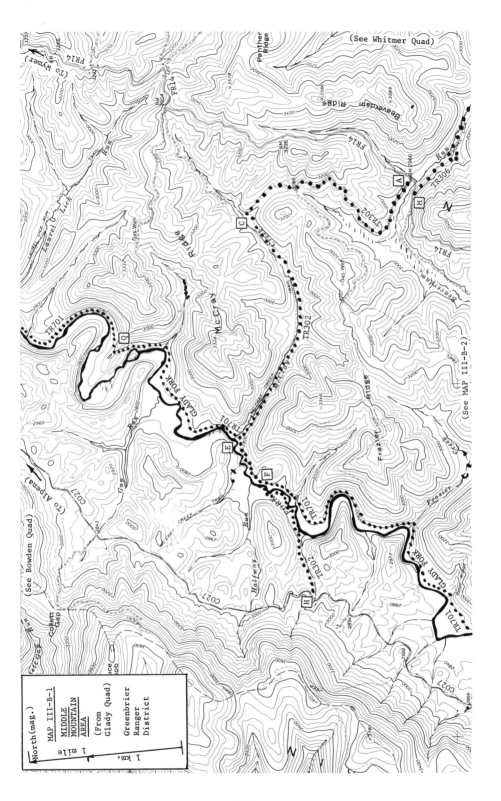

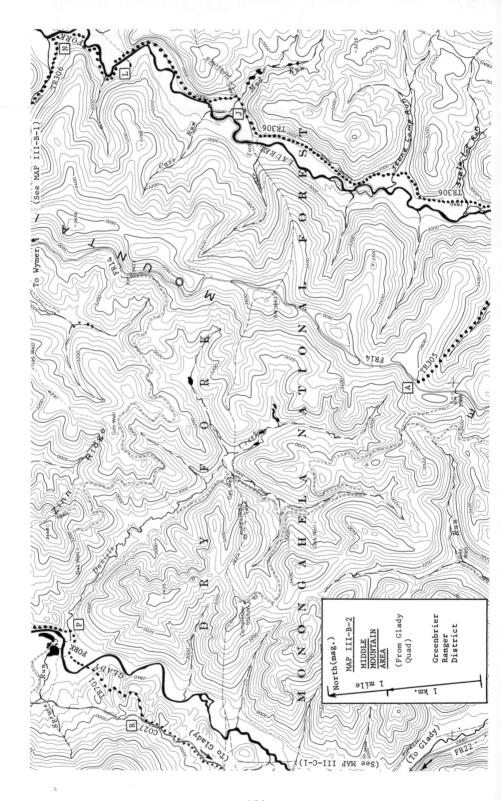

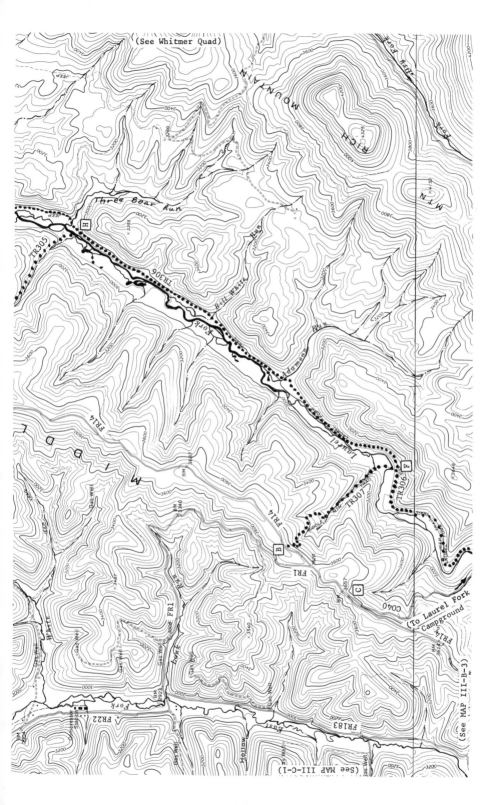

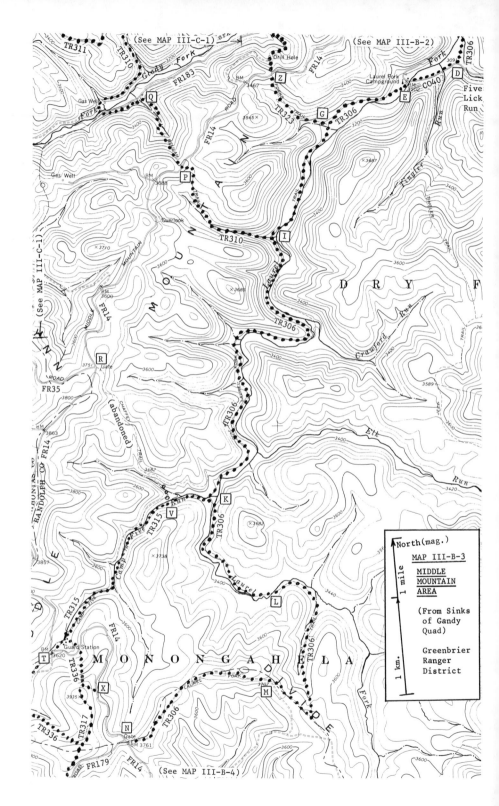

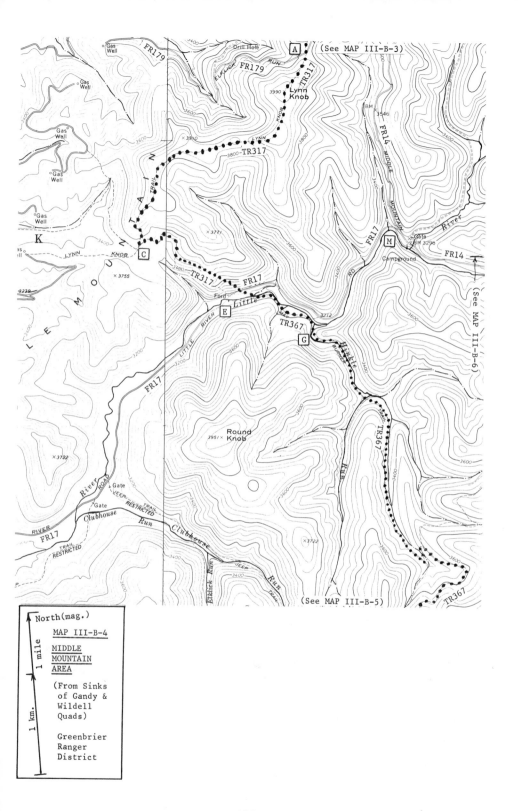

(See MAP III-B-3)

North(mag.)

MAP III-B-4

MIDDLE
MOUNTAIN
AREA

(From Sinks
of Gandy &
Wildell
Quads)

Greenbrier
Ranger
District

193

Shaver's Fork from High Falls Trail (TR345). Photo by Allen de Hart

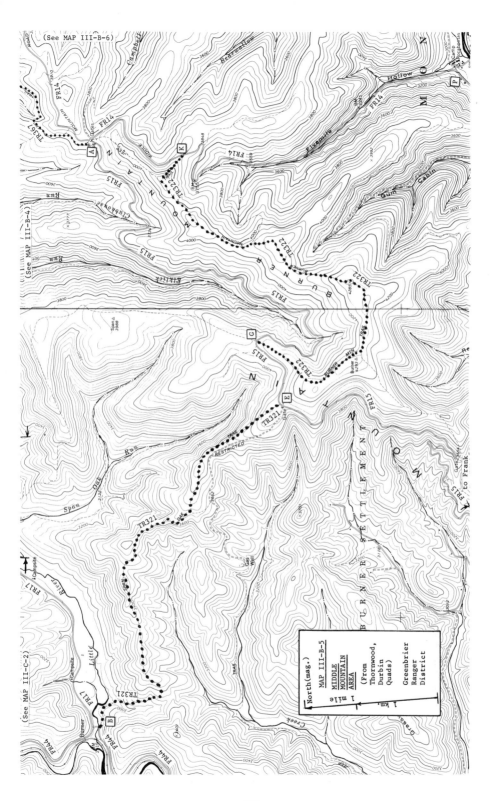

(See MAP III-B-6)

(See MAP III-B-4)

(See MAP III-C-2)

North (mag.)

MAP III-B-5

MIDDLE
MOUNTAIN
AREA

(From
Thornwood,
Durbin
Quads)

Greenbrier
Ranger
District

1 mile

1 km.

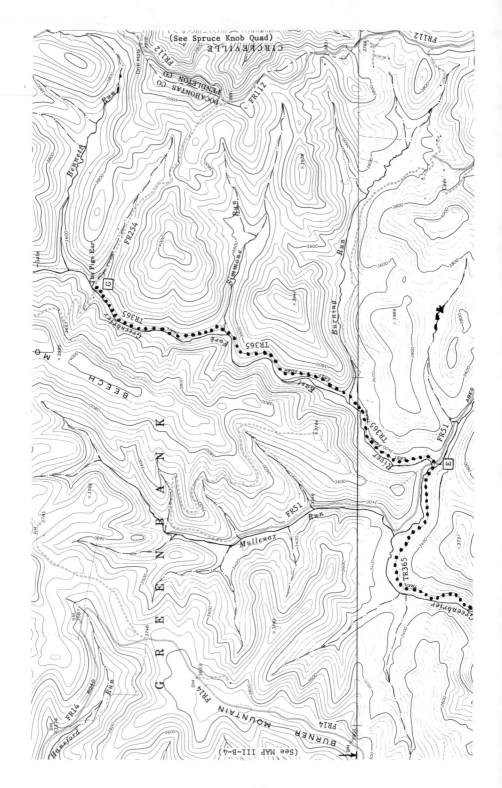

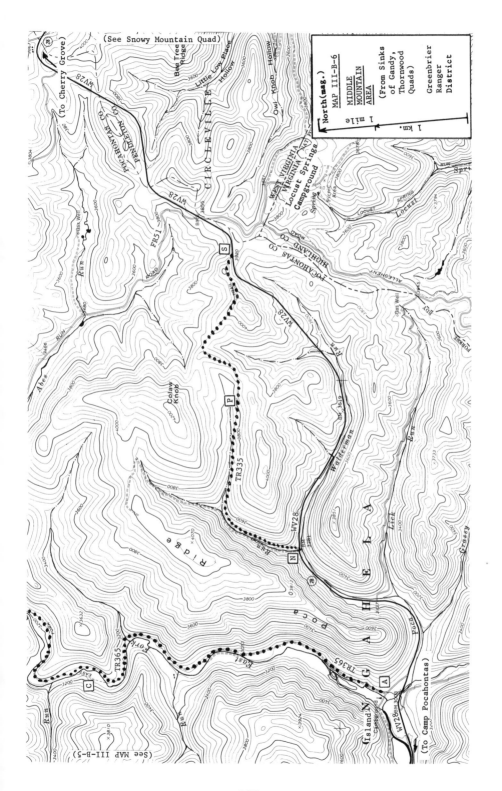

(III-C) SHAVERS FORK AREA

The Shavers Fork Area contains one of West Virginia's most attractive streams and has a great deal of natural appeal and has much to offer. It is largely uninhabited and supports several hundred bears and much other wildlife. The 140-acre tract of virgin spruce and hardwoods preserved in Gaudineer Scenic Area is worth a visit. A miniature Niagara Falls 15ft high just below the mouth of Falls Run (on Shavers Fork) is an outstanding scenic point. It is known as "High Falls of the Cheat". Backpackers will find camp-sites nearby. See TR345.

(Note: The 1969 USFS North Half [1/2"=1.0mi] Map erroneously reversed the names of Fall Run and Red Run. The USGS Beverly East topo is correct.)

Access Roads:

(Note: Many roads in this area are being used for traffic related to mining of privately owned coal. Exercise caution.)

FR27-	Gaudineer Road proceeds N from US250 near Gaudineer Scenic Area. It provides access to Allegheny Trail (TR701) and John's Camp Trail (TR341).
CO22-	Glady-Bemis Road, also provides access to Allegheny Trail (TR701). The portion from Bemis over Cheat Mountain is rec-ommended for 4-wheel-drive vehicles only.
FR44-	Glady-Durbin Road provides access to High Falls Trail (TR345) on the E side of Shaver's Mountain which connects to Allegheny Trail (TR701).
FR92-	Cheat Mountain Road proceeds N from US250 along the crest of Cheat Mountain and is the high elevation terminus of Stonecoal Trail (TR360). FR92 now connects to CO37 (via former FR185) along the Right Fork of Files Creek which runs E from US250-219 at Dailey. This road provides access to the trailless area of Cheat Mountain S of Bemis.
FR209-	Shaver's Fork Road leaves US250 a few miles N of Cheat Bridge and follows the W side of Shaver's Fork, dead-ending in 3.0mi. This road provides access to Stonecoal Trail (TR360).
FR317-	John's Camp Road continues E from the end of Gaudineer Road (FR27) for 0.5mi, dead-ending at the start of John's Camp Trail (TR341).
FR47-	Whitmeadow Run Road goes E off FR92, 4.0mi N of US250. Its dead-end is the E terminus for Whitmeadow Ridge Trail (TR361).
FR49-	Crouch Run Road goes E off FR92 6.7mi N of US250. The E terminus of Crouch Ridge Trail is on Crouch Run Road.
FR188-	Yokum Run Road goes E off FR92 6.7mi N of US250. The lower mile is rough.
FR210-	McGee Run Road goes E off FR92 9mi N of US250. The E end of Yokum Ridge Trail is on FR210 near Shavers Fork.

Campgrounds:

There are not any improved campgrounds on middle or upper Shaver's Fork area. The most developed USFS campground nearby is Stuart Recre-ation Area, E of Elkins and off US33. (See Cheat Ranger District.) Less developed, but closer, is the Laurel Fork Campground, described on page 173 and below. It is on FR40, E off FR14, between Glady and Sinks of Gandy. There are scattered roadside camping spots (without water) along FR92 and FR209. The map of Greenbrier Ranger District on page 163-165 shows nine campgrounds in the Middle Mountain area just E of the Shavers Fork area, but only two of these are actually campgrounds. They are Laurel Fork Campground (TR306, 19 sites, water April 1 to Dec.1, restroom, no fee, and open all year), and Island Campground (TR365, 6 sites, restroom, no water, no fee, and open all year). All others are dispersed undeveloped campsites which may or may not have water, and none have restrooms. There is a private campground, Whittaker Camping Area, 2mi SW of Cass. It is fully developed with electric hookups and hot shower (Tel. 304-456-3218).

Motels, Restaurants and Stores:
Other than Elkins, there is a motel and restaurant at Dailey (US219, S of Elkins); Bartow (US250/WV92); and Pocahontas Motel and Restaurant (US250/FR92, between Cheat Bridge and Huttonville). The later is open April 1 to Nov. 30, and usually closes at 8 PM. In addition to Elkins, there are supply stores with gasoline along US219, US250, and US33. Small country grocery stores are usually closed after 5 PM, and are not open on Sundays or holidays. The only developed picnic area in the district is Gaudineer Knob Picnic Area of FR27, off US250 and W of Durbin.

CHESTNUT RIDGE TRAIL (TR327)   5.5mi(8.8km)
SCENERY: 2 (wooded)   NOTE: M,(2)
DIFFICULTY: II (moderate)   SKI-:   S4
CONDITION: B (average)   ELEV: 3780/2400
MAPS: USFS(A), Mill Creek, III-C-3 in this Guide
SEGMENTS:
   (1) FR92 to TR328 (former McGee Run Trail)   0.8mi
   (2) TR328 to TR331 (former Laurel Run Trail)   1.7mi
   (3) TR331 to Shavers Run Road   3.0mi
   Chestnut Ridge Trail starts at FR92 near the junction of FR92 and FR47. It travels W through the head of McGee Run and along the crest of Chestnut Ridge to Shavers Run Road 39/1. (The USFS announced, in 1998, that plans were being made for partial relocations of this trail.)

   Access: The S trailhead [A] is about 3.5mi N of US250 along FR92, just before FR47 turns off to the right.
The N trailhead [F] is along Shavers Run Road, 39/1, just before a bridge over Shavers Run.

   Segment 1: Starting at FR92 [A] the trail proceeds downhill and joins with, and follows, Riffle Creek wildlife access road to the right (N) at 0.6mi. Arrive at a 3-road intersection at 0.7mi and follow the left road (W). Pass the junction [B] with (former) McGee Run Trail (TR328) at 0.8mi.

   Segment 2: Pass (former) Laurel Run Trail (TR331) at 2.5mi [D].

   Segment 3: Continue on the road to where it leaves a wildlife plot at 3.0mi and becomes a woodland trail. Follow Chestnut Ridge to a left switchback at 4.9mi and a right switchback at 5.0mi. Cross a fence and enter open land at 5.4mi and meet Shavers Run Road at 5.5mi [F] by Shavers Run Bridge.

ALLEGHENY TRAIL (TR701) 25.1mi(40.2km)
SCENERY: 1 (exceptional)   NOTE: B,H,M,(0)
DIFFICULTY: III (strenuous)   SKI-: S2
CONDITION: A-B (good-average)   ELEV: 4190/2700
MAPS: USFS(A), Glady, Durbin, Beverly East, Wildell, III-C-1 &
       III-C-2 in this Guide
SEGMENTS: (1) Durbin,US250 to Exit US250   2.7mi
           (2) Exit US250 to FR27   6.0mi
           (3) FR27 to TR341 (John's Camp Run Trail) 3.5mi
           (4) TR341 to TR345 (High Falls Trail)   8.3mi
           (5) TR345 to CO22   4.6mi

This portion of Allegheny Trail lies between US250 in Durbin and CO22 in Glady. The first 6.6mi is the approach and ascent to the crest of Shavers Mountain, and the remaining 18.5mi follows up and down, or around the sides of, 16 knobs (including Gaudineer Knob). Among the oldest, highest, and most remote trails in the district, it follows the former Shavers Mountain Trail (TR332) and North-South Trail (TR688) for long segments. It has two shelters and is ideal for backpacking or cross-country skiing. In Durbin are stores, post office, laundry, restaurant, and telephone. In Glady is a small store, usually open from 11 AM to 3PM, and a telephone.

Access: The S trailhead is at the junction of US250 and River Road (CO250/2) at the E end of Durbin (not shown on Map III-C-2). The trail follows US250 W 0.6mi to a junction (on the left) with West Fork Trail (TR312) at Pocahontas Road (CO250/ 13). (For a long loop of about 48mi, backpackers can follow West Fork Trail to Glady and return on Allegheny Trail to reduce the ascent distance to Shavers Mountain. See West Fork Trail on page 207.)

Parking is a problem at the N trailhead on Glady-Bemis Road (CO22).

Segment 1: From the junction with West Fork Trail (TR312), continue on US250 0.6mi to cross Greenbrier River Bridge. At 2.5mi leave US250 (0.2mi N of Back Mountain Road, CO1) and turn right.

Segment 2: After 1.1mi, cross Fill Run. Begin an ascent, and at 4.4mi, meet Simmons Road (CO250/1, a gravel road that goes 0.5mi to the left to US250 and goes right to the MNF boundary). Turn right onto Simmons Road, go 0.7mi, turn left off the road, and ascend steeply on switchbacks to the top of Shavers Mountain at 6.6mi. [A] (Map III-C-2) (From the left is a 0.2mi access trail from Gaudineer Knob Road, FR27, near US250.)

Segment 3: For the next 2.2mi the trail parallels FR27, but is on the E slope of the mountain. In Gaudineer Scenic Area the trail partially follows Gaudineer Trail (TR373) which has exceptionally tall virgin red spruce, maple, cherry and birch. After a few yd. on FR27, turn right off the road and continue on Allegheny Trail. At 12.2mi is Johns Camp Shelter (sleeps 6) and the junction with Johns Camp Trail (TR341) [C]. A small spring is in front of the shelter, and a greater source of water is 300yd W on Johns Camp Trail. (Johns Camp Trail is 0.8mi along Johns Camp Run to its W trailhead at FR317. On FR317 it is 0.5mi to a junction with FR92 and 6.1mi to US250.)

Segment 4: Leave the shelter and ascend for 0.8mi to Allegheny Trail's highest point [F] (el.4193ft) on Shavers Mountain. From here it is another 0.8mi N to an E outcropping with panoramic views. After another 2.3mi are additional views to the E. At 16.2mi is the old unmarked Helmick Trail which leads off to the left. (On this trail it is about 0.5mi to a small stream

West Fork Trail (TR312) Tunnel. Photo by Allen de Hart

and a clearing large enough for several tents.) Another potential campsite is in a saddle at 17.7mi at the crossing of former Camp 48 Trail. (A streamlet is 0.2mi W of the saddle.)

From here the trail gradually ascends and descends a high knob to cross an old road at 18.8mi. (To the W about 0.3mi is a clearing suitable for a campsite, but intermittent water is about 0.1mi farther.) After traversing another knob the trail descends to Wildell Shelter (sleeps 6) [F](Map III-C-1), which is off the trail to the E in a saddle. There is not any water.

From Wildell Shelter the trail gradually ascends another knob, descends a steep slope, and crosses High Falls Trail (TR345) [H] at 20.5mi. Here is a large and popular campsite area, with water available 0.2mi E on a steep grade of High Falls Trail. (The High Falls Trail E trailhead is 1.0mi to FR44, and the W trailhead is 1.9mi at High Falls on Shavers Fork.)

Segment 5: Allegheny Trail continues through a mixed hardwood forest, then through a timbered area where it sporadically follows old logging and farm roads on private property. The trail begins its final descent at 24.5mi, enters an open area on an old road, and follows it to a gate at Elliots Ridge Road (CO22) [J] at 25.1mi. From here the trail turns E and goes 0.3mi on CO22 to Glady crossroads.

JOHN'S CAMP RUN TRAIL (TR341)   0.8mi(1.3km)

SCENERY: 2 (wooded)   NOTE: B,H,M,(1)
DIFFICULTY: II (moderate)   SKI-:   S2
CONDITION: B (average)   ELEV: 3820/3640
MAPS: USFS(A), Wildell, III-C-2 in this Guide
SEGMENTS: (1) FR317 to TR701 (Allegheny Trail)   0.8mi

John's Camp Trail connects Allegheny Trail (TR701) with John's Camp Road (FR317), joining Allegheny Trail 1.3mi N of Gaudineer Road (FR27). At this trail junction is John's Camp Shelter which sleeps 6.

Access: The W trailhead [M] is at the E end of FR317, a 0.5mi-long road that joins FR27 3.4mi N of Gaudineer Scenic Area.

Segment 1: From FR317 [M], John's Camp Trail ascends on a jeep road, bearing right at a fork, until leaving the road at 0.3mi. At 0.4mi is a spring. The trail crosses a small stream at 0.6mi, and meets Allegheny Trail (TR701) at 0.8mi [C].

HIGH FALLS TRAIL (TR345)   2.5mi(4.0km)

SCENERY: 1 (exceptional)   NOTE: B,M,(2)
DIFFICULTY: II (moderate)   SKI-:   S4
CONDITION: B (average)   ELEV: 3620/2900
MAPS: USFS(A), Wildell, Beverly East, III-C-1 in this Guide
SEGMENTS: (1) FR44 to TR701 (Allegheny Trail) 1.0mi
                (2) TR701 to High Falls   1.5mi

High Falls Trail (formerly Beulah Siding Trail) is blue-blazed and easy to follow. The lower (SE) portion crosses open fields and is relatively flat, while the upper section, ascending Shaver's Mountain, is steep. (Together with Beulah Trail [TR310], this trail forms an excellent connection between the Middle Mountain area and the Shaver's Mountain Trail system.)

Access: To get to the E trailhead from the N, drive S on FR44 from the junction of FR223/FR44 near Glady for 3.9mi. From the S drive 3.5mi N on FR44 from the junction of FR44 and FR35. The trailhead is marked with a trail sign reading: "High Falls Trail, 1mi to Shaver's Mtn. Trail" on the E side of FR44. The trail starts out on the W side of FR44 across from the trail sign. (Note that the trailhead for Beulah Trail is 0.6mi N of High Falls Trailhead along FR44.)

Segment 1: From FR44, High Falls Trail starts out as an overgrown road [P]. After 0.2mi it fords a small stream (West Fork of the Glady). It continues to follow the road through fields with scattered hawthorne to West Fork Trail (TR312) (formerly the CSX RR grade). At the junction with West Fork Trail, look up to the saddle on Shaver's Mountain. This is where you are going. After crossing West Fork Trail the trail goes 0.1mi to cross a small stream. Soon, the trail leaves the field and enters the woods. From this point the trail becomes progressively steeper. It is rocky in parts. The junction with Allegheny Trail (TR701) [H] is marked with two USFS signs reading: "High Falls Trail" and "Wildell Shelter, John's Camp Shelter, Gaudineer Road".

Segment 2: High Falls Trail continues ahead. After 0.2mi in a rocky gradual descent, the trail turns right on an old logging road, but after 300yd the trail turns left off the road. Through a forest of cherry and birch, the trail rapidly descends to a RR [R] along Shaver's Fork at 2.0mi. On the RR it is 0.5mi downstream to spectacular High Falls of the Cheat [T]. The popular falls area may be crowded on summer weekends. Across the river, and a few yards upstream, is a small waterfall on the lower end of Fall Run. Backtrack for a round-trip of 5.0mi.

STRIP MINE TRAIL (TR350)   4.0mi(6.4km)

SCENERY: 1 (exceptional)	NOTE: B, M, W
DIFFICULTY: II (Moderate)	SKI : S4
CONDITION A (good)	ELEV: 4285/3940

MAPS: USFS(A) Snyder Knob
SEGMENTS: (1) Summit Fork Parking Area to FR227   4.0mi

This unique trail provides exposure to the history of Fort Milroy, the 40,827-acre Mower Tract purchased by the USFS in 1986, and the results of strip-mining. The USFS has constructed a parking area between White Top Mountain (el.4100ft), a strategic look-out at the beginning of the Civil War, and the Fort Milroy Cemetery. Southwest of the cemetery the USFS has extended a gravel road to a strip-mining area for a parking area and trailhead of Strip Mine Trail (TR350). At the SE corner of the parking lot is a pit latrine. Although there are some scenic views here toward the E, the astonishing views come later when you arrive on open strip-mining spaces between Barton Knob and Lambert Run. Crouch Knob (el.4529ft) can be seen to the SW.

Access: To get to the NE trailhead drive 9.4mi W on US250 from the Greenbrier Ranger District office in Bartow. Immediately after crossing Shavers Fork Bridge turn left off US250 onto FR245. After 0.5mi turn right onto a steep and rough road and drive 0.5mi to a parking area and a signboard of information. To the right, N, is the Confederate lookout that was lost to Col. Nathan Kimball. Turn S and ascend to pass Fort Milroy Cemetery, partially destroyed by strip-mining, and ascend to the NE trailhead.

Access to the SW trailhead is gained by driving 4.0mi farther on US250 and turning left at Cromer Top on FR227. (FR92 is opposite, to the right and N.) Follow FR227 for 2.2mi to a strip mine road on your left and a flat area for parking. (There may not be any signs.)

Segment 1: From the NE parking area pass through an opening in a fence and go through a stand of Scotch pines in a flat area. Enter a hardwood forest at 0.3mi and turn right. Follow the blue blazes, mainly on an old logging road. There are slight ascents and descents. Go straight at a logging road junction at 1.2mi. At 1.7mi turn left and descend. Turn left again at 1.9mi. Watch closely for a few turns on and off the old road, but at 2.1mi reach a strip mine road. Turn right. Follow the road W, partially through sections of forest, but mostly in open areas formed by strip-mining. Ascend and reach FR227, the SW trailhead, at 4.0mi.

STONECOAL TRAIL (TR360)   4.0mi(6.4km)

SCENERY: 2 (wooded)   NOTE: B,M (0)
DIFFICULTY: II (moderate)   SKI-:   S3
CONDITION: C (poor)   ELEV: 4160/3650
MAPS: USFS(A), Mill Creek, Wildell, III-C-3 in this Guide
SEGMENTS: (1) FR92 to FR209   4.0mi

Stonecoal Trail, a West Va. Department of Natural Resources hunter-access trail, connects the Cheat Mountain Road (FR92) with the W side of Shaver's Fork and Shaver's Fork Road (FR209).

Access: The NW trailhead [H] is on FR92, 3.2mi from US250/ WV92. The E trailhead (not shown on Map III-C-3) is on FR209, 1.0mi from US250/WV92. Parking space is available.

Segment 1: Starting from the NW [H] FR92, follow the crest of the ridge through a forest of hardwoods and red spruce, and pass a number of wildlife food plots. At 2.2mi the blue blazes may be sparse or absent, but the trail descends on the S slope of the ridge toward a stream. At 3.0mi the trail curves E, away from the stream, and descends rapidly to FR760 at 3.8mi. Turn right and go 0.2mi to FR209.

WHITMEADOW RIDGE TRAIL (TR361)   4.6mi(7.4km)

SCENERY: 2 (wooded)   NOTE: B,M,S (0)
DIFFICULTY: II (moderate)   SKI-:   S4
CONDITION: B (average)   ELEV: 4160/3480
MAPS: USFS(A), Mill Creek, Wildell, III-C-2 & -3 in this Guide
SEGMENTS: (1) FR92 to FR47   4.6mi

Whitmeadow Ridge Trail (also called Whitmeadow Hunter Access Trail) is a SE-NW hunters' trail from the Cheat Mountain N-S ridgeline to the banks of Shavers Fork NW of Dublin. Its entire distance is through a mixed forest.

Access: The NW trailhead [K](Map III-C-3) is on FR92, 1.3mi N of the junction with FR47.
The SE trailhead [N](Map III-C-2) is at the E end of FR47, 2.2mi from FR92.

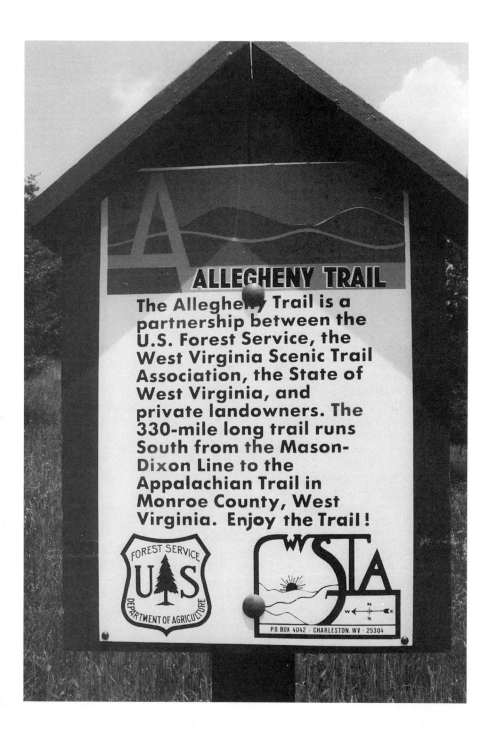

WV92 parking area for Allegheny Trail (TR701). Photo by Allen de Hart

Segment 1: Starting from FR92 [K], ascend gradually 0.4mi to a trail junction and turn left, E. From this point, stay on the ridge, follow the blue blazes for 2.3mi, then begin a descent. Cross FR409 (not shown on Map III-C-2) and descend more steeply on a rocky treadway to an old RR grade [P]. (To the left (N) it is 0.5mi to the E end of FR49 at Shavers Fork.) Continue to the right and parallel to Shavers Fork in a rhododendron grove. Reach FR47 and a parking area [N] near the mouth of Whitmeadow Run.

CROUCH RIDGE TRAIL (TR362)   2.9mi(4.6km)

SCENERY: 1 (exceptional)   NOTE: B (1)
DIFFICULTY: II (moderate)   SKI-:   S4
CONDITION: B (average)   ELEV: 4120/3560
MAPS: USFS(A), Mill Creek, Wildell, III-C-2 & -3 in this Guide
SEGMENTS: (1) FR92 to FR49   2.9mi

This trail formerly had a NW entrance on FR188 and joined Crouch Hunter Access Trail in a ridge saddle. Now its trailhead is on FR92. It is similar in terrain and vegetation to Whitmeadow Ridge Trail. Birch, maple, hemlock and red spruce are mixed.

Access: The NW terminus [M](Map III-C-3) is on FR92, 0.05mi N of the junction with FR49.

The SE terminus [R](Map III-C-2) is on FR49, 2.7mi from FR92.

Segment 1: Starting from FR92 [M](Map III-C-3), follow the crest of the ridge with four knobs and shallow saddles for 2mi to a junction [S](Map III-C-2) with Turkey Trail (TR363) (not shown on Map III-C-2). (Formerly a 0.7mi hunters' access trail, Turkey Trail goes NE around a knob and rapidly ascends to Yokum Run and FR188.) Turn right at the junction and follow Crouch Ridge Trail to immediately begin a descent into a cove of tall red spruce. At 2.9mi cross Crouch Run to FR49 [R]. (It is 1.2mi to the end of FR49 at Shavers Fork.)

YOKUM RIDGE TRAIL (TR372)   1.4mi(2.2km)

SCENERY: 2 (wooded)   NOTE: B,M (0)
DIFFICULTY: II (moderate)   SKI-:   S4
CONDITION: B (average)   ELEV: 3940/3360
MAPS: USFS(A), WILDELL, III-C-2 in this Guide
SEGMENTS: (1) FR92 to FR210   1.4mi

Yokum Ridge Trail is the most northern in a series of trails which extend from the crest of Cheat Mountain on perpendicular ridges. Near their E termini they all drop to rocky Shavers Fork. All these trails (Stonecoal, Whitmeadow, Crouch, and Yokum) have bear, deer, turkey and other wildlife.

Access: The W trailhead [U] is on FR92, 0.9mi N of FR188.

The E trailhead [W] is on FR210, 1.8mi from FR92 (9mi N of US250).

Segment 1: From FR92 [U] follow the trail through mixed hardwoods and red spruce on an even contour for 0.6mi to a fork. (To the right is a short cut to Yokum Ridge Spur, a 0.8mi descent in a cove to Yokum Run and FR188.) Take the left fork and descend gradually 0.2mi to a junction with Yokum Ridge Spur trail (TR369) (not shown on Map III-C-2) before a final descent to FR210 [W]. (The length of Yokum Ridge Spur Trail is 0.8mi.) To the left is a parking area, and to the right is an oxbow of Shavers Fork.

WEST FORK TRAIL (TR312)   25.5mi(40.8km)

SCENERY: 1 (exceptional)   NOTE: B,M,S,(0)
DIFFICULTY: II (moderate)   SKI-:   S1
CONDITION: A (good)   ELEV: 3130/2730
MAPS: USFS(A), Beverly East, Glady, Wildell, Durbin, III-C-1, III-C-2
in this Guide
SEGMENTS: (1) Cheat Junction to TR701/CO22   2.7mi
             (2) TR701/CO22 to TR345 (High Falls Trail)   4.6mi
             (3) TR345 to Durbin   18.2mi

In 1986 the USFS purchased the right-of-way of the abandoned CSX Railroad from Greenbrier Junction at Shavers Fork to the town of Durbin. Since then, all rails and ties have been removed, trestles restored, gates installed, and a gravel base has been graded for hiking, bicycling and cross-country skiing. Motorized travel is prohibited. Space for campsites is allowed along the trail with the exception of the tunnel area and the narrow fenced strip between Glady and High Falls Trail. It was named the West Fork Trail because its longer distance parallels the West Fork of the Greenbrier River, and another section parallels the West Fork of Glady Fork. If the trail bypasses the tunnel the distance is 25.7mi.

From its N terminus along Shavers Fork to Glady, the spectacular trail ascends gently through woodlands on a grassy treadway, and tunnels through Shavers Mountain to return S. After a bucolic section from Glady to the High Falls Trail crossing, it is an unnoticeable descent for 18.2mi in a mixture of woods, meadows, beaver ponds, pools and rock slopes. The trail's highest point, also undiscernable in elevation is at Lynn Divide where the waters of Glady Fork flow N and the waters of the Greenbrier flow S. Wildflowers and wildlife are prominent on the trail, and the fall season foliage colors are out-standing.

Two loops could be formed for the N section of the trail. One loop uses High Falls Trail from FR44 ([P]Map III-C-1)) for 2.5mi to High Falls [T] on Shavers Fork, continue downstream 1.4mi to milepost 49 and the N terminus [J] of West Fork Trail, pass through Glady (or use the tunnel) and return to FR44 [P] for a 11.6mi loop.

The other loop uses High Falls Trail from FR44 [P] for 1mi to join Allegheny Trail (TR701), goes N 3.9mi to Glady [J] for a junction with West Fork Trail, and turns S to rejoin High Falls Trail. A return to FR44 [P] makes a 9.3mi loop. It is 4mi to Glady from the High Falls Trail trailhead on FR44, which becomes CO22/2. (A small store is open 9 AM to 3 PM in Glady.)

Access: Access to the N terminus requires a hike from CO22 (0.7mi W of Glady at the former RR loading dock) to the SW trailhead for backtracking. Because the USFS discourages the use of the tunnel (near [J]), the best parking area for the N access is 0.5mi S of Glady on SR27 to a parking area near private homes. (There is a question of safety in hiking through the tunnel. Water cannot drain from the tunnel because the USFS has made earthen barriers at the entrance, and there is some crumbling of the tunnel's lining.)

Access at the S terminus is at the junction of US250 and CO250/13 in Durbin.

Segment 1: Starting from Greenbrier Junction ([S]Map III-C-1), there are no major overlooks into Shavers Fork canyon, but the sounds of the rapids can be heard for nearly 2mi. After 1.3mi is an open area, the site of Cheat Junction where a former RR spur curved across the river to join the main line to Bemis. At 2.7mi is a former loading dock [L] and access to CO22 (0.7mi W of Glady). Here is the takeout point if you are not entering the tunnel.

Segment 2: If passing through the tunnel, climb over the earth-and-rock barriers at the tunnel entrance at 3.1mi; exit at 3.3mi. (The tunnel may have water pockets as deep as 1ft; a flashlight is advisable though both ends of the tunnel provide some light.)

At 3.8mi pass a parking area near private homes (the S end of Glady Fork Road, CO27) in Glady. Begin a narrow channel of RR grade on scenic hillside pasturelands. Cattle, sheep, and deer graze on both sides of the fenced and gated trail. Pass a gate and graveyard at 4.1mi, and a junction with High Falls Trail (TR345) at the former Beulah Station at 7.3mi. (It is 0.4mi E to FR44 [P].)

Segment 3: At 8.1mi cross a glade, a forest logging road at 8.6mi, and reach a meadow with a hawthorne grove at 10mi. Other vegetation includes ash, maple, hemlock, cattails, and wildflowers. There are old and new beaver dams in the area. The former Wildell RR junction is at 10.5mi, where a gate and parking area is near a dirt road which goes E 0.2mi to FR44.

Trestles over Greenbrier River are crossed at 13.5mi ([Q] Map III-C-2) and 13.7mi before a gate crossing to Mill Run Road at 15.5mi [T]. The dirt road goes E 0.1mi to FR44 and a popular spring. Other trestles are crossed near the confluence with Iron Bridge Run at 16.5mi [X], at 18.7mi with Little River (not on Map III-C-2), and at 23.9mi with Mountain Lick Run. Between the trestle crossings are excellent views of river, pools for fishing, wildflower meadows, and rock formations. At 21.5mi is a trail access a few yd. to FR44 (Braucher on the topo map). The trail passes under the US250 bridge at 25mi, passes a gate and ends at 25.5mi at a parking area by Pocahontas Road (CO250/13). (Across the street, US250, is Highland Street which connects with FR44.)

ALLEGHENY TRAIL (TR701)   11.0mi(17.6km)

SCENERY: 2 (wooded)   NOTE: B,M (6)
DIFFICULTY: III (strenuous)   SKI-:   S2
CONDITION: B (average)   ELEV: 3080/2640
MAPS: USFS(A,B), Bowden, Glady, III-B-1, III-B-2 & III-C-1 in this Guide
SEGMENTS: (1) CO22 to TR302 (McCray Run Trail)   5.6mi
          (2) TR302 to US33   5.4mi

This section of well-marked Allegheny Trail extends from Glady to the N boundary of Greenbrier Ranger District at US33. It follows downstream, for the first 2.0mi on paved Glady Road (CO27) (Map III-C-1), and for most of the remaining route, on an old RR grade. At a few points it leaves the RR grade and becomes steep, rocky or rough. Forest vegetation includes red spruce, hemlock, mixed hardwoods, and rhododendron.

Access: The S access is CO22, 0.3mi W of the Glady crossroads with CO27 (near [J] Map III-C-1). Parking at Glady is roadside parking, either at the trailhead or at the community's single crossroads of CO22 and CO27. Here is a small store, usually open from 11 AM to 3 PM, and a public telephone.

The N access is on the E side of Glady Fork Bridge on US33, between Alpena and Wymer. About 1.5mi E on US33 is a country store with a telephone. About 1.3mi W on US33 is Alpine Lodge and Restaurant.

Segment 1: From near Glady [J] follow blazes N on CO27 and, after 2.1mi, leave the road [R](Map III-B-2) to the right, into the National Forest and descend steeply to a crossing of Glady Fork at 3mi. Except at one point near the junction [F](Map III-B-1) of McCray Run Trail (TR302), Allegheny Trail is on a level grade before McCray Creek.

Segment 2: From 5.6mi [F] to 6.1mi [E] follow McCray Run Trail. (McCray Run Trail has an E terminus on FR14 and a W terminus on CO27.) At 7.1mi Allegheny Trail breaks away from the river and ascends a ridge [Q]; at 8.6mi is another break (not on Map III-B-1) before descending to Laurel Lick Run. From Laurel Lick Run the trail leaves the RR grade, ascends and then descends to a meadow where it crosses Nichols Lane Run at 10.8mi. After 0.2mi the Greenbrier Ranger District section of Allegheny Trail is completed at US33. (Allegheny Trail continues downstream from here in Cheat Ranger District.)

A restoration lake by Strip Mine Trail (TR350). Photo by Allen de Hart

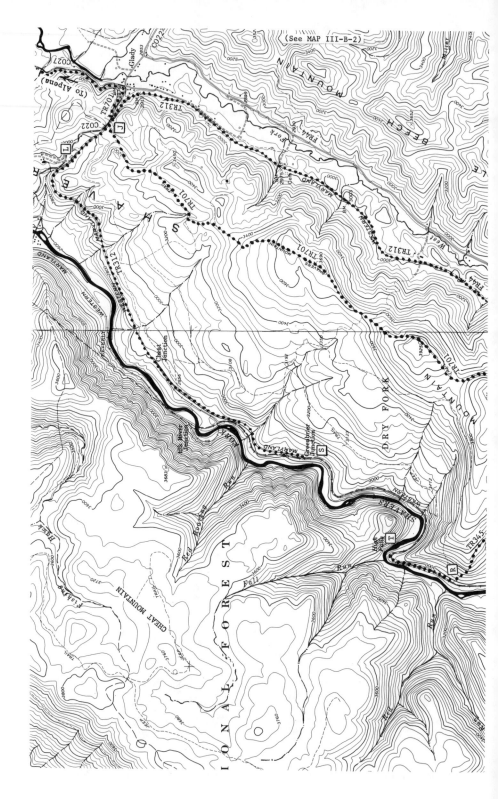

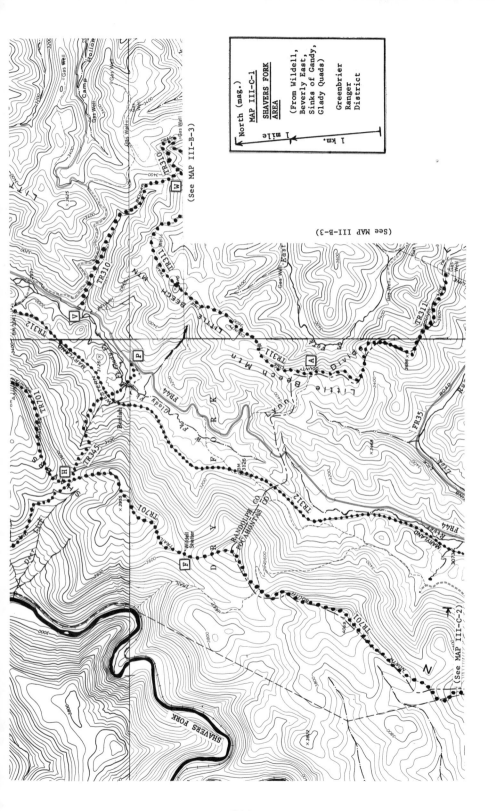

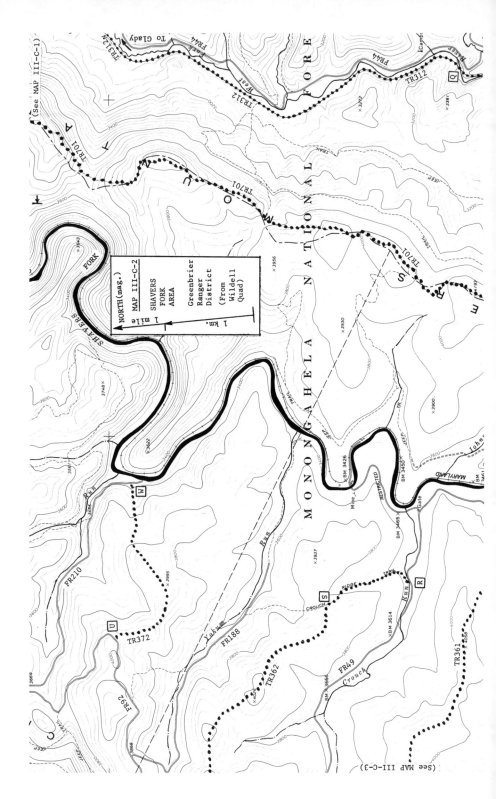

MAP III-C-2

SHAVERS
FORK
AREA

Greenbrier
Ranger
District
(From
Wildell
Quad)

NORTH (mag.)

1 mile

1 km.

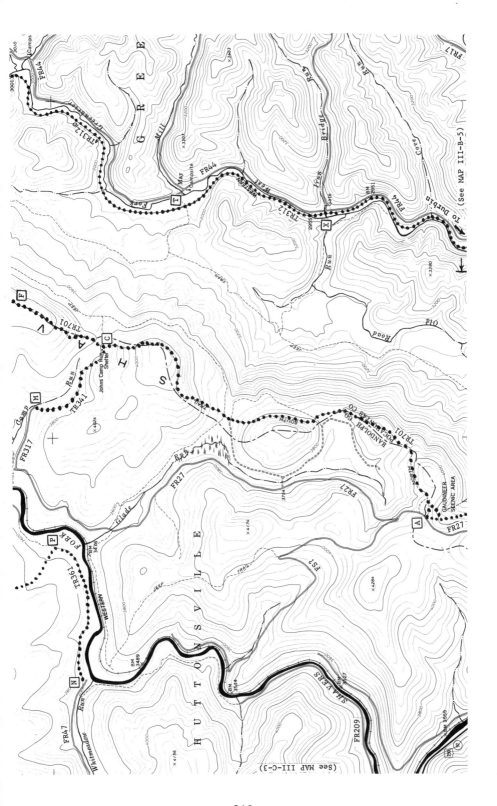

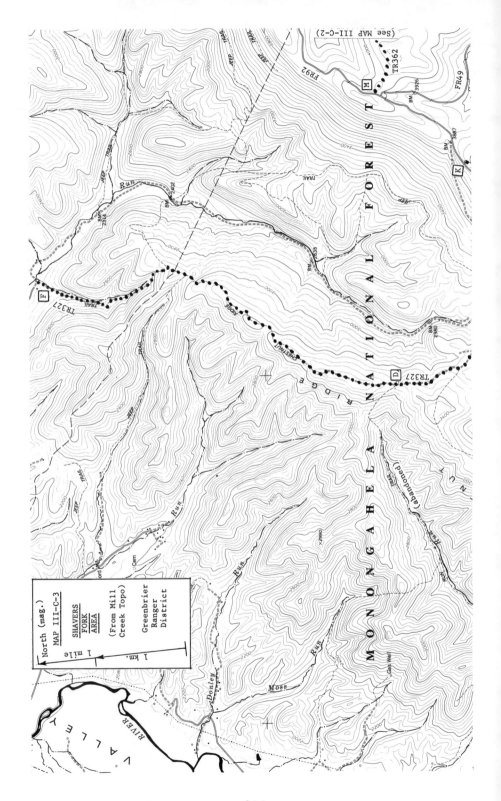

North (mag.)

MAP III-C-3

SHAVERS
FORK
AREA

(From Mill
Creek Topo)

Greenbrier
Ranger
District

1 Km.
1 mile

214

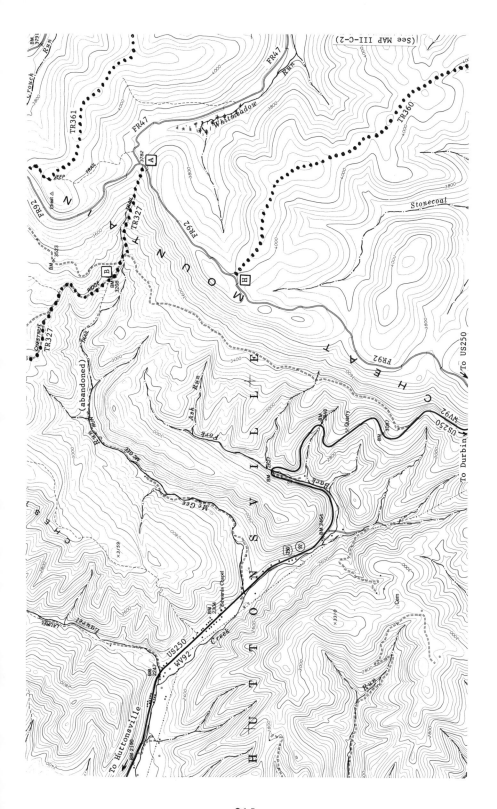

215

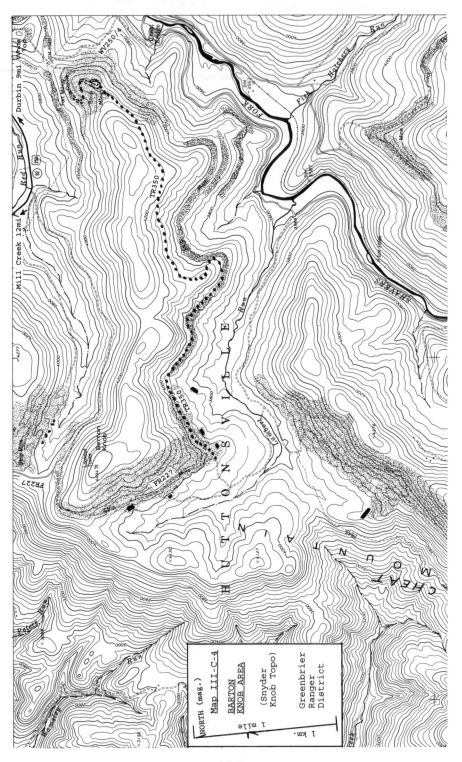

NORTH (mag.)

Map III-C-4

BARTON KNOB AREA

(Snyder Knob Topo)

Greenbrier Ranger District

1 mile

1 KM.

216

MARLINTON RANGER DISTRICT

Marlinton Ranger District adjoins three other districts: Greenbrier on the N, Gauley on the W, and White Sulphur on the S. The E boundary adjoins George Washington National Forest in Virginia. Near the center of the district the Greenbrier River Valley separates the district from its highest and most rugged Gauley and Yew mountains in the W from Buckley, Marlin, Brushy, and Middle Mountains in the E. Its highest peak is Red Spruce Knob (el.4703ft) NW of Marlinton. In the district's N border is the state's oldest state forest, Seneca State Forest (Tel. 304-799-6213), and its S border has Watoga State Park (Tel. 304-799-4087), the state's oldest and largest state park. Although its major trail network is in the Tea Creek and Tea Creek Mountain area in the W of the district, a 40-mi section of Allegheny Trail weaves through the district's center. The trail intersects trail networks in both Seneca State Forest and Watoga State Park. As in other districts, some forest roads are unplowed in the winter. Such road offer ski-touring opportunities. One of the best is Highland Scenic Highway (WV150) from Cranberry Mountain Nature Center on WV39 to US219 N of Marlinton.

There are four developed campground in the district, all with user fees except Bird Run. They open March 15 and close December 15. They are:

| Bird Run | (12 sites) | Pocahontas | (9 sites) |
| Day Run | (12 sites) | Tea Creek | (29 sites) |

All have water, toilets and picnic tables. There is an undeveloped campground at Handley Public Hunting and Fishing Area E of Tea Creek Campground and W of Marlinton on Williams River Road. Convenient to hikers in the S area of the district are developed campgrounds (one with hot showers) at Lake Sherwood Recreation Area in White Sulphur Ranger District. Additionally, there are two campgrounds in Watoga State Park both with flush toilets and hot showers, and a section of rental cabins. A less developed, smaller, campground is found in Seneca State Forest; it has picnic areas and rental cabins.

Ski-Touring in Marlinton Ranger District

Highlands Scenic Highway (WV150) is a high-elevation highway from US219 N of Marlinton to the Cranberry Mountain Nature Center. It is not plowed in winter, and was designed to provide scenic vistas. It is sure to delight skiiers of all ability levels. For snow conditions call Marlinton Ranger District at Tel. 304-799-4334.

Greenbrier River Trail

West Virginia has acquired ownership of an abandoned RR grade along scenic Greenbrier River. A 75.2mi trail that makes use of this grade is complete. Use of the trail is restricted to hiking, bicycling, horseback riding, cross-country skiing and camping. No motorized vehicles are allowed. When fully developed, it should be one of the state's most outstanding trails. Although the trail is not a USFS trail, it is a major trail resource within the proclamation boundary of the MNF. It connects with Allegheny Trail (TR701) at Sitlington (see Map III-A-1). Marlinton Ranger District contains 3.6 miles of Greenbrier River Trail (between Marlinton and Clover Lick). To get to the Clover Lick access point, drive W from WV28 on Laurel Creek

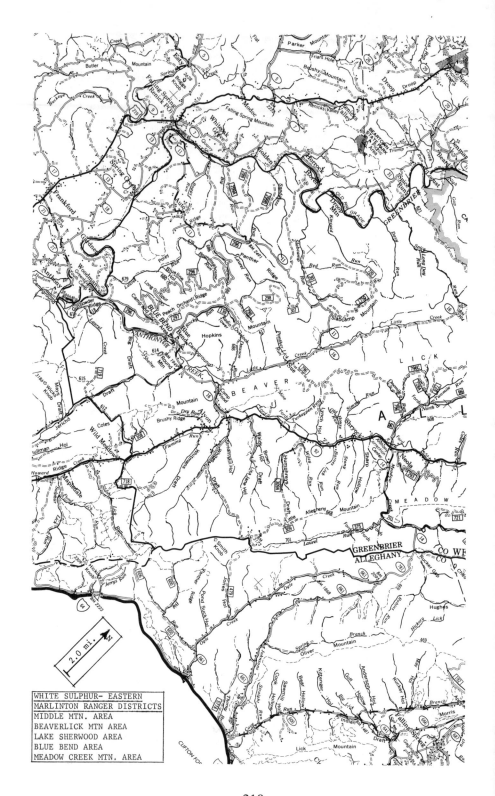

WHITE SULPHUR- EASTERN
MARLINTON RANGER DISTRICTS
MIDDLE MTN. AREA
BEAVERLICK MTN AREA
LAKE SHERWOOD AREA
BLUE BEND AREA
MEADOW CREEK MTN. AREA

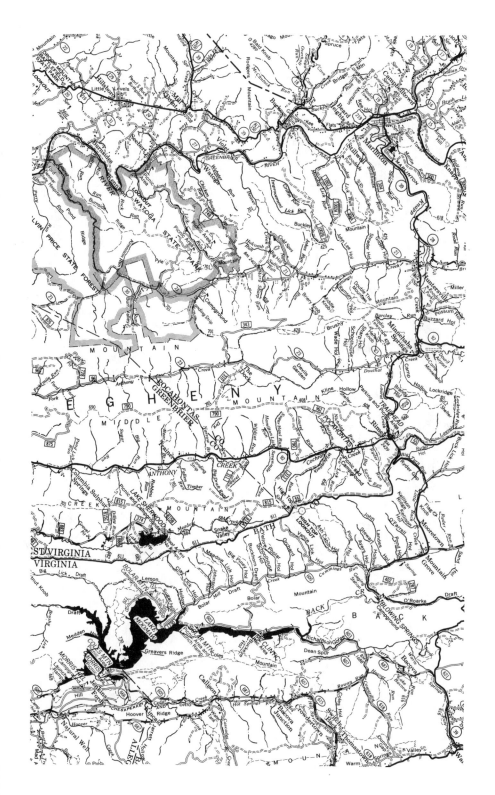

Swinging Bridge over Anthony Creek for Blue Bend Loop Trail (TR614).
Photo courtesy of USFS

Road (CO114) for 4.1mi. The other access point in Marlinton Ranger District is within the town of Marlinton.

Greenbrier River Trail passes (across Greenbrier River from) Watoga State Park and Seneca State Forest. The status of the trail can be learned from Greenbrier State Forest, HC-30, Box 154, Caldwell, WV 24925 (Tel. 304-536-1944) or Watoga State Park, HC-82, Box 252, Marlinton, WV 24954 (Tel. 304-799-4087 or Tel. 1-800-CALL-WVA).

Greenbrier River Trail is scenic and usable for its entire distance. Repairs have been made to correct damage from the floods of 1985 and 1996. It is popular with hikers, mountain bikers and equestrians. Descent from Cass to North Caldwell is easy and gradual. Access to Cass is 1.0mi S on Deer Creek Road (CO1/13), and access from North Caldwell is 1.4mi off US60 on Stone House Road (CO-38). The trail parallels the river on the W side, except between the community of Clawson (S of Cass) and the community of Watoga (E of Mill Point). The town of Marlinton is about half way between Clawson and Watoga. (see Map III-A-1).

The trail passes through a few small towns, and traverses 35 bridges and two tunnels as it winds along the valley.

Primitive camping is available along the trail, and facility camping is available at Greenbrier State Forest, Watoga State Park, and Seneca State Forest.

Maps needed for Greenbrier River Trail are: USFS(A), Lewisburg, White Sulphur Springs, Anthony, Droop, Denmar, Hillsboro, Marlinton, Edray, Clover Lick, and Cass. Another good trail map is "Secondary Base Series Map" of the S half of the MNF. (See pages 15 and 218-219.) Greenbrier State Forest (address above) offer a free map and trail guide. Access points and nearby roads are shown.

ALLEGHENY TRAIL (TR701)   40.3mi(64.5km)

SCENERY: 1-2 (exceptional-wooded)   NOTE: B,H,M,S,(8)
DIFFICULTY: II (moderate)   SKI-:   S4
CONDITION: A-B (good-average)   ELEV: 3420/2220
MAPS: USFS(A): Clover Lick, Marlinton, Lake Sherwood, Minnehaha
        Springs
SEGMENTS: (1) CR23 to Watoga SP (CR21/4)   4.2mi
          (2) CR21/4 to Huntersville (CR21/WV39)   13.7mi
          (3) CR21/WV39 to Thorny Creek (WV28)   10.6mi
          (4) WV28 to Seneca State Forest (FR1/4)   5.4mi
          (5) FR1/4 to Sitlington (CR12)   6.4mi

Allegheny Trail in Marlinton Ranger District is described in two parts, mainly because Huntersville is nearly halfway, and is the only resupply point on the route. The first part is 17.9mi from near "The Dock" to Huntersville, and the second part is 22.4mi from Huntersville to Sitlington, near Dunmore. Its route is on new routes, old and new bridges and trails, old and new USFS roads, state park and forest trails and roads, and short pieces of county and state highways. The highest point on the trail is 3420ft in elevation at the lookout tower in Seneca State Forest. Developed campground facilities and a restaurant are in Watoga State Park, but they are open only in the summer and parts of the spring and fall. (For more detailed description and mapping, secure *Hiking Guide to the Allegheny Trail* described on page 48 in this Guide.)

Access: The S trailhead is at "The Dock", which got its name from a former timber loading point, and which is now only a place by the roadside for parking. It is also the junction where Allegheny Trail arrives from the E on gated FR310 and continues W on a gated and grassy forest road. Although the trail does not enter Marlinton Ranger District until crossing Brushy Mountain Road (FR343) 1.4mi W, "The Dock" is the most convenient access point because FR343 may be gated and closed.

The N trailhead is at the Greenbrier River Bridge on CR12, 3.3mi W of Dunmore.

Segment 1: Starting from the S ("The Dock"), follow the old gated forest road W through a pine plantation on former Brushy Mountain Trail to a meadow. After crossing North Fork of Anthony Creek the trail ascends to Beaver Lick Mountain ridge and crosses Brushy Mountain Road. The trail descends on former Beaver Creek Trail into Marlinton Ranger District. It then follows downstream, and crosses Beaver Creek to a large grassy developed meadow (formerly a landing strip), and to the edge of Beaver Creek Campground of Watoga State Park.

Segment 2: For the next 3.4mi the trail ascends to connect with park trails and an entrance road, and reenters the MNF on Pyle Mountain. After 2.7mi, and a number of switchbacks, the route descends to cross a bridge (built in 1991) over Beaver Creek. An ascent on more switchbacks follows to approach the ridge crest of Buckley Mountain, where, for more than 7.0mi, the trail remains until descending E in Gilden Hollow. Upon reaching CR21, the route is left on the road into Huntersville at 17.9mi. Groceries, gasoline, post office, and public telephones are available here.

Segment 3: The second part of the trail is more isolated. It has a shelter and touches a state highway only once. From Huntersville the trail follows WV39 W for 0.9mi, where a right turn onto WV28 leads 0.5mi to the forest entrance on the left. The ascent to the Marlin Mountain ridgeline is steep, but once there the undulations are minor or moderate for 6.0mi. Marlin Mountain shelter (no water, sleeps six), is 4.5mi after beginning on the ridgeline. From the shelter the trail continues on a forest road for 3.0mi before descending to cross Marlin Lick Run. From here it ascends again before descending to Thorny Creek. There, a WV28 bridge crosses Thorny Creek.

Segments 4 & 5: The remainder of the trail is another 11.4mi, most of which passes through Seneca State Forest on Thorny Creek Mountain. This part of the trail, as with Marlin and Buckley Mountain ridges, has wild turkey, deer, owls, and other wildlife. Through a mainly hardwood forest there are ferns, mountain laurel, and wildflowers such as wildpink.

(IV-A) BIRD RUN AREA

In the NE corner of Marlinton Ranger District is Bird Run Campground (formerly CCC Camp Copperhead) on the N side of Bird Run. It is on WV84, 1.6mi NE of Frost and 3.1mi from the Virginia state line. The clear stream drains from the Paddy Knob area of the Allegheny Mountains range between Virginia and West Virginia. Bird Run Trail (TR486), whose 4.0mi route was from Bird Run Campground to Paddy Knob (el.4477ft), has been dropped from the USFS trail system. Because Paddy Knob is a scenic area, hikers may drive there on FR55 from WV84 near the state line. Not only is this part of FR55 an easy access for hunters, the road can be an attractive route for naturalists, birders, and hikers from one end of the district to the other.

Another nearby trail, 4.1mi Sugar Camp Trail (TR406) has been removed from the trail system inventory. It has been converted to a permanent linear wildlife opening because half of the trail was made a system road in the mid 1980s. The USFS states that the linear opening will actually improve conditions because it will be mowed every other years. Hikers can easily reach the wildlife route on FR55, 2.1mi W of WV84. But 1.0mi of FR441 on the W half is used for an access to Flame Azalea Trail added to the trail system in 1991 and described below.

FLAME AZALEA TRAIL (TR410)   0.3mi(0.5km)

SCENERY: 1 (exceptional)   NOTE: (0)
DIFFICULTY: I (leisurely)   SKI-: S4
CONDITION: A (good)   ELEV: 3080/3035
MAPS: USFS(A), Paddy Knob
SEGMENTS: (1) FR441 to FR441   0.3mi

Flame Azalea Trail is one of the shortest and most unique in the MNF. No other forest trail has such a concentration of orange, yellow, and red hues of the wild *Rhododendron calendulaceum*. After a timber harvesting in the early 1980s it was discovered, developed, and since maintained by a group of professors and students from Louisburg College in North Carolina. Some of the more than 150 azaleas are 12ft tall and others are low, dense, and profuse. Some, mainly yellow, are at the uncut timber edge. Growing among the azaleas are rosebay rhododendron, dogwood, locust, oaks, minnie-bush, ferns and more than 50 species of wildflowers.

Access: To reach the trailhead, drive 1.5mi N on WV92 from Frost. At a gated forest road (FR441) is parking for two vehicles. FR441 is part of the former Sugar Camp Trail. Its gate is supposed to be locked year-around. Follow FR441 1.0mi to the trailhead on the left.

Segment 1: The loop trail follows old logging roads in a cove favored by afternoon sunshine.

(IV-B) LAUREL CREEK AREA

Laurel Creek headwaters are between Lockridge Mountain on the W and the Allegheny Mountains on the E between Virginia and West Virginia. The stream is joined by Cochran Creek, which flows through Pocahontas Campground, near the junction of WV39 and WV92. Together they parallel the highway for 3.0mi, flow into Douthat Creek, and after another mile flow through Minnehaha Springs. Along the way, on the S side of Laurel Creek, Middle Mountain forms an 18-mile ridge ending near Neola.

LAUREL CREEK TRAIL (TR466)   8.0mi(12.9km)

SCENERY: 2 (wooded)   NOTE: B,H,M,(5)
DIFFICULTY: II (moderate)   SKI-: S2
CONDITION: A (good)   ELEV: 3000/2410

MAPS: USFS(A), Minnehaha Springs, IV-B-1 in this Guide
SEGMENTS: (1) WV39 to Shelter   4.5mi
               (2) Shelter to WV39   3.5mi

Laurel Creek Trail was completed by Older American Workers in 1975, and was classified as a National Recreation Trail. But in the late 1980s the USFS removed this status, as it is authorized to do, after 10 years. Maintenance continues, however, to be of good quality. The trail follows along Laurel Creek as it flows through a flat-bottomed, narrow valley. Several wildlife meadows, bordered by red pine, are located along the upper third of the stream, and a large pine plantation occupies a former meadows immediately N of WV39. A loop trail, it ascends from Laurel Creek to Lockridge Mountain, passes a shelter, and returns to the point of origin.

Access: The trailhead is at the Rimel parking area [A] on WV39, 0.8mi W of the Virginia state line and 0.5mi W of the WV39-WV92 intersection.

Segment 1: Proceeding counterclockwise, Laurel Creek Trail leads E from the parking area, crosses Lockridge Mountain Road (FR345), then goes around a slope to an abandoned RR grade along Laurel Creek. This is a grassy, and sometimes wet, lane through the woods. Branches of the grade go up into unnamed side-streams S of Lockridge Run, and make interesting side trips. After 2.4mi on this grade the trail turns up Lockridge Run [E], where it follows on the SW side. After reaching new growth from a clear-cut in the early 1980s, the trail turns W. At the end of the new growth the trail goes S on the E side of Lockridge Mountain. The trail passes S of a wildlife clearing, and an Adirondack shelter [S] (sleeps 8) at 4.5mi.

Segment 2: From the shelter, Laurel Creek Trail passes a wildlife water hole and continues meandering on the E side of Lockridge Mountain. At 7.5mi the trail crosses Lockridge Mountain forest road, passes by a wildlife water hole, and descends in a cove for a return to the parking area.

TWO LICK TRAIL (TR456)   4.3mi(6.9km)

SCENERY: 2 (wooded)	NOTE: (0)
DIFFICULTY: II (moderate)	SKI-: S4
CONDITION: A (good)	ELEV: 3030/2490

MAPS: USFS(A), Mountain Grove
SEGMENTS: (1) Campground to campground   4.3mi

Although this is the only trail at Pocahontas Campground, it is a good base camp (see facilities in the introduction of this chapter) for other trails such as Laurel Creek Trail (TR466) and Middle Mountain Trail (TR608). Also, it is only 6.5mi S on WV92 where Allegheny Trail (TR701) crosses the highway at Bear Branch parking area in White Sulphur Ranger District.

Access: At Pocahontas Campground on WV92, 1.8mi S of WV39, Two Lick Trail begins on the left at the entrance.

Segment 1: Cross Cochran Creek on a footbridge, and pass through a mature white pine and hemlock stand in the bottomland. At 0.1mi the trail divides to form a loop. If choosing counterclockwise ascend SE on a ridge. At 1.7mi the trail curves left from the ridge and passes the headwaters of Two Lick Run on a W slope. After a rocky 0.3mi, it reaches another ridge and curves left. After a slight ascension to a knob, a descent begins with switchbacks. At 4.1mi the trail crosses Two Lick Run to the left of a grazing field and returns to the campground.

MIDDLE MOUNTAIN TRAIL (TR608) (N Section)   4.6mi(7.4km)

SCENERY: 2 (wooded)   NOTE: B,H,W,(1)
DIFFICULTY: II (moderate)   SKI-:   S4
CONDITION: A/B (good-average)   ELEV: 3220/2410
MAPS: USFS(A), Minnehaha Springs, Mtn. Grove, Lake Sherwood
SEGMENTS: (1) WV39 to FR790/TR608 (S Section)   4.6mi

Middle Mountain Trail follows Middle Mountain for 17.0mi, from Rimel (near the junction of WV39 and WV92) S to Neola at WV92. The N 4.6mi are maintained by Marlinton Ranger District (formerly as TR408) and the remainder (S Section) of the trail is maintained by White Sulphur Ranger District. Wildlife clearings are found at 2.5mi, 4.0mi, and 4.3mi, starting from the N entrance. The entire trail is waterless except for the crossing of Laurel Creek at the N entrance and N Fork of Anthony Creek at the S entrance.

Access: The N trailhead is across WV39 from the spacious Rimel parking area, 4.0mi E of Minnehaha Springs on WV39, the same space as described above for Laurel Creek Trail (TR466).

Divide Road (FR790) is the S terminus (and the N terminus of TR608 (S Section) (White Sulphur Ranger District). From the S trailhead, FR790 leads 3.0mi to WV92 at a point 3.5mi S from the Rimel intersection of WV39 and WV92. FR790 is gated and locked.

Segment 1: The blue blazed trail begins in a white pine forest. After crossing Laurel Creek on a timber bridge, Middle Mountain Trail climbs moderately for the first 0.8mi. (At 0.6mi is an old woods road where the trail turns sharply right.) At 0.8mi the trail levels off. A shelter (sleeps 8) is found at 3.5mi; water is not available. However, there are water holes for wildlife at 0.6mi, 1.6mi, 2.5mi, and 3.5mi. At 4.4mi Divide Road (FR790) is reached. From here the trail ascends steeply for 0.2mi to its S terminus and the N terminus of TR608 (S Section). Allegheny Trail (TR701) meets TR608 2.7mi S of FR790. Neola is 13.4mi S.

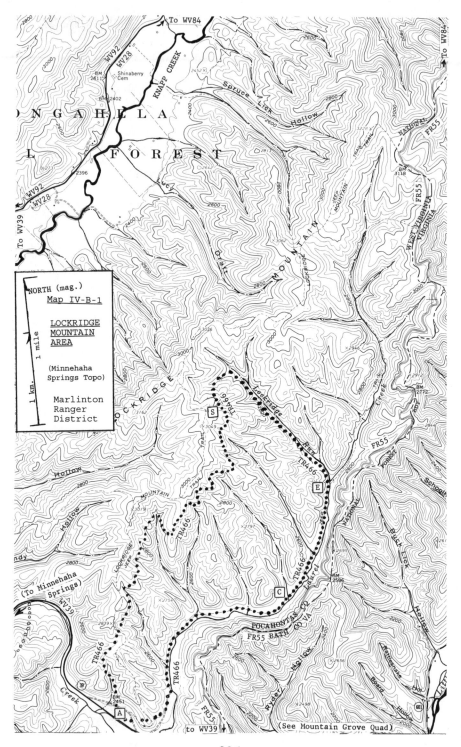

NORTH (mag.)

<u>Map IV-B-1</u>

<u>LOCKRIDGE
MOUNTAIN
AREA</u>

(Minnehaha
Springs Topo)

Marlinton
Ranger
District

View from cliff of High Rock Trail (TR409) off Highlands Scenic Highway. Photo by Allen de Hart

(IV-C) HIGHLAND SCENIC HIGHWAY, PARKWAY SECTION

Highland Scenic Highway (WV150) is a 45-mi natural area route from Richwood to US219 on Elk Mountain, N of Marlinton. It has a distinctive yellow and green logo marker, and is also WV39/55 from Richwood to Cranberry Mountain Nature Center, a distance of 22mi. From the Nature Center to US219 on Elk Mountain, the 23mi section is a parkway. It is exceptionally different because it is the only USFS-managed parkway in the nation. Restricted by law to passenger cars and recreation vehicles (commerical usage is by permit only), it is the state's highest, longest, and most limited access parkway.

Among the points of interest are trailheads, overlooks, remote forest roads, grazing fields, and parking spots for nature study or hunting. Listed below are some of the major points of interest. Because the Parkway is not plowed during winter, it is usually closed from mid-December into March. At that time the Parkway can be used for ski-touring.

The S half of the Parkway is the E-W boundary between Marlinton and Gauley ranger districts, but from the intersection with Williams River Road (FR96) N to US219 the Parkway is in Marlinton Ranger District.

There are four major overlooks for vehicular parking: all are on the E side of the Parkway in Marlinton Ranger District. One overlook, Red Lick, has had a picnic area and pit toilets since the mid 1980s, but in the early 1990s the USFS began constructing a small picnic shelter and pit toilets at the other three overlooks. Instead of constructing and blending the facilities within the shrubbery, the USFS has destroyed the scenic integrity of the overlooks. For example, the conspicuous toilet at Little Laurel Overlook is in the parking area. The Parkway is particularly colorful with spring flowers, banks of crown vetch and mosses, and autumn foliage. Cranberry Wilderness is on the W side of the Parkway and a large sanctuary for bear is on the E side.

Near WV150 are two USFS, and one state, campgrounds. The most developed is Tea Creek Campground, 0.1mi W on FR86 at the bridge over Williams River. The other is Day Run Campground 3.0mi SE on FR86 and 1.2mi S on FR216. The undeveloped state campground is 4.0mi N of Day Run on CO17/4 and CO17/1 to Handley Wildlife Management Area.

Points of Interest from Cranberry Mountain Nature Center (WV150/39/55) on WV150 to Elk Mountain (US219) are listed below.

Point of Interest	Milepost
Highrock Trail (TR409)	3.3
Cranberry Glades Parking Area and Overlook (TR411)	4.8
Forks of Cranberry Trail (TR245) Gauley R. Dist. side	5.2
Williams River Valley Overlook and Black Mtn. Trail (TR412)	6.2
Big Spruce Overlook and Black Mountain Trail (TR412)	7.9
North-South Trail (Gauley Ranger District side)	8.6
FR461 and North Fork Trail (TR272)	10.0
FR86 and Williams River	13.3
Williams River Trail (TR487) and Parking Area	13.4
Little Laurel Overlook and Tea Creek Mtn. Trail (TR452)	16.8
Gauley Mountain Trail (TR438)	17.3
Red Spruce Knob Trail (TR405)	17.7
Red Lick Overlook	20.1
US219 at Elk Mountain (6.6mi N of Marlinton)	23.0

HIGH ROCK TRAIL (TR409)   1.6mi(2.5km)
SCENERY: 1 (exceptional)   NOTE:B,M (0)
DIFFICULTY: I (leisurely)   SKI-:S4
CONDITION: A (good)   ELEV:4440/4350
MAPS: USFS(A), Hillsboro, II-A-8 in this Guide
SEGMENTS: (1) WV150 to views   1.6mi
     On top of High Rock Ridge, High Rock Trail follows an easy treadway
to an outstanding view of Greenbrier River Valley.
     Access: High Rock Trail is accessed from a parking area, 3.3mi N of
Cranberry Mountain Nature Center on Highland Scenic Highway (WV150).
     Segment 1: The trail is well designed through a forest of oak, beech,
maple, and other hardwoods. Wildflowers and ferns are prominent. Old timber road crossing are noticeable. A high cliff marks the trail's dead-end at
views of Lick Run Valley, Bald Knob, and Rodgers Mountain (to the SE).

CRANBERRY GLADES OVERLOOK TRAIL (TR411) 0.3mi(0.5km)
SCENERY: 1 (exceptional)   NOTE: M (0)
DIFFICULTY: I (leisurely)   SKI-: S4
CONDITION: A (good)   ELEV: 4520/4420
MAPS: USFS(A), Hillsboro, II-A-8 in this Guide
SEGMENTS: (1) WV150 to Overlook   0.3mi
     Cranberry Glades Overlook Trail was constructed by the Youth Conser-
vation Corps (YCC) in 1975. The trail has a 1-yd wide gravel surface. On
clear days the entire Cranberry Glades, including part of the boardwalk, and
Blue Knob in Gauley Ranger District can be seen.
     Access: The trailhead is at a 16-car parking lot [I] on Highland Scenic
Highway (WV150) 4.8mi from Cranberry Mountain Nature Center. It is near
the head of Black Mountain Run.

BLACK MOUNTAIN TRAIL (TR412)   4.7mi(7.6km)
SCENERY: 1 (exceptional)   NOTE: M (1)
DIFFICULTY: II (moderate)   SKI-: S4
CONDITION: A (good)   ELEV: 4545/3880
MAPS: USFS(A), Hillsboro, Woodrow, II-A-6 in this Guide
SEGMENTS:
(1) Williams R. Valley Overlook to Big Spruce Overlook   2.4mi
(2) Big Spruce Overlook to Williams R. Valley Overlook   2.3mi
     Constructed between 1991 and 1994, the Black Mountain Loop Trail
was designed for day-hiking between Williams River Valley Overlook and
Big Spruce Overlook, both on the Highlands Scenic Highway (WV150).
(Note: The contour interval on Map II-A-6 is 40ft instead of 20ft.)
     Access: The S Terminus, Williams River Valley Overlook, is 6.2mi N
on WV150 from Cranberry Nature Center. The N terminus, Big Spruce
Overlook, is 7.9mi N on WV150 from Cranberry Nature Center.
     Segment 1: From Williams River Valley Overlook the trail ascends to
a ridge, but quickly begins a descent on rocky switchbacks. At 0.3mi it turns
left (N) and stays generally level through rhododendrons, birch, beech, and
red spruce forest. Most of the distance is on an old RR grade. At 2.1mi it

ascends a rocky area to a boardwalk with observation decks. To the left it is 160yd to an exit at Big Spruce Overlook.

Segment 2: To continue on the loop, cross Highlands Scenic Highway and turn left (S). Enter a forest of red spruce and scattered hardwoods. Descend gradually on a narrow and rocky treadway. At 2.9mi and 3.2mi are sections of seepage. Pass a rock pile at 3.4mi. Lengthy beds of mosses and wood sorrrel are on the trail. After patches of rhododendron and mountain laurel ascend easily to Highlands Scenic Highway at 4.7mi, across the road from Williams River Valley Overlook.

RED SPRUCE KNOB TRAIL (TR405)   1.2mi(1.9km)

SCENERY: 1 (exceptional)   NOTE: M (0)
DIFFICULTY: I (leisurely)   SKI-: S4
CONDITION: A (good)   ELEV: 4703/4320
MAPS: USFS(A), Woodrow, IV-D-1 in this Guide
SEGMENTS: (1) WV150 to Red Spruce Knob   1.2mi

Opened in 1991, this unique mossy pathway leads to the district's highest peak. The habitat of Virginia flying squirrels, the trail makes a loop at the mountain top. Once the site of a fire tower, the area now is a dense red spruce forest with a view only toward the E. Views are of Crooked Fork Valley, Old Field Fork Valley, and (on a clear day) Snowshoe Ski Resort on Cheat Mountain.

Access: The trailhead is at a parking area, 0.9mi N of Little Laurel Overlook on Highland Scenic Highway (WV150).

Segment 1: After entering the woods, the trail ascends left and follows switchbacks to the ridge line. (Another trail, from the parking entrance, goes right and descends to Old Gauley Road, which, after 1.0mi, joins FR115. It is used mainly for ski-touring.)

IV-D TEA CREEK AREA

Marlinton Ranger District's major trail network is in the Tea Creek Area, adjacent to the N side of Gauley Ranger District's Cranberry Wilderness Area. The Tea Creek Area is a semi-primitive, non-motorized environment for dispersed recreation, wildlife habitat, and nature study. Some Tea Creek trails have a history of nearly 50 years; others are as recent as 1992. Tea Creek Trail (TR454), traditionally considered to be among the oldest, has been the passage of pioneers, hunters, fishermen, lumbermen, trappers, and railroaders. Flash floods and beaver dams have changed the routes of wagon roads, creek flow, railroad grades, and the trail. Over the years, other trails, like tributaries, have been added to form a diverse network to make it easier to explore the area's natural beauty.

Tea Creek receives its name from its water's amber color, which comes from conifer tannin or sedimentary rocks, or both. At the confluence of Tea Creek with Williams River is Tea Creek Campground, long the site of pioneers, hunters, and lumber camps. In recent years it has been expanded to accommodate visitors seeking ideal sites to hunt, fish, and hike the 40mi of foot trails.

Although Tea Creek Campground is open year around, services are provided from March 15 to mid-December. Helpful to the hikers is the district's free trail map. Trails are blazed with blue plastic diamond-shaped markers.

Access to the campground is on Williams River Road (FR86), 1.0mi W of an intersection with Highland Scenic Highway--Parkway Section (WV150).

BANNOCK SHOALS RUN TRAIL (TR446)   4.8mi(7.7km)

SCENERY: 1 (exceptional)   NOTE: B,M (1)
DIFFICULTY: II (moderate)   SKI-:   S1
CONDITION: A (good)   ELEV: 4000/3000
MAPS: USGS(A), Woodrow, Sharp Knob, IV-D-1, -3 in this Guide
SEGMENTS:
    (1) Tea Creek Campground to TR445 (Tea Creek Trail)(former)   0.3mi
    (2) TR445 to TR209 (Turkey Mtn. Trail)(former)   3.9mi
    (3) TR209 to TR448 (Saddle Loop Trail)/TR449 (Bndy. Trail)   0.6mi

Following an easy grade on former FR135 this gated and gravelled trail is excellent for a hiking climb to Turkey Mountain ridge of Gauley Ranger District and Turkey Mountain (a different mountain range) in Marlinton Ranger District. It can be used by equestrians and skiers. Except for near the campground, the trail is the border between the Gauley and Marlinton ranger districts.

Access: The S access is in the campground at the gate ⬚F along Williams River, upstream of the mouth of Tea Creek.

The N access is difficult; drive 2.3mi S of Slaty Fork on US219 and turn right onto FR24, a gravel road up to Gauley Mountain. After 4.3mi turn left onto FR135 which meanders 6.0mi through old strip mines.

Segment 1:   Starting at Tea Creek Campground ⬚F(Map IV-D-1), the partially grassy trail parallels Williams River.

Segment 2:   After TR445, the trail curves N up Upper Bannock Shoals Run. Vegetation is mainly maple, oak, yellow and black birch, beech, ferns, and roadside wildflowers. At 1.5mi the trail crosses Upper Bannock Shoals Run in a horseshoe curve, the first of two in the ascent. After 0.8mi farther, the sharp curve switchbacks to the stream and gorge, where it follows past the headwaters to a junction ⬚E (Map IV-D-3) with Turkey Mountain Trail (TR209) at 4.2mi.

Segment 3:   Farther on the ridge top the trail meets Saddle Loop Trail (TR448) and Boundary Trail (TR449) ⬚G. Either TR448 or TR449 could be followed back to Tea Creek Campground without backtracking.

TURKEY POINT TRAIL (TR447)   1.5mi(2.4km)

SCENERY: 1 (exceptional)   NOTE: B,M,W (0)
DIFFICULTY: II (moderate)   SKI-:   S4
CONDITION: A (good)   ELEV: 4360/4200
MAPS: USFS(A), Woodrow, IV-D-1, IV-D-3 in this Guide
SEGMENTS:
    (1) Turkey Pt. Connector Trail to TR448 (Saddle Loop Trail)   0.7mi
    (2) TR448 to TR449 (Boundary Trail)   0.8mi

An isolated trail on the crest of scenic Turkey Mountain (different from Turkey Mountain in Gauley Ranger District), it is accessible by climbing the mountain on the 0.6mi Turkey Point Connector Trail, or on either the Saddle Loop Trail (TR448) or Boundary Trail (TR449) on easy terrain from the N terminus of Bannock Shoals Run Trail (TR446).

Access: The S access [X] may confuse you because, after the ascent on Turkey Point Connector Trail, there are signs which may indicate "Turkey Loop," "Turkey Point Trail," or "Turkey Loop Connector." Not all the blue plastic diamond-shaped blazes indicate turns where signs may be missing from damage by bears. If in doubt, remember to keep right at any of three junctions (the third of which will be Saddle Loop Trail) until you reach the N terminus [Y] with Boundary Trail.

Segment 1: Starting from Turkey Point Connector Trail [X], traverse N along the ridge line (el. 4000+ft), where there are exceptional views of Tea Creek drainage and Tea Creek Mountain. Hemlock, red spruce and rhododendron are scattered among the hardwoods, a habitat for bear, turkey, deer and squirrel. After 0.7mi reach Saddle Loop Trail [Z].

Segment 2: Continue NE from Saddle Loop Trail. After reaching Boundary Trail [Y], it is 1.1mi left (W) along TR449 to Bannock Shoals Run Trail ([G] of Map IV-D-3). (You could also proceed 2.8mi further NE via Boundary Trail to Tea Creek Trail (TR454) which returns 4.5mi to Tea Creek Campground.)

SADDLE LOOP TRAIL (TR448)   1.7mi(2.7km)

SCENERY: 1 (exceptional)   NOTE: B,M (0)
DIFFICULTY: II (moderate)   SKI-:   S4
CONDITION: A (good)   ELEV: 4060/3920
MAPS: USFS(A), Woodrow, Sharp Knob, IV-D-1, -3 in this Guide
SEGMENTS:
(1) TR447 (Turkey Pt. Trail) to TR446 (Bannock Shoals Run Trail)   1.7mi

Serving as a connector between Turkey Point Trail (TR447), Bannock Shoals Run Trail (TR446) and Boundary Trail (TR449), Saddle Loop Trail is only part of the loop. A delightful treadway, it has a generally even terrain through hemlock and red spruce near Turkey Point Trail to an open and old logging road near Bannock Shoals Run Trail.

Segment 1: From Turkey Point Trail [Z] follow a winding course among hardwoods, dense rhododendron and rocks. After 1.0mi from Turkey Point Trail the trail joins an old logging road, crosses a footbridge over a stream, and follows a forest road with flowering plants and ferns. Near the stream area is a good campsite. Bannock Shoals Run Trail [G](Map IV-D-3) is reached at 1.7mi.

BOUNDARY TRAIL (TR449)   3.9mi(6.2km)

SCENERY: 1 (exceptional)   NOTE: B,M (3)
DIFFICULTY: II (moderate)   SKI-:   S4
CONDITION: A (good)   ELEV: 4360/3840
MAPS: USFS(A), Woodrow, Sharp Knob, IV-D-1, -2, -3 in this Guide

Tea Creek Mountain Trail (TR452). Photo by Allen de Hart

SEGMENTS:
(1) TR448 (Saddle Loop Trail) and TR446 to TR447 (Turkey Pt.Tr.)   1.1mi
(2) TR447 to TR454 (Tea Creek Trail)   2.8mi
    Boundary Trail receives its name from the USFS boundary S of Yew Mountain. It connects Bannock Shoals Run Trail (TR446--formerly FR135), and Saddle Loop Trail (TR448) on the W with Tea Creek Trail (TR454) on the E. Part of the route is new (1991), and another part is a pioneer roadbed and old RR grade.
    Segment 1: Starting from the W (TR448 and TR446) [G](Map IV-D-3), the route ascends moss-covered rocks, and through rhododendron and hemlock. Later the trail is more open, with some new growth and then a return to rhododendron. At 1.1mi is a junction [Y](Map IV-D-1), to the right, with Turkey Point Trail (TR447).
    Segment 2: For the next 2.8mi the trail descends on a rocky flank, among large boulders, and a variety of hardwoods before joining an old road [R](Map IV-D-2). (This road is accessible from private lands and FR135 E of South Fork Mountain. Evidence of ATV and mountain bike usage may be noticeable.) At 3.1mi is an old RR grade used for logging, and a rocky stream (sometimes dry) under the shadow of Buck Knob. At 3.8mi is another rocky streambed, after which the trail curves right to cross Tea Creek and an old RR grade. Then it meets Tea Creek Trail (TR454) [T].
    Options here are: take Tea Creek Trail upstream for 1.7mi to a shelter, and another 0.7mi to FR24, the N terminus of TR454; or take Bear Pen Ridge Trail (TR440) and Gauley Mountain Trail (TR438) out to WV150 (Highland Scenic Highway) for 5.0mi; or take Tea Creek Trail downstream for 4.5mi in a return to the Tea Creek Campground.

TEA CREEK TRAIL (TR454)   6.8mi(10.9km)
SCENERY: 1 (exceptional)   NOTE: B,M,H (13)
DIFFICULTY: III (strenuous)   SKI-:   S4
CONDITION: A (good)   ELEV: 4400/2980
MAPS: USFS(A), Woodrow, Sharp Knob, IV-D-1, -2, -3 in this Guide
SEGMENTS:
(1) Tea Creek Campground to TR453 & TR450 (North Face Trail)   2.9mi
(2) TR453 & TR450 to TR449 & TR440 (Bear Pen Ridge Trail)   1.5mi
(3) TR449 & TR440 to FR24   2.4mi
    A victim of storm and flood (1981, 1984, 1985--some of the most recent), this historic trail is no stranger to relocations. It is the trunk line, and the longest trail in the Tea Creek network. It is also the most popular with evidence that near the confluence of Tea Creek and Tea Creek's right fork, it has been the weekend home of many backpackers. There is an Adirondak-style trail shelter here. Although it ascends over 1,420ft in elevation, it is hardly noticeable until it leaves the stream and climbs to Flat Ridge on Gauley Mountain. A cool trail, where sunlight is filtered by yellow birch, rosebay rhododendron, and hemlock, mist rises from the rocky creek and tumbling tributaries. At least a dozen rock hops are required, depending on washed-away footbridges.
    Access: The S trailhead is at the junction [B] (Map IV-D-1) of Tea Creek Mountain Trail (TR452) and Williams River Trail (TR487) 0.1mi E of the Tea Creek Campground parking lot.

The N terminus [F] (Map IV-D-2) is on FR24 which leads 3.6mi E to meet US219 at a point 2.4mi S of Slaty Fork.

Segment 1: Starting from Tea Creek Campground parking lot, walk 0.2mi SE, crossing the Tea Creek footbridge, to [B] (Map IV-D-1). Here Tea Creek Trail and Tea Creek Mountain Trail turn left, up the side of the mountain. Tea Creek Trail is immediately left of Tea Creek Mountain Trail. For the first 0.4mi the trail is high and dry from a steep embankment of the creek. Then it follows irregular sections of an old RR grade and crosses Lick Creek and other small tributaries. At 2.9mi is the cascading confluence [G] with Right Fork of Tea Creek Trail (TR453) and North Face Trail (TR450). A trail shelter is located here.

Segment 2: For the next 1.5mi to Bear Pen Ridge Trail (TR440) [E] (Map IV-D-2) and Boundary Trail (TR449) [T], the trail is rocky with frequent rock hops of Tea Creek, and may have wet treadway.

Segment 3: Ascent becomes more noticeable for the next 1.7mi as the trail makes a final crossing of Tea creek, and switchbacks to a shelter (sleeps 8) [D] near a area flattened from strip mining. An old, easy, road among Scotch pine is the route for the remaining 0.7mi to FR24 [F].

TEA CREEK MOUNTAIN TRAIL (TR452)   4.6mi(7.4km)

SCENERY: 1 (exceptional)   NOTE: B,M (0)
DIFFICULTY: III (strenuous)   SKI-:   S4
CONDITION: A (good)   ELEV: 4535/2980
MAPS: USFS(A), Woodrow, IV-D-1 in this Guide
SEGMENTS;
(1) Tea Creek Campground to TR450 (North Face Trail)   1.5mi
(2) TR450 to WV150   3.1mi

Tea Creek Mountain Trail switchbacks up the SW arm of the mountain to the main ridge line, an ascent of 1,370 ft in elevation within 1.9mi. Less traveled and without water, it provides more solitude. Two trails, North Face Trail (TR450) and Right Fork of the Tea Creek Trail (TR453) meet TR452, coming from the N. Less ascent would be involved by beginning this trail at its E trailhead.

Access: The E access [D] is on WV150 near the S terminus of Right Fork of Tea Creek Trail (TR454). A parking area is on the N side of WV150 across from Little Laurel Overlook on Highland Scenic Highway (WV150).

The W access is 0.2mi S of Tea Creek Campground parking lot at the junction [B] of Williams River Trail (TR487) and Tea Creek Trail (TR454).

Segment 1: From Williams River Trail (TR487) [B], the trail ascends steadily to a first knob at 0.6mi, followed by a shallow saddle. The climb continues to another knob and makes a junction with North Face Trail (TR450), [L] 0.9mi after the first knob.

Segment 2: On the mountain crest are rock outcroppings, dense rhododendron, and a mixture of red spruce and hardwoods. At 3.9mi is the high point [E], a round knob which precedes a switchback descent to the parking area opposite Little Laurel Overlook [D] (Map IV-D-1) along Highland Scenic Highway (WV150).

NORTH FACE TRAIL (TR450)   3.1mi(5.0km)

SCENERY: 2 (wooded)   NOTE: B,M (2)
DIFFICULTY: III (strenuous)   SKI-:   S4
CONDITION: A/B (good-average)   ELEV: 4000/3400
MAPS: USFS(A) Woodrow, IV-D-1 in this Guide
SEGMENTS:
(1) TR452 (Tea Creek Mtn. Trail) to TR454 (Tea Creek Trail)/TR453
    (Right Fork, Tea Creek Trail)   3.1mi
    As with many other trails in the Tea Creek area network, the North Face
Trail mainly follows an old wet and rocky RR grade. It can be combined with
a section of Tea Creek Mountain Trail (TR452) and Tea Creek Trail (TR454)
to form a day hike loop of 7.5mi. Its forest hardwoods are mainly cherry and
birch, a change from oak and maple before a 1930s fire.   Rhododendron
thickets are in the damp coves, and deer may be seen on grassy spots of the
trail.
    Segment 1: A counterclockwise route ascends on Tea Creek Mountain
Trail (TR452) for 1.5mi to the junction ⌊L⌋ with North Face Trail. It descends
to a more even contour and after 1.0mi crosses a stream. On the steep north
face of Tea Creek Mountain the trail curves around a ridge to cross Lick
Creek ⌊W⌋ at 1.8mi. After the cascading stream, the trail drops rapidly until
leveling off for the last 0.5mi to Right Fork of Tea Creek Trail (TR453) and
Tea Creek Trail (TR454) ⌊G⌋. A trail shelter is just before the junction.

RIGHT FORK OF TEA CREEK TRAIL (TR453) 3.4mi(5.4km)

SCENERY: 2 (wooded)   NOTE: B,M (0)
DIFFICULTY: III (strenuous)   SKI-:   S4
CONDITION: A (good)   ELEV: 4270/3550
MAPS: USFS(A), Woodrow, IV-D-1 in this Guide
SEGMENTS:
(1) TR454/TR450 (North Face Trail) to TR439 (Red Run Trail)   1.7mi
(2) TR439 to The Meadows   1.2mi
(3) The Meadows to WV150   0.5mi
    Frequently the second-most used choice by hikers to the center of the
Tea Creek Trail area, Right Fork of Tea Creek Trail (as seen on the network
signs) follows most of the S side of the Right Fork of Tea Creek. Most of its
entire route is on old RR grades. Red Run Trail (TR439) joins it (as a connector to Gauley Mountain Trail) halfway along its route.
    Access: The N access ⌊G⌋ is from Tea Creek Trail (TR454) (2.9mi from
Tea Creek Campground). The N end of North Face Trail (TR450) is also at
this junction. A trail shelter is nearby. (See map)
    The S access is near the parking area ⌊D⌋ opposite Little Laurel Over-
look on Highland Scenic Highway (WV150).
    Segment 1: Starting near the confluence of Tea Creek and Right Fork
of Tea Creek ⌊G⌋, the trail follows upstream on the S side of Right Fork of
Tea Creek on a moderate old RR grade. Vegetation is rhododendron, hemlock, black cherry, maple, and birch. After 1.6mi the trail crosses the stream
⌊H⌋ and soon meets Red Run Trail (TR439) before crossing Red Run⌊I⌋ .
    Segment 2: At 2.9mi it meets Right Fork Connector Trail ⌊U⌋ (0.6mi to
Gauley Mountain Trail (TR438)), and The Meadows ⌊C⌋, a 0.2mi spur to a
swampy area, but not a developed trail.

Segment 3: The trail then briefly ascends and descends to the parking area [D] across WV150 from Little Laurel Overlook.

RED RUN TRAIL (TR439)   2.5mi(4.0km)
SCENERY: 2 (wooded)   NOTE: B,M (0)
DIFFICULTY: II (moderate)   SKI-: S4
CONDITION: A (good)   ELEV: 4350/3820
MAPS: USFS(A), Woodrow, IV-D-1 in this Guide
SEGMENTS:
(1) TR453 (Rt.Fork, Tea Cr.Tr.) to TR438 (Gauley Mtn. Trail)   2.5mi

An excellent connector, and less traveled route, to the heart of the Tea Creek valley from Gauley Mountain Trail (TR438) is Red Run Trail. The well graded trail goes through birch, rhododendron, ferns, shamrock and red spruce (from which the red tannin gives the trail its name).

Access: The E trailhead is at Gauley Mountain Trail [N] (where it is 2.5mi from Highland Scenic Highway).

The W trailhead [I] is at the junction with Right Fork of Tea Creek Trail (TR453).

Segment 1: Starting from the stream's confluence [I], the trail switchbacks. It stays on the N side of Red Run for 1.0mi on a rocky old RR grade. After crossing Red Run on a footbridge, the trail ascends moderately to Gauley Mountain Trail (TR438) [N].

BEAR PEN RIDGE TRAIL (TR440)   3.5mi(5.6km)
SCENERY: 1 (exceptional)   NOTE: B,M,H, (0)
DIFFICULTY: II (moderate)   SKI-: S4
CONDITION: A/B (good-average)   ELEV: 4480/3880
MAPS: USFS(A), Woodrow, Sharp Knob, IV-D-1, -2 in this Guide
SEGMENTS: (1) TR438 (Gauley Mtn. Tr.) to TR454 & TR449 3.5mi

This trail is one of the least used, but one of the most different from the other trails in the Tea Creek trails network. It, as all the other network trails, can be used as portions of loops with multiple choices. Except for its final descent to Tea Creek it remains above 4,000ft in elevation.

Access: Its NW terminus is an intersection [E](Map IV-D-2) with Tea Creek Trail (TR454) (4.5mi from Tea Creek Campground). The E end of Boundary Trail (TR449) (3.8mi from FR135) is a short distance E along TR454 in a grassy area.

The S access [M] (Map IV-D-1) is along Gauley Mountain Trail (TR438) (1.5mi S from FR24, or 3.7mi N from WV150).

Segment 1: Starting from Gauley Mountain Trail [M], the trail ascends gradually on an old RR grade to the N ridge line above Red Run. A trail shelter is located on this ridge. After 1.5mi W it changes to a footpath among Pottsville sandstone. Forest vegetation includes red spruce, cherry, maple, and hemlock. At 2.5mi the trail joins an old logging road on a knob, descends, and soon turns NE for a descent down the mountainside to Tea Creek Trail [E](Map IV-D-2).

GAULEY MOUNTAIN TRAIL (TR438)   5.2mi(8.3km)
SCENERY: 2   (wooded)   NOTE: B,M (0)
DIFFICULTY: II (moderate)   SKI-:   S1
CONDITION: A/B (good-average)   ELEV: 4440/4220
MAPS: USFS(A), Woodrow, Sharp Knob, IV-D-1, -2 in this Guide
SEGMENTS:
(1) WV150 N to Right Fork Connector   0.4mi
(2) Right Fork Connector to TR439 (Red Run Trail) [L] 2.2mi
(3) TR439 to TR440 (Bear Pen Ridge Trail)   1.1mi
(4) TR440 to Gauley-Tea Connector [J]   0.6mi
(5) Gauley-Tea Connector to FR24   0.9mi

Following an old RR grade on a generally even contour on the W side of the mountain for the first half, and the E side for the second half, the trail stays over 4,000ft in elevation. Sometimes with wet spots, the trail weaves around ridges and into coves above headwaters. Red spruce groves, hardwood forests, and wildflowers such as trillium and blue beads are common. The trail is used for hiking, backpacking, bicycling, and ski-touring. There is some sameness of terrain, vegetation, and elevation on the trail, but the variety of wildflowers, ferns, and summer songbirds make it more appealing. The usually cool air and lack of insects are other appeals.

Access: The easiest S access is on a side road [Q](Map IV-D-1) off Highland Scenic Highway (WV150), 0.5mi E of Little Laurel Overlook [D].

The N trailhead [A], (Map IV-D-2) is on FR24, 0.2mi E of the N terminus [F] of Tea Creek Trail (TR454).

Segment 1: Starting from the S, after the first 0.4mi the trail meets Right Fork Connector Trail (which leads to The Meadows [E]), a 0.2mi spur trail to a swampy area that is undeveloped, and Right Fork of Tea Creek Trail (TR453).

Segment 2: At 2.2mi is a junction [L] with Red Run Trail (TR439) (which descends to join Right Fork of Tea Creek Trail).

Segment 3: From here, Gauley Mountain Trail shifts to the E side of the wide mountain top with hardly a notice to meet Bear Pen Ridge Trail (TR440) [M] at 3.3mi.

Segment 4: At 3.9mi is a junction [J] (Map IV-D-2) with Gauley-Tea Connector Trail, a shorter distance to Tea Creek Shelter than continuing on to FR24.

Segment 5: The trail's N end is over an earthen barrier at FR24 [A].

WILLIAMS RIVER TRAIL (TR487)   3.0mi(4.8km)
SCENERY: 2   (wooded)   NOTE: M (0)
DIFFICULTY: I (easy)   SKI-:   S1
CONDITION: A/B (good-average)   ELEV: 3160/2990
MAPS: USFS(A), Woodrow, IV-D-1 in this Guide
SEGMENTS:
(1) Tea Creek Campground to Handley Wildlife Management Area   3.0mi

Williams River Trail also follows an old RR grade, but in contrast to all the other trails in the Tea Creek network, it is the lowest in elevation and cannot form a loop. Of its 3.0mi, 2.2mi is in the national forest.

Access: The SE terminus [K] is in the state's Handley Wildlife Management Area with camping facilities. The SE end can be approached by following FR86 upstream from Tea Creek Campground, turning left onto CO17-4 and left again at CO17-1.

Access at the NW end is from the parking area $\boxed{A}$ at Tea Creek Campground. To reach the campground, turn off WV150 onto FR86 just W of where WV150 crosses Williams River. Drive 1.0mi N of FR86. (See trailhead information for TR454.)

An intermediate access is on the N side of the Highland Scenic Highway bridge over Williams River.

Segment 1: From the Tea Creek Campground parking area the trail goes upstream on an old RR grade along the N side of Williams River. It goes through open forests and meadows to the deadwaters of Williams River. Along the way are songbirds, butterflies, and wildflowers. The trail passes under the WV150 bridge at 1.0mi, at a spur trail to a parking area from WV150 at 1.2mi, and leaves the national forest on an approach $\boxed{F}$ to Little Laurel Creek at 2.2mi. From here it slightly ascends on an old road to go between two small lakes in Handley Wildlife Management Area.

Beaver Tale Trail at Blue Bend Recreation Area. Photo courtesy USFS

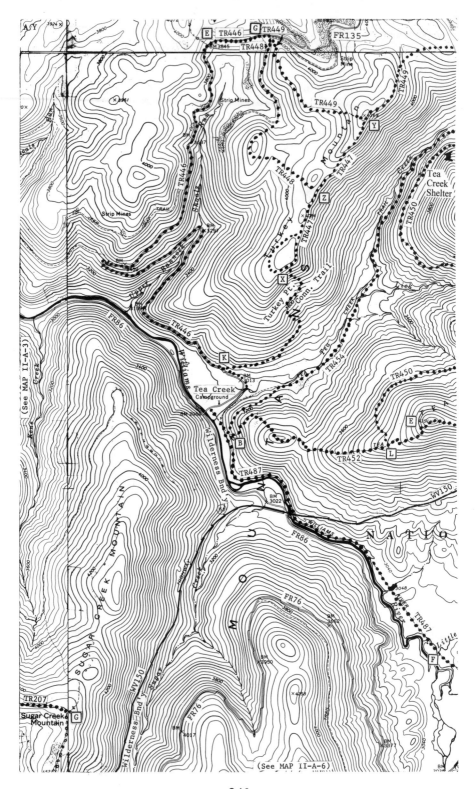

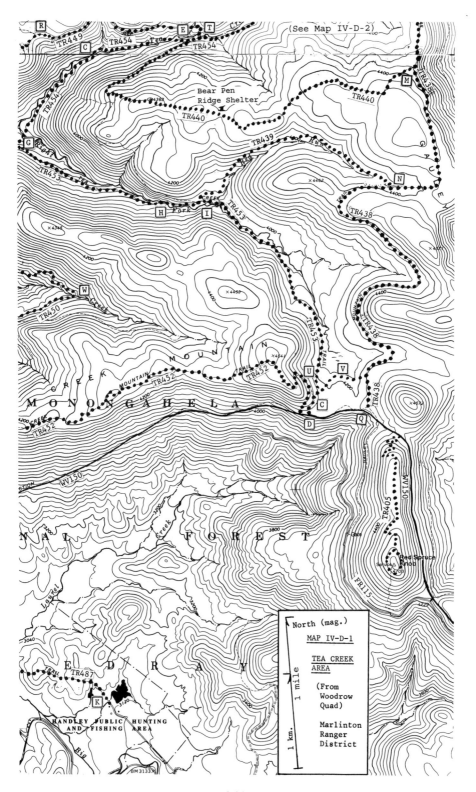

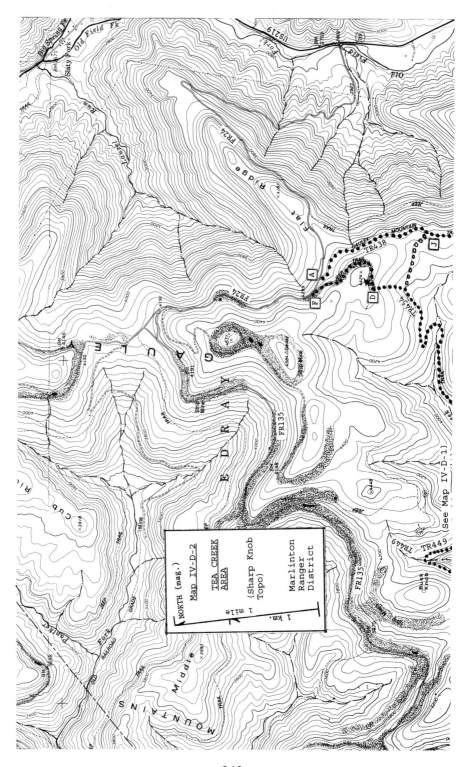

NORTH (mag.)

Map IV-D-2

TEA CREEK
AREA

(Sharp Knob
Topo)

Marlinton
Ranger
District

1 Km.   1 mile

POTOMAC RANGER DISTRICT

Potomac Ranger District is in the NE corner of the MNF and SE of Cheat Ranger District. Between them is the Canaan Valley area and the Dry Fork Valley of Cheat River. The District is contiguous with Greenbrier Ranger District on the SW corner at the Virginia state line. Most of the District is in the Potomac River drainage, but drainage from the Dolly Sods and Flatrock Plains areas flows W to the Dry Fork of Cheat River.

The outstanding scenery in this high, rugged country has caused the Spruce Knob-Seneca Rocks National Recreation Area (NRA), the Dolly Sods Scenic Area and the Dolly Sods Wilderness to be established in this district. Four localities are of special significance to hikers:
- North Fork Mountain and South Branch of the Potomac;
- Spruce Knob (highest point in W.Va.), Seneca & Gandy Creeks;
- Dolly Sods Wilderness and Scenic Area;
- Roaring Plains and Flatrock Plains.

The first two, with the exception of Gandy Creek, are units of National Recreation Areas. Each of these areas offers a largely interconnected system of trails, though there is no trail system linking the four areas. Hikers will find Seneca Rocks Discovery Center a source of information about the district. An interpretive trail from the Discovery Center to an observation deck near the top of Seneca Rocks is also a source of information. A new USFS land acquisition of 6,168 acres in Dolly Sods North opens an outstanding additional exploratory area full of open heath, scattered spruce and spectacular views. (It also contains some unexploded WWII shells that the USFS is working to locate and eliminate before formal hiking trails are developed in the area.) It may eventually be given Wilderness status, so treat it as such. (See page 21)

All these areas are popular to hikers and campers who regard these high rugged mountains as a retreat from nearby metropolitan areas. Other recreational activities are rock climbing at Seneca Rocks, fishing at Spruce Knob Lake (the MNF's highest in elevation), canoeing and kayaking in the South Fork and North Fork of the South Branch, and snow skiing on unplowed forest roads. For spelunkers, the most worthwhile caves are commercially owned, but check with the district headquarters or West Virginia Geological and Economic Survey (Tel. 304-594-2331) for more information on the many non-commercial caves in the area.

The district has five developed campgrounds with a total of more than 180 sites, the largest number in any MNF district. Their seasons of use range from mid-March to mid-December. Campers should contact the district ranger office for individual campground schedules and fees. All campgrounds have user fees except Gatewood. The campgrounds are:

Big Bend (45 sites) (picnic tables, no showers, water, flush toilets);
Gatewood (6 sites) (picnic tables, no water, vault toilets);
Red Creek (12 sites) (picnic tables, hand pump at well, vault toilets);
Seneca Shadows (80 sites, 13 with electrical hookups) (picnic tables, water, flush toilets, hot showers),
Spruce Knob Lake (43 sites) (picnic tables, hand pump at well, vault toilets)

The newest area, Seneca Shadows, is off US33, 1.0mi S of Mouth of Seneca. The group tenting area there offers a great view of Seneca Rocks.

View of Seneca Rocks Discovery Center from the top of Seneca Rocks.
Photo by Allen de Hart

Reservations for Seneca Shadows are made through National Recreation Reservation Service, Tel. 877-444-6777 or through the Internet address http://www.ReserveUSA.com. Dogs must be on leashes in campgrounds.

Four developed picnic areas are:
- Dolly Sods Picnic Area (tables, toilets, but no tested water) on FR19 near the intersection with FR75;
- Seneca Rocks (tables, toilets, water) at Seneca Rocks Discovery Center;
- Smoke Hole (tables, toilets, water, pavilion) on CO2 near Upper Tract;
- Spruce Knob (tables, toilets, water, pavilion) on top of Spruce Knob and on FR104 near the intersection with FR112. There are also picnic tables on top of Spruce Knob.

Ski-Touring in Potomac Ranger District
Some unplowed forest roads used for ski-touring in winter are:
- FR104 from Spruce Knob Observation Tower to FR112;
- FR112 from FR104 W to CO29 (9mi);
- FR131 from FR112 to a dead-end (4mi);
- FR70 from FR19 to a dead-end on Flatrock Plains (4mi);
- FR19 from FR75 to Laneville (4mi down a long mountain),
- FR75 from FR19 to near Bear Rocks (7mi on generally level, windswept terrain).

Trails that are good for ski-touring include Tom Lick Trail (TR559), Seneca Creek Trail (TR515) and other trails within the Seneca Creek back-country area.

For more information on the district contact the District Ranger, Potomac Ranger District, MNF, HC59, Box 240, Petersburg, WV 26847 (Tel. 304-257-4488).

Seneca Rocks Discovery Center
Seneca Rocks Discovery Center, near the intersection of WV28 and US33, is one of the MNF's most popular attractions, more than 140,000 visitors annually. By the summer of 1999 the Center will have interpretive displays, an auditorium for presentations and videos, a classroom for crafts and other classes, an interpretive information store, and a climbing wall. Information by USFS staff, books and other literature on outdoor activities, history, wildlife, geology are also available there. A major display of artifacts found during the dig before the buildings were built will show parts of the lifestyles of prehistoric occupants of the area. The Discovery Center is open 9 AM to 5:30 PM daily, spring, summer and fall.

The popularity of the Discovery Center is associated with Seneca Rocks itself, a magnificent, sheer, Tuscarora sandstone outcropping which towers 960ft above the valley floor. It is a landmark of natural beauty whose gradations of color change according to sunshine and sunsets. It is favored by about 8,000 rock climbers as being among the best in the eastern US. Although there are separate trails for climbers, a 1.3mi trail (described below) is available for hikers. It leads to an observation deck near the top. Other attractions within a few miles of the Discovery Center are Seneca Caverns (commercial) and Smoke Hole Caves, both on WV28. Fishing is popular in nearby North Fork of the South Branch of the Potomac. Motels, restaurants, and general stores are nearby. The telephone number of the Discovery Center is 304-567-2827. General management guidelines set by the USFS emphasize

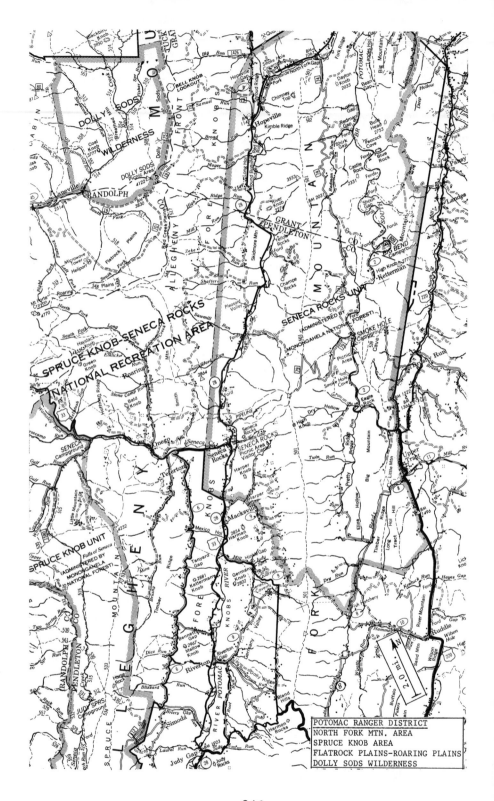

POTOMAC RANGER DISTRICT
NORTH FORK MTN. AREA
SPRUCE KNOB AREA
FLATROCK PLAINS-ROARING PLAINS
DOLLY SODS WILDERNESS

the Seneca Rocks area as one of high density in a self-contained recreation environment.

The Seneca Indians, of Iroquois stock, called themselves "people of the mountains", and many legends exist about their early history in the Mouth-of-Seneca area. For them the valley provided a major route, the Seneca Trail, along the Potomac River to the E. A creek, bearing their name, flows into the North Fork at the S side of the Discovery Center.

Seneca Rocks community has had its share of natural and human calamities. For example, the Seneca Rocks Visitor Center, which first opened in 1968, was severely damaged by the flood of 1985. Reopened and expanded to increase the capacity from 80 to 320 in 1991, it mysteriously burned to the ground on May 26, 1992. The flood also redesigned the valley floor with a loss of life, homes, farmland, roads, bridges, and vegetation. On the walls of Seneca Rocks are memorial plaques for those who have died on the climbs. It is a dangerous place; it is legend that even Seneca Princess Snowbird saved her betrothed from falling. Then on October 22, 1987, the rock's most famous central spire "The Gendarme" collapsed from erosion and fell to the bottom of the E face.

SENECA ROCKS HIKING TRAIL (TR563)   1.3mi(2.1km)

SCENERY: 1 (exceptional)	NOTE: M,(0)
DIFFICULTY: II (moderate)	SKI-: S4
CONDITION: A (good)	ELEV: 2300/1560

MAPS: USFS(A,B), Upper Tract, V-A-2 in this Guide
SEGMENTS: (1) Seneca Rocks Visitor Center to Platform   1.3mi

This interpretive trail is the most heavily used foot trail in the MNF. Its major appeal is the ascention to the North Peak of Seneca Rocks for spectacular views of Seneca Rocks, North Fork Valley, and W to the Allegheny Mountains. For those who wish to rest, in this nearly 700ft elevation ascent, there are seven bench sites along the way. In addition to interpretive signs describing geology, history, soil, and botany, there are protective signs at ecologically sensitive and dangerous walking areas.

Access: Seneca Rocks Discovery Center [C] is on WV28/55 N of the intersection with US33 at Seneca Rocks. The trailhead is at a sign on the E side of the S parking area.

Segment 1: From the S parking area the trail goes through a meadow to cross a high footbridge over the North Fork of the South Branch of the Potomac River. There are excellent upstream and downstream views from the bridge. A short distance after crossing the bridge, the trail turns left from a junction with a side trail, right, used by rock climbers, that leads toward Roy Gap. The remainder of the trail is a gradual ascent with switchbacks, past rock formations, and through a beautiful forest of oak, hickory, maple, locust, redbud and scattered hemlock. The trail ends at an open observation platform at the N edge of North Peak of Seneca Rocks. Backtracking is necessary.

(V-A) NORTH FORK MOUNTAIN AREA

The North Fork Mountain Area is part of the Seneca Rocks Unit of a National Recreation Area. On its ridgecrest is the district's longest trail, the high, dry, 23.8mi North Fork Mountain Trail (TR501)--one of the best foot trails in this part of the country. Outside Magazine (4/96) named it the best trail in West Virginia. North Fork Mountain slopes more gradually on its E side toward the South Branch of the Potomac River, and on whose riverside are Eagle Rock, Smoke Hole Picnic Area, and Big Bend Campground. The crest of the W side of the trail has a number of large, long, sandstone outcroppings. From them are uncountable spectacular views of North Fork of the South Branch of the Potomac River, Germany Valley, Seneca Rocks, Fore Knobs and Champe Rocks. Beyond, on the horizon, can be seen Spruce Knob, Flatrock Plains, Roaring Plains, Dolly Sods and Allegheny Front.

Accessing North Fork Mountain Trail are Landis and Redman Run Trails, both from CO28/11 on the E side. There are no official access trails on the W side. Another trail in the area is South Branch Trail (TR539), which ascends Cave Mountain from Smoke Hole Picnic Area.

NORTH FORK MOUNTAIN TRAIL (TR501)   23.8mi(38.1km)

SCENERY: 1 (exceptional)	NOTE: B,M,W,(0)
DIFFICULTY: II (moderate)	SKI-: S2-S4
CONDITION: A (good)	ELEV: 3795-1120

MAPS: USFS(A,B), Petersburg West, Hopeville, Upper Tract, Circleville, V-A-1, V-A-2, V-A-3 and V-A-4 in this Guide

SEGMENTS: (1) US33 to FR79   10.1mi
               (2) FR79 to TR507 (Redman Run Trail)   5.6mi
               (3) TR507 to TR502 (Landis Trail)   4.4mi
               (4) TR502 to CO28/11 (formerly FR74)   3.7mi

Except for the lack of water, the trail is ideal for a 2-3 day backpacking trip. Once on top of the mountain, the trail is moderately level and easy to follow. Rock outcroppings a few yards off the trail offer vantage points for spectacular views both E and W and along the N-S range of the cliffs on the W side of the mountain. Vegetation is mainly hardwoods with fern beds and acres of wildflowers such as spring beauty. Deer and turkey are likely to be seen, and sometimes wild goats forage on the trail. Except for a 2mi section of dirt road on the N side of the radio antenna, and a 1-mile section of fire lane on the S side of the radio antenna, the trail is a beautiful forested footpath. The treadway of the blue-blazed trail is well-designed, and only rocky on its descent to CO28/11.

Backpackers may be interested in commercial shuttle services for North Fork Mountain Trail. Shuttle services drive you from your car at one end of the trail to the other end of the trail. They also offer water-drops at the end of FR79, but this still requires that you carry at least a gallon of water on the first leg of your trip (more on hot days). Contact the Potomac Ranger District office for information on shuttle-services.

Warning: Bits and pieces of North Fork Mountain Trail cross private property, some of which is indicated on the maps in this Guide. All of this private property is on the southern third of the trail. The heavy and growing usage the trail receives has created concerns among landowners about trampling of vegetation (especially the more sensitive plants) along the trail. Hikers and backpackers should realize what they have to lose by even minor carelessness and take extra precautions to stay on the trail. Short side excursions to the spectacular overlooks along the trail are extremely tempting. But most of these can be done by walking on rocks or rock-hopping. Make sure

North Fork Mountain looking south from Chimney Rocks (TR501). Photo by Bruce Sundquist

you take great pains to avoid any damage to the sensitive plant-life in this harsh environment when you take these side trips. You should take pains to minimize your impact on all trails on the MNF, but the North Fork Mountain Trail requires an even greater level of caution. If you plan a trip involving the S third of the trail you would be well advised to call the Potomac District Ranger Office to make sure the sections you are interested in are open.

Access: The S (US33) trailhead is at the ridge crest of North Fork Mountain on US33 (9.0mi W of Franklin, 5.0mi E of Judy Gap). There is a small parking lot on the side of the road at either end of the curve.

The FR79 trailhead, near the midpoint of the trail, is 3.5mi up the mountain on FR79 from a junction with CO28/11 (formerly FR74), Smoke Hole Road. Access to this junction is S from WV28 near Cabins, or N from US220 at Upper Tract. It is near Smoke Hole Picnic Area. From this point N, Redman Run and Landis Trails provide access.

The N trailhead is 0.3mi S along CO28/11 from WV28 (and E of Smoke Hole Caverns). Parking is available for 5-8 cars at this trailhead which is marked by a hiker sign. Up the trail 50yd is a larger trail sign and space for a few tents (commonly used by people who arrive Friday evening for a weekend on North Fork Mountain Trail). A spring house and spring are on the bank near the S side of the bridge over the North Fork of the South Branch of the Potomac 0.2mi from the trailhead. Locals fill drinking-water containers there (1998). See Map V-A-4.

Segment 1: Starting from the S trailhead at US33, the trail ascends through a grassy area and enters the woods on an old road. Signage may be sparse because the first 0.4mi of trail is on private property. Blue blazes start after 0.4mi. Soon, to the left, are spur trails leading to scenic views of Germany Valley and Spruce Mountain. After 1.7mi the footpath becomes a woods road and a more even treadway. Laurel, flame azaleas and wintergreen border the trail. Here, as elsewhere on the trail, it follows the leeward side of the ridge, except along a short segment at 9.5mi. It passes under a power line at 3.3mi, and enters an area where the road has been used for logging. Chestnut oak and black birch are common in this area. A timber road descends left into Germany Valley at 4.3mi. (It was once used to drive cattle to markets to the E.) Another timber road descends right for 2.3mi to Reeds Creek Road (CO8).

At 4.5mi is a hang glider launching ramp on your left, and an access road on private property, also on your left. From here the trail becomes a footpath, well-designed and easy to follow. It skirts E of a rocky knob at 5.0mi; it arrives at a patch of blueberries, mountain laurel and spring beauty in a rocky area with vistas at 5.8mi. On approaching 7.5mi there is evidence of private development on the left. After leaving the boundary markers, it gradually ascends to an outcropping at 8.2mi where Seneca Rocks can be seen far below. The trail then skirts right (E) of High Knob, and descends to a saddle before beginning a steep ascent on an old jeep road. It reaches a pipeline swath and a gravel forest road (FR79) at 10.1mi. It follows FR79, and after 0.5mi, passes a radio tower (el. 3795ft), the trail's highest point.

Segment 2: The trail follows FR79 down the E slope for 1.4mi before re-entering the forest on the left at a curve in FR79. It goes through hardwoods and wildflowers, and passes an abandoned trail (Kimble Trail) that is 1.5mi from CO28/11 (formerly FR74) on the right at 14.2mi. At 15.7mi is a junction with Redman Run Trail (TR507) on the right. (Redman Run Trail descends 1.6mi to CO28/11.)

Segment 3: The trail continues N on the leeward side of the mountain among hardwoods, rhododendrons and laurel. It passes a large rock formation on the left at 17.5mi. After a slight descent to 18.7mi, there is a formation of sandstone, sculptured by wind and ice to a honeycomb shape. The views to the left, of the Potomac River Valley, are one of the highlights of the trip. After a passage through an open forest, the trail reaches Landis Trail (TR502) at 20.1mi. (Landis Trail descends steeply in sections for 1.4mi to CO28/11 [formerly FR74].)

Segment 4: About 0.2mi beyond the junction with Landis Trail is a campsite. More scenic views are to the left from 20.4mi to 20.5mi, and another campsite is at 20.9mi. At 21.1mi is a 0.1mi spur trail to the left (uphill) to Chimney Top, part of an area called Chimney Rocks. (This spectacular rock outcrop can be seen from WV28. It offers one of the more spectacular view in the MNF. To the W can be seen Allegheny Front [Dolly Sods, Red Creek Plains, Flatrock Plains]). To the E can be seen the next five or more ridges. To the S can be seen the northern half or more of North Fork Mountain. To the N can be seen the continuation of North Fork Mountain, the spectacular cut of North Fork of the South Branch of the Potomac through North Fork Mountain, and the small towns on the W side of Petersburg. Please do not camp at or near Chimney Rocks. Leave this area open for all to visit without feeling like they are intruding.

The problem (at least for south-bound hikers) is finding the rocks. When you hike up from the N trailhead to the first overlook, you still have about 0.3mi to go. Continue S along North Fork Mountain Trail until you see hints of a high point through the trees. Continue on for another 100yd to where the ridgeline can be seen descending to the S. Watch carefully for the faint traces of a side-trail angling back (NW) up the mountain. It was marked by a small, toppled cairn in late 1998. The narrow path leads 0.1mi up to a ridge-line rock outcrop. Two higher rocks are separated from these ridge-line rocks. Even further out (W) are several more rock pinnacles that are somewhat lower than the first pair.

The trail skirts E of Chimney Top and begins a descent at 21.3mi, about 0.3mi N of Chimney Rocks (not as shown on Map V-A-4). Views to the left are of New Creek Mountain. Along this 1800ft. descent, the trail changes from a pine-needle-covered path to a rocky (small pieces of deep-red shale-like rock) path. It is steep only in a few spots as it switchbacks through pine, hardwoods and laurel. It arrives at CO28/11 at 23.8mi.

LANDIS TRAIL (TR502)   1.4mi(2.3km)
SCENERY: 2 (wooded)   NOTE: B,M,W,(0)
DIFFICULTY: II (moderate)   SKI-:   S4
CONDITION: A (good)   ELEV: 2800/1670
MAPS: USFS(A,B), Hopeville, Petersburg W, V-A-4 in this Guide
SEGMENTS: (1) CO28/11 to TR501 (North Fork Mtn. Trail)   1.4mi

Access: The E terminus of Landis Trail is at a trail sign on CO28/11 (formerly FR74). Three cars can park at this terminus.

Segment 1: The trail ascends on a mossy and rocky treadway among oak, maple, and laurel. The junction with North Fork Mountain Trail

(TR501) is on the E slope of the mountain. An established camp site with room for 4 tents, but no views, is 0.2mi N along TR501 from Landis Trail.

REDMAN RUN TRAIL (TR507)   1.6mi(2.6km)
SCENERY: 2 (wooded)   NOTE: B,(0)
DIFFICULTY: II (moderate)   SKI-:   S4
CONDITION: A (good)   ELEV: 3000/2100
MAPS: USFS(A,B), Hopeville, V-A-3 & V-A-4 in this Guide
SEGMENTS: (1) CO28/11 to TR501 (North Fork Mtn. Trail)   1.6mi

The USFS maps show the trail which, at its lower end, is a gravel road. The trail is well-blazed and well-maintained, but westbound hikers could miss the departure from the gravel road.

Access: The S terminus of the trail is at a Hiker sign on CO28/11. Several cars can park here. The drive along CO28/11 is scenic, but the road is narrow and the curves are sharp.

Segment 1: Starting from CO28/11, Redman Run Trail begins as a gravel road. Halfway up the trail, after the gravel road veers right, watch for Redman Run Trail to make an abrupt left turn off the road at a faded double blue blaze and continue on up to North Fork Mountain Trail (TR501), slightly S of a camp-site and an overlook.

SOUTH BRANCH TRAIL (TR539)   3.5mi(5.6km)
SCENERY: 2 (wooded)   NOTE: B,M,(0)
DIFFICULTY: II (moderate)   SKI-:   S4
CONDITION: B (average)   ELEV: 2100/1270
MAPS: USFS(A,B), Upper Tract, V-A-3 in this Guide
SEGMENTS: (1) Picnic Area (S) to Picnic Area (N)   3.5mi

South Branch Trail is on the W slope of Cave Mountain, just E of North Fork Mountain. Signs should be in place.

Access: South Branch Trail begins at the S end of Smoke Hole Picnic Area and ends at the N end of the Picnic Area, forming essentially a complete loop. Park cars at the Picnic Area.

Segment 1: Beginning at the S end of the Picnic Area, the trail ascends through a mixed hardwood stand, crosses a few intermittent streams and bears left (N). It crosses the side of Cave Mountain through woods and old fields overgrown with cedar. It then drops down to a meadow and an old home place. From here it goes through the field diagonally to a jeep road which it follows down the mountain. At a switchback on the lower end of the road, the trail leaves the road and heads left (S). South Branch River is below on the right. The trail follows the river on a rocky treadway, crosses a power line and a pipeline swath, and ends at the N end of the Picnic Area.

North Fork Mountain Trail (TR501) looking north to Chimney Rocks. Photo by Barry Adams

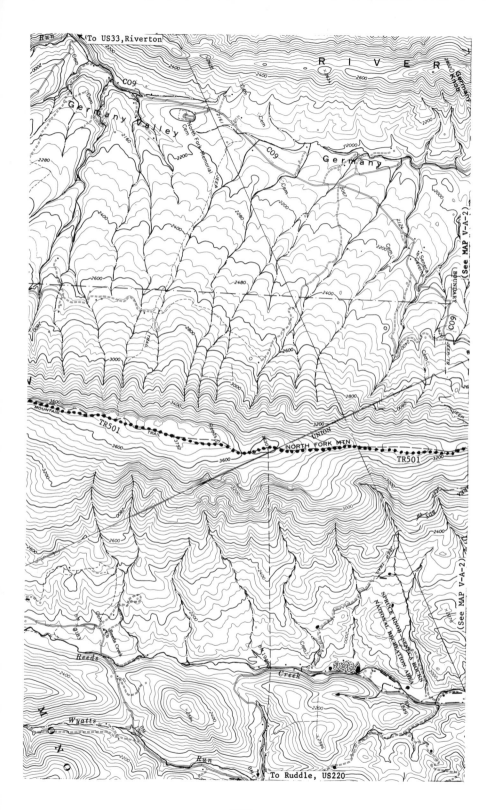

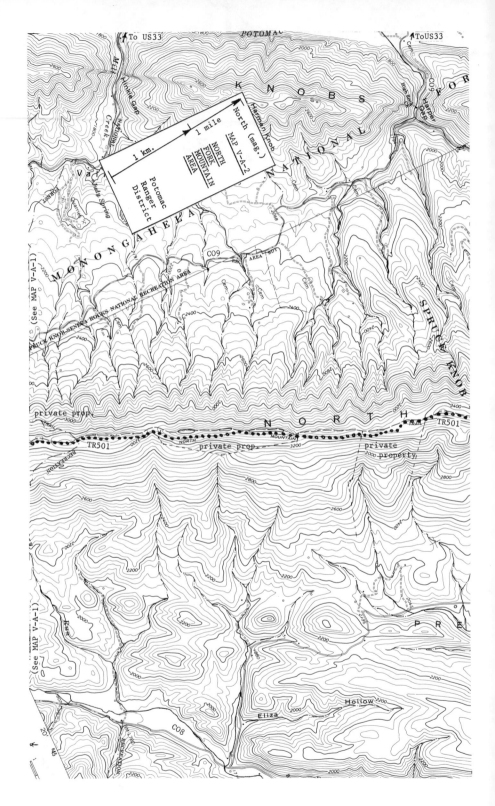

MAP V-A-2

NORTH FORK MOUNTAIN AREA

Potomac Ranger District

North (mag.)

1 mile

1 km.

(See MAP V-A-1)

(See MAP V-A-1)

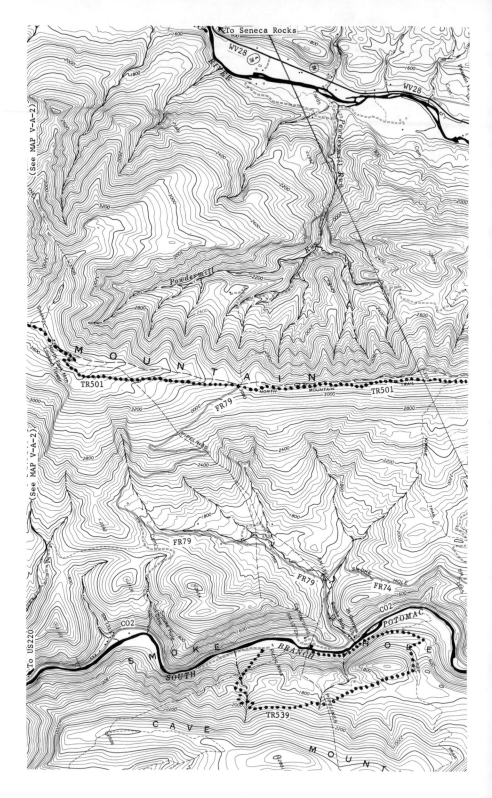

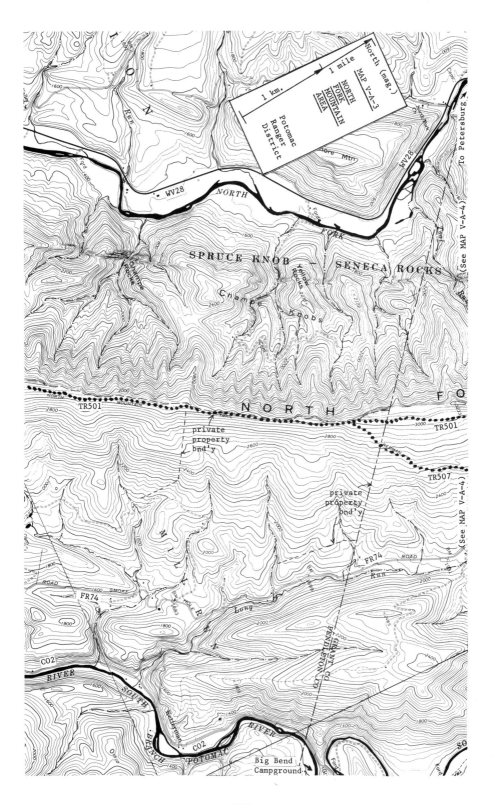

MAP V-A-3

NORTH
FORK
MOUNTAIN
AREA

Potomac
Ranger
District

North (mag.)

1 mile

1 km.

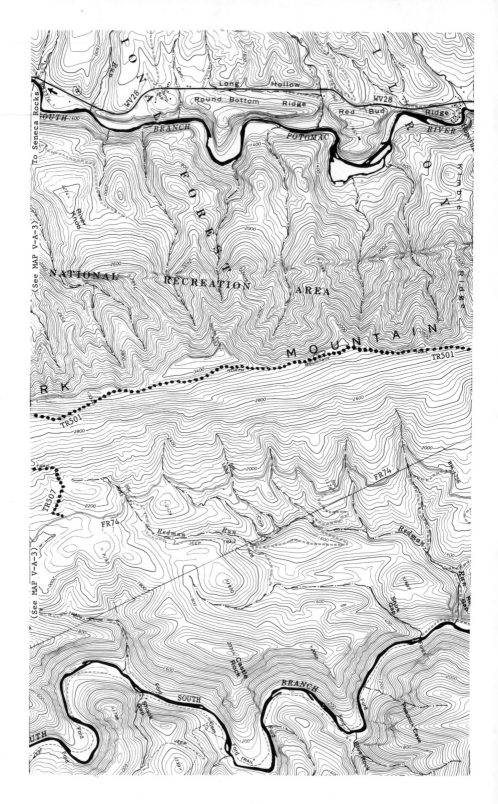

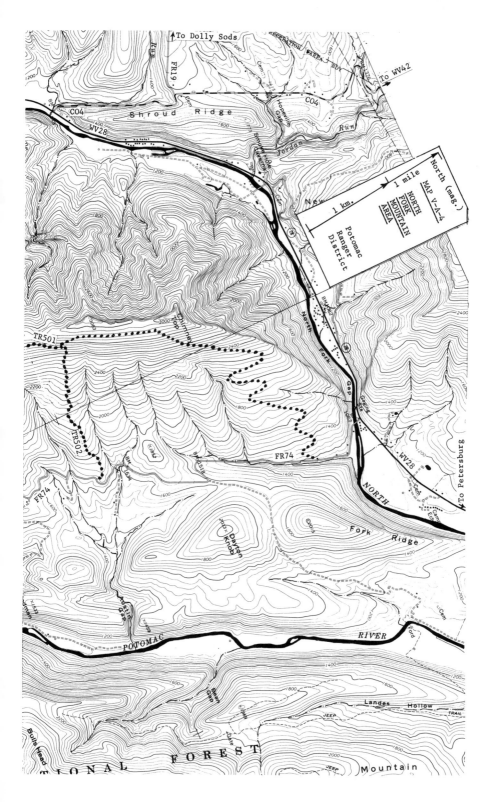

(V-B) SPRUCE KNOB AREA

This area is composed of the Spruce Knob unit of the National Recreation Area (NRA) and contiguous areas. Attractions of the area include Spruce Knob (el.4863ft), the state's highest mountain top, and other similar rugged areas; the Seneca Creek Backcountry, and Allegheny Mountain Trail (TR532), the district's second longest. Contiguous with the NRA are trails from the Gandy Creek area to the W, and from Grassy Mountain to the S. Campgrounds in the area are located at Spruce Knob Lake (FR1) and Gatewood (FR131). (The Seneca Campground along CO7 was washed away in the 1985 flood, and will not be rebuilt. Replacing it with expanded facilities is Seneca Shadows Campground, 1.0mi S of Seneca Rocks on WV28/ US33.) A developed picnic area is on FR104, the road from FR112 to Spruce Knob. Picnic facilities are available at the parking circle of Spruce Knob. The Spruce Knob Area is an excellent place to explore--with or without trails. Woods are open, and streams and ridges are easy to follow. Except on system USFS roads, all motorized vehicles are prohibited.

In the early to mid-1990s the USFS made changes in the Seneca Creek trail system. Some trails were combined or renamed, but none of the locations changed. Horton Trail (TR530) now goes from the trailhead on CO29 (near Whitmer/Horton) to Seneca Creek where it ends. Huckleberry Trail (TR533) was extended and goes from Spruce Knob to Seneca Creek Trail (TR515) near Upper Seneca Falls. Also, Little Allegheny Trail (TR535) was renamed as part of Allegheny Mountain Trail (TR532), making it 12.4mi. Lumberjack Trail (TR534) has been extended 2.0mi NE to a flat area on Spruce Mountain range. (Some old USGS topo maps incorrectly show this as Huckleberry Trail.) A new trail, High Meadows Trail (TR564) was created at the NE end of Lumberjack Trail to form a loop by descending to juncture with Huckleberry Trail.

The shortening of "Horton-Horserock" to "Horton" reflects the shortened segment need because it never went to Horserock. Horserock (which is the rocky saddle of Spruce Mountain) is where the Horton-Riverton (also called Whitmer-Riverton) Trail once crossed. The USFS claims the Horton-Horserock is not historic, but rather was penned when the Riverton link was abandoned.

Hikers will also notice the replacing of signs in the Seneca Creek trail system. Trailhead signs have the trail name, number, and the distance to several major destinations or trail junctions. All mileages are rounded to the nearest one-half mile, and blazes are plastic diamond-shaped blue. Reflecting these changes is the revised USFS and NRA map.

JUDY SPRINGS TRAIL (TR512)   0.7mi(1.1km)

SCENERY: 1 (exceptional)   NOTE: B,M,S,(1)
DIFFICULTY: II (moderate)   SKI-:   S3
CONDITION: B (average)   ELEV: 3890/3400
MAPS: USFS(A,B), Whitmer, Spruce Knob, V-B-2 in this Guide
SEGMENTS: (1) TR533 (Huckleberry Trail) to Judy Springs   0.7mi

The primary attractions of Judy Springs Trail are the high mountain pasture with great views at the top end of the trail, and the former Judy Springs Campground at the lower end. The meadow at Judy Springs is no

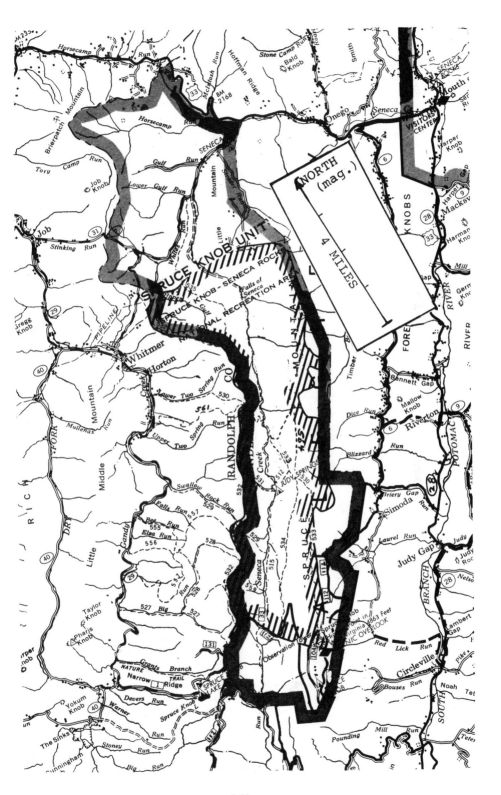

longer a campground with a well pump. Hikers continue to use the meadow on both sides of Seneca Creek for setting up tents. Judy Springs water is dependable, even in dry weather, and is always very cold.

Access: See Huckleberry Trail (TR533) for the turn-off to Judy Springs ⒜. Near the N edge of the upper pasture a sign reads: "Judy Springs- 1 mile".

Segment 1: Starting from TR533 ⒜ leave Huckleberry Trail (TR533) and go 10yd along the N edge of the pasture before taking a diagonal to the left. Arrows and rock cairns mark the trail as it descends SW across a pasture. The trail then enters the woods and follows an old road a short distance to a large meadow on the E and W bank of Seneca Creek ⒝. Judy Springs is 30yd to the left on a spur trail. After continuing a few yards, cross a footbridge over Seneca Creek to a meadow and Seneca Creek Trail (TR515).

SENECA CREEK TRAIL (TR515)   5.0mi(8.0km)

SCENERY: 1 (exceptional)   NOTE: B,M,S,(1)
DIFFICULTY: I (leisurely)   SKI-: S1
CONDITION: A (good)   ELEV: 3890/2500
MAPS: USFS(A,B), Spruce Knob, Whitmer, Onego, V-B-2 and V-B-3 in
       this Guide
SEGMENTS: (1) FR112 to TR559 (Tom Lick Run Trail)   1.1mi
          (2) TR559 to TR529 (Swallow Rock Trail)   1.1mi
          (3) TR529 to Judy Springs   1.3mi
          (4) Judy Springs to TR530 (Horton Trail)   1.5mi

Seneca Creek Trail follows Seneca Creek from its S headwaters N to Horton Trail (TR530). (The former N section of TR515 is no longer maintained from the junction of TR515/TR530 to White's Run Road.) It appears to be the most popular trail in the area.

Numerous springs flow into Seneca Creek. Those from the W drain through woods; those from the E may flow across pastureland. Overall, this is an exceptional mountain stream, with old crossties and the remnants of the RR adding history and interest.

Access: The S trailhead ⒜(Map V-B-3) is 4.0mi E of Spruce Knob Lake and 5.0mi W of Spruce Knob on FR112 (formerly FR103). Park cars at the USFS parking area. A bulletin board gives emergency information and a trail map. Access road FR112 is not plowed in winter beyond the junction of FR1 and FR112.

Segment 1: Starting from the S ⒜, Seneca Creek Trail is an old road near the E bank of Seneca Creek. It is closed to vehicles. Seneca Creek is small at first, flowing through young spruce groves and meadows. The trail fords small streams flowing in from the E. At 0.9mi a sign identifies Tom Lick Run Trail (TR559) ⒝ which ascends 1.1mi W to Allegheny Mountain Trail (TR532).

Segment 2: At 1.5mi is a beaver dam and pond off the W side of the trail. Another small stream, coming in from the E, is crossed at 2.1mi. A short distance farther (0.1mi) is the junction with Swallow Rock Run Trail (TR529) ⒞ which ascends 1.0mi W to Allegheny Mountain Trail. No bridge crosses Seneca Creek to TR529.

Segment 3: About 2.7mi before Judy Springs ⒝, the trail fords ⒟ to the W bank of Seneca Creek, by now of moderate size, and continues directly into a large meadow at 3.5mi. Judy Springs (Map V-B-2) is on the E side of Seneca Creek. To get to Judy Springs Trail (TR512), which connects with Huckleberry Trail (TR533), cross the bridge over Seneca Creek. After crossing the bridge, a side trail bears off to the right and leads 30yd to the gushing Judy Springs.

Segment 4: Near the lower end of this meadow, at 3.6mi, a sign indicates the start of Bear Hunter Trail (TR531) which ascends W to join Allegheny Mountain Trail (TR532). Seneca Creek Trail continues N from this sign on an old logging RR bed along Seneca Creek and is easy to follow downstream.

At 3.7mi, the trail crosses from the W to E bank of Seneca Creek. At 4.1mi it recrosses [C] to the W side. At 4.8mi the trail again crosses to the E. This is a short distance above Upper Seneca Creek Falls (highest falls on the creek). A large overhang can be seen on the W side of the Falls. To the right is the junction [D] with Huckleberry Trail (TR533). Follow Seneca Creek Trail downstream for 0.2mi to a junction [L] with Horton Trail (TR530). Seneca Creek Trail ends at this point.

BIG RUN TRAIL (TR527)   3.1mi(5.0km)
SCENERY: 2 (wooded)   NOTE: B,M,(5)
DIFFICULTY: II (moderate)   SKI-:   S2
CONDITION: A (good)   ELEV: 3955/3270
MAPS: USFS(A,B), Spruce Knob, V-B-3 in this Guide
SEGMENTS: (1) FR112 to TR528 (North Prong Trail)   1.5mi
                    (2) TR528 to CO29   1.6mi

Big Run Trail connects Gandy Creek with FR112 (FR103 on old maps). Many areas along this trail are suitable for camping, with springs, near the upper trailhead below FR112, at the junction with North Prong Trail (TR528) and along North Prong Trail (TR528).

Access: The upper (SE) trailhead [E] is 2.5mi NE of Spruce Knob Lake on FR112, 0.6mi NE of the intersection of FR1 and FR112 and 0.3mi E of FR131 (to Gatewood Campground). Parking space is found near the trail signs. The S trailhead of Allegheny Mountain Trail (TR532) is nearby.

The lower trailhead [H], on CO29, is marked by a hiker symbol sign, TR527.

Segment 1: From the SE terminus [E], Big Run Trail makes a descent through the woods to a spring, turns left, then follows a small stream on the N side. The valley is open and pleasant. Watch for a double blaze (turn) at 0.4mi. At 1.3mi a sign at the fork [F], where the trail meets TR528, points back to the junction [E] with Allegheny Mountain Trail (TR532).

Segment 2: TR527 continues on down Big Run from [F], with stream crossings at 1.4mi, 1.54mi, 1.6mi, 2.1mi and 2.4mi. Nearing Gandy Creek, the trail follows an old road through a field to a footbridge across Gandy Creek to CO29 [H].

NORTH PRONG TRAIL (TR528)   2.8mi(4.5km)
SCENERY: 2 (wooded)   NOTE: B,M,(2)
DIFFICULTY: II (moderate)   SKI-:   S2
CONDITION: B (average)   ELEV: 4120/3500

MAPS: USFS(A,B), Spruce Knob, V-B-3 in this Guide
SEGMENTS:
    (1) TR527 (Big Run Trail) to TR556 (Elza Trail)   1.2mi
    (2) TR556 to TR532 (Allegheny Mtn. Trail)   1.6mi

    North Prong Trail was formerly called Leading Ridge Trail. Campsites, with springs, are found near both ends of the trail.

    Access: The SW terminus [F] of this trail is on Big Run Trail (TR527), 1.5mi NW of its upper end.

    The NE terminus [K] is along Allegheny Mountain Trail (TR532). These three trails can be combined to form a pleasant circuit hike starting from FR112.

    Segment 1: Starting from the SW [F], North Prong Trail ascends along North Prong with several crossings. At 0.7mi, at a clearing, is a fork. Follow the N branch which runs into an old road at 1.2mi at a bridge over North Prong [I]. Elza Trail (TR556) comes in from the N here.

    Segment 2: Continue NE (not crossing bridge) to where you encounter old beaver ponds and an open valley. At 1.6mi [J] the road turns into the woods, bearing SE. It ascends the hill to a clearing at 2.3mi. Continue SE to Allegheny Mountain Trail (TR532) [K] by a stand of pines, a clearing and a spring.

SWALLOW ROCK TRAIL (TR529)   3.2mi(5.1km)

SCENERY: 1-2 (exceptional-wooded)   NOTE: B,M,(5)
DIFFICULTY: II (moderate)   SKI-: S2
CONDITION: A (good)   ELEV: 3974/3050
MAPS: USFS(A,B), Whitmer, Spruce Knob, V-B-2 and V-B-3 in this
        Guide
SEGMENTS: (1) CO29 to TR532 (Allegheny Mtn. Trail)   2.3mi
            (2) TR532 to TR515 (Seneca Creek Trail)   0.9mi

    The stream along Swallow Rock Trail is spring-fed. The trail is fine for ski touring.

    Access: The lower (NW) trailhead [E](Map V-B-2) is on CO29, 4.7mi S of Whitmer. CO29 is snowplowed early to Little Italy and later beyond that. Several cars can park along the road. The trail starts from a scenic area just below Gandy Creek Bridge. At the trailhead is a hiker symbol with the trail number. A USFS sign up the trail says: "Swallow Rock Trail, Allegheny Mountain Trail".

    Segment 1: From the NW terminus [E] Swallow Rock Trail starts up hill just N of Gandy Creek Bridge. Turn S and follow the trail up and over a ridge to Swallow Rock Run. The trail crosses the run in a camping area [F] and follows the S side of the run to a fork. At this fork the trail takes the right (SE) branch. After 0.2mi from the fork the trail crosses to the left bank where it continues 15-20yd from the stream. At 1.7mi from Gandy Creek the trail enters a small clearing and continues along the right (S) fork across the clearing and into the woods. From here, continue along the main branch S, ascending to the ridge top and Allegheny Mountain Trail (TR532) [L] (Map V-B-3). There is a grassy clearing at this junction and an arrow pointing SE to Seneca Creek. The junction with TR532 is marked with a 4x4 post with arrows and the trail number.

Segment 2: The trail continues SE to Seneca Creek and Seneca Creek Trail (TR515) [C]. No bridge crosses Seneca Creek.

HORTON TRAIL (TR530)   3.5mi(5.6km)

SCENERY: 1-2 (exceptional-wooded)   NOTE: B,M,(2)
DIFFICULTY: II (moderate)   SKI-:   S4
CONDITION: B (average)   ELEV: 3800/2840
MAPS: USFS(A,B), Whitmer, V-B-2 in this Guide
SEGMENTS:
    (1) CO29 to TR532 (Allegheny Mtn. Trail)   2.4mi
    (2) TR532 to TR515 (Seneca Creek Trail)   1.1mi

Horton Trail was formerly named Horton-Riverton Trail and later Horton-Horserock Trail. The trail traverses the Spruce Knob Unit from Gandy Creek near Horton, across Allegheny Mountain to Spruce Knob Mountain.

Access: The NW trailhead [H](Map V-B-2) is 1.5mi S of Whitmer along CO29. (Groceries are available in Whitmer.) Beyond Horton, CO29 crosses Lower Two Springs Run. About 0.1mi beyond is a hiker symbol. Nearby is parking in a grove of pine and spruce. To the E, up the dirt road on the S side of the run, is space for car-camping and tent-camping.

Segment 1: Starting from the NW [H] Horton Trail follows the old logging road up Lower Two Springs Run. Beyond the parking area take the S fork of this road (do not ford the run) up the narrow valley. The foot trail with some visible rock grading follows the run 40ft up on the S bank. Remains of an old logging road are seen in places. The grade is gentle. The stream is spring-fed. The faint intersecting trail [I] , shown on the topo at 0.7mi, is unmarked. At the fork [J] at 1.5mi is an old healed blaze on a small forked maple on the left side of the trail. On the ridge between the forks of the run is a rhododendron thicket and small rock outcrop. The trail in this area is not obvious with snow cover.

Ascend the right (S) fork, following along the right side of the run. At a second fork, 0.4mi from the first one, are three old slash marks on a tree. Follow the left fork to intersect Allegheny Mountain Trail (TR532) [K] at the ridge top, just above a spring and pond. A sign says: "Allegheny Mountain Trail".

Segment 2: From the junction with TR532, the trail diagonals SSE, downhill, to cross Seneca Creek [L] just below the Upper Seneca Creek Falls and meet Seneca Creek Trail (TR515).

BEAR HUNTER TRAIL (TR531)   1.0mi(1.6km)

SCENERY: 1-2 (exceptional/wooded)   NOTE: B,M,(2)
DIFFICULTY: II (moderate)   SKI-:   S4
CONDITION: A (good)   ELEV: 4020/3400
MAPS: USFS(A,B), Whitmer, V-B-2 in this Guide
SEGMENTS: (1) Judy Springs to TR532 (Allegheny Mtn. Trail)   1.0mi

Access: A sign indicates the beginning of Bear Hunter Trail on the NW side of Judy Springs meadow where Seneca Creek Trail leaves the meadow [B].

Segment 1: Bear Hunter Trail crosses a run and ascends toward Allegheny Mountain. After 0.7mi the trail crosses to the S side of the run,

Seneca Creek near former Judy Springs campsites (TR515).
Photo by Roger Spencer

near the end of a cove. Near the top of the mountain the trail turns left, SW, before reaching Allegheny Mountain Trail (TR532) [M].

ALLEGHENY MOUNTAIN TRAIL (TR532) 12.4mi(19.8km)
SCENERY: 1 (exceptional) NOTE: B,M,(0)
DIFFICULTY: III (strenuous) SKI-: S2-S4
CONDITION: A/B (good/average) ELEV: 4250/2170
MAPS: USFS(A,B), Whitmer, Spruce Knob, Onego, V-B-1, V-B-2 and
      V-B-3 in this Guide
SEGMENTS:
    (1) FR112 to TR559 (Tom Lick Run Trail)   2.1mi
    (2) TR559 to TR528 (North Prong Trail)   0.2mi
    (3) TR528 to TR557 (Leading Ridge Trail)   0.5mi
    (4) TR557 to TR529 (Swallow Rock Trail)   0.5mi
    (5) TR529 to TR531 (Bear Hunter Trail)   1.4mi
    (6) TR531 to TR561 (Spring Ridge Trail)   1.5mi
    (7) TR561 to TR530 (Horton Trail)   0.2mi
    (8) TR530 to CO7   6.0mi

Allegheny Mountain Trail is not to be confused with Allegheny Trail (TR701) which runs the entire length of the MNF, or with Allegheny Mountain Trail (TR611) in White Sulphur Ranger District. In 1991 the Little Allegheny Trail (TR553) name was deleted by the USFS and its 4.5mi were added to Allegheny Mountain Trail, making it the second-longest trail in the district. Following a NE-SW ridge from near Spruce Knob Lake to near the confluence of Whites Run and Seneca Creek, 75% of the trail distance is on an old forest road. The S section from FR112 to Spring Ridge Trail (TR561) receives moderate vehicle usage by the W.Va. Department of Natural Resources to maintain the grassy wildlife fields. All other vehicles are prohibited. Its seven trail junctions provide options for various short loops to Seneca and Gandy creeks, or longer combinations. The route as far NE as Horton Trail (TR530) is suitable for ski-touring. Wildlife which may be seen on the trail includes deer, raccoon, wild turkey, grouse, bear and fox.

Access: The S trailhead [E](Map V-B-3) is on FR112, 0.6mi NE of the FR1-FR112 intersection, 2.5mi NE of Spruce Knob Lake.

The N trailhead [A](Map V-B-1) is on CO7, 2.1mi S from US33, W of Onego.

Segment 1: Starting from the S (FR112) [E](Map V-B-3), at 1.0mi is a small field on the E side of the trail, and roads lead off both E and W. The trail continues on the road following the ridge. At 1.5mi the road forks. A sign points to the E fork as Allegheny Mountain Trail. At 2.1mi Tom Lick Trail (TR559) [N](Map V-B-3) comes in from Seneca Creek (E).

Segment 2: A short distance beyond, the trail again forks [K]. A small grove of pines and a field are on the W side of the road. A pond and spring are below this point a short distance on the E side of the road. Another spring is at the S end of the clearing on the W side of the trail. Camping is not recommended in the clearings along the trail since they are maintained for wildlife habitat. They must be mowed periodically; no rocks, firewood, or other obstacles should be left in them. The W fork at this point [K] is North Prong Trail (TR528). The E fork continues as Allegheny Mountain Trail.

Segment 3: The trail continues on the E side of the ridge, past a clearing on the W side of the trail, with a road, Leading Ridge Trail (TR557) [O], leaving the N corner of the clearing.

Segment 4: At 3.3mi is a clearing [L] on the E side of the trail. Signs mark this junction with Swallow Rock Trail (TR529).

Segment 5: At 0.4mi farther on the trail (from [L]) is a spring. At 4.7mi is a trail junction with a clearing [M](Map V-B-2) on the W side of the road. On the NE side is a junction with Bear Hunter Trail (TR531), which descends to Judy Springs.

Segment 6: From Bear Hunter Trail (TR531) [M], Allegheny Mountain Trail continues N and, after 1.6mi, meets Spring Ridge Trail (TR561) [O] coming up from the W.

Segment 7: Here Allegheny Mountain Trail swings E and crosses Horton Trail (TR530) [K] after 0.2mi. (Horton Trail was formerly called Horton-Horserock Trail.)

Segment 8: From here on, the trail becomes more narrow and less-well maintained. At 7.9mi the trail reaches the former Little Allegheny Trail (TR535) [N] and turns right. After 2.0mi along the ridge, the trail crosses a gas pipeline clearing [D](Map V-B-1) with excellent vistas W and E. From this point the trail gradually descends through a scenic forest of hardwoods, mountain laurel and huckleberry. At 11.2mi switchbacks begin [B] in rhododendron groves, and at 12.3mi the trail opens to a meadow with a huge apple tree. The trail turns left to a footbridge over White's Run [A]. A parking area is 0.1mi downstream.

HUCKLEBERRY TRAIL (TR533)   5.2mi(8.3km)

SCENERY: 1 (exceptional)   NOTE: B,M,(1)
DIFFICULTY: II (moderate)   SKI-:   S4
CONDITION: B (average)   ELEV: 4840/3085
MAPS: USFS(A,B), Spruce Knob, V-B-2, V-B-3 in this Guide
SEGMENTS:

    (1) Spruce Knob to TR534 (Lumberjack Trail)   3.8mi
    (2) TR534   to TR512 (Judy Springs Trail)   0.2mi
    (3) TR512   to TR564 (High Meadows Trail)   0.8mi
    (4) TR564   to TR515 (Seneca Creek Trail)   0.4mi

Huckleberry Trail runs from the parking lot of the Spruce Knob observation tower to Seneca Creek Trail (TR512) at Upper Seneca Creek Falls. It goes NE on a rocky treadway, through dense groves of conifers, in open heath meadow, descends to former grazing lands, and terminates at Seneca Creek. (See the introduction to Spruce Knob Area above about the incorporation of a section of Horton-Horserock Trail.) Potential campsites are found at 0.3mi, 0.7mi, 1.1mi, 1.8mi, 2.3mi and 3.1mi.

Access: The upper (S) trailhead [P](Map V-B-3) is at the parking area on top of Spruce Knob (just N of the observation tower). Get there by taking FR104, a spur road off FR112. It is 8.2mi from Spruce Knob Lake Campground.

The N terminus is on an embankment at Seneca Creek [D](Map V-B-2), near Upper Seneca Creek Falls.

Segment 1: Starting from the parking area [P](Map V-B-3) at the S terminus, walk 0.2mi to a sharp left turn. (To the right is a faint path in a thicket to a spring in a spruce grove.) In the huckleberry fields where there are good views, the trail is marked by rock cairns. At 1.9mi are remnants of a small plane crash, and at 2.0mi is a low place with a spruce grove. After a descent in a rocky area, the trail crosses Lumberjack Trail (TR534) [G](Map V-B-2), right and left, at 3.8mi.

Segment 2: The trail continues to descend on an old rocky road with a large pasture to the left. At 4.0mi the trail meets Judy Springs Trail (TR512) on the left [A]. (Judy Springs is 0.7mi from here.)

Segment 3: For the next 0.8mi the trail goes through an open forest with a rocky treadway, enters a grazing field of wildflowers with rock cairns, and descends rapidly to a small stream where it meets High Meadows Trail (TR564) coming in from the right.

Segment 4: From the juncture with TR564 Huckleberry Trail deswcends parallel to a stream but leaves it to the right for a juncture with Seneca Creek Trail (TR515) at 5.2mi [D]. (Downstream 0.2mi on Seneca Creek Trail is the junction with Horton Trail (TR530) [L].

LUMBERJACK TRAIL (TR534)   5.3mi(8.5km)

SCENERY:	1-2 (exceptional-wooded)	NOTE: B,M,(0)
DIFFICULTY:	II (moderate)	SKI-: S2
CONDITION:	B (average)	ELEV: 4100/3950

MAPS: USFS(A,B), Spruce Knob, Whitmer, V-B-2 and -B-3 in this Guide

SEGMENTS:	(1) FR112 to TR533 (Huckleberry Trail)	3.3mi
	(2) TR533 to TR564 (High Meadows Trail)	2.0mi

The trail N from FR112 follows an old RR grade through a northern hardwood forest along the N slope of Spruce Knob Mountain. Lumberjack Trail is not as frequently used as Seneca Creek Trail (TR515). It is marked with sporadic blue blazes and is easy to follow for its entire length.

Access: The S trailhead [Q](Map V-B-3), just S of the prominent switchback on FR112, is marked by a hiker symbol with the trail name further down the trail. This is 4.5mi E from Spruce Knob Lake. Parking is possible along FR112.

Segment 1: Starting from the S [Q], follow the old RR. Beyond an old field at 0.6mi is a spring area in a hemlock grove on the W side of the trail. The spring drains into a "lost creek" in a narrow ravine. Occasional sinks are found nearby, and just before the trail swings NE the stream goes underground. Several hundred yards N is another sink into which a spring flows. The trail along the old RR is marked by arrow signs (pointing S) as it leaves the stream valley. Old crossties and bridge footings mark this portion of the trail which is somewhat soggy in wet weather. At 3.3mi is the junction with Huckleberry Trail (TR533) [G](Map V-B-2).

Segment 2: Lumberjack Trail continues NE on the old RR grade. It is wet and rocky in a number of sections. At 3.8mi and 4.5mi are parts of old crossties preserved in wet areas. Most of the passage is through hardwoods with the exceptions of red spruce at 4.4mi and 5.3mi. Its NE end is at an open plateau with wildflowers and scattered trees and shrubs. Deer and wild turkey have been seen here. At the end of the trail, High Meadows Trail (TR564) begins its descent to meet Huckleberry Trail (TR533).

BEE TRAIL (TR555)   1.4mi(2.2km)
SCENERY: 1-2 (exceptional-wooded)   NOTE: B,M,(1)
DIFFICULTY: II (moderate)   SKI-:   S4
CONDITION: A (good)   ELEV: 4130/3100
MAPS: USFS(A,B), Whitmer, V-B-2 and V-B-3 in this Guide
SEGMENTS:
(1) CO29 to TR557 (Leading Ridge Trail) & TR556 (Elza Trail)   1.4mi
    This trail, as with Elza Trail (TR556), is ideal for connector routes to
Leading Ridge Trail (T557) from Whitmer Road, CO29.
    Access: The NW trailhead [P] (Map V-B-2) is on Whitmer Road
(CO29), 2.5mi N of Big Run Trail (TR527).
    Segment 1: Starting from the NW [P], Bee Trail crosses Gandy Creek
on a footbridge to a grassy field, and then enters a forest of cherry, maple,
birch and scattered groves of red spruce. For the first 0.8mi it follows an old
forest road, after which the footpath steepens. At 1.1mi it reaches an easy-to-
miss junction to the right of the former Bee Trail route to Elza Trail. After
ascending 0.4mi in open woods, the trail enters a wildlife field and joins
Leading Ridge Trail [R].

ELZA TRAIL (TR556)   2.0mi(3.2km)
SCENERY: 1-2 (exceptional-wooded)   NOTE: B,M,(2)
DIFFICULTY: II (moderate)   SKI-:   S4
CONDITION: A (good)   ELEV: 4000/3150
MAPS: USFS(A,B), Whitmer, Spruce Knob, V-B-2 and V-B-3 in this
        Guide
SEGMENTS:
    (1) CO29 to TR557 (Leading Ridge Trail)   1.5mi
    (2) TR557 to TR528 (North Prong Trail)   0.5mi
    Access: The lower (NW) trailhead [Q] (Map V-B-2) is on CO29, 6.0mi
S of Whitmer. A hiker symbol is on the E side of the road, and a trail sign
down the jeep road says, "Elza Trail".
    Segment 1:   From CO29 the trail continues on a jeep trail across the
creek and then leaves the road at an apple tree on the left. After crossing the
run, it follows the ridge toward the top of the hill, then along the contour on
the N side of the ridge. The trail crosses the run and continues on the N side
of the run to its head. It then bears right and climbs the grade and intersects
with a spur trail, formerly Bee Trail (TR555) and, after a few yards, with
Leading Ridge Trail (TR557) [R](Map V-B-3). Signs should be in place.
    Segment 2:   Continue beyond TR557 and TR555 through a small
wooded patch and down the access road. A small pond is on the right. At the
E end of the trail is a bridge and the junction [I] with North Prong Trail
(TR528).

LEADING RIDGE TRAIL (TR557)   5.1mi(8.2 km)
SCENERY: 2 (wooded)   NOTE: B,M,W,(1)
DIFFICULTY: II (moderate)   SKI-:   S3
CONDITION: A (good)   ELEV: 4220/3210

Huckleberry Trail (TR533). Photo by Charles Webb.

MAPS: USFS(A,B), Whitmer, Spruce Knob, V-B-2 and V-B-3 in this Guide
SEGMENTS:
    (1) CO29 to TR556 (Elza Trail)   2.8mi
    (2) TR556 to TR555 (Bee Trail)   0.7mi
    (3) TR555 to TR532 (Allegheny Mtn. Trail)   1.6mi
    The trail is a wide grassy road used for access to wildlife plots by the West Va. Department of Natural Resources.

Access: The lower (W) trailhead [S](Map V-B-3) is marked by a hiker symbol on the E side of CO29 where it crosses the bottom land through the woods to cross Gandy Creek.

Segment 1: Starting from the W [S] Leading Ridge Trail first reaches the junction with Elza Trail (TR556) [R] at 2.8mi.

Segment 2: From Elza Trail the trail continues to a junction with Bee Trail (TR555) [R](Map V-B-2) at 3.5mi.

Segment 3: The trail ends at the intersection with Allegheny Mountain Trail (TR532). [O](Map V-B-3)

TOM LICK TRAIL (TR559)   1.1mi(1.8km)

SCENERY: 2 (wooded)   NOTE: B,M,(1)
DIFFICULTY: II (moderate)   SKI-: S2
CONDITION: A (good)   ELEV: 4010/3710
MAPS: USFS(A,B), Spruce Knob, V-B-3 in this Guide
SEGMENTS:
(1) TR515 (Seneca Creek Trail) to TR532 (Allegheny Mtn. Trail) 1.1mi

Access: The SE trailhead [B] at Tom Lick Trail is 0.9mi along Seneca Creek Trail (TR515) from the Seneca Creek trailhead at FR112. Signs marking this trailhead are on the W side of Seneca Creek Trail (TR515).

The NW terminus [N] at Allegheny Mountain Trail (TR532) may also be signed.

Segment 1: Starting from the SE, Tom Lick Trail passes through an open area and crosses a bridge. It then follows a wide access road used for W.Va. Department of Natural Resources wildlife management.

SPRING RIDGE TRAIL (TR561)   3.2mi(5.1km)

SCENERY: 2-3 (wooded-developed)   NOTE: B,M,W,(1)
DIFFICULTY: II (moderate)   SKI-: S2
CONDITION: A (good)   ELEV: 4120/2880
MAPS: USFS(A,B), Whitmer, V-B-2 in this Guide
SEGMENTS: (1) CO29 to TR532 (Allegheny Mtn. Trail)   3.2mi

Spring Ridge Trail is an old timber access road, blocked to vehicle traffic, that winds up the mountain to Allegheny Mountain Trail (TR532). The trail does not have open areas for views, but it has numerous wildflowers and provides pleasant ski touring (downhill only) from Allegheny Mountain Trail.

Access: The W trailhead [R] of Spring Ridge Trail is along CO29, 1.5mi S of Whitmer.

The E trailhead [O] is along Allegheny Mountain Trail (TR532) 0.2mi SW of the intersection of TR532 and Horton Trail (TR530).

SHORT TRAIL (TR562)   0.5mi(0.8km)
SCENERY: 2 (wooded)   NOTE: B,M,W,(0)
DIFFICULTY: II (moderate)   SKI-:   S4
CONDITION: A (good)   ELEV: 4000/3850
MAPS: USFS(A,B), Spruce Knob, V-B-3 in this Guide
SEGMENTS: (1) Spruce Knob Lake Campground to FR112   0.5mi
    This is primarily an access for campers to Gatewood Trail.
    Access: Across from the entrance to Spruce Knob Lake Campground, a hiker symbol marks the NW trailhead.
    Segment 1: Walk through a mixed forest of beechnut and oaks, and conifers such as red spruce, to FR112. Across the road and into the forest, the trail makes a junction with Gatewood Trail.

HIGH MEADOWS TRAIL (TR564)   1.9mi(3.0km)
SCENERY: 1 (exceptional)   NOTE: B, M
DIFFICULTY: II (moderate)   SKI :   S4
CONDITION: A (good)   ELEV: 4100/3365
SEGMENTS:
(1) TR534 (Lumberjack Trail) to TR533 (Huckleberry Trail)   1.9mi
    This partially new, and sections of old, trail routes with different names provides the most scenic of all Seneca Creek and valley views. On the former pastoral slopes the trail descends rapidly past posts or cairns. Spectacular views can be seen almost any time. Fall foliage colors are at their peak during the first two weeks in October.
    Access: The upper (E) trailhead is at the N trailhead of Lumberjack Trail (TR534) on an old RR grade. The lower (W) trailhead is by a stream to juncture with Huckleberry Trail (TR533) $\boxed{E}$.
    Segment 1: At a plateau on Spruce Mountain, where Lumberjack Trail ends, continue left on an old RR grade/road to follow blue blazes and arrows, but after a few yards turn left off the grade into a hardwood forest. Meander to a fence which is briefly followed at 0.2mi. Descend steeply through yellow birch, cherry and maple. At 0.6mi exit the woods on a grassy knoll for views of the major section of Seneca Creek Valley and the Allegheny Mountains beyond.
    Watch for blue blazes on posts and cairns on the descent. Arrive at an old road where you slightly ascend, but watch for a sudden right to turn off the road. At 1.3mi exit to another grassy slope. Follow cairns, then enter the forest again among hemlock and maple at 1.5mi. After a cascading stream, descend to enter a pastoral slope with post markers. Pass an old cattle salt feeder and juncture with Huckleberry Trail (TR533) $\boxed{E}$, left and right, at 1.9mi.

GATEWOOD TRAIL (I-51)   2.4mi(3.9km)
SCENERY: 2-3 (wooded-developed)   NOTE: B,M,(1)
DIFFICULTY: II (moderate)   SKI-:   S2
CONDITION: A (good)   ELEV: 3980/3620
MAPS: USFS(A,B), Spruce Knob, V-B-3 in this Guide
SEGMENTS: (1) Sawmill Run Road to same spot   2.3mi
           (2) Sawmill Run Road to FR112   0.1mi

This loop trail was formerly an interpretive trail with marked stations.

Access: The trail begins on Sawmill Run Road (CO10) ⊤, just E of the Shot Cherry Cabin, 0.5mi SE from the junction with FR112 (FR103 on old USFS maps). A wide curve in the road offers parking for a few cars.

Segment 1: Starting clockwise from CO10 ⊤, the trail takes off to the NW, ascending through mixed hardwoods and a beech stand. (If hiked counterclockwise the ascent is not as steep.) It then descends through a small stand of pines. Just left (W) up the hill past a small pond is access (via Short Trail) to FR112 and to Spruce Knob Lake Campground. This passes through a W.Va. Department of Natural Resources demonstration area.

Gatewood Trail then descends to an open area, and back into a wooded area. A spring is nearby, off to the right. A chestnut rail fence and stile are at the edge of the wooded area. Cross at this point and parallel the fence through an open area, with spruce interspersed, to where the trail bears left and crosses the run. The trail may not be as obvious here through the Big Run Grazing Allotment. It passes through clumps of hawthorn and through some spruce planting to a fence. To protect the fence, cross at the stile. On the other side of the fence, bear right and cross the footbridge. At Big Run Ⅴ turn SW and follow the old RR grade along Big Run to an obvious point where the trail leaves the grade and ascends through a red pine plantation. (If you continued on the grade, you would reach Sawmill Run Road [CO10].) Continue N through the pine plantation, across the log road and eventually come out onto a field. Cross the field. The trail continues past a blaze on a large tree at the edge of the field and ascends the hill, skirting the old clear-cut along the ridge. The trail is easy to follow through the forest to the log landing, and the path ⊤ to Sawmill Run Road, the point of origin.

BACK RIDGE TRAIL (TR526)   5.0mi(8.0km)

SCENERY: 2-3 (wooded-developed)   NOTE: B,W,(3)
DIFFICULTY: II (moderate)   SKI-: S4
CONDITION: B (average)   ELEV: 3963/2497
MAPS: USFS(A,B), Spruce Knob, Snowy Mountain
SEGMENTS: (1) WV28 to Rt28/10   5.0mi

Big Run, the stream immediately W of Back Ridge Trail, is beautiful with falls, cascades and pools. The old RR grade along this stream is well-traveled by fishermen. The upper 170yd of this grade is almost nonexistent. Use the creek bed as a trail here. This area has many campsites along Big Run and is popular with fishermen. Trash and debris mar the scenery.

Access: The lower trailhead is 6.8mi W of Cherry Grove where WV28 crosses Big Run. (This is 0.6mi W of the turnoff to Spruce Knob Lake, Saw Mill Run Road and Hunting Ground which leads to the upper trailhead.) The trail at this point is an old logging RR and road. Several cars can park here. The foot trail begins just beyond the first ford.

Parking space is available for about 3 cars at the upper trailhead along Rt28/10.

Segment 1: Starting from WV28, follow the old RR grade upstream for 1.3mi, and rock-hop or wade Big Run three times before beginning an ascent of Back Ridge. The trail makes a gradual traversing ascent of Back Ridge. It is a little-traveled, rocky, graded path through shrubby oak. In this first section is one old large oak along the trail and numerous laurel thickets near the crest. As the crest is gained, a road shown as a trail on the topo comes in from the E. Back Ridge Trail then continues N along this road. Within the next 0.5mi, two logging roads drop down on the W side of the ridge and dead-end.

Near the upper trailhead are fine views to the E of high farm country. The view at the trailhead is particularly nice. A sign here reads: "Back Ridge Trail, TR526, State Rd.28". This point is 3.0mi SE of the junction of FR1 and FR112 (2.0mi SE of Spruce Knob Lake) along the road intersecting WV28 (Rt28/ 10) a few miles W of Cherry Grove. One mile S of the N terminus is a vista intentionally created as part of a timber sale. A beautiful view of Spruce Mountain and North Fork Mountain are seen from this point.

SPRUCE KNOB LAKE TRAIL (No #)   1.0mi(1.6km)
SCENERY: 1 (lake area)   NOTE: M, W, (0)
DIFFICULTY: I (easy)   SKI :   S4
CONDITION: A (good)   ELEV: 3840/3825
MAPS: USFS(A), Spruce Knob
SEGMENTS: (1) Lake Parking Area and return   1.0mi

Access: On FR1, a short distance W of the Spruce Knob Lake Campground, turn left to the lake where there is a parking lot and picnic area.

Segment 1: From the parking lot, circle the lake on a foot trail (no bikes or horses). If crossing the dam, turn left after the crossing, and cross a boardwalk at 0.3mi. After slightly ascending on a tiered boardwalk descend to a meadow at the lake's headwaters at 0.5mi. The remainder of the trail passes through wildflowers, ferns, yellow birch and red spruce. Return to the picnic area and parking area.

High Meadows Trail View (TR564). Photo by Amy Seibert-Carrier

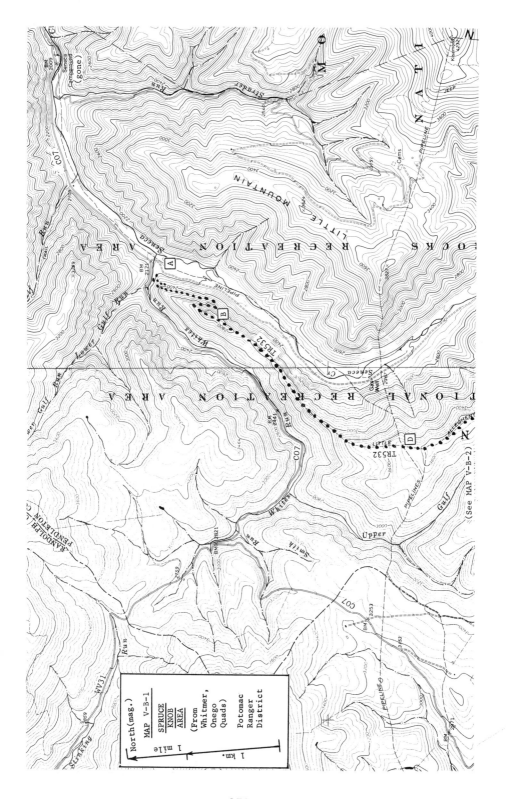

MAP V-B-1

SPRUCE
KNOB
AREA

(From
Whitmer,
Onego
Quads)

Potomac
Ranger
District

North(mag.)

1 mile

1 Km.

(See MAP V-B-2.)

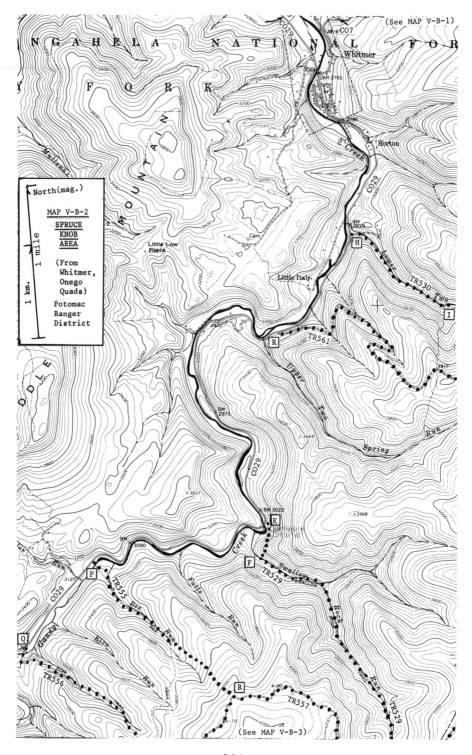

(See MAP V-B-1)

(See MAP V-B-3)

MAP V-B-2

SPRUCE
KNOB
AREA

(From
Whitmer,
Onego
Quads)

Potomac
Ranger
District

North(mag.)

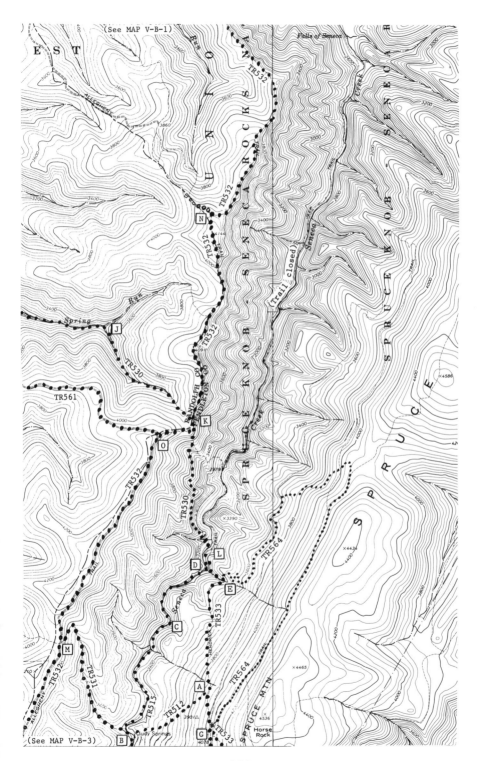

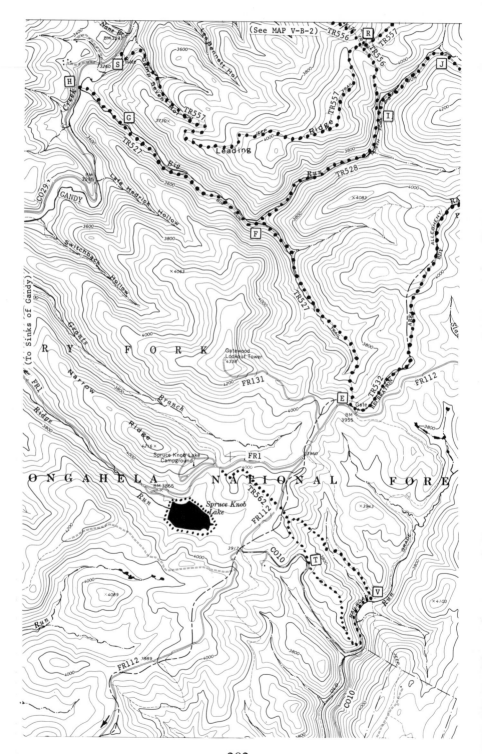

(See MAP V-B-2)

282

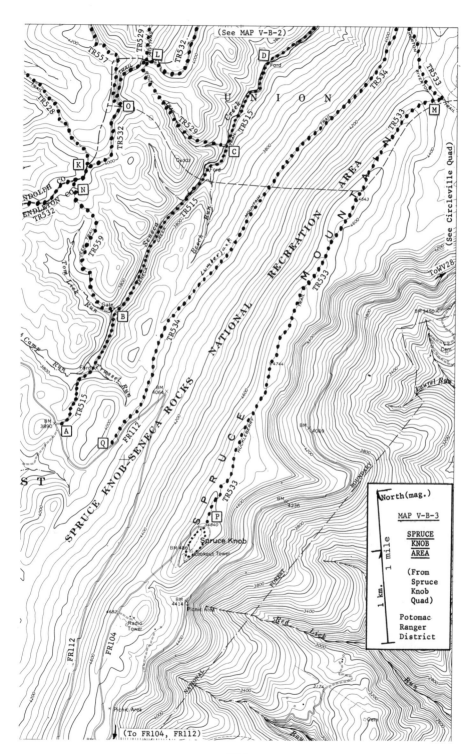

(V-C) FLATROCK PLAINS AND ROARING PLAINS

Anyone who has ever looked at a relief map of West Virginia spots this area immediately: it may be the most rugged in the entire state. The highest point (Mt. Porte Crayon--Thunder Knob) is only 93ft lower than Spruce Knob. Broad views and scenery in this area rival almost anything else the MNF has to offer. Like Dolly Sods, it is full of 3-sided spruce, heath, and boggy areas. However it has fewer open meadows and windswept rock formations, even though it has a similar geology. It also has fewer visitors than Dolly Sods, but it has become quite popular. Signs of bear are far more common in this area than in northern Dolly Sods. Since the early 1970s when this hiking guide was first written, significant transformations have occurred. Brushy areas have become oak forest; spectacular views have disappeared behind tall spruce; red spruce are reclaiming what they once dominated completely and vegetation is becoming dense, reflecting the rebuilding of soil. The term "Plains" is now only marginally appropriate. Mt. Porte Crayon is now so heavily vegetated as to be virtually inaccessible to hikers. Also its views are largely gone.

Trails described here were originally explored, mapped and described by Helen McGinnis as part of her early 1970s study that ultimately led to Congress declaring Dolly Sods a Wilderness Area. The area's ruggedness demands more hiking experience than usual. In the past decade the USFS and volunteers from hiking groups have done a lot of trail maintenance and improvements in the area. Trails are now all signed at trailheads, and trails are marked with blue plastic diamond blazes. Topographic maps (Laneville, Onego, Harman, and Hopeville) are essential.

Experienced hikers accustomed to off-trail hiking will find some of the area a delight. However much of the area now has such dense vegetation (especially spruce) that off-trail hiking is difficult or impossible. Old abandoned RR grades are common. Worthy of particular note:
- spectacular views from Green Knob, just S of Haystack Knob
- the vicinity where the eastern continental divide intersects the pipeline swath.

General Description

This area encompasses 17.7sq.mi of federal land in Randolph and Pendleton counties. The largest portion is drained by the South Fork and other tributaries of Red Creek, notable Flatrock Run and Big Run, but streams in the SE part flow into Dry Fork River, Roaring Creek and Seneca Creek. The eastern continental divide (Allegheny Front) runs through Roaring Plains and Red Creek Plains.

The high plateau that is so well defined in the watershed of the main (N) fork of Red Creek is more eroded here, leaving Roaring-, Flatrock-, and Red Creek Plains as flat topped ridges. The steep slopes below the ridge tops are covered predominantly with northern hardwoods on the W, and with oaks on Allegheny Front above the Fore Knobs. On the high plains are dense stands of spruce and rhododendron, thickets of mountain laurel, small bogs, meadows, and outcrops of conglomerate with bands of rounded white pebbles. Meadows of blueberry heath with scattered azaleas, mountain laurel and red spruce are a favorite of visitors. Trillium, bleeding hearts (very common) and pink lady slippers normally bloom in late May. Azaleas normally bloom in early to mid June. Laurel bloom in mid- to late June. Rhododendron bloom in mid-July. A cold spring could move these dates back a week or more. Adjacent private lands include many open pastures. In scenic grandeur the Plains rival the northern Dolly Sods area and the open parts of the summit of Cabin Mountain.

A 66-foot-wide gas pipeline swath mars the wild character of Roaring- and Flatrock Plains. FR70, a 3.5mi-long gravel road, gated to public vehicular travel, provides access to the swath and a microwave relay station on Flatrock Plains. These facilities were built by Atlantic Seaboard Corporation under lease arrangements with the USFS. The only recreation facilities are hiking trails and the Dolly Sods Picnic Area. Campsites tend to be small (typical capacity: 3-4 tents). The largest (and most spectacular) sites are on the pipeline swath where it crosses the top of Allegheny Front (el.4495ft) and the large adjacent meadow just to the N.

The area contains 60% (4.5sq.mi) of the federally owned commercial quality timber in the Red Creek drainage. An intermediate cut is found along the lower part of the South Fork below FR19. Logging and timber-stand improvement (girdling of undesirable trees) has been carried out in the drainage of Flatrock Run. Commercial timber is also found in the watershed of Long Run, a tributary of Roaring Creek.

The area is underlain by as many as five potentially mineable coal seams--the Bakerstown, Upper Freeport, Hughes Ferry (Iaeger), Sewell, and Fire Creek. With the purchase of the mineral rights to 24.3sq.mi of federal land in the Dolly Sods area, the USFS became the owner of coal under most of the 17.7sq.mi.

Although the pipeline swath and microwave tower disqualify this region as a potential Wilderness area, it is still exceptionally scenic and largely undeveloped. It deserves special management to retain these qualities. The 1986 Monongahela National Forest Land Management Plan recognized this need to some extent by establishing a 0.6sq.mi semi-primitive non-motorized area near Mt.Porte Crayon, and by classifying 12.1sq.mi for semi-primitive, non-motorized recreation. ATVs and motorcycles have damaged the area E of Mt. Porte Crayon. (They apparently gain access via adjacent private property.)

Allegheny Front

One of the most interesting features of the area is the mountain ridge on its E edge. Allegheny Front is the eastern continental divide in this region, and is also part of the reason for the scenery and uniqueness of the Dolly Sods area and the Spruce Knob area, two of the more popular and scenic areas on the MNF. Allegheny Front is the backbone ridge of the Appalachian Mountains in W.Va. (and Pa.) and affects weather patterns in this part of the U.S. significantly. Tree species E of the Front are somewhat different from those W of the Front, reflecting the generally drier climate E of the Front. It is fascinating to approach the ridgetop from the W and watch how vegetation changes dramatically over a very short distance, from lush and dense to sparse and stunted at the ridgetop. The Front often blocks the eastward motion of clouds, resulting in more rain to the W than to the E.

The E portion of South Prong Trail (TR517) follows along the top of Allegheny Front, but much of this is in trees with only a few good views. The most interesting part of the Front is the 1.5mi between where TR517 drops N off the Front and where the pipeline swath crosses, in particular the large (0.4

x 0.7mi) flat meadow just E of where the pipeline swath crosses the eastern continental divide at el.4495ft. The pipeline swath, from here E down to where it drops steeply off Roaring Plains [Q], is also one of the most impressive parts of the region. Boulders beside the swath offer spectacular views of Smith Mountain and its picturesque high-mountain pastures, Seneca Rocks, practically all 24mi of North Fork Mountain (near the E horizon), Chimney Rocks, the Spruce Knob area, Roaring Creek Valley, Fore Knobs and more. The portion of the swath near where the eastern continental divide crosses it can be camped on. It is grassy, level, and smooth, and offers spectacular views. Due to the exposure, do not camp on the swath in windy or rainy weather. Small, sheltered campsites are found adjacent to the swath. Water is usually available from the tiny stream crossing the swath, as indicated on the map.

The meadow contains grasses and blueberry heath with scattered azaleas, mountain laurel and red spruce. A grassy old jeep trail (blocked by a large boulder) leaves the pipeline swath near the SE rim of the meadow and extends out onto the meadow and then branches. (See o o o o on the map.) There are numerous little paths, so stay on these to keep the meadow at its scenic and natural best. Seneca Rocks is visible from points along the former jeep trail. Shortly beyond where it divides is a spectacular overlook at the meadow's SE rim. From here, even the North Fork of the South Branch of the Potomac River is visible 3000ft below you. There is probably no other view with a 3000ft. drop on the MNF. About 100yd E of the main overlook are grassy, well-used campsites [Y] among tall hardwoods. Beyond are bogs [X] usually containing running water. Hours could be spent roaming around the meadow, especially in June when azaleas and mountain laurel bloom.

From the E tip of the meadow [W] very experienced hikers sometimes walk off-trail along the ridgetop 0.9mi N to South Prong Trail (TR517). The N 0.5mi is a narrow pile of flat boulders, nearly vegetation-free, with views E.

SOUTH PRONG TRAIL (TR517)   5.7mi(9.2km)

SCENERY: 2 (wooded)   NOTE: B,M,(3)
DIFFICULTY: II (moderate)   SKI-: S4
COND: B (average)   ELEV: 4130/2950
MAPS: USFS(A,B), Laneville, Hopeville, V-C-1 & V-D-2 in this Guide
SEGMENTS: (1) FR19 (W) to FR70   2.7mi
          (2) FR70 to FR19 (E)   3.0mi

South Prong Trail receives its name from South Fork of Red Creek, near the W part of the trail. The E half is high on Red Creek Plains, where it parallels FR70. A loop can be made by using FR19, the access route for the trail's termini. Because the E portion runs along the top of Allegheny Front (eastern continental divide) for 2.5mi, it offers a number of impressive views. The number of views has decreased over the past two decades due to growth of red spruce. Blue plastic blazes mark this well-used trail.

Access: The E end of the trail is at a parking area (capacity: 6 cars) on FR19 [V] (Map V-D-2) 0.4mi SW of Dolly Sods Picnic Area, and 0.2mi E of the FR70-FR19 intersection.

South Prong Trail (TR517) on Red Creek Plains.
Photo by Steve Swingenstein

The W terminus of South Prong Trail is on FR19 [A](Map V-C-1) 1.0mi from the Red Creek bridge in Laneville. The parking area (capacity: 8-10 cars) is also the access point for Boar's Nest Trail (TR518), but these two trails begin at separate spots.

Segment 1: Starting from the W terminus [A], South Prong Trail descends from the parking lot gate on a logging road. Rock-hop or wade across South Fork of Red Creek. A good campsite is near the grade at this crossing. The trail turns left at the pilings of an old bridge over the South Fork, and switches back to climb the hill on the other side on old RR grades. (If hiking in the reverse direction, the old RR grades are more difficult to distinguish.) The trail continues uphill, re-crosses South Fork [B], and crosses FR70 [C]. (FR70 continues 1.7mi N to FR19.) Since FR70 is gated to cars at FR19, hikers have the choice of getting back to FR19 by walking 1.7mi along FR70 or 3.0mi on TR517 (the far more scenic alternative).

Segment 2: South Prong Trail E of FR70 is a scenic old trail, with blueberry patches, small bogs, hardwoods, spruce, rhododendrons, laurel and good views from conglomerate outcrops. The first 0.4mi follows close to a small, clear stream that runs most of the year. A large meadow (with camp-sites) is found along the upper reaches of this stream. The trail reenters the woods 0.1mi before reaching the top of Allegheny Front. Where the trail direction turns from SE to N atop Allegheny Front, the map shows a trail continuing E. This route is no longer visible. Red spruce and laurel dominate the remainder of the trail. The best view [D] is to the NW, N and NE (even Chimney Rocks of North Fork Mountain is visible). It is 15yd off the W side of the trail, 2.0mi before FR19. The turnoff (no clear path, but marked by a cairn?) is just before an unusually steep 30-yd. descent. About 100 yd. before this steep descent is an easy side-trail leading 20yd E to a good view (on clear days) of North Fork Mountain. This turnoff is marked by a flat white sand patch (10 ft. diameter) on the E side of the trail. A second good overlook to the W is 1.1mi before FR19 at a large rock outcrop [E] that the trail winds through. One campsite is 0.25mi before the E end of the trail, on the W side of the trail. Another small campsite, 30yd from the E trailhead, would be suitable for Friday-night arrivals. The last 0.3mi of trail is very wet for some days after a rain. About half of this wet section is paved with planks resting on cross-logs.

BOAR'S NEST TRAIL (TR518)   2.7mi(4.3km)

SCENERY: 1-2 (exceptional-wooded)   NOTE: B,M,(2)
DIFFICULTY: II (moderate)   SKI-: S4
CONDITION: B (average)   ELEV: 4290/2950
MAPS: USFS(A,B), Laneville, V-C-1 in this guide
SEGMENTS: (1) FR19 to FR70   2.7mi

Boar's Nest Trail gets its name from a saloon that once was nearby. Laneville residents did not want disreputable establishments within the town, forcing thirsty loggers looking for a little fun after days of hard work in back-country camps to go up or down Red Creek. (There once was a similar tavern called "Pig's Ear" near Cheat Bridge in the Shaver's Fork watershed.) The trail is blazed bright blue.

Access: This trail's N terminus [G] is on the S side of FR19 at a parking area 1.0mi from the Red Creek Bridge in Laneville. Trail signs mark the parking area. The W terminus of South Prong Trail (TR517) uses the same parking area. Capacity: 8-10 cars.

The S terminus [M] is on FR70, 3.mi S of FR19 and 1.3mi S of TR517 [C].

Segment 1: The N terminus [G] is about 5yd from FR19 in the parking lot. From the N terminus Boar's Nest Trail descends in a rocky area to cross South Fork of Red Creek. Rock-hopping is the usual method of crossing, but knee-deep wading in fast, cold water could easily be necessary. On the S side of the South Fork is a small cave that could shelter you for the night. The trail goes steeply uphill to the right of the cave and then curves back to the left [I] above an unnamed tributary of South Fork. The trail climbs along an old RR grade paralleling the tributary of South Fork before curving away to the left on a footpath in dense red spruce. (Follow blazes carefully and do not get side-tracked onto old logging roads.)

As you climb higher, the hardwood forest turns to dense rhododendron and laurel thickets with scattered three-sided spruce. Near the top [K] is a spectacular view of Dolly Sods, Cabin Mountain, and Allegheny Front to the NW. A short distance after the view is a small campsite on top of a large flat rock. The view is great but the location is exposed. After this area, there are no further campsites before FR70 because the land is alternately rocky and boggy. No blazes mark this section, but the trail is clear and easy to follow. Before reaching FR70, the trail drops steeply down hill and crosses the headwaters of South Fork of Red Creek. Several small roadside campsites are found within 0.1mi NE and SW of the junction [M] along FR70. The sign at the FR70 terminus points 3.0mi NE to FR19, 1.5mi NE to South Prong Trail (TR517), and 0.5mi SW to Roaring Plains Trail (TR548).

FLATROCK RUN TRAIL (TR519)   5.1mi(8.2km)
SCENERY: 2 (wooded)   NOTE: B,M,(1)
DIFFICULTY: III (strenuous)   SKI-: S4
CONDITION: B (average)   ELEV: 4620/2420
MAPS: USFS(A,B), Laneville, V-C-1 in this Guide
SEGMENTS: (1) FR32-2 to TR548 (Roaring Plains Trail)   5.1mi

This trail begins as FR1517 in a privately-owned pasture [S] just W of Laneville. Only one car is permitted to park at this trailhead, so this could create problems on a good weekend. (Because the USFS has a user agreement with the landowner, it is wise for hikers to pick up litter, close gates you open, and otherwise strive to maintain good relations with landowners.) Sink holes can be seen in the pasture's Greenbrier Limestone. The trail climbs through hardwood forests, past the falls and cascades on the Right Fork of Flatrock Run and ends on the top of Roaring Plains. There are fine views near the top. The route involves a greater change in elevation (2200ft) than any other trail in the MNF. The middle portion, which cuts steeply across the switchbacks of an old RR grade, can be difficult to follow.

Access: The lower (N) end [S] is the jeep road beginning at the gravel road (FR32-2) on the S side of Red Creek. If you are coming from the E, this road curves down from WV45 35yd W of the point where the gas pipeline swath, marked by upright pipes painted orange and white, crosses under the pavement. If you are driving from Harman on WV32, FR32-2 begins 4.0mi N of the junction with US33. The trail begins opposite the sign marking the driveway to the James D. Jordan home. The USFS has acquired a right-of-way for foot travel only. The right-of-way agreement specifies that access can be obtained by walking up the driveway (located next to where some gas pipes are enclosed in a small fenced-in area) between the Red Creek Stables horse barn and the owner's house. Proceed past the barn up a farm road to USFS property. This lower portion of the trail is often muddy and rutted from horse use.

Segment 1: Flatrock Run Trail leaves the road on a switch-back just below the right fork of Flatrock Run and climbs steeply to Flatrock Plains. It crosses the Right Fork of Flatrock Run at 3.1mi. The upper (S) end of the trail is signed at Roaring Plains Trail (TR548) [U].

An easy-to-miss spot coming uphill is where the trail leaves the abandoned RR grade, 0.25mi beyond the cascading Right Fork of Flatrock Run.

ROARING PLAINS TRAIL (TR548)   3.3mi(5.3km)

SCENERY: 1 (exceptional)   NOTE: B,M,(0)
DIFFICULTY: II (moderate)   SKI-: S1
CONDITION: B (average)   ELEV: 4690/4200
MAPS: USFS(A,B), Laneville, V-C-1 in this Guide
SEGMENTS: (1) TR519 (Flatrock Run Trail) to FR70   3.3mi

This trail passes through beautiful stands of young spruce, rhododendron thickets, meadows and small bogs. Late June offers spectacular displays of mountain laurel. The trail is blazed and easy to follow. Much of the pathway is rocky.

Access: The E trailhead [O] is on FR70 where it meets a gas pipeline swath and turns NW along the swath. This point is 3.4mi along FR70 from its gated intersection with FR19. A large USFS sign marks this trailhead.

Segment 1: From the E trailhead [O] the trail leads SW through rhododendron and spruce. A small campsite (capacity: 4 tents) is 10yd. from the trailhead on the S side of the trail. Water is nearby. A less-desirable campsite is 0.2mi from the trailhead on the W side of the trail. An obvious side trail leads 20yd into the cluster of sites (capacity: 4 tents). The last sure water is 35yd to the right in the headwaters of South Fork. Ascend through woods. After 0.6mi reach the top of Roaring Plains [V] and turn right (W) in a flat boggy area and follow an obscure RR grade. Continue W on this old RR grade for 2.8mi, staying on top of Roaring Plains. Near the W edge of the Plains the old RR grade becomes Flatrock Run Trail (TR519) [U]. An arrow and a trail sign marks where Flatrock Run Trail begins its 2,200ft descent to Laneville.

Note: Despite what the map suggests, no readily passable trails go from the E end of the trail ([O] or [V]) down to Roaring Creek or Smith Mountain, except on the pipeline swath. The area near, and S of, Mt. Porte Crayon (0.8mi W of TR519 [U]) has informal trails and rugged terrain to challenge experienced hikers. Hikers are often unable to reach the top of Mt. Porte Crayon.

Stream by Flatrock Run Trail (TR519). Photo by Monika Vucic

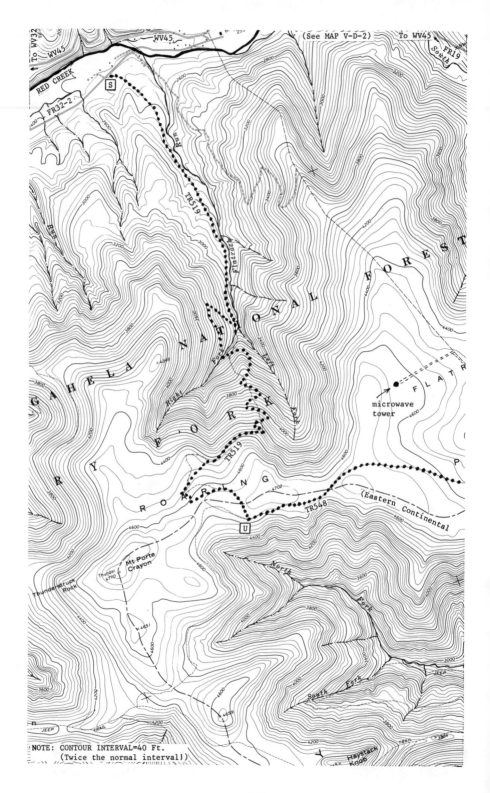

NOTE: CONTOUR INTERVAL=40 Ft.
(Twice the normal interval!)

292

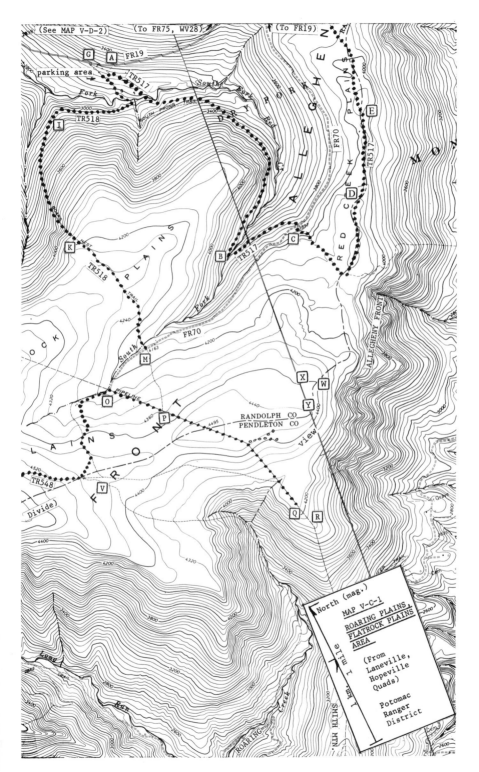

(V-D) DOLLY SODS AREA

"Dolly" comes from the name of a German farmer (Dahle) who used to farm an area near the present Rohrbaugh Plains Trail (TR508). "Sods" is a colloquial expression for high pasture land. Parts of Dolly Sods were grazed into the mid-1960s.

More than 30mi of USFS trails are found within the Dolly Sods area. This area includes the 16sq.mi Dolly Sods Wilderness, the 3.75sq.mi Dolly Sods Scenic Area, and the upper Red Creek USFS purchase of 6,168 acres (9.6sq.mi) in 1992. These occupy the USFS land N of FR19 and W of FR75 (although a portion of the Scenic Area extends E of FR75). Virtually all of this area is within the drainage of the North Fork of Red Creek above Laneville. Access to the new property is from FR75. Formal (USFS) trails on the new upper Red Creek area have not yet been developed pending the location and elimination of unexploded shells from the area. (During WWII the entire Dolly Sods area was used as a firing range for mortars and similar arms.) However the area is being well-used by hikers, backpackers, hunters and fishermen. The USFS requests that no camping or fire-building take place in this area. Treat the area as if it were a Wilderness (See page 21).

The USFS maintains the popular 12-unit Red Creek Campground, the Dolly Sods Picnic Ground, and Northland Loop Interpretive Trail, as well as FR75 within the Scenic Area. Camping and open fires, except at designated sites, are prohibited within the Scenic Area. Camping is permitted within the Wilderness, but is not permitted within 100yd of a road or 35yd from a live stream or trail. Dogs must be on leash in Dolly Sods. Trails are well-used, so treadways are usually evident. But do not get too careless. The USFS gets lots of complaints from people who lose their way in Dolly Sods. (See page 21 regarding Wilderness trail-marking standards.)

Access (East and South): Laneville Road (WV45) provides access from WV32 2.0mi S of the S rim of Canaan Valley. Paved WV45 changes into gravel FR19 at the bridge over Red Creek near the Laneville wildlife manager's cabin and the S trailhead of Red Creek Trail (TR514). From the E, WV28/7 (Jordan Run Road, shown as Rt.4 on some maps) leads N from WV28 9.0mi W of Petersburg and connects to both FR19 and FR75. FR19 is 1.0mi and FR75 is 8.0mi from WV28. People coming from the NE, E and S and arriving late in the day would normally spend the night at Red Creek Campground along FR75.

Regardless of where you plan to start, a tour of the entire length of the area by vehicle is a must. Follow FR19 up to its junction with FR75, and continue N on FR75 for 7.7mi to Bear Rocks parking area. Along the way are numerous trailheads for Dolly Sods trails, a spectacular overlook, Bell Knob Lookout Tower, and Red Creek Campground (see Maps V-D-1 and -2). The spectacular overlook to the E is shortly after the FR19/FR75 junction. A trail leads to the edge of the overlook from a parking area. As you continue N on FR75, a side road (2.2mi from FR19) (foot travel only) leads 0.4mi NE to Bell Knob Lookout Tower. Both the steps to the tower, and the tower itself, are locked. After passing Red Creek Campground (4.9mi N of FR19), you encounter the unique ecology of the area, the subarctic plains for which the area is known. In the area around Bear Rocks (2.8mi N of Red Creek Campground) huge rock formations form cliffs which provide views of ridges to the E extending many miles N and S. Vegetation is severely stunted, and few trees grow on the expanse of boggy plain. The sight is both beautiful and foreboding because of the obvious weather extremes it must take to produce such an environment. (Dolly Sods was once a dense forest of giant spruce trees. After logging, a fire burned the thick soil (mainly partially decomposed spruce needles) to bed rock. This blackened the air of states to the east for weeks in the 1930s.) The cross-country hike to Stack Rock is well worth the effort, being more remote and yielding similar spectacular views. Follow the route indicated on Map V-D-1 between Bear Rocks and Stack Rocks. Note that Stack Rocks is not on USFS land. It has not been posted in the past. But watch for, and obey, any posting signs.

Wilderness Management Policies: Before visiting the Dolly Sods Wilderness, the Dolly Sods Scenic Area or the northern portion of Dolly Sods, please read the section of this Guide on Wilderness management policies and how to treat Wilderness. (See page 21) The MNF manages Wilderness in far different ways than it manages non-Wilderness. Wilderness visitors need to understand these differences, the reasons for them, and what Wilderness is all about.

GEOLOGY OF THE DOLLY SODS AREA
The geologic formations exposed in the Dolly Sods area were deposited in the Mississippian and Pennsylvanian Periods, 330 to 290 million years ago (when North America was much closer to Africa). After deposition ceased, they were uplifted and gently folded.

The oldest geologic series in the immediate vicinity of the Dolly Sods is the Greenbrier Limestone, which underlies pastures near Laneville (a community in Red Creek Valley with an elevation of about 2500ft.). Above it is an alternating series of green and red shales and beds of sandstone--the Mauch Chunk. The Mauch Chunk is seen in the canyon of the north fork of Red Creek and on the steep slopes leading up to Roaring Plains and Flatrock Plains of the South Fork. Its elevation is about 3200ft.

Above that are layers of sand, gravel, shale (originally mud), and coal (originally peat from dense swamp forests). The lowest of these deposits (Pottsville Series) is exposed along the tops of Allegheny Mountain and Cabin Mountain, both over 4000ft in elevation. It often forms small cliffs that are eroded into unusual sculpture at Bear Rocks on the Allegheny Mountains and rocky knobs on the Cabin Mountain range. Other boulders are among the huckleberry patches of Rohrbaugh Plains of the Allegheny Mountains. These rock forms can be seen along Rohrbaugh Plains Trail. Because the deposit is down-warped, it also is exposed in the canyon below, where it causes the waterfalls and cataracts just below the Forks of Red Creek. Plant fossils--the impressions of leaves and hardened sandstone preserving the inner cores of ancient branches, roots, and trunks--can be found at the Forks of Red Creek. Please leave them where you find them for others to enjoy.

The youngest and highest rocks (over 4000ft in elevation) in the Dolly Sods (Conemaugh Series) underlies most of the extensive grass land in the northern end of the North Fork watershed and also much of the Roaring- and Flatrock Plains. It includes some coal seams. Sediment deposition ceased in the Permian Period about 235 million years ago, and erosion cut steep-walled canyons in the newly raised land.

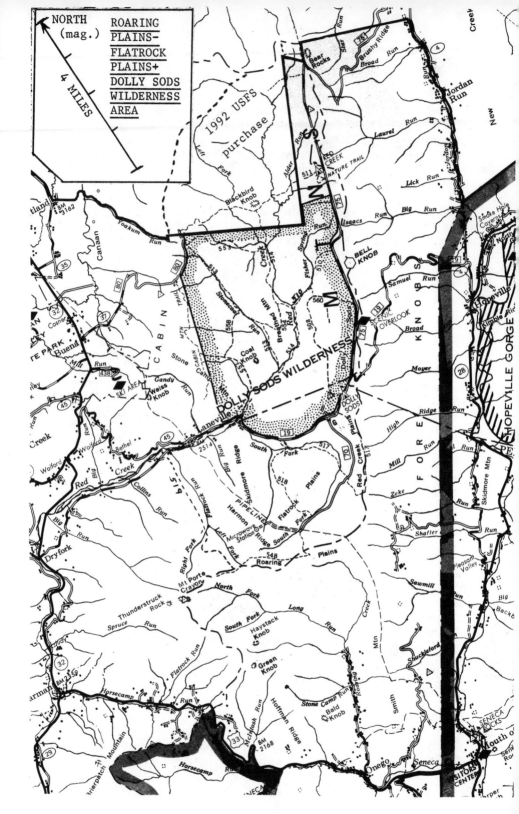

Red Creek Canyon from the sandstone cliffs along Rohrbaugh Plains Trail (TR508). Photo by Steve Swingenstein and Bill Battenfelder

297

One interesting geologic feature of the Dolly Sods "high country" dates from a much later period--the sorted patterned ground or "rock glaciers". Most often these are tongues of boulders extending down gentle slopes from the shattered sandstone and conglomerate outcrops from which they originated. The blocks within these "sorted stripes" are often aligned with their long axes parallel to the borders of the stripes. Sometimes the stripes take a sinuous path or interconnect with others. Where the ground is almost level, polygonal patterns of large rocks may be observed. Sorted patterned ground is thought to be caused by the action of ice, although the mechanism is not well understood. Although the continental glaciers of the Pleistocene Ice Age (about one million years ago) never came closer to West Virginia than central Pennsylvania, tundra conditions apparently prevailed considerably S.

ROHRBAUGH PLAINS TRAIL (TR508)   3.5mi(5.6km)

SCENERY: 1 (exceptional)   NOTE: B,M,(0)
DIFFICULTY: II (moderate)   SKI-:   S2
CONDITION: C (poor)   ELEV: 4010/3480
MAPS: USFS(A,B), Hopeville, V-D-2 in this Guide
SEGMENTS:
   (1) FR19 to TR560 (Wildlife Trail)   3.0mi
   (2) TR560 to TR510 (Fisher Springs Run Trail)   0.5mi

Rohrbaugh Plains Trail runs along the W edge of the plateau E of Red Creek Canyon. There are a few wildlife game food plots along the way, particularly at 2.7mi and 2.9mi. A good campsite is 2.5mi from the S trailhead and at the junction with Wildlife Trail (TR560) at 3.0mi. There is a large rock outcrop at 2.3mi from the S end of the trail on the W, and at 3.1mi on the E side. Portions of the trail are very rocky. Southbound hikers will find that, S of the sandstone cliffs, the trail deteriorates to many side trails. Blazes, if any, are obscure. Farther S, the left turn off the woods road is easily missed.

Access: The S terminus [A] is on FR19, 0.2mi NE of Dolly Sods Picnic Ground. It is signed, and parking is available 50yd N of the picnic area.

The N terminus is at Fisher Spring Run Trail (TR510) near Fisher Spring Run.

Segment 1: From the S end [A] on FR19, the trail winds downhill through spruce and rhododendron and passes through a young timber area. Beyond this area, the trail re-enters older timber and then joins an old RR grade [B] just beyond the first of three moderately large tributaries of Red Creek. It follows this grade to Fisher Spring Run.

An outstanding view is available where the trail swings left to some sandstone cliffs overlooking Red Creek between 2.2mi and 2.4mi from FR19. Just beyond this, the trail rejoins the RR grade which also was used as a road serving several wildlife game food plots. Coming from the S the trail crosses diagonally through the first clearing and skirts just below the second clearing. About 70yd S of the second clearing, the access road [C] leaves Rohrbaugh Plains Trail and is now maintained as Wildlife Trail (TR560). This point is easy to miss, but it is marked by a trail number on an arrow.

Segment 2: TR508 continues N on the unimproved RR grade to Fisher Springs Run Trail [D]. (Good campsites are found within 0.3mi N of this junction on TR510.)

FISHER SPRING RUN TRAIL (TR510)   2.3mi(3.7km)

SCENERY: 1 (exceptional)   NOTE: B,M,(2)
DIFFICULTY: II (moderate)   SKI-: S4
CONDITION: B (average)   ELEV: 3960/3230
MAPS: USFS(A,B), Blackbird Knob, Hopeville, V-D-2 in this Guide
SEGMENTS: (1) FR75 to TR508 (Rohrbaugh Plains Trail)   1.2mi
          (2) TR508 to TR514 (Red Creek Trail)   1.1mi

Fisher Spring Run Trail is one of the more heavily used in the Dolly Sods area, and is easy to follow, except near where it crosses Fisher Spring Run.

Access: Its NE terminus is at FR75 [F], 0.9mi N of the road to (former) Bell Knob Tower, and just S of the only significant jog in FR75.

Segment 1: Starting from FR75 [F], the trail leads W and then SW through open hardwood forest to the junction [D] with Rohrbaugh Plains Trail (TR508).   Traveling E, people often miss this junction and wind up on TR508. Good campsites are found along the last (E) 0.3mi of TR510.

Segment 2: For the next 0.3mi W from TR508 [D], the trail follows an old RR grade. Then it begins to drop steeply into the rocky basin of Fisher Springs Run, with numerous switchbacks. The trail is rocky in spots. The topo does not show the switchbacks or the crossing of Fisher Spring Run. This is because the November 1985 flood caused a huge washout 0.2mi from the junction with Red Creek Trail (TR514), forcing a major rerouting of the lower end of the trail. Watch carefully for a rerouting around the washout. The junction [G] with Red Creek Trail is on a steep bank of Red Creek. (However, note that TR514 [not TR510] descends to Red Creek, contrary to what is shown on the Hopeville topo.) No campsites are found along this lower segment of TR510, but good campsites are found on flat ground near the Red Creek Trail crossing of Red Creek on both sides of Red Creek as far upstream as the first large falls.

BLACKBIRD KNOB TRAIL (TR511)   2.2mi(3.5km)

SCENERY: 1 (exceptional)   NOTE: B,M,(2)
DIFFICULTY: II (moderate)   SKI-: S4
CONDITION: B (average)   ELEV: 3970/3650
MAPS: USFS(A,B), Blackbird Knob, V-D-1 in this Guide
SEGMENTS:
(1) FR75 (Red Creek Campground) to TR514 (Red Creek Trail)   2.2mi

Blackbird Knob Trail is used to gain access to numerous scenic views, the N end of Red Creek Trail (TR514), campsites at the Forks of Red Creek, and for viewing open country for which Dolly Sods is well-known. Since forest vegetation in this area is sparse, good views of the surrounding hills are seen along much of the trail's length. Mountain laurel, azaleas and blueberry are common. Some of the trail is rocky and eroded due to very heavy use, although considerable maintenance has been done in recent years to reduce erosion. Stay on the trail to minimize erosion.

Access: The E trailhead is on FR75, 50yd N of the signed entrance to Red Creek Campground. [A]   Cars can be parked on the E side of FR75, across from the E trailhead. This lot holds about 15 cars and is often filled. Parking in Red Creek Campground is for campers only.

The campground has a hand-powered water pump and pit toilets. The water has somewhat of an iron taste so consider extracting water from Alder Run.

Segment 1: Starting from FR75, Blackbird Knob Trail skirts a spruce-covered knob just N of Red Creek Campground. A number of side trails and campsites are found on this knob. The trail offers a splendid view from a sandstone outcrop at 0.4mi amid blueberries and . Shortly before crossing Alder Run, the trail skirts around the S side of a beaver pond with several dams, lodges, and canals. Crossing Red Creek is usually easy on large stones, but this crossing can be dangerous in high water. The floods of 1996 created a steeply cut S bank here, so use caution for safety, and care to avoid erosion. Just after the Red Creek crossing [C] are a few campsites--mostly over-used. Other campsites are available along the S edge of the meadow encountered immediately after climbing out of the steep portion of Red Creek Valley. These are scenic and not over-used, but you need a collapsible water jug for getting water from Red Creek. The trail meets Red Creek Trail (TR514) [E] on the S side of Blackbird Knob where there is an old trail sign and the official end of Blackbird Knob Trail.

(An extension of Blackbird Knob Trail [formerly part of American Discovery Trail] continues W, crossing Left Fork of Red Creek. Numerous small but popular campsites are found upstream and downstream of this crossing. Then the trail climbs steadily to an old jeep trail running N-S along the top of Cabin Mountain. The junction is 200yd S of Harman Knob. Harman Knob's rock outcrop is 40yd W of a high point on the old jeep trail. It offer spectacular views of Canaan Valley and the upper reaches of the watershed of the Left Fork of Red Creek. Numerous views and scenic meadows are also found along much of the Blackbird Knob Trail extension.)

BIG STONECOAL TRAIL (TR513)   4.4mi(7.1km)

SCENERY: 1 (exceptional)   NOTE: B,M,(5)
DIFFICULTY: III (strenuous)   SKI-:   S4
CONDITION: B (average)   ELEV: 3930/2890
MAPS: USFS(A,B), Hopeville, Blackbird Knob, Blackwater Falls,
          V-D-2 in this Guide
SEGMENTS:
(1) TR514 (Red Creek Tr.) to TR554 (Rocky Point Trail)   1.3mi
(2) TR554 to TR558 (Dunkenbarger Trail)   0.6mi
(3) TR558 to TR553 (Breathed Mtn. Trail)   2.5mi

Access: Former FR80 from Canaan Valley to TR553/TR513 is now private.

Segment 1: Big Stonecoal Trail begins at Red Creek Trail (TR514) [H] 1.5mi upstream from the wildlife manager's cabin [I] near FR19. The trail crosses North Fork of Red Creek (no bridge) and follows an old logging road overlooking falls and cascades on Big Stonecoal Run. At 1.3mi is a junction with Rocky Point Trail (TR554) [J] which leads SE, then N to Red Creek Trail (TR514). Campsites are located off Rocky Point Trail about 0.3mi S of the trail junction.

Segment 2: From [J], Big Stonecoal Trail continues on a spruce-lined RR grade to an old logging campsite. (This is the only campsite until after the junction [K] with Dunkenbarger Trail [TR558] where there are good sites along the stream.) About 0.2mi from TR554 is a large waterfall. About 20yd beyond the old logging campsite the trail crosses to the W side of Big Stonecoal Run and enters the open plateau country where beaver ponds can be seen. Sometimes these ponds flood the trail. If so, please walk in the water to minimize damage to fragile vegetation. The junction $\boxed{K}$ with Dunkenbarger Trail (TR558) is fairly clear.

Segment 3: The trail crosses back to the E side of the stream 0.25mi beyond TR558. Here it follows an old RR grade for most of the next 1.5mi well above Big Stonecoal Run. It then skirts the edge of a red pine plantation for 0.3mi, turns sharply left, and descends to a stream crossing beside a large spruce. Just before the stream crossing are excellent level campsites in the pine stand beside the trail. This is the last good site before it climbs to another RR grade and proceeds on to a junction with Breathed Mountain Trail (TR553) $\boxed{L}$ and an old USFS road (formerly FR80). This last stretch is rocky and sometimes wet. A large USFS sign with map are found at the junction with TR553. (The former FR80 can be followed N to a saddle just beyond Harman Knob.)

RED CREEK TRAIL (TR514)   6.1mi(9.8km)

SCENERY: 1 (exceptional)   NOTE: B,M,(2)
DIFFICULTY: III (strenuous)   SKI-: S4
CONDITION: B (average)   ELEV: 3930/2620
MAPS: USFS(A,B), Laneville, Hopeville, Blackbird Knob,
        V-D-1 & V-D-2 in this Guide
SEGMENTS:
    (1) FR19 to TR552 (Little Stonecoal Trail)   0.5mi
    (2) TR552 to TR513 (Big Stonecoal Trail)   1.0mi
    (3) TR513 to TR510 (Fisher Springs Run Trail)   1.6mi
    (4) TR510 to TR554 (Rocky Point Trail)   0.5mi
    (5) TR554 to TR553 (Breathed Mtn. Trail)   1.4mi
    (6) TR553 to the "Forks"   0.1mi
    (7) "Forks" to TR511 (Blackbird Knob Trail)   1.0mi

Red Creek Trail generally follows North Fork of Red Creek from the wildlife manager's cabin $\boxed{I}$ (Map V-D-2), near the bridge on FR19, to Blackbird Knob Trail (TR511) $\boxed{E}$ (Map V-D-1) N of the Wilderness Boundary. The USFS requests that no new campsites be made in the lower 0.5mi of the trail. Crossing Red Creek anywhere in the Red Creek Trail area could be dangerous during periods of high water. In January of 1996 the trail was scoured by flood waters. So the trail was rerouted uphill to prevent damage to unstable sections of the blowouts. Wilderness management policy is to let natural processes dominate as much as possible, so be prepared to accept the challenges that this entails.

Access: A dozen or so cars can be parked along the driveway of the wildlife manager's cabin (small brown/yellow building) just E of the WV45 bridge over Red Creek (the start of FR19).

Segment 1 & 2: Starting from the S $\boxed{I}$ (Map V-D-2) Red Creek Trail begins as an abandoned road/RR grade. The grade extends for 1.0mi beyond the cabin (passing Little Stonecoal Trail (TR552) $\boxed{M}$ at 0.5mi), and then continues along Red Creek (but switchbacking up the hill for a stretch to avoid a flood washout) to the S end of Big Stonecoal Trail (TR513) [H] 1.5mi from the cabin. No bridge crosses Red Creek here, but there are campsites.

Segment 3: Red Creek Trail continues to follow the abandoned RR grade for 0.2mi and climbs the slope to the right. The trail continues high above Red Creek to the junction [G] with Fisher Spring Run Trail (TR510). (Halfway between Big Stonecoal and Fisher Spring Run, Red Creek Trail crosses a medium-sized run which provides the best rest stop in the section. As you leave this point, you will see the run become a beautiful waterfall off to your left.) There are no campsites between Big Stonecoal Trail and Fisher Spring Run.

Segment 4: From the junction [G] with TR510, Red Creek Trail descends to Red Creek where there are a number of nice campsites along both banks of Red Creek. A side trail leads N along the E bank of Red Creek for 0.2mi to a waterfalls. Red Creek Trail crosses Red Creek and ascends the W side of the canyon on a rough and rocky treadway, cutting across switchbacks of the RR grade. About 0.2mi above the crossing, it meets Rocky Point Trail (TR554) [N] coming in from the left.

Segment 5: From the junction with TR554, Red Creek Trail continues to climb for 100yd to a level old RR grade. From here the trail continues almost level to where it meets Breathed-Mountain Trail (TR553) [O] just before the Forks of Red Creek.

Segment 6: Red Creek Trail then continues along the old RR grade for another 0.1mi and crosses the Left Fork just upstream from the junction [P] of Left Fork of Red Creek and Red Creek (commonly called the "Forks" or the "Forks of Red Creek" by trail users). There are many campsites along five of the six stream banks in the vicinity of [P], though many suffer from over-use-- as do most streamside campsites in Dolly Sods. Some campsites have been closed in order to allow them to recover. The Forks also offers three swimming holes, several waterfalls, fossils in the main Red Creek stream bed, and a natural water slide that drops about 15 vertical feet (over a distance of about 80ft) into a large swimming hole just upstream of an impressive waterfall in a scenic setting. Needless to say, the "Forks" is popular. Good camping manners are absolutely essential here to keep the area looking good. Floods in 1985 and 1996 made major changes to the Forks, especially to Left Fork.

Segment 7: Beyond [P], the trail goes 70yd NW along the N bank of Left Fork. Then it climbs steeply N to the plateau on a rough and rocky treadway. On the plateau are broad scenic vistas, and attractive meadows (blueberry, azaleas, laurel and scattered red spruce). Backpackers often camp along the edges of these meadows to avoid over-used sites and crowds at the "Forks". Informal side trails leading to some of these sites can be seen. (Using these sites requires collapsible water jugs to gather water from the Left Fork of Red Creek.) The trail continues N toward Blackbird Knob where it ends at Blackbird Knob Trail (TR511) [E] (Map V-D-1) just S of the top of Blackbird Knob.

Rocky Point, a huge outcrop accessible by a steep 40yd scramble from Rocky Point Trail (TR554) in Dolly Sods Wilderness. Photo by Steve Swingenstein

LITTLE STONECOAL TRAIL (TR552)   1.8mi(2.9km)

SCENERY: 1 (exceptional)   NOTE: B,M,(2)
DIFFICULTY: II (moderate)   SKI-: S4
CONDITION: B (average)   ELEV: 4000/2740
MAPS: USFS(A,B), Laneville, V-D-2 in this Guide
SEGMENTS:
(1) TR514 (Red Creek Trail) to TR558 (Dunkenbarger Trail)   1.8mi

Little Stonecoal Trail is steep and rocky and does not have good campsites until the junction with Dunkenbarger Trail (TR558). The lower end goes
through a forest cathedral in a steep-walled stream valley, quite different from
the open spruceheath found in the N part of Dolly Sods Wilderness. It follows Little Stonecoal Run to the boundary of USFS land some distance
beyond the junction with TR558. (Beyond this point the trail continues on
private land to TR513 and TR553.) The section of TR552 N of
Dunkenbarger Trail is not maintained, and has not been surveyed for
unexploded ordinance.

Access: Little Stonecoal Trail has its S terminus at Red Creek Trail
(TR514) [M] 0.5mi upstream from the wildlife manager's cabin [I].

Segment 1: From Red Creek Trail (TR514), Little Stonecoal Trail
crosses an upper meadow, descends an embankment, and goes through woods
on the E edge of a larger lower meadow to the bank of Red Creek. Here the
trail crosses Red Creek and climbs the opposite bank upstream from the
mouth of Little Stonecoal Run. This stream crossing can be difficult or dangerous during high water.

One mile from Red Creek, the trail leaves the narrow canyon of Little
Stonecoal Run to enter a less-steep E slope before it meets Dunkenbarger
Trail [Q]. An excellent campsite is just E of the trail junction [Q] (S of
TR558; N of TR552).

BREATHED MOUNTAIN TRAIL (TR553)   2.5mi(4.0km)

SCENERY: 1 (exceptional)   NOTE: B,M,(0)
DIFFICULTY: III (strenuous)   SKI-: S4
CONDITION: B (average)   ELEV: 3950/3500
MAPS: USFS(A,B), Blackwater Falls, Blackbird Knob, V-D-2 in this
      Guide
SEGMENTS:
(1) TR513 (Big Stonecoal Trail) to TR514 (Red Creek Trail)   2.5mi

Breathed Mountain Trail has its NW terminus on Cabin Mountain at a
junction with Big Stonecoal Trail (TR513) [L]. It leads SE through open
meadows, extensive areas of huckleberries, shady stands of young hardwoods,
spruce and pine, and alongside several beaver ponds. (Beaver ponds occasionally grow and cause problems on the trail.)

(A private ski trail is expected to be built from the knob 0.6mi WSW of
the W trailhead of Breathed Mountain Trail to the trailhead [L]. Another ski
trail is planned to go from there to the base of Cabin Mountain near Yoakum.)

Access: (No car access. Former FR80 is now private.)

Segment 1: Starting from the NW [L], the first 0.75mi from FR80 is a
jumble of boulders, and does not offer good campsites. A short wet area at
0.75mi has some semi-submerged logs serving as a wet bridge. At 1.5mi is
the first beaver pond meadows. Side trails lead 30yd NE for better views of

this large, impressive complex of beaver dams, lodges and canals. The trail then rises slightly to cross a ridge through a hardwood forest and then continues through a stand of pines which offer an excellent campsite (although there is not any close water). The trail then passes through open blueberry heath with excellent views. More beaver ponds and several good campsites can be found within 0.2mi of where the trail descends steeply over large rocks to Red Creek Trail (TR514) [O]. This area is just below the "Forks" where Left Fork of Red Creek joins Red Creek.

ROCKY POINT TRAIL (TR554)   1.8mi(2.9km)

SCENERY: 1 (exceptional)   NOTE: B,M,(0)
DIFFICULTY: II (moderate)   SKI-: S2
CONDITION: A (good)   ELEV: 3580/3350
MAPS: USFS(A,B), Hopeville, V-D-2 in this Guide
SEGMENTS:
(1) TR513 (Big Stonecoal Trail) to TR514 (Red Creek Trail)   1.8mi

Rocky Point Trail follows an old logging RR grade from Big Stonecoal Trail (TR513) [J] to Red Creek Trail (TR514) [N]. It is now one of the most popular trails on Dolly Sods because it provides access to spectacular views from a huge flat rock outcrop. The trail is easy to follow and does not include steep grades except for a few dips that once had RR bridges. However ballast rocks make a rough treadway, and rhododendron often squeeze the W half of the trail.

Several campsites are found about 60yd off the trail (to the E) in a former pine plantation that is just N of the rock outcrop. The plantation floor is brush-free but covered with pine needles. The side trail to the campsites is 0.25mi from the junction with Big Stonecoal Trail (TR554). The only water for these campsites is from Big Stonecoal Run (at a waterfall 0.2mi N of the junction of TR554 and TR513).

Rocky Point is an impressive outcrop of Pottsville sandstone that offers the most spectacular views in the southern (forested) portion of Dolly Sods Wilderness. Magnificent view of Red Creek Canyon makes the scramble to the top of the rocks worth the effort. The trail treadway itself offers no views.

Segment 1: Starting from Big Stonecoal Trail [J], watch for informal side trails (scramble routes) leading up to the broad, flat top of the rocks. The first is at 0.5mi (0.1mi before the southernmost point [R] in Rocky Point Trail) and the second is at the southernmost point in the trail. A trail also leads to the rocks from the campsites in the pine plantation about 70yd N of the rocks. These pines are visible from the top of the rocks, but the trail between the campsites and the rocks is not simple to locate. If you wish to avoid the steep scramble to the top of the rocks (and the associated risks), go via the campsites.

Beyond the southernmost point [R] on Rocky Point Trail, look for more comfortable footpaths along the edges of the rock ballast. The trail is tree-shaded except for a 0.2mi stretch near Rocky Point [R]. About 100yd before the junction with Red Creek Trail (TR514) an old logging RR grade angles off slightly to the left.

DUNKENBARGER TRAIL (TR558)   1.6mi(2.6km)
SCENERY: 1 (exceptional)   NOTE: B,M,(1)
DIFFICULTY: II (moderate)   SKI-:   S2
CONDITION: B (average)   ELEV: 3670/3620
MAPS: USFS(A,B), Laneville, Blackwater Falls, V-D-2 in this Guide
SEGMENTS:
(1) TR513 (Big Stonecoal Trail) to TR552 (Little Stonecoal Trail)   1.6mi
    Dunkenbarger Trail connects Little Stonecoal Trail (TR552) [Q] to Big
Stonecoal Trail (TR513) [K]. The trail is signed at both ends and is blazed,
but is easy to lose in the central portion where it crosses Dunkenbarger Run.
    Segment 1: When traveling NE, immediately after crossing Dunken-
barger Run [S], the trail curves right at a post and backboard for a campsite
and then turns sharply left.

WILDLIFE TRAIL (TR560)   1.2mi(1.9km)
SCENERY: 2 (wooded)   NOTE: B,M,(0)
DIFFICULTY: II (moderate)   SKI-:   S2
CONDITION: A (good)   ELEV: 4010/3600
MAPS: USFS(A,B), Hopeville, V-D-2 in this Guide
SEGMENTS: FR75 to TR508 (Rohrbaugh Plains Trail)   1.2mi
    This wooded trail follows a former access road serving several wildlife
food plots which were developed and maintained for habitat improvement.
    Access: A parking lot for a dozen or so cars is found along FR75 at the
trailhead.
    Segment 1: Starting at FR75 [T], head W to Rohrbaugh Plains Trail
(TR508) [C]. An excellent overlook of Red Creek Canyon is found on a large
sandstone outcrop 0.2mi S of [C] along TR508. To the SW can be seen the
overlook along Rocky Point Trail.

NORTHLAND LOOP INTERPRETIVE TRAIL (#I-52) 0.3mi(0.5km)
SCENERY: 1 (exceptional)   NOTE: M,(0)
DIFFICULTY: I (leisurely)   SKI-:   S4
CONDITION: A (good)   ELEV: 3870/3820
MAPS: USFS(A,B), Blackbird Knob, V-D-1 in this Guide
SEGMENTS: (1) FR75 to FR75   0.3mi
    Northland Loop Interpretive Trail begins and ends on FR75. It is
located within Dolly Sods Scenic Area between the N boundary of Dolly Sods
Wilderness and Red Creek Campground. The trail skirts the edge of Alder
Run Bog as shown on the map. Interpretive signs explain the flora and fauna
of the area.
    Access: Parking is provided for about 10 cars at each of the two trail-
head parking lots along FR75. The trail is 0.4mi S of Red Creek Campground.

Overlook at Rocky Point in Dolly Sods (TR554).
Photo by Steve Swingenstein and Andy DeCissio

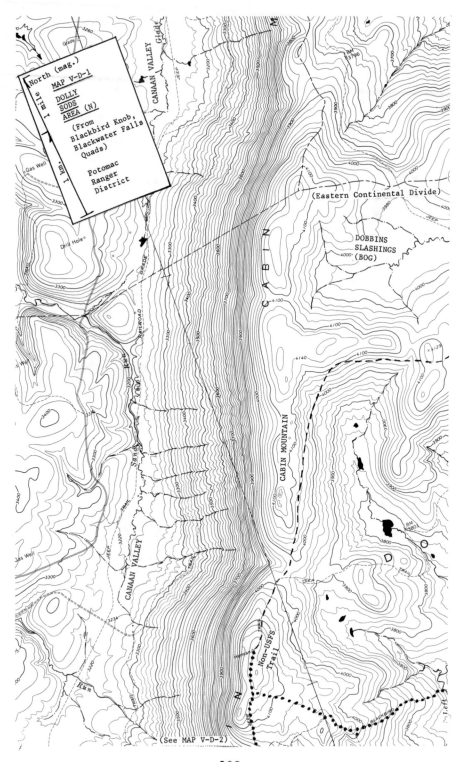

North (mag.)

MAP V-D-1

DOLLY
SODS
AREA (N)

(From
Blackbird Knob,
Blackwater Falls
Quads)

Potomac
Ranger
District

(Eastern Continental Divide)

DOBBINS
SLASHINGS
(BOG)

CABIN MOUNTAIN

CANAAN VALLEY

CANAAN VALLEY

Non-USFS Trail

(See MAP V-D-2)

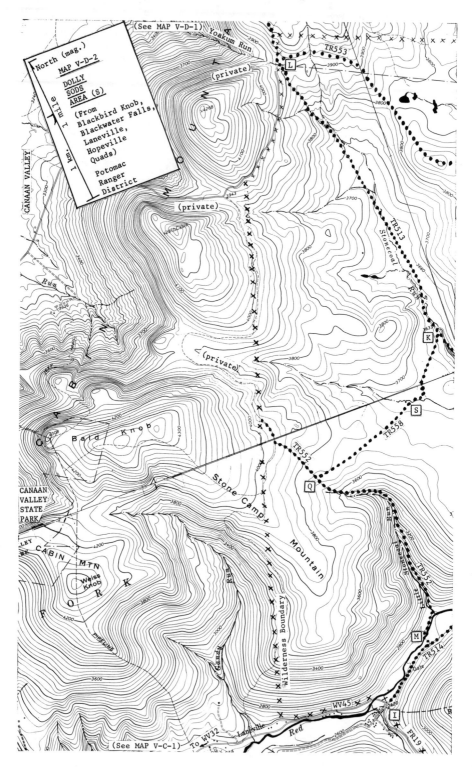

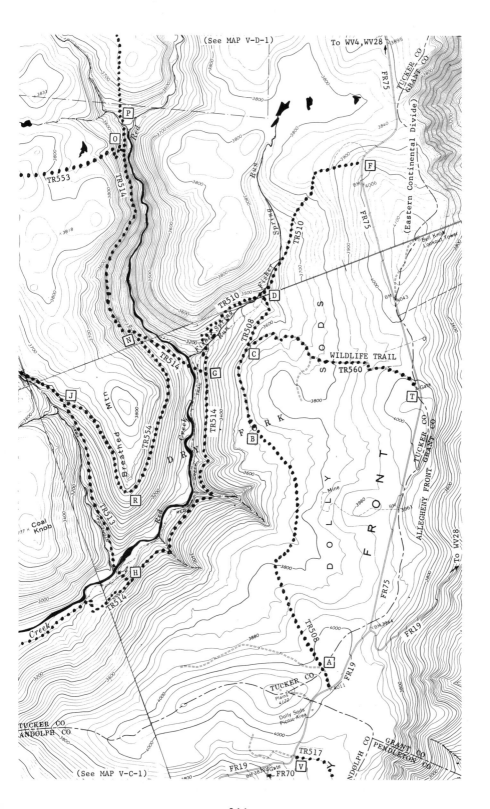

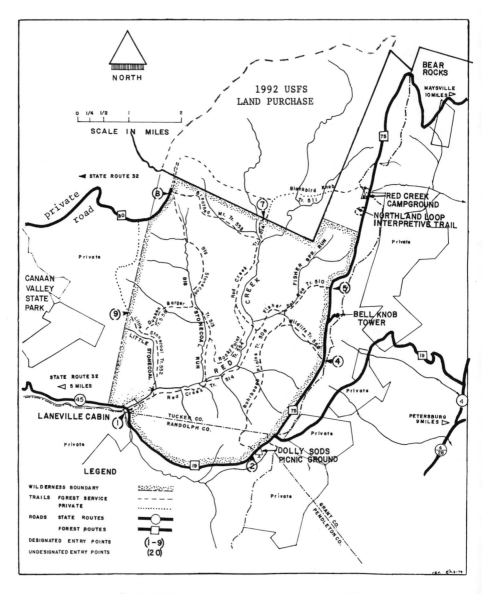

DOLLY SODS WILDERNESS

312

WHITE SULPHUR RANGER DISTRICT

White Sulphur Ranger District is the southernmost, and the smallest, of the MNF's six districts. Its address is 410 E Main St., White Sulphur Springs, WV 24986, Tel. 304-536-2144. Mainly in Greenbrier County, its E boundary is on the Allegheny Mountains, the boundary between West Virginia and Virginia. On the N it adjoins Marlinton Ranger District, Watoga State Park, and Calvin Price State Forest. Greenbrier River forms the W boundary. Its S border is six miles N of White Sulphur Springs. The district is best known for Lake Sherwood Recreation Area near the Virginia border, and Blue Bend Recreation Area along Anthony Creek. Traversing Brushy Mountain, Middle Mountain, and Meadow Creek Mountain is the 17.7mi Allegheny Trail (TR701). A second long trail is the 17.8mi Middle Mountain Trail (TR608) from Neola to Rimel.

During the 1980s the district promoted its trail system with improved maintenance and signage. But the improvements did not increase usage. It was discovered that only a small percentage of the public used the trails. Another disappointment by the district was the lack of funding needed for maintenance. As a result, the district abandoned nine trails and cut mileage on two others in the early 1990s. Dropped are Camp Wood Trail (TR618), Civil War Trail (TR686), Coles Mountain Trail (TR612), Dilly Trail (TR682), Rider Trail (TR629), Slab Camp Trail (TR617), Spice Ridge Trail (TR621), Snake Valley Trail (TR684), and Wild Meadow Trail (TR670). On the 11.5mi Allegheny Mountain Trail (TR611) 8.0mi were abandoned, and of the 5.5mi Laurel Run Trail (TR679) 3.2mi were abandoned. One new trail was added--the Connector Trail (TR604)--a 1.9mi route between Allegheny Mountain Trail and Meadow Creek Mountain Trail (TR610). Also, Snake Valley Trail was somewhat rerouted and became Meadow Creek Trail--keeping the same trail number. But the most remarkable advancement in the district's trail system was with Allegheny Trail. Not only was the treadway in excellent condition, but two new footbridges were constructed over Anthony Creek and Meadow Creek. Additionally, a large parking area was created on WV92, and Allegheny Trail information signage was constructed. The remaining trails in the district are well maintained, and Lake Sherwood Trail (TR601) continues to be one of the most used in the MNF.

The major streams of this area are the Greenbrier River, its tributary Anthony Creek, and the North Fork of Anthony Creek (which feeds into Anthony Creek at Neola).

The district has two developed campgrounds. A section of each campground is open year-round. Other sections are open usually from Memorial Day to Labor Day. The campgrounds are:
Blue Bend Recreation Area (user fee)
    Blue Meadow   (18 sites) picnic tables
    Blue Bend   (22 sites) picnic tables, showers
Lake Sherwood Recreation Area (user fee)
    Meadow Creek   (36 sites) picnic tables, showers
    Pine Run   (35 sites) picnic tables, showers
    West Shore   (25 sites) picnic tables, showers
(All of the above five campgrounds have water and toilets.)

Campground reservations can be made for Lake Sherwood via check or credit card through National Recreation Reservation Service, Tel. 877-444-6777 or via Internet http://www.ReserveUSA.com. Other sites are on a first-come-first-served basis. At both recreation areas are large picnic grounds with pavilions. Trail map/brochures are available for both recreation areas.

Visitors may also enjoy a visit to Watoga State Park and the adjacent Calvin W. Price State Forest. The address is Marlinton, WV 24954 (Tel. 304-799-4087). The park is 9.0mi S of WV39 on CO21. It is also 2.0mi W of US219 on CO27. The total size of this park and forest is 32.4sq.mi.

Another area of interest is the 75.2mi Greenbrier River Trail in Greenbrier River State Park. It offers hiking and bicycling on an abandoned Chesapeake and Ohio RR right-of-way along scenic Greenbrier River. The portion of the trail closest to White Sulphur Ranger District runs along the W bank of Greenbrier River, so strictly speaking it is not within the District. However anyone thinking of hiking in White Sulphur Ranger District should be aware of this trail. A more complete description of Greenbrier River Trail is found in the introduction to Marlinton Ranger District (page 217). Access points in White Sulphur Ranger District are at:

- Anthony--Anthony Station Road (CO21/2) (see Map VI-B-2 and Anthony Creek Trail (TR618));
- Renick/Falling Spring--Auto Road (CO11).

Bridges span Greenbrier River at both these points.

(VI-A) MIDDLE MOUNTAIN AND LAKE SHERWOOD

Middle Mountain and Lake Sherwood Area is connected by Allegheny Trail (TR701). The connector is from Lake Sherwood Valley on Meadow Creek, a long section of Meadow Creek Mountain, a descent to Anthony Creek Valley, and then up and over Middle Mountain. Allegheny Trail runs jointly for 1.8mi with Middle Mountain Trail (TR608). These major connections, plus the network of trails branching from the 3.7mi Lake Sherwood Trail which circles the lake, make for ideal short or extended walks or backpacking trips. Lake Sherwood is a popular family recreation area, with facilities for camping, fishing, swimming, hiking, and picnicking. The 165-acre lake was constructed in 1958 and named for the property's former owners, the Sherwood Land, Mineral, and Timber Company. The lake is 2700ft. in elevation and located between the Allegheny Mountains range between Virginia and West Virginia, and Meadow Creek Mountain. It is 11mi NE on Lake Sherwood Road (CO14) from Neola and WV92.

MIDDLE MOUNTAIN TRAIL (TR608), (S Section) 13.1mi(21km)

SCENERY: 2 (wooded)   NOTE: B,M,W (1)
DIFFICULTY: III (strenuous)   SKI-: S3-4
CONDITION: A (good)   ELEV: 3565/2028
MAPS: USFS(A), Lake Sherwood, Ruckers Gap, Alvon, Mtn. Grove, VI-A-4 in this Guide

SEGMENTS:
(1) CO14/FR96 to FR875   4.6mi
(2) FR875 to TR701 (Allegheny Trail (S))   4.0mi
(3) TR701 (S) to TR701 (Allegheny Trail (N))   1.8mi
(4) TR701 (N) to FR790   2.7mi

Middle Mountain Trail follows Middle Mountain for 17.5mi from near Neola, S, to Rimel, N. White Sulphur Ranger District maintains the S 13.1mi section, and Marlinton Ranger District maintains the N 4.6mi section. Except for North Fork of Anthony Creek at the S trailhead, and Laurel Creek at the N trailhead, the trail is without water, and hikers should prepare accordingly.

Access: There are three vehicular accesses to this section. The S trailhead C is on North Fork Road (CO14/FR96), 0.5mi W of Neola at WV92. Access is across Anthony Creek on a low-water bridge. Parking space is small and is a few yards upstream from the trailhead.

Another S access is on FR875 B on top of Middle Mountain. It is gated Coles Run Road, 3.7mi from WV92, and 2.4mi N of Neola. A scenic gravel road, it is open to vehicles from September 1 to December 31. Walking is essential at other times.

The N trailhead is the gated and locked 3.0mi Divide Road (FR790), 3.5mi S from the Rimel intersection of WV39 and WV92.

Segment 1: From the S terminus C, Middle Mountain Trail follows an old logging road across North Fork of Anthony Creek and, after 100yd, comes to a clearing. Here, marked by a sign and an arrow, it leaves the old road uphill to the E. At this point it is a blue-blazed foot trail. It is a gentle climb up the side of a steep slope where there are frequent views of mountains and North Fork valley. Among open woods the prominent wildlife are deer and wild turkey. The first of 4 switchbacks is a switch right, 1.2mi from the trailhead; the last switchback is at 1.7mi E. Major hollows are signed along the ridge. Among them are Hatfield Hollow, Lynch Hollow, and Coles Run. (Hikers traveling N to S should use caution where the trail leaves the main ridge, right, to descend to the North Fork. This is 0.5mi S of the Hatfield Hollow sign. A game trail continues S along the main ridge.) At 2.9mi is a wildlife water pond, and wildlife clearings are at 4.2mi, 4.4mi, and 4.6mi. Also at 4.6mi is a gate B and junction with Coles Run Road (FR875).

Segment 2: From the intersection of the trail and FR875, Middle Mountain Trail continues N on the ridgeline. At 5.3 is a wildlife water pond, and 8.5mi is a wildlife clearing. At 8.7mi the Allegheny Trail (TR701) from the E joins Middle Mountain Trail.

Segment 3: The two trails continue jointly for 1.7mi, after which Allegheny Trail turns W.

Segment 4: From this point, Middle Mountain Trail continues N on the ridgeline for 2.7mi to meet Divide Road (FR790). Along the way, at 12.5mi, is a wildlife clearing. At 12.9mi is a junction with the old Divide Road, the boundary of Marlinton and White Sulphur ranger districts. The road junction was relocated 0.2mi N because of a timber sale in the 1980s. From this point the N section of the trail continues 4.6mi to the Rimel parking area on WV92/39.

MEADOW CREEK MOUNTAIN TRAIL (TR610)   3.5mi(5.6km)

SCENERY: 1 (exceptional)
DIFFICULTY: II (moderate)
CONDITION: A (good)
MAPS: USFS(A), Lake Sherwood, Mountain Grove, VI-A-2 in this Guide
SEGMENTS: (1) TR701 (Allegheny Trail) to FR311   2.2mi
          (2) FR311 to TR604 (Connector Trail)   1.3mi

NOTE: B,M,(0)
SKI-:   S2
ELEV: 3574/3200

Meadow Creek Mountain Trail runs along the top of Meadow Creek Mountain on FR815 and FR311. Public use of the grassy road is presently restricted during the deer hunting (gun) season. (Trail plans call for separating the trail from the roads and possible designating the roads as a mountain bike route.) Being a ridge top route, water is scarce, but campsites are plentiful. The trail has large grass openings for visual variety, and is suitable for ski-touring.

Access: The recommended S access [O] is via Upper Meadow Trail (TR672), 1.7mi from Lake Sherwood Recreation Area.

The N access [Q] is via Meadow Creek Trail (TR684) and W on Connector Trail (TR604).

Segment 1: At the junction [O] of Upper Meadow Trail and Allegheny Trail (TR701) is a metal map which displays the trail system. For the first 1.0mi Allegheny Trail and Meadow Creek Mountain Trail are together. Then Allegheny Trail turns left onto a footpath. At 2.2mi Meadow Creek Mountain Trail joins FR311 where there is another metal map.

Segment 2: From here to Connector Trail [Q] are several large grass openings. On clear days some of these openings afford good views into Virginia, including Westvaco in Covington.

LAKE SHERWOOD TRAIL (TR601)   3.7mi(6.0km)
SCENERY: 1 (exceptional)   NOTE: B,M,S,(4)
DIFFICULTY: I (leisurely)   SKI-:   S4
CONDITION: A (good)   ELEV: 2720/2700
MAPS: USFS(A), Lake Sherwood, IV-B-2 in this Guide
SEGMENTS:
   (1) Picnic Area S to TR685 (Virginia Trail)   0.9mi
   (2) TR685 N   to TR684 (Meadow Creek Trail)   1.4mi
   (3) TR684   to Picnic Area   1.4mi

Lake Sherwood Trail encircles the Lake. It connects the three campgrounds with the boat dock, swimming area, and picnic area. It is an easy walk in casual footwear and can be completed in 1.5 hours. It is the principal means of access to Virginia Trail (TR685) and Meadow Creek Trail (TR684). The trail is well-signed, well-blazed and well-used.

Access: Day visitors should park in the picnic area [K] at the hiking trailhead. To get to this trailhead, enter Lake Sherwood Recreation Area on CO14/1 and take the first right into Pine Knoll Picnic Area, and then turn right again 70yd into the picnic area. This road ends in a loop with numerous parking spaces. The trailhead is on the lake side of this loop.

Segment 1: Cross the dam and a footbridge over the spillway [L] at 0.5mi. At 0.9mi juncture with the Virginia Trail (TR685). (It ascends to Allegheny Mountain Trail, a trail unrelated to the Allegheny Trail on the W ridge from the lake area.)

Segment 2: Continue counterclockwise and cross a small stream at 1.5mi.

Segment 3: At 2.3mi cross a footbridge over Meadow Creek to a fork in the trail. To the right is Meadow Creek Trail (TR684); Lake Sherwood Trail continues left. After 0.2mi pass a boat access in Meadow Creek Campground. The trail also passes through Pine Run Campground and West Shore Campground to complete the loop.

Bridge below dam of Lake Sherwood and on Lake Sherwood Trail (TR601). Photo courtesy of USFS

MEADOW CREEK TRAIL (TR684)   2.7mi(4.3km)
SCENERY: 2 (wooded)   NOTE: B,M,(7)
DIFFICULTY: II (moderate)   SKI-:   S4
CONDITION: A (good)   ELEV: 3080/2670
MAPS: USFS(A), Lake Sherwood, Mountain Grove, IV-B-2 in this Guide
SEGMENTS: (1) Lake Sherwood to Connector Trail (TR604)   2.7mi
    Meadow Creek Trail, formerly Snake Valley Trail, was built by the
W.Va. Department of Natural Resources to make the upper Meadow Creek
more accessible to hunters and fishermen. Native trout may be found in pools
along the creek and the area is noted for deer, beaver (dams), turkey and
grouse. Water is frequently available. There are seven creek crossings and no
bridges.
    Access: The S (CO14) trailhead is accessible by driving to Neola on
WV92 and then going NE on CO14 (Lake Sherwood Road) for 11mi. On
entering Sherwood Recreation Area follow the signs to the trailhead [A] which
is near the bridge at the N end of the lake. You could also take Lake Sherwood Trail (TR601) in either direction around the lake to the start of Meadow
Creek Trail.
    Segment 1: The trail starts from Meadow Creek Bridge [A] at Lake
Sherwood Recreation Area, runs up the stream bottom, and then climbs to the
top of Allegheny Mountain to meet Connector Trail (TR604) [D].

UPPER MEADOW TRAIL (TR672)   1.2mi(1.9km)
SCENERY: 2 (wooded)   NOTE: B,M,(0)
DIFFICULTY: II (moderate)   SKI-:   S2
CONDITION: A (good)   ELEV: 2970/2680
MAPS: USFS(A), Lake Sherwood, IV-B-2 in this Guide
SEGMENTS: (1) CO14 to TR610 (Meadow Creek Mtn. Trail)   1.2mi
    Rhododendrons line the lower end of the trail. Great views are found
further up. For the most part, the trail travels through fairly mature forest.
The trail has one switch-back. The upper end of the trail passes through a
1980 ice-damage salvage clear-cut.
    Access: Upper Meadow Trail starts in the service area of Lake Sher-
wood that is located N of the lake on Sherwood Lake Road (CO14). Traveling N on CO14, the SE trailhead is signed on the left side of the road, directly
across from the picnic area entrance.
    The NW terminus [O] at TR610 is also signed.
    Segment 1: Starting from the SE terminus, the trail leads through the
group camping/amphitheater area, and then climbs the E slope of Meadow
Creek Mountain to the crest where it joins Meadow Mountain Trail (TR610).
[O]

VIRGINIA TRAIL (TR685)   0.6mi(1.0km)
SCENERY: 2 (wooded)   NOTE: B,M,(1)
DIFFICULTY: I (leisurely)   SKI-:   S3
CONDITION: A (good)   ELEV: 3050/2670
MAPS: USFS(A), Rucker Gap, IV-B-2 in this Guide
SEGMENTS:
(1) TR601 (Lake Sherwood Trail) to TR611 (Allegheny Mtn. Trail)   0.6mi

Virginia Trail follows an old trail used by early settlers. The old trail went from their farms in Meadow Creek Valley across Allegheny Mountain to a store in Virginia. The present trail links Lake Sherwood Trail (TR601) and Recreation Area to the summit of Allegheny Mountain and Allegheny Mountain Trail (TR611). The trail is heavily used. The George Washington National Forest in Virginia is planning a link trail from Lake Moomaw to Lake Sherwood via Virginia Trail. (See pages 218-219.)

Access: The trail's NW end $\boxed{H}$ is 0.1mi beyond and SE of the dam spillway $\boxed{L}$ on Lake Sherwood Trail (TR601).

Segment 1: Starting from the NW $\boxed{H}$, the foot trail joins an old road after 0.1mi and passes an old quarry at 0.2mi and a spring at 0.3mi. Shortly beyond the spring, the trail leaves the road and goes 0.3mi SE to Allegheny Mountain Trail (TR611) $\boxed{I}$. Going uphill (SE) you encounters a fork. Bear right. At the summit of Allegheny Mountain, at the junction with Allegheny Mountain Trail, you can enjoy splendid views of Lake Sherwood and Lake Moomaw during leafless seasons.

ALLEGHENY MOUNTAIN TRAIL (TR611) 3.6mi(5.8km)

SCENERY: 1 (exceptional)   NOTE: B,M,W,(0)
DIFFICULTY: II (moderate)   SKI-: S2
CONDITION: A (good)   ELEV: 3214/3040
MAPS: USFS(A), Mountain Grove, VI-A-2 in this Guide
SEGMENTS: (1) TR685 (Virginia Trail) to TR604 (Connector Trail) 3.6mi

Allegheny Mountain Trail is a segment of an old fire trail built by the CCC. The old fire trail is still evident. It went from Ruckers Gap N on the Virginia-West Virginia state line for 11.5mi to High Top Lookout. The prime attraction of this trail is the great views of Lake Sherwood in West Virginia and Lake Moomaw in Virginia. The contrasting geology between the states is evident and educational. The trail map/brochure is helpful in illustrating the area trail network.

Access: The S entrance $\boxed{I}$ is from the Lake Sherwood Recreation Area via Lake Sherwood Trail (TR601) and Virginia Trail (TR685).

The N entrance $\boxed{F}$ is via Lake Sherwood Trail, Meadow Creek Trail (TR684), and Connector Trail (TR604).

CONNECTOR TRAIL (TR604) 1.9mi(3.0km)

SCENERY: 2 (wooded)   NOTE: B,M,(2)
DIFFICULTY: II (moderate)   SKI-: S2
CONDITION: A (good)   ELEV: 3480/3000
MAPS: USFS(A), Mountain Grove, VI-A-2 in this Guide
SEGMENTS:
  (1) TR610 (Meadow Creek Mtn. Trail) to TR684   1.4mi
  (2) TR684 (Meadow Creek Trail) to TR611 (Allegheny Mtn. Trail)   0.5mi

Connector Trail connects Meadow Creek Mountain Trail (TR610), Meadow Creek Trail (TR684), and Allegheny Mountain Trail (TR611). The use of the trails listed above, plus a part of Lake Sherwood Trail, all of Virginia Trail, and all of Upper Meadow Trail can form loops of 10.0mi or 13.0mi.

Segment 1: Starting from the NW at its junction $\boxed{Q}$ with Meadow Creek Mountain Trail (also FR815), it travels SE on an old road, past a wildlife opening and a water impoundment, and on through attractive hardwood forest. The trail reaches the valley floor before connecting with Meadow Creek Trail $\boxed{D}$. Two stream crossings provide beautiful views of mountain laurel, which bloom in June and July.

Segment 2: The trail narrows after leaving Meadow Creek Trail. It winds it's way gently up to Allegheny Mountain Trail. $\boxed{F}$

LITTLE ALLEGHENY MOUNTAIN TRAIL (TR668)   4.2mi(6.8km)
SCENERY: 1 (exceptional)   NOTE: B,M (1)
DIFFICULTY: II (moderate)   SKI-:   S3-4
CONDITION: B (average)   ELEV: 3341/2130
MAPS: USFS(A), Rucker Gap, Alvon
SEGMENTS: (1) CO14 to FR309   4.2mi

Access: The N trailhead can be reached by driving to Neola on WV92 and taking CO14 E toward Lake Sherwood. After 1.5mi up CO14 on the right is a sign marking the trail with mileages. A small area at the trailhead off the road is available for parking. Also at this location is a small stream which drains a USFS watershed, and flows year-round.

The S terminus, Little Allegheny Road (FR309), is open to public travel, but is a narrow 4WD road. Humphrey's Draft Road (FR687) is gated, closed to vehicular traffic, and is often impassable even to 4WD vehicles. Its W origin is at WV92 near Young's Campground.

Segment 1: The trail follows an old logging road for 170yd; as the road passes a wildlife clearing on the right, the foot-trail departs left. The first mile of foot-trail rises at a moderately steep grade and there are two switchbacks in this climbing section. The stream at the first switchback is the last water for the remainder of the trail. There are two scenic overlooks to the right of the trail at the 0.8mi mark. The main ridge of Little Allegheny Mountain is reached after 1.2mi and the trail widens into an old logging road at 1.5mi where it continues for the remaining length of the trail. Throughout the third mile, clear-cuts left of the trail offer scenic vistas. Along the fourth mile of trail several wildlife openings, ranging in size from 0.3 to 3 acres, offer areas for camp sites. The trail ends on Little Allegheny Road (FR309).

ALLEGHENY TRAIL (TR701)   17.7mi(28.3km)
SCENERY: 1 (exceptional)   NOTE: B,M,(0)
DIFFICULTY: III (strenuous)   SKI-:   S4
CONDITION: A (good)   ELEV: 3565/2212
MAPS: USFS(A), Lake Sherwood, Mountain Grove, Rucker Gap,
        VI-A-1, VI-A-2, VI-A-3 in this Guide.
SEGMENTS:
        (1) Laurel Run at CO14 to TR610 (Meadow Creek Mtn. Trail)   5.6mi
        (2) TR610 to TR672 (Upper Meadow Trail)   2.3mi
        (3) TR672 to WV92   3.4mi
        (4) WV92 to TR608 (Middle Mtn. Trail)   2.6mi
        (5) TR608 to The Dock on CO23   3.8mi

This section of yellow-blazed Allegheny Trail in White Sulphur Ranger District ascends and descends Meadow Creek Mountain and Middle Mountain with an average elevation of 2600ft. The trail is partly on old forest roads, hand-dug new footpaths, and older trails. Most of the distance is in an open hardwood forest of mainly oak, maple and hickory. Scattered white- and Virginia pines, mountain laurel, and patches of blueberries are throughout. In the coves are rhododendron and hemlock. Wildlife likely to be seen are deer, wild turkey, grouse, and skunk. There is one wildflower meadow between Anthony Creek and WV92, and a major scenic outlook on Meadow Creek Mountain. Both Meadow Creek and Anthony Creek have first class footbridges.

Access: The S end of the trail is Laurel Run parking lot on CO14, 2.5mi E of Neola. Another 6.1mi S is completed upstream of Laurel Run to the top of Allegheny Mountain for entrance into Virginia and George Washington National Forest. From there another 9.4mi has been completed in Virginia. The route descends to cross I-64, Exit #2 at Jerry's Run. Contact the West Virginia Scenic Trails Association. For trail information: Elsa Nadler, Tel. 304-293-5967 (W); 304-599-4917 (H). For ordering guidebooks: Vicky Shears, 463 Cobun Ave., Morgantown, WV 26501, Tel. 304-296-7249.

The N trailhead easiest for parking is at "The Dock" on CO23, 7.0mi SW of Minnehaha Springs. (See Marlinton Ranger District.)

Between the N and S trailheads is an access [P] (Map VI-A-3) at the WV92 parking lot, 7.4mi N of Neola.

Segments 1 & 2: Starting from the S [A] (Map VI-A-3), Allegheny Trail leaves the Laurel Run parking lot at CO14, goes 0.1mi W on CO14 to cross Meadow Creek on a footbridge, and begins an ascent. For the first 1.6mi the trail switchbacks up nearly 1,000ft in elevation to a scenic outlook. From here it follows the ridgeline of Meadow Creek Mountain for 7.3mi before leaving the ridge to the W. Along the way, after 6.3mi from the overlook, is a junction [O] (Map VI-A-2) with Upper Meadow Trail (TR672), which descends SE for 1.7mi to CO14 at Lake Sherwood.

Segment 3: About 0.4mi farther NE along Meadow Mountain from TR672, Allegheny Trail descends a ridge on switchbacks from Meadow Creek Mountain to Anthony Creek [Z], where it crosses on a footbridge. Ahead it passes through a meadow of thick grasses and wildflowers to WV92 at 11.3mi. On the W side of WV92 is a large parking area with trail information.

Segment 4: From WV92 the trail parallels Bear Creek for 0.6mi before switchbacking to the top of Middle Mountain where it meets Middle Mountain Trail (TR608) at 13.9mi.

Segment 5: The trail turns right and after 1.8mi on the ridge on an easy treadway, it leaves the ridge to the W on the former Dock Trail/FR310. After a descent of 2.0mi the trail crosses Douthat Road (CO23) at The Dock--a parking area only. (It received its name from many years ago for the location of a timber loading dock.) There is another 1.4mi of Allegheny Trail in White Sulphur Ranger District before it enters Marlinton Ranger District on Brushy Mountain, but The Dock is the most convenient place to park.

Boating at Lake Sherwood Recreation Area. Photo courtesy of USFS

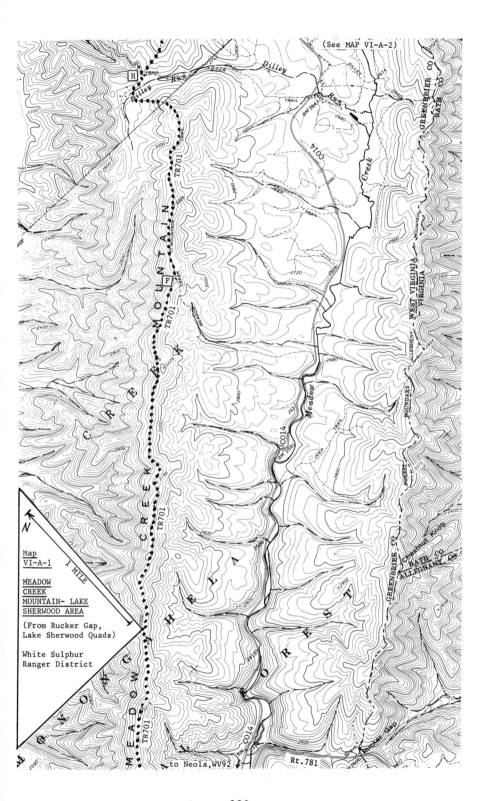

Map
VI-A-1

MEADOW
CREEK
MOUNTAIN- LAKE
SHERWOOD AREA

(From Rucker Gap,
Lake Sherwood Quads)

White Sulphur
Ranger District

N

1 MILE

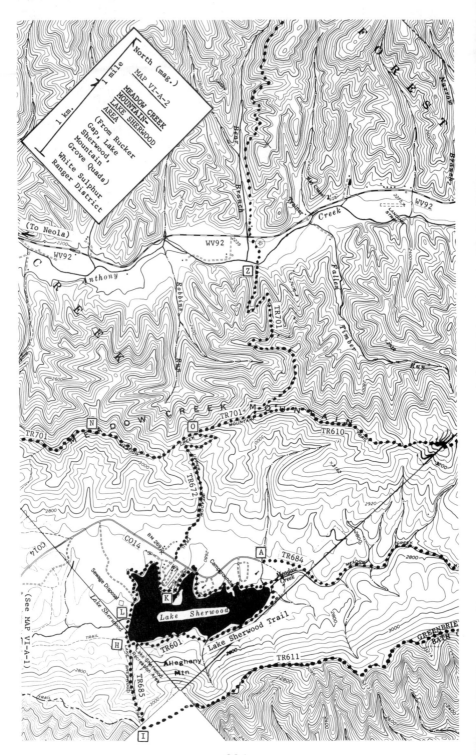

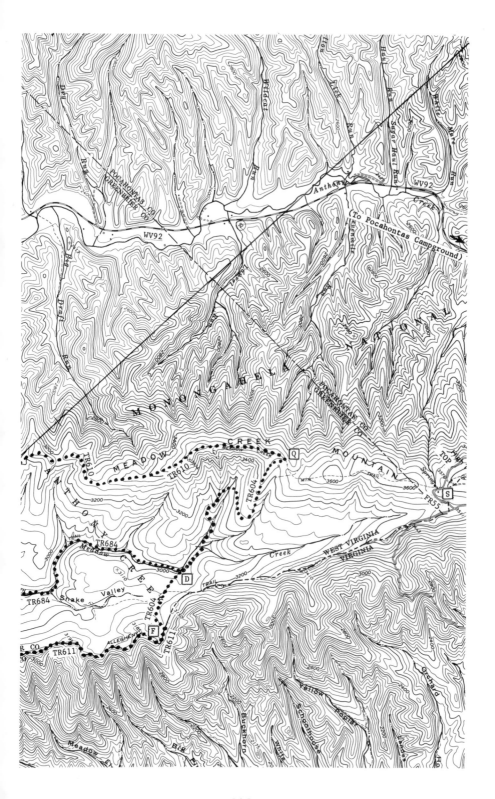

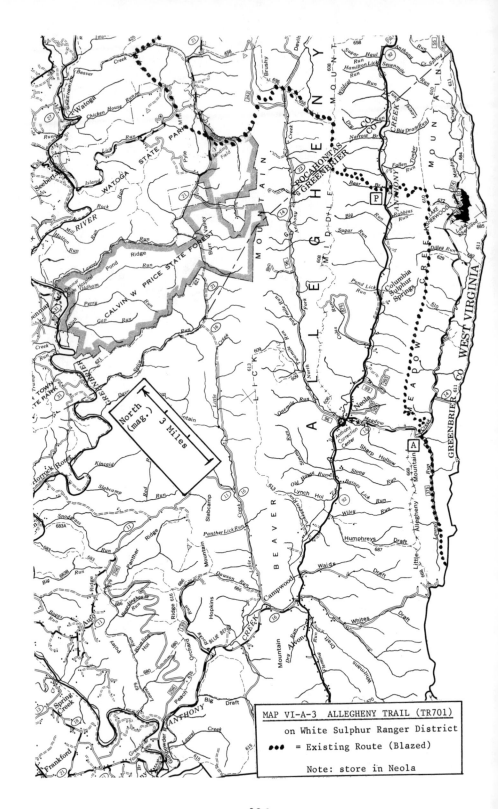

MAP VI-A-3 ALLEGHENY TRAIL (TR701)

on White Sulphur Ranger District

••• = Existing Route (Blazed)

Note: store in Neola

326

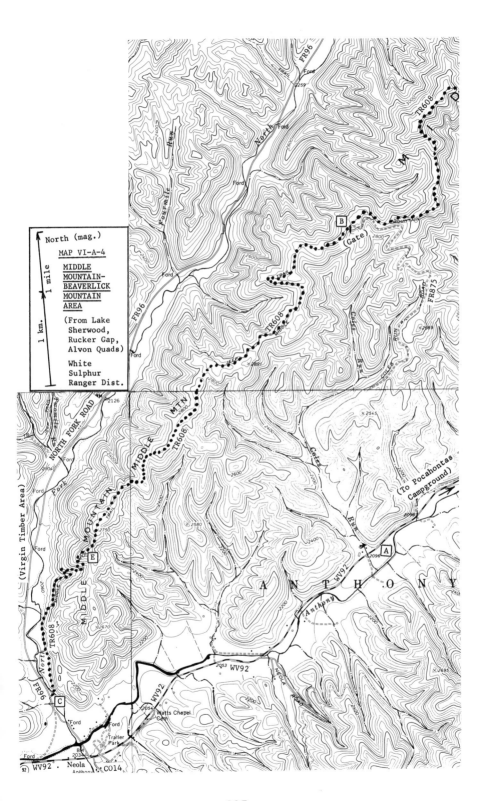

North (mag.)

MAP VI-A-4

MIDDLE
MOUNTAIN-
BEAVERLICK
MOUNTAIN
AREA

(From Lake
Sherwood,
Rucker Gap,
Alvon Quads)

White
Sulphur
Ranger Dist.

(VI-B) BLUE BEND AREA

The Blue Bend area is a rugged, wild 7.3sq.mi area located in the extreme SE corner of White Sulphur Ranger District, N of the town of White Sulphur Springs.

The USFS maintains two excellent campgrounds on Anthony Creek, Blue Bend and Blue Meadow. These two campgrounds are on opposite sides of Big Blue Bend Road (CO16/2). The former is popular with the trailer-type campers, while the latter is favored more by tenters. The Blue Meadow area even has a few "walk-in" campsites for tenters, i.e. those that cannot be driven to. Blue Meadow is open and grassy, and Blue Bend is in deep forest and more private. Both are within walking distance of a swimming hole on a bend of Anthony Creek. Anthony Creek is popular with fishermen, and is frequently stocked with trout.

The USFS has restored the 0.3mi Beaver's Tail Trail for the visually handicapped. It is across the road from the Blue Meadow Campground and makes a loop between the parking lot and the river. It has Brailled interpretive signs and plants with odors such as wild phlox, spicebush, and wild rose. A National Recreation Trail, it is supported by the Lewisburg Lion's Club and clubs of District 29-N. It does not have a trail number. It is located on the Anthony topo map.

The forests are typical of the drier portions of the MNF, including oaks, hickory, black locust, sassafras, white pine and hemlocks. The slopes above the S bank of Anthony Creek are extremely steep and often overgrown with rhododendron thickets. The narrow bottomland along the S side of the creek near the swimming hole support a mature forest of white pine and hemlock-- one of the most beautiful in the MNF. In wetter portions, low-growing poison ivy is encountered.

Most of the area is shown on Maps VI-B-1.

BLUE BEND TRAIL (TR614)   5.0mi(8.0km)
SCENERY: 1 (exceptional)   NOTE: B,H,M,(0)
DIFFICULTY: II (moderate)   SKI-: S4
CONDITION: A (good)   ELEV: 2930/1920
MAPS: USFS(A), Anthony, VI-B-1 in this Guide
SEGMENTS:
    (1) Campground to TR618 (Anthony Creek Trail)   1.5mi
    (2) TR618   to Campground   3.5mi

Blue Bend Trail (formerly Round Mountain Trail) is an easy loop to follow, well marked and well used.

Access: The trailhead is in the Day-Use Parking lot of Blue Bend Recreation Area. Several shorter trails are also in the immediate area. From the trailhead it goes through the picnic area and over the swinging bridge above Anthony Creek.

Segment 1: Proceeding counterclockwise towards the right, the trail follows Anthony Creek downstream for 1.5mi, passing under many large white pines and hemlock, before turning up the mountainside at the mouth of Big Draft. A camp site for a medium-sized group is found here. [A] Anthony Creek Trail (TR618) comes in from the SW here.

Segment 2: Blue Bend Trail makes four switchbacks in climbing the steep mountainside, but it is wide and the grade relatively easy. On reaching the top, it levels off and follows the ridge top. At 2.8mi $\boxed{B}$ is an Adirondack shelter (capacity: eight). Water is sometimes available from a small spring in the ravine 70yd below the shelter. It is not dependable in dry weather.

Segment 3: The trail leads NE from the shelter over the top of Round Mountain. There are no views when the leaves are on the trees. Beyond the summit, the road descends rapidly. Blue Bend Trail turns left off the old road and becomes a one-lane foot path again. As it reaches the end of Round Mountain ridge $\boxed{C}$, spectacular views of the Anthony Creek Valley towards Neola are offered. These overlooks are not protected by railings, and the footing is loose. From here back to the recreation area, the trail descends sharply and is much steeper. Toward the bottom, near the swimming hole, it passes through a cathedral-like grove of white pine and hemlock just after an impressive laurel and rhododendron canopy.

SOUTH BOUNDARY TRAIL (TR615)   4.8mi(7.7km)

SCENERY: 2   (wooded)   NOTE: B,M,W,(1)
DIFFICULTY: II-III (moderate-strenuous)   SKI-:   S4
CONDITION: A   (good)   ELEV: 3120/1800
MAPS: USFS(A), Anthony, White Sulphur Springs, VI-B-1 in this Guide
SEGMENTS: (1) CO36/1 to TR618 (Anthony Creek Trail)   4.8mi

South Boundary Trail roughly follows the S proclamation boundary of the MNF. In late June mountain laurels flank the trail with bands of pink; later in summer other flowers and blueberries are seen.

Access: The E end is well signed on Big Draft Road (CO36/1).

The W end is a junction with Anthony Creek Trail (TR618) which ends at CO21 at Anthony Station $\boxed{I}$.

Segment 1: Starting from the E, South Boundary Trail begins at CO36/1 as a foot path that climbs up a ridge and proceeds along its top N and W through small oaks and larger white pines. At 0.8mi $\boxed{H}$ the trail drops to a low point on the ridge, and crosses FR719 near the head of Laurel Creek watershed.

South Boundary Trail continues straight ahead toward the top of Greenbrier Mountain $\boxed{J}$ on an old road. At 1.8mi, near the top of the ridge, the trail turns right and leaves the old road, narrowing to a footpath again. Beyond its top of Greenbrier Mountain (no views in the summer), the trail widens into a two-track woods road and makes a gradual descent. After 1.0mi the woods road ends, and a foot trail turns right, and descends steeply on the side of a slope. It makes a switchback on top of the spur reaching to the mouth of Laurel Creek, and two more switchbacks as it descends to Anthony Creek where it meets Anthony Creek Trail (TR618) $\boxed{P}$.

ANTHONY CREEK TRAIL (TR618)   3.8mi(6.1km)

SCENERY: 1 (exceptional)   NOTE: B,M,S,(3)
DIFFICULTY: II (moderate)   SKI-:   S4
CONDITION: A (good)   ELEV: 1920/1800
MAPS: USFS(A), Anthony, VI-B-1 in this Guide

SEGMENTS:
  (1) TR614 (Blue Bend Trail) to TR615   3.1mi
  (2) TR615 (South Boundary Trail) to CO21   0.7mi
        Anthony Creek Trail is a level trail through impressive hardwood forest
along Anthony Creek. It extends from the W extremity of Blue Bend Trail
(TR614) to the Greenbrier River, connecting Blue Bend Campground with the
town of Anthony. It offers hikers and fishermen access to numerous fishing
holes and dispersed camp sites along Anthony Creek. It includes a ford of
Anthony Creek that may be difficult to cross during periods of high water.
For much of its length, the trail follows an old logging RR grade used in the
early 1900s. Anthony Creek Trail was reconstructed by the Youth Conservation Corps.
        Access: The E (TR614) terminus is near the mouth of Big Draft Run
on Anthony Creek [A]. To get there, park at Blue Bend Recreation Area,
cross the suspension footbridge over Anthony Creek, turn right onto Blue
Bend Trail (TR614) and travel 1.5mi W to the point where Blue Bend Trail
turns left and climbs sharply uphill.
        The W end is along CO21 at Anthony Station [I] on the E side of the
bridge over Greenbrier River.
        Segment 1: Starting from the E [A], Anthony Creek Trail leads down-
stream along Anthony Creek, fording Big Draft Run. Wading is required.
The trail enters an old tram road at 0.2mi and follows this intermittently all
the way to the Greenbrier River. At 0.5mi is rock cribbing for 50 feet on the
right side of the trail, and at 0.6mi is a good fishing hole. The trail crosses a
stream and hollow at 1.2mi [R] and another good fishing spot in Anthony
Creek at 1.3mi. The trail crosses a small run at 1.5mi and a larger one at
2.0mi. A good camping spot is on the right side at 2.5mi, and the trail crosses
Laurel Creek at 2.7mi [S]. At 3.1mi the trail intersects South Boundary Trail
(TR615) [P].
        Segment 2: A ford of Anthony Creek (30yd wide) is found at 3.2mi;
this ford is often difficult to cross in spring due to high water. Several good
swimming holes, fishing holes, and camping spots are located in the vicinity
of this ford and downstream from it. The trail continues another 0.6mi to
CO21/2 at the bridge from Anthony, on the E side of Greenbrier River [I].
Across the bridge is a junction with 75mi-long Greenbrier River Trail in
Greenbrier River State Park.

LAUREL RUN TRAIL (TR679)   3.9mi(6.2km)
(This trail, described in the previous edition of this guide, is now overgrown
from lack of maintenance and should be considered as being abandoned.)

Anthony Creek Foot Bridge on Allegheny Trail (TR701) near the parking lot on WV92. Photo by Allen de Hart

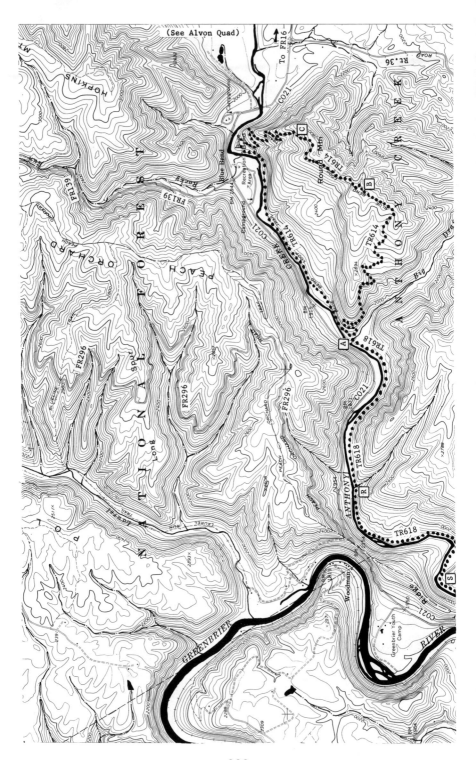

(See Alvon Quad)

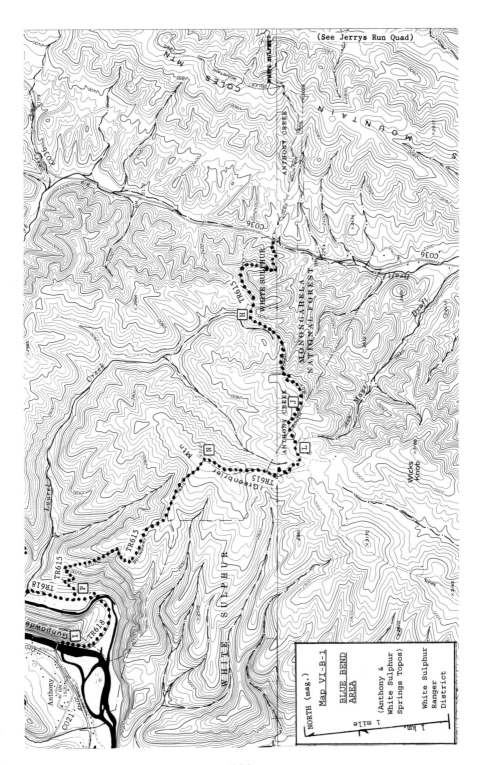

(See Jerrys Run Quad)

NORTH (mag.)

Map VI-B-1

BLUE BEND
AREA

(Anthony &
White Sulphur
Springs Topos)

White Sulphur
Ranger
District

1 mile

1 km

333

ABOUT THE WEST VIRGINIA HIGHLANDS CONSERVANCY

The West Virginia Highlands Conservancy was founded in 1967. Its goal is the preservation and conservation of natural, scenic, and historical areas of significance within the West Virginia Highlands region. The Highlands Conservancy has pursued numerous projects, using such means as letter-writing campaigns, giving testimony at hearings, press releases, publishing newsletters, guides and proposals, preparing and giving slide-show presentations, workshops, field trips, and giving financial aid to other conservation organizations in the Highlands--all on a membership fee of only $15/year/member. Examples of projects the West Va. Highlands Conservancy has completed, or is working on, include:

- Wild- and scenic river corridor protection for parts of the New, Gauley, Bluestone, Meadow and Greenbrier Rivers;
- Worked to prevent the logging of Blackwater Canyon and move it into public ownership;
- Wilderness status for the Dolly Sods Area, the Otter Creek drainage, the Laurel Fork Valley and part of the Cranberry Backcountry;
- Seeking protection of the Canaan Valley and the Dobbins Slashings portion of the Dolly Sods area from flooding by a proposed peaking-power project and from environmentally unsound development;
- Participation in the land management planning process for the Monongahela National Forest;
- Efforts to prevent construction of the Corridor H Highway as an unnecessary and environmentally destructive project;
- Efforts to protect the farmlands and the town of St. George in the upper Cheat River valley from being flooded by a dam at Rowlesburg;
- Participation in lawsuits to enforce surface-mining and water-quality laws being ignored by the State,
- Legislation establishing groundwater quality standards.

The 700 members are mainly outdoor-oriented people of West Virginia and nearby areas who appreciate the natural values that the West Virginia Highlands now contains. The Conservancy sponsors special weekends in the spring and fall of each year, featuring outings, tours, speakers and fellowship.

Conservancy members receive *The Highlands Voice*, a monthly 12-16-page newsletter containing articles on a variety of outdoor topics and conservation issues of importance to the Highlands. Members may also participate in special events such as hikes and similar outings.

To join the WVHC, copy and complete the form at the end of this Guide.

ABOUT THE WEST VIRGINIA SIERRA CLUB

The Sierra Club is a grassroots environmental organization founded in 1892 by writer and naturalist John Muir. It was Muir's belief that if people could experience wilderness and understand its value, that they would work to preserve and protect it. Membership nationwide now exceeds 650,000.

The Club is organized into regions, chapters and local groups. The WV Chapter now has three groups, the Monongahela Group in north-central WV, the Eastern Panhandle Group, and the Charleston Area Group. A student section, the Sierra Student Coalition, is active at West Virginia University. The Chapter's membership is 1300 at the end of 1998.

The West Virginia Sierra Club has adopted "Conservation 2000: Priority Conservation Issues for 1998-2000". This long-term conservation agenda focuses on five broad areas: Mountaintop Removal/Mining, MNF/Public Lands, Wildlife, Transportation/Sprawl, and Water Quality. Within these broad areas are specific concerns such as Corridor H, Blackwater Canyon, and logging on public lands.

The Club played a key role in the public review and redrafting of the 1986 MNF Land and Resource Management Plan for the MNF. The Club is also working to protect Blackwater Canyon, expand Dolly Sods Wilderness Area, and to minimize the impacts of timbering and other commercial activities in the MNF.

A major new MNF project is Mon Trails for the Millennium (MTM). This project will place renewed emphasis on the wild areas of the Mon. These are the Congressional Wilderness areas and the Wildlands (also called management prescription 6.2). Outings, trail work, and advocacy will target the Wilderness and Wildlands through the new millennium. Goals are protection of roadless areas, expansion of Wilderness, and recognition of semi-primitive ("backcountry-style") recreation values.

The Chapter's active and diverse outings program covers the areas of environmental education/nature study, conservation issues, service, and of course, fun. Outdoor recreational outings are conducted year round, with activities such as hiking, backpacking, camping, canoeing, kayaking, climbing, nature study, bicycling, and ski-touring.

The Mon Trail Recovery Project was organized after the November 1985 flood by WV Sierra Club volunteers, in cooperation with the USFS, to repair flood damage to the MNF Trail System. In its first year, 90 volunteers from all over WV and surrounding states logged over 1800 hours working on 90 miles of trail. The Mon Trail Project now continues well into its second decade of trail maintenance and construction in the MNF.

WV Sierra Club publishes a bimonthly newsletter, the *Mountain State Sierran*, highlighting conservation issues, outings, and other activities. For information or membership forms, write to WV Sierra Club, P.O. Box 4142, Morgantown WV 26504, Web site: http://www.wvsierra.org, or call 304-466-6431 or 304-789-6277.

WEST VIRGINIA TRAILS COALITION

The Coalition provides information on the Allegheny Trail, the Mary Engles Trail, greenway efforts for the Charleston Area, and information on trails in general. Its address is 302 21st St. Room 207 (or P.O. Box 487), Nitro, WV 25143 (Tell. 304-755-4878) or send E-mail to wvtc@wvtrails.com or see their web site at http://www.wbtrails.com. Karen Morris is the director. Dues are $10/year for individuals.

WEST VIRGINIA SCENIC TRAILS ASSOCIATION (WVSTA)

WVSTA is developing the Allegheny Trail (TR701). To subscribe to their newsletter, join or help, send $8 to WVSTA, Box 4042, Charleston, WV 25364 (See http://www.wvonline.com/wvsta/ and pages 33 and 48.).

Pink Lady's Slipper (Cypripedium acaule), an orchid seen all over the MNF.
Photo by Sayre Rodman

INDEX

339

WEST VIRGINIA HIGHLANDS CONSERVANCY MEMBERSHIP APPLICATION

NAME_____

STREET_____

CITY_____STATE_____ZIP_____

TELEPHONE_____   Check one of the following:

Category	Individual	Family	Organization
Senior/Student	$12	-	-
Regular	15	$25	$50
Associate	30	50	100
Sustaining	50	100	200
Patron	100	200	400
Mountaineer	200	300	600

What is your intended relationship to the Conservancy?
_____Sympathetic with basic purposes but unable to be active
_____Willing to help out in minor projects
_____Want to be an active participant
_____Other (Describe)_____

What other outdoor- and conservation groups do you belong to?

_____

What skills and experience do you have that might be of value to the Conservancy?

_____legal	_____photography	_____history
_____government	_____trip leading	_____field investigations
_____speaking	_____geology	_____computer
_____printing	_____forestry	_____other
_____typing	_____minerals	_____

Give details on the above_____

Check off those items below which reflect your interests.

_____hiking	_____forestry	_____Seneca Rocks-Spruce Knob
_____fishing	_____wildlife	_____Cranberry Back Country
_____hunting	_____Shavers Fork	_____Dolly Sods Area
_____climbing	_____hiking trails	_____Otter Creek Area
_____canoeing	_____Canaan Valley	_____Scenic Rivers
_____camping	_____sight-seeing	_____strip-mining issues
_____caving	_____water quality	_____
_____others (describe)		_____

DATE_____SIGNATURE_____

Send your completed application to the address on the title page of this Guide.

Make checks payable to West Virginia Highlands Conservancy.

NOTES